Inclusive Ethics

Inclusive Ethics

Extending Beneficence and Egalitarian Justice

Ingmar Persson

UNIVERSITY PRESS

Great Clarendon Street, Oxford, OX2 6DP,
United Kingdom

Oxford University Press is a department of the University of Oxford.
It furthers the University's objective of excellence in research, scholarship,
and education by publishing worldwide. Oxford is a registered trade mark of
Oxford University Press in the UK and in certain other countries

© Ingmar Persson 2017

The moral rights of the author have been asserted

First Edition published in 2017

Impression: 1

All rights reserved. No part of this publication may be reproduced, stored in
a retrieval system, or transmitted, in any form or by any means, without the
prior permission in writing of Oxford University Press, or as expressly permitted
by law, by licence or under terms agreed with the appropriate reprographics
rights organization. Enquiries concerning reproduction outside the scope of the
above should be sent to the Rights Department, Oxford University Press, at the
address above

You must not circulate this work in any other form
and you must impose this same condition on any acquirer

Published in the United States of America by Oxford University Press
198 Madison Avenue, New York, NY 10016, United States of America

British Library Cataloguing in Publication Data

Data available

Library of Congress Control Number: 2016952214

ISBN 978-0-19-879217-8

Printed in Great Britain by
Clays Ltd, St Ives plc

Links to third party websites are provided by Oxford in good faith and
for information only. Oxford disclaims any responsibility for the materials
contained in any third party website referenced in this work.

Contents

Acknowledgements vii

Introduction 1

Part I. The Inclusiveness of Benefiting and Reasons of Beneficence

1. Two Aspects of Things Being Intrinsically Valuable for Us: Well-Being and Autonomy 27
2. Defence of an Inclusive View of Benefiting and Reasons of Beneficence 48
3. Three Problems of Procreation: Replaceability, the Asymmetry, and the Non-Identity Problem 77
4. The Repugnant Conclusion and the Non-Transitivity of Value Relations 103
5. The End of Life and of Consciousness 119
6. The Inclusion of Non-Human Animals 137

Part II. Extreme Egalitarianism

7. The Ground for the Justice of Equality 149
8. The Badness of Unjust Inequality 172
9. Prioritarianism and Its Problems 183
10. Some Alternative Bases of Equality 208

Part III. Philosophical Thinking about How to Live

11. On the Usefulness of the Principles of Beneficence and Justice 225
12. The Point of Moral Philosophy 235
13. Beyond Ethical Inclusiveness: The Philosophy of Life 247

References 263
Index 269

Acknowledgements

This book is based on a number of papers that I have published during the last twenty years or so. In many cases what has been harvested from them has only been smaller bits, or has undergone significant revision. These are marked as references in the text. But in a few cases, I have derived larger bits without much revision. Thus, the argument against transitivity in 4.2 appears in a fuller form in Chapter 9 of *From Morality to the End of Reason: An Essay on Rights, Reasons and Responsibility*, Oxford University Press, 2013. The defence of egalitarianism in Chapter 7 is found in 'A Defence of Extreme Egalitarianism', in N. Holtug and K. Lippert-Rasmussen (eds) *Egalitarianism: New Essays on the Nature and Value of Equality*, Oxford University Press, 2007. The account of when one unjust inequality is worse than another in Chapter 8 has earlier been published as 'The Badness of Unjust Inequality', *Theoria*, 69 (2003). The criticism of prioritarianism in 9.2 comes from 'Prioritarianism and Welfare Reductions', *Journal of Applied Philosophy*, 29 (2012).

During the last couple of years when I have been putting together this book, I have greatly benefited from discussions on the various issues it contains with Roger Crisp, David DeGrazia, Jeff McMahan, Derek Parfit, Melinda Roberts, Julian Savulescu, Shlomi Segall, Victor Tadros, and Larry Temkin. I am also very grateful to two anonymous readers for OUP for constructive criticisms, and to OUP's excellent philosophy editor, Peter Momtchiloff, for skilfully guiding me through the production of this book—like my earlier OUP books—in every way an author would want. There is of course a much larger number of people from whom I benefited through all the years when I worked on the papers on which the book is based. The fact that I do not now repeat my thanks to them does not mean that I am no longer grateful to them. Finally, I would like to express my gratitude to the Uehiro Foundation for Ethics and Education for generously providing financial and academic support through the Oxford Uehiro Centre for Practical Ethics.

Introduction

The Inclusiveness of Ethics

The title of this book, *Inclusive Ethics*, is meant to designate an ethics that develops and defends a morality that regulates actions affecting anything which has or could have consciousness.[1] Such a morality is inclusive compared to most existing moralities. It is a plausible hypothesis that morality originated as something quite exclusive: in order to promote unity and cohesion within human groups, so as to make them more successful in struggles with other human groups, and natural adversaries and adversities. Thus, morality was restricted to in-groups and excluded various kinds of outsiders. It promoted unity and cohesion within in-groups by generally prohibiting harmful acts against their members, and by encouraging cooperation between them, but it did not prohibit harming members of other groups, or encourage cooperation with them.

The morality expounded in this book is also more inclusive than a more wide-ranging morality according to which all that has consciousness or will have consciousness independently of what is done matters in itself at the time of action, since it takes *possible* conscious beings or individuals, who *could*—but perhaps will not—be made to exist with consciousness, to matter morally in themselves. Entities which do not carry with them this possibility of consciousness—whether they be organic and biologically alive, or inorganic and non-living—cannot morally matter in themselves, though they can morally matter extrinsically because of their relations to individuals who do matter morally in themselves. Thus, having intrinsic moral importance or significance is anchored in the possibility or actuality of consciousness, according to the morality here advanced. This is because entities with these relations to consciousness are the only entities *for* which things can be intrinsically good or bad at some point.

However, I believe not just that only entities for which things can be intrinsically good or bad at some point—because they could then have consciousness—have intrinsic moral significance, but that *all* such entities have such significance. I cannot see what justification there could be for excluding some of them—for instance, those who do not exist—from such significance. I am a bit uncomfortable with saying that possible individuals who might begin to exist and acquire consciousness have moral

---

[1] It seems reasonable to take 'ethics' to differ from 'morality' by being a more 'theoretical' enterprise which explores various aspects of morality—meta-morality, if you like—but I do not propose any clear distinction between 'inclusive ethics' and 'inclusive morality'.

status or standing, since this manner of speaking may seem to suggest that these possible beings somehow exist. Consequently, I shall reserve these expressions for individuals who currently exist and have at least a potential to acquire consciousness, and for whom things can be made intrinsically good or bad in virtue of this fact, while I shall use the notion of having (intrinsic) moral importance or significance in itself more broadly, to apply also to possible individuals who might develop consciousness.

Personal and Impersonal Values

By a 'morality' is usually meant a set of norms to the effect that some *acts* (or act-related reactions or attitudes, like desires, intentions and emotions) are morally right or wrong, or morally ought or ought not to be done (or held). I shall however be talking primarily about *the moral value of outcomes*, which may be outcomes of morally appraisable acts, but may also be outcomes of non-moral, natural processes. These outcomes are of value because they contain individuals for whom things can be of value. This claim relies on a distinction between *personal* value and *impersonal* value. When we say that the fact that an outcome contains as much of what is good *for* you as it contains of what is good *for* me makes it twice as good as it would have been had it contained such goodness for only one of us, we invoke an impersonal value alongside the personal value for each of us—for the outcome is not twice as good *for anybody*. This impersonal value is distinct from the personal values or benefits of which it consists as a whole is distinct from its constituents.

However, the impersonal value that an outcome has in this way is only weakly impersonal in the following sense: in so far as an outcome is impersonally better (worse) than another in virtue of the amount of personal value that it contains, it is necessarily better (worse) *for* someone that it obtains. As will be seen in Part II, the value of justice or fairness is impersonal in a stronger way for which this implication does not hold: when one outcome is better than another in virtue of featuring a distribution of personal values that is closer to being just or fair, it may not be better for anyone that it obtains.

The impersonal value that an outcome has in virtue of containing some amount or set of benefits, and a more or less just or fair distribution of these benefits, is a *moral* value. This means, as I see it, that it has an essential connection to the primary subject of morality, namely actions, consisting in that these features of outcomes necessarily provide moral reasons for action. Since I am inclined to say that moral actions are necessarily concerned with what benefits and harms beings, I am committed to the view that impersonal values that are moral necessarily encompass personal values.

We should also distinguish the (intrinsic) value that existence has for an individual in an outcome from the comparative issue of whether this individual has been made better off or, in other words, has been benefited, by enjoying the benefits that this outcome offers. This distinction can be masked by the fact that the verb 'benefit' has both a 'state' sense—the sense in which we are benefited by having the benefits that we have, that is, something of intrinsic value for us—and an 'event' sense, the sense in which we are benefited when we become better off than we would otherwise be. The view that whenever the sum or set of benefits of a state increases, somebody is benefited in the event sense presupposes that somebody can be benefited not just if they already exist and receive additional benefits, but also by beginning an existence that is good for them. A main claim of Part I of this book is that this view is true.

Even if this is so, it should however not be taken for granted that the strength of a moral reason is *proportional* to the value increase of the outcome. This is so according to consequentialist moral theories like utilitarianism, but not if deontological principles like the act-omission doctrine and the doctrine of the double effect are true. These doctrines imply that, although an outcome in which, say, five innocent people survive benefits people more and, thus, has a greater value in respect of the benefits that it contains than an outcome in which one person survives, we ought morally to forgo the former outcome rather than to *cause* the death of the one, at least in circumstances in which we have to save the lives of the five *by means of* causing the death of the one.

Having discussed and rejected these deontological principles elsewhere (2013), I shall not now do so systematically. Placing this controversy in the background, I shall focus on the personal and impersonal value of outcomes and largely refrain from arguing for more precise normative claims about the strength of moral reasons to act that presuppose the falsity of these deontological principles. It is rather uncontroversial that the value that outcomes have in virtue of the benefits that they contain buttress moral reasons and that the reasons get stronger if the value is greater, though the strength of reasons might not *match* the degree of outcome value, as some consequentialists would have it. However, some other consequentialists believe that we have more reason to do what benefits some individuals simply for the reason that they are identical us, or closely related to us. In Persson (2005: pt. IV) I rejected this idea, contending that personal identity has no rational significance. This is another issue that will not be at the centre of attention here.

Two Aspects of Things Going Well or Badly for Us: Well-being and Autonomy

As already remarked, there would be no outcomes of moral value—and consequently nothing that morally ought to be done—if there was nothing that was intrinsically good or bad for individuals, nothing personally good in itself. What is intrinsically good for us is, for example, the satisfaction of intrinsic desires for the pleasures of food and drink, comfortable shelter, sex, and health, and the satisfaction of special interests which vary from individual to individual, like artistic, intellectual, or athletic interests. In so far as this satisfaction is *felt or experienced*, it constitutes what I shall refer to as our *well-being*. These feelings or experiences of satisfaction are desired for their own sakes, or liked (in themselves), and this is necessary for their qualifying as our well-being, which by definition is something that is intrinsically good for us. Well-being, then, consists in the having of feelings or experiences that we desire to have for their own sakes and that are therefore intrinsically good for us. It follows that individuals can have well-being only if they have desires and (sensory) consciousness—since well-being consists in the felt or experienced—not merely in the actual or factual—satisfaction of their desires.

The well-being that I have talked about so far is something positive and could be contrasted to 'ill-being', the felt frustration of certain desires, like the desire to avoid for their own sakes pain and other unpleasant sensations such as itches and nausea and, consequently, activities that generate them. This felt frustration is properly called *suffering*, but ill-being also comprises *boredom*, that is, the feeling that we are prone to have when we are aware of lacking an opportunity to do anything that we take an interest in doing. However, I shall in general use 'well-being' in a wider way, to cover not only positive well-being, but also the balance between well-being and ill-being, whether or not there is a net surplus of (positive) well-being.

Still, I think that there is more to the notion of things having intrinsic value for us, or going well for us, than well-being. The purely factual satisfaction—without our awareness of the satisfaction—of our intrinsic desires for how things go for us beyond our current experiences, and their immediate continuation, can also be a part of the value that things have for us. Possible examples are the satisfaction of desires to the effect that our friends do not deceive us so cleverly that we never disclose their deceit, or that after our death our property be put to the uses specified in our last wills. But if the factual satisfaction of intrinsic desires which are not at all about our having certain experiences can be a part of what makes things go well for us, the factual satisfaction of desires which are about our having certain experiences, but stretch beyond the immediate continuation of our present experiences, can surely also be a part of what makes things go well for us. The goals that we have in life—even the hedonist goal to lead a life which maximizes the net balance of our pleasurable experiences—are desires of this 'trans-experiential' type.

To my mind, the factual satisfaction of all such trans-experiential desires cannot plausibly be included in our well-being, although the satisfaction that we could *feel* because we (truly or falsely) believe that our friends are loyal, or that our wills will be fulfilled once we are deceased can be part of our well-being. When we form and act on such trans-experiential desires, we exercise our *autonomy*, and when these exercises are successful to the extent that the desires formed are factually fulfilled, this is good for us, provided the desires acted on meet conditions such as being informed, rational and free. Thus, I would like to distinguish between two senses or aspects in which things can go well for us: how well they *experientially* go for us—this is our degree of well-being—and how well things *actually* go for us because we successfully exercise our autonomy with respect to how things go for us beyond the immediate continuation of our current experiences. In other words, I propose a distinction between an 'inner' and 'outer' aspect of things in the world being of intrinsic value for us, or benefiting us.[2] By our 'welfare', I mean how things go for us in these two respects (in order not to confuse this term with 'well-being', think of it as shorthand for 'faring well in the two respects of well-being and autonomy'). Chapter 1 is dedicated to working out this account of welfare in further detail.

The term 'autonomy' is however ambiguous: it designates not merely the capacity to form and implement desires about ourselves beyond the immediate future, but also a *right* or *permission* that we are granted to exercise this capacity within certain limits, provided that it is exercised in a rational, informed, and free fashion. There is the problem of delimiting the extent of this right or permission, since in most cases our exercising autonomy in the sense of satisfying our desires about things relating to ourselves is likely to have effects on others as well. The way that we dress, the goods that we buy, the jobs and hobbies that we choose, and so on, are likely to affect others in some ways, benefiting or harming them at least marginally. But sometimes when we propose to go about our way, we shall harm others so seriously that it is not morally permissible to let us go ahead. The question then arises what the criterion of this prohibitive seriousness is. This is a question that has been much discussed in the context of J. S. Mill's principle of liberty (1859), which declares that it takes harm to others—not just damage to our own good—to make interferences with our liberty or autonomy permissible. But the crux is, what kind of harm to others?

I believe that common-sense morality incorporates a theory of negative (claim-) rights that answers this question. The idea would be that as long as you do not infringe the rights of others, you act within the boundaries of your autonomy even if what you do has other harmful consequences for them. Such an appeal to rights, however, will not do in the present context, since their existence is denied in Chapter 7 (see also Persson, 2013: ch. 2). But to provide a satisfactory account of the limits of our permission to exercise our autonomy would take a more or less complete moral theory, which this work does not have the ambition to present. I believe however that such a moral theory would comprise reasons for inclusive benefiting, as defended in Part I, and reasons for distributing benefits as equally as possible, as defended in Part II. This moral theory may leave less scope for our autonomy than common-sense morality, first, because it rejects rights—which generally allow us to hold on to things, though

---

[2] Cf. Shelly Kagan's (1992: 188–9; 1994: 317ff.) distinction between our well-being, or how well off *we* are, and the value that *our lives* have for us, or how well they are going. I am unhappy with this terminology because, although I am inclined to agree that the facts on which our well-being turn are intrinsic or internal facts about us, they are also facts about our lives: it is a fact about our lives that we are now feeling pleasure or pain, for instance. I would rather appeal to another distinction Kagan draws (1992: 188) and claim that they are 'internal' aspects of our lives because they are internal or intrinsic facts about us. Consequently, our well-being would be restricted to internal aspects of our lives—our experiences in fact—whereas successful exercises of our autonomy may include relational facts about us that refer to things external to us. I tentatively suggest in Chapter 5 that in order to be parts of our lives these relational facts—like the internal facts—must obtain while we are biologically alive and must make some difference to how we act and react. Having our testaments fulfilled does not do so and, thus, is not part of our lives. Therefore, the phrase 'the value of life' is not adequate for my purposes and, thus, its vagueness does not matter.

others may need them more—and, secondly, because it does not recognize making exceptions in our own favour for reasons of personal identity. This is because, as already mentioned, I have elsewhere (2005: pt. IV) argued that personal identity is of no rational significance. But these are matters that will not be pursued here.

So, I shall not attempt to make the boundaries of our permission to exercise autonomy precise. Nor shall I attempt to explicate the conditions that our exercises must meet to fall under this permission and, thus, to qualify as 'autonomous', conditions like being rational, well-informed, and free or unconstrained. Hopefully, these omissions will not be felt too sorely.

Person-affecting Reasons of Beneficence and Reasons of Autonomy

Suppose that overall things would be going well for you in the future were you to go on living. Then killing you now deprives you of the benefits that you would otherwise have had.[3] This is a major reason—*a reason of beneficence*—against such an act of killing. It is, more precisely, a *person-affecting* or *person-regarding reason* against killing you, since it is worse *for you* to be killed than not to be killed under these circumstances.[4] It is not an impersonal reason to the effect that the future outcome will be worse due to its sum or set of benefits being reduced.

I shall argue that there would be such a person-affecting reason not to kill you even if you were to have no conception of your possible future beyond the immediate continuation of your present experiences and, consequently, no desires that it go one way rather than another. But if you do have autonomous desires with respect to your possible future, this supplies a further moral reason not to kill you—alongside the reason of beneficence to the effect that it deprives you of future benefits—*a reason of respect for your autonomy*. These reasons may conflict, for instance, in case you want to die now, although you realize that you would have ahead a life that would be good for you. If your reasons for wanting to die are good enough for this desire to be considered autonomous—say, if you want to die because this is necessary to save other lives,

---

[3] When I discuss the badness of death, I assume that death involves a permanent loss of consciousness. As will transpire in 5.1, this is not logically necessary: conceivably, your consciousness could flow on, though you die if the areas of your brain that are the seat of your consciousness are transplanted to another body, or kept alive in a vat, as your body dies.

[4] It would be more apt to talk about 'individual-affecting' and 'individual-regarding' reasons, since I employ the term 'individuals'—or 'beings'—for all kinds of beings with consciousness, regardless of the sort of consciousness (cf. DeGrazia, 2005: 273 and McMahan, 2009: 50), but 'person' in the Lockean sense of 'self-conscious' beings, who have a capacity to conceive of themselves as being in psychological states and as existing as such not only in the present, but in the past and future as well. Accordingly, I should have used the term 'individual values' instead of 'personal values' because I believe these values to be within the reach of all individuals who are capable of some kind of feeling and desire. But this would be a break with firmly established usages, and it would jar with the contrast 'impersonal'. So, I have kept the established terminology, though it is misleading.

or to further some other impersonally worthwhile cause—then it is reasonable to respect your autonomy and let you die, and even to assist you in your action.

If someone is prevented from coming into existence then, I shall contend, this is also an action that could deprive this individual of future benefits; thus, there could be a person-affecting reason of beneficence not to prevent this from happening. That is to say, I shall contend that this act of prevention can harm someone, and that this individual can be benefited by beginning to exist; it is not just the case that this event would boost the impersonal value of the outcome by increasing the sum or set of benefits that it contains and, thus, would constitute an impersonal reason not to prevent your existence. Keep in mind that to describe the sum or set of benefits of an outcome as having increased is consistent with denying that anyone has been benefited (in the event sense) by the increase. This is precisely because the increase may have come about by someone's entering existence, and it is controversial whether someone's entering existence could be said to be a shift to the better (or worse) for this individual. According to the view that I shall arrive at in Chapter 2, this ontological change can indeed make someone better off; hence, impersonal reasons to increase the sum or set of benefits of an outcome could give way to person-affecting reasons to the effect that this benefits someone (but as will transpire, there are other moral reasons that are purely impersonal, namely reasons of just equality).

Benefiting and Harming

There is however a noteworthy asymmetry between benefiting and harming individuals on the assumption that life in general is better than non-existence. Under these circumstances, the instrumental badness of preventing your (further) existence is greater than the instrumental goodness of causing you to (continue to) exist, since the former act is sufficient for preventing your future benefits, while the latter is not sufficient to ensure them. Thus, it is in general easier to harm us than to benefit us, given that our lives are as a rule good. Since it also takes less effort to avoid doing something than to do something, I believe that we have here an explanation of why common-sense morality features stronger reasons—in the shape of negative rights—not to harm us than to benefit us (see Persson and Savulescu, 2012: 12–20).

There are two natural ways in which the event notion of harming (or benefiting) can be understood. An event (which could be an act) E harms a patient,[5] Pat, just in case it makes her worse off either than (1) she *is* at the time of the occurrence of E, or than (2) she *would have been* had E not occurred. Neither alternative is adequate. Against (1) it could be adduced that you can harm Pat not only by causing her current level of welfare to drop, but also by preventing it from rising, by preventing her from receiving benefits

---

[5] I shall sometimes use 'patient'—and at other times 'victim'—as the opposite of 'agent', that is, to refer to an individual being affected by an act.

already in the pipeline. Then you surely harm Pat, though you leave her on the same level as she was just before your act (or even on a higher level).

Option (2) takes care of this problem, but it succumbs to another difficulty. Suppose that if Pat had not been made worse off than she is by an event E_1 at t, she would instead have been made worse off to the same extent by another event E_2 at t. Then it is not true that E_1 makes Pat worse off than she would have been had it not happened, since E_2 would then have happened in its place and made Pat just as much worse off than she is. Yet, it seems that E_1 harms her because it is *it* and not E_2 that makes her worse off than she is at t.

Faced with an example of this sort, David Boonin (2014: 57–60) thinks that advocates of a counterfactual account should bite the bullet. His example is that if Hit Man 1 had not shot Pat dead, Hit Man 2 would instead have shot her dead at the same time. Then Hit Man 1 does not make Pat worse off than she would otherwise have been, but to me it seems perfectly clear that *he* harms her, since he is the one who kills her. Otherwise, who harmed Pat? Surely, it was not Hit Man 2, but Hit Man 1 who killed her. To my taste, to deny that Hit Man 1 harmed Pat is a bullet too hard to bite; so, (2) must be rejected as well.

It might be thought that a disjunction of (1) and (2) could provide an adequate definition of harming: E harms Pat just in case E makes Pat worse off either than she is at its occurrence, or than she would have been had E not occurred. But then it would seem that E's benefiting Pat would consist in E's making Pat better off either than she is at its occurrence, or than she would have been had E not occurred. However, these definitions imply that one and the same event can both benefit and harm Pat. Imagine that E_2 would have made Pat worse off not to the same extent as E_1, but to a *greater* extent. Then E_1 harms Pat according to the given disjunctive definition of harming, since it makes her worse off than she is at its occurrence, but E_1 also benefits Pat according to the parallel definition of benefiting because it makes her better off than she would have been had E_1 not occurred, since then E_2 would instead have occurred, making her worse off to a greater extent. This seems like an unacceptable result.

To handle this difficulty, it might be suggested that we should exchange the counterfactual condition in the disjunction for a condition which refers to E's preventing Pat from becoming better off than she is at its occurrence. Then we obtain the following definition: E harms Pat just in case E makes Pat worse off than she is at its occurrence, or prevents Pat from becoming better off than she then is. The parallel definition of benefiting would be: E benefits Pat just in case E makes Pat better off than she is, or prevents Pat from becoming worse off than she is. E_1 neither makes Pat better off than she is, nor prevents her from becoming worse off than she is; so, it does not benefit her. It simply harms her, albeit it also prevents her from being even more harmed by E_2. This seems to answer the objection in the preceding paragraph.

The suggested definition of benefiting also takes care of another case that is problematic for a counterfactual account. Suppose that you have been considering giving Pat a gift—for example, some golf clubs—that would make her better off than she is.

Then, at the last moment, you change your mind and refrain from turning over the gift to Pat. This makes Pat worse off than she would otherwise have been—that is, than she would have been had you turned over the gift—but you do not seem to harm Pat. Rather, you simply refrain from benefiting her. Thus, leaving her worse off than she would otherwise have been is not a sufficient condition of harming her.

Defending a counterfactual account against this kind of example, Boonin replies (2014: 53n) that an account which states that an *act* harms Pat if it makes her worse off than she would otherwise have been is not vulnerable to this kind of counterexample, since refraining from acting is not acting. However, refraining from giving Pat a gift could manifest itself in an act, for instance the act of holding on to the gift (the clubs) when they would have been transferred to Pat had you let go of them. Again, this is not harming Pat: it is refraining from benefiting her because it is refraining from making her better off than she is. Nor does refraining from making somebody better off imply *preventing* them from becoming better off. The latter implies that there are benefits under way that come from a different source than your own present agency. A counterfactual condition, on the other hand, implies that by hanging on to your gift, you would be harming Pat, since you make her worse off than she would otherwise have been.[6]

However, the suggested definitions stand in need of further adjustment. Imagine that E would not entirely block the benefits under way, but would diminish them, although Pat will still be better off than she is. Is it then not true that E would harm Pat, though she will end up better off than she is, which implies that she is benefited? If E in itself harms Pat—say, by being painful—I think that we would be inclined to say yes. But if E in itself benefits Pat—for example, by being pleasant—I think that it goes against the grain to say without qualification that it harms her, even though it prevents her from becoming as much better off as she would otherwise have been. To deal with this complication, I believe that we have to operate with a *general* notion of harming of which there are two species: *qualified* harming, or harming by benefiting, and *unqualified* harming, or harming without benefiting. I propose the following definition of general harming:

> (H) E harms Pat just in case E makes Pat either worse off than she is at the occurrence of E, or prevents her from becoming as much better off than she is as she would have been had E not occurred.

The harming is qualified if E in itself is a benefit, that is, is intrinsically good for Pat, and unqualified if it is not, that is, is intrinsically bad or neutral. Notice that even if E in itself is a benefit, it can make Pat worse off than she currently is by removing greater benefits that she already enjoys. Corresponding definitions of benefiting could of course be supplied. According to these, the harmful event E_1 earlier considered which

---

[6] We must imagine that you do not in this situation cause Pat any frustration or suffering by clinging to your would-be gift. Then you might indeed harm her, by making her worse off than she was. To rule this out, we might for instance imagine that, unbeknownst to her, you were about to drop the golf clubs from an aeroplane onto the golf course where Pat is.

prevents the more harmful E_2 would in fact be qualified benefiting, benefiting by harming. In this sense, it is not unacceptable if an event both benefits and harms. But what I henceforth mean by 'benefiting' and 'harming' is the unqualified form.

There is, however, still one respect in which (H) is unspecified, namely about *the time* at which Pat is made worse off or prevented from being as much better off. We can make a rough distinction between what harms her in the longer and shorter run. Imagine that the fact that Pat comes down with the flu today prevents her from taking a flight tomorrow to some pleasant holiday destination. This makes us inclined to say that the flu harmed her. But imagine further that the plane crashes and nobody survives, so that if Pat had not come down with the flu today, she would have been killed tomorrow. She survives for a longer period thanks to the flu, and is better off than she would otherwise have been tomorrow evening. This may tip us in favour of the view that the flu rather benefited her. It did indeed *in the longer run*, assuming that the life that she goes on to lead after tomorrow is overall good for her. But it is still true that the flu harmed her *today*.

Often when we talk about what benefits or harms individuals, we are talking about what benefits or harms them in a shorter run because we cannot tell how they will be affected by events in a longer run. It may even be hard to ascertain whether events benefit or harm individuals in the immediate future, since it may well be hard to tell what would have happened had they not occurred. But, of course, it is more important what benefits or harms us in a longer than in a shorter run.

When I say that what benefits you in the event sense makes you better off than what you would otherwise be and that what harms in this sense makes you worse off than what you would otherwise be, this should be taken as an abbreviation for (H) and its positive counterpart. The event notions of benefiting and harming are comparative: they consist in your being better or worse off than you would be in some alternative situation. They do not imply that you are in a state in which something benefits you, that is, is intrinsically good for you, or harms you, that is, is intrinsically bad for you. The state of being benefited, on the other hand, does precisely this, but it is also implicitly comparative in the sense that if you have a benefit, it follows that you are better off than you would be without it, everything else being the same. However, to say that a claim *implies* a comparison is not to say that it *is* a comparative claim, that the comparison exhausts its content. Furthermore, the state sense differs from the event sense in that it implies no comparison to an *actual* state of affairs with respect to which there is a *change*.

The Inclusive View of Benefiting and Person-affecting Reasons of Beneficence

Since the event notion of benefiting someone involves a comparison to a state of affairs with respect to which there is a change to the better for this individual, the claim that you can benefit individuals by causing them to exist implies a comparison of the value of existence for these individuals with the value of non-existence for them. There has been a change with respect to the state of affairs or fact that they did not exist. On my view, the value of non-existence is intrinsically *neutral* in the sense that the fact that somebody does not exist is neither intrinsically good nor bad for the non-existent. The value of an outcome or result that contains some individuals *having* benefits (in the state sense) is intrinsic. It has this value in itself, however it arose—even if it arose by the individuals being created, and we hold that non-existence cannot be evaluatively compared to a state of existence and, thus, that individuals cannot be benefited by being created. Therefore, the claim that the value of an outcome in respect of its sum or set of benefits can be boosted by creating new individuals who enjoy benefits does not presuppose that the newcomers have been benefited by being created. It can be a claim about the impersonal, intrinsic value that an outcome possesses in virtue of the fact that the sum or set of benefits that it contains is higher than that of another outcome.[7]

When we start existing depends on which theory of our nature and identity we accept. I shall argue in Chapter 2 that, according to *biological views* which identify us with our human organisms, we start existing two to three weeks after conception when a cluster of cells has formed an integrated multi-cellular organism to the extent that neither monozygotic nor conjoined twins could come forth. By contrast, according to *psychological views*, we cannot begin our existence earlier than at the point at which the first signs of consciousness emerge, which is considerably later, probably around the mid-term of a pregnancy.[8]

Suppose that advocates of psychological views were to maintain that the survival of human foetuses does not morally matter in itself until they acquire consciousness because prior to this event none of us exists. Then the reply could be that before the occurrence of this event, *something* exists, namely some human organisms or animals (to which we would be identical on biological views) that have a potential to develop consciousness. Why does it not matter morally in itself whether these organisms *continue* to exist and actualize their potential for consciousness? It is hard to imagine that it could make much of a difference to the moral importance of the continuation of existence whether or not the first rudimentary conscious episodes have appeared. Granted, it makes a moral difference whether more sophisticated forms of consciousness have developed, for instance whether consciousness has developed to the point at which there could be plans about how to live in the future, and an individual endowed with autonomy is present. But that does not happen until years after birth, and we

---

[7] As we shall see in more detail further on, even such an acute philosopher as Temkin seems to overlook this point, since he writes that bringing someone into existence 'does *not* itself *benefit* the person and hence does not, itself, make the outcome better' (2012: 412n). This is a *non-sequitur*: even if the bringing of someone into existence is not regarded as benefiting this individual, it could be taken as making the outcome better by increasing the amount of benefits that it contains because there is an impersonal moral reason—as opposed to a person-affecting reason—to do so.

[8] I discuss these views of our identity more fully in (2005: pt. IV).

surely want to affirm that there are beings of moral importance in themselves well before that point, beings that there could be person-affecting reasons of beneficence not to kill.

It might be claimed, alternatively, that we begin to exist already at conception because at that point something with a potential to develop into a full-blown human being with consciousness is formed. But I shall argue that this is not so, even on a biological view of our nature and identity: at that point there is no entity that will later be a full-blown human being. There is merely a set of cells from which such a being *originates*. At this point, the being who will later be conscious is merely possible, not actually existent.

A main claim of Part I of this book is, however, that there being such a possibility of a being with consciousness emerging is sufficient for there being something which morally matters in itself. For then there is the possibility that somebody will have well-being, experiences of personal, intrinsic value. If this is so, (action-)events which promote or prevent the actualization of this possibility of consciousness will have *extrinsic* value for the possible subject of consciousness: positive extrinsic value if they ensure that a possibility of a worthwhile existence is actualized, and negative extrinsic value if they prevent this. In other words, these events can benefit or harm this subject, making it better or worse off on the assumption that the value of non-existence is neutral. Thus, we arrive at an *inclusive (or wide) view of benefiting and harming* and, since it would be gratuitous to deny that there are moral reasons in favour of benefiting and against harming *all* beings who can be benefited or harmed, we arrive at an *inclusive person-affecting view of reasons of beneficence* which extends the applicability of these reasons to possible conscious beings.

Consider two ways of increasing the value of an outcome, A, in respect of the benefits contained in it: (i) by creating an outcome, B, in which the same individuals exist as in A, but at a higher level of welfare, or (ii) by creating an outcome C in which the same individuals exist as in A at the same level of welfare, but some *additional* individuals have also been made to exist at some positive level of welfare. Even if we do not accept the inclusive person-affecting view of benefiting, it cannot be denied that both (i) and (ii) are ways of increasing the amount or set of benefits in the outcome. According to the inclusive person-affecting view, however, whenever the amount or set of benefits increases, someone is benefited; and it is true not only of B, but also of C, that it is better *for someone* that this outcome obtains in place of A. According to a *narrow person-affecting view*, this is true only of B, since this view denies that individuals can be benefited by being made to enter existence.

But, on this view, is it true not merely that C contains a greater sum or set of benefits, but also that it is *better* than A in virtue of this fact, as B presumably is? Temkin's answer seems to be 'no'. He expounds an 'Essentially Comparative View of Utility', according to which 'to improve an outcome regarding utility one must (generally) increase the utility of some of those already living in that outcome' (2012: 411). ('Utility' may be taken to mean the same as 'benefits'.) On this view, he writes, 'the notions of "*more* utility" and "*better* regarding utility" come apart' (2012: 413), leaving room for the possibility that, although C contains 'more utility' than A, it is not 'better regarding utility'. I take this to be because there would be no moral reason to do what increases the sum of benefits when this does not benefit anyone, that is, when the increase is achieved by causing somebody to exist.

There are, then, two claims that should be kept apart here. The narrow person-affecting view claims: (1) only individuals who exist at the time of action, or who will exist independently of this action—*independent individuals*—can be benefited or harmed by the action, not individuals whose coming into existence is dependent on the action; only actions which do not determine whether or not they begin to exist can benefit or harm individuals. This is a claim about the concept of benefiting (and harming) but, like the inclusive person-affecting view, this narrow view also makes a claim about moral reasons of beneficence, to the effect that (2) they are person-affecting, that is, what we have moral reasons of beneficence to do is only to benefit individuals and avoid harming them, not to increase the sum of benefits (to an extent which goes beyond benefiting individuals). It follows from (1) and (2) that we have no reasons of beneficence to affect changes such as the one from A to C. If so, we have to abandon the view that C is *better* than A in respect of benefits, since the value in question is plausibly a moral value. C just contains more benefits, as Temkin puts it.

It could be objected to (2) that we have moral reasons of beneficence to do what increases the sum or set of benefits even when this does not benefit anyone, though weaker reasons than we have when someone is benefited (see e.g. DeGrazia, 2005: 277–8). These reasons to increase the set of benefits might be called *impersonal* reasons of beneficence, as opposed to person-affecting reasons which are about benefiting individuals (in the event sense). It would then follow that whenever the set of benefits of an outcome increases, the outcome becomes morally better in respect of benefits. By contrast, an inclusive view of person-affecting reasons renders such impersonal reasons superfluous.

However, I am inclined to hold that reasons of beneficence are always person-affecting. To my mind, it is implausible to claim that we would have moral reason to do what increases the set of benefits even if this were not to benefit anyone. For this implies that we have a moral interest in boosting the amount of benefits that is independent of our concern that individuals be benefited. But familiar dispositions associated with morality such as altruism, benevolence, sympathy, compassion, and so on, are all concerns that beings be benefited, or not harmed. Their object is not anything as abstract as sets or sums of benefits for which individuals are seen as mere 'containers' or 'receptacles'. Benefiting individuals is not ordinarily conceived as a means of increasing the sum of benefits; it is a moral end in itself.[9]

---

[9] Presumably this is what Temkin has in mind when he criticizes an 'impersonal view of utility' for not being fundamentally concerned with people, but rather regarding them as mere 'vessels' or 'generators' of utility (2012: 412–13). This is however misconceived as a criticism of the inclusive (or wide) person-affecting view, as Parfit also notes (1987: 400).

To be sure, if it is claimed, as is done in this book, that the objects of altruism, etc. should include possible individuals, this requires an expansion of the natural range of these attitudes. However, the same is true if their range is held to cover independently existing individuals who will come into existence in the future, but few could stomach leaving these individuals outside the scope of morality. Such extensions, though they do not invite themselves spontaneously, are nevertheless not extensions to a different kind of entity than individuals, like sets of benefits.

There is another scruple about the impersonal view that is misguided. Temkin asks: if 'more of the good is better than less of the good' and 'it doesn't matter *whose* goods it is... why should it matter if the good is anybody's at all?' (2012: 413n). We must remember that the goodness that we are assembling into impersonal sets is personal goodness, goodness *for somebody*. So, it *must* be somebody's goodness. Moreover, in so far as this goodness consists in well-being, it is a matter of experiential states and, as I shall argue in 5.2, such states must have a physical subject. However, even if benefits are always benefits for someone, 'more benefits' does not imply '(morally) better in respect of benefits'—the latter requires in addition that we take there to be a (moral) reason to produce more benefits, a reason which may be person-affecting or impersonal.

I have expressed my allegiance to the view that such reasons are person-affecting, that (2) is true, and that there are no impersonal reasons of beneficence. But by opposing (1) I endorse an inclusive view of benefiting and harming, according to which we can benefit and harm beings by bringing them into existence. In conjunction with (2), this yields an inclusive view of person-affecting reasons of beneficence but, as indicated, the precise strength of these reasons depends on where the truth lies in the consequentialism/deontology and the agent-neutrality/agent-relativity debates which are beyond the scope of the present work. However, it is rather uncontroversial that there are moral reasons to benefit and not to harm—as opposed to impersonal moral reasons to increase the sum or set of benefits—so for the vindication of an inclusive view of person-affecting reasons, the crux is the denial of (1), that is, a defence of an inclusive view of benefiting, and that is the main objective of Part I.[10] If it is maintained that in the case of some beings—say, possible beings—who can be benefited or harmed, there are no moral reasons to benefit them and against harming them, a justification must be produced for this exclusion. I cannot see what such a justification could be,

---

[10] Temkin seems to construe the wide (inclusive) person-affecting view differently than I do, since he writes that 'the question of whether causing someone to exist can benefit that person is extraneous to the notion of a Wide Person-Affecting View' (2012: 437n). This strikes me as strange because he appears to take the narrow person-affecting view to deny that you can benefit individuals by causing them to exist (2012: 412n), and one would expect the wide person-affecting view to contradict the narrow person-affecting view. Furthermore, he writes that the wide view 'focuses on how people are affected for better or worse... in different outcomes whether or not they are the *same* people' (2012: 437), whereas the narrow view focuses on people who are the same in different outcomes. But when judging that one outcome is better or worse than another in respect of benefiting people, how can you disregard whether people in one outcome are the same as people in the other outcome, unless you hold that causing to exist can benefit and harm?

since person-affecting reasons of beneficence simply are reasons to benefit and avoid harming, and should apply wherever benefiting and harming is possible.

There is one principle of person-affecting reasons of beneficence that is close to being uncontroversial, namely that the more independently individuals are benefited by an outcome, the more of a reason of beneficence there is to produce it, other things being equal. Yet, this has been denied by some, like Elizabeth Anscombe (1967) and John Taurek (1977), who argue that the number of individuals affected does not morally matter. Such a view has implausible corollaries, for example that if we cannot save one who has a good life, the outcome would not be worse if we let everyone else with lives that are equally good die! What leads to such an implausible view seems to be the failure to realize that *two* kinds of value are involved in such outcomes, an impersonal and moral value alongside a personal value, that an outcome can have more or less value, though there is nobody *for* whom it has more or less value.

In support of his view, Taurek points out that when five people lose their equally good lives or experience the same sort of pain, nobody experiences anything that is five times as bad as what one person who experiences this would experience (1977: 307–8). But although it is no doubt true that there is not anything that is five times as bad *for* anyone, it could still be true that the *impersonal or moral badness* of five individuals being afflicted by something that is bad for each of them, like pain, is five times as great as the impersonal or moral badness of one individual being afflicted to this degree. Each individual's being afflicted by pain is morally bad—that is, it provides a moral reason for others to alleviate it—and, when five of them are thus afflicted, all together the moral badness of this state of affairs could be five times greater without it following that there is any pain for anyone that is five times as great, and whose personal badness is five times as great, as it would be were the five instances of this pain to occur in one life rather than in separate lives. Certainly, a sceptic could doubt or deny that there is more of a moral reason to mitigate a pain afflicting five than to mitigate the same sort of pain afflicting only one individual on one occasion but, if this is to be plausible, it cannot be merely on the ground that in the former case there is no pain that is longer or worse for anyone. Also, it should not be on a ground so radical that it leads to questioning the existence of all moral reasons to assist others in pain.

To repeat, the inclusive view of person-affecting reasons of beneficence—together with its companion, the inclusive view of benefiting—that I shall be defending should be distinguished from the view that there are impersonal reasons to do what increases the set or sum of benefits, whether this be by acts that make independent individuals better off, or that create new individuals who are well off. On the impersonal view, even if individuals cannot be benefited by being made to enter existence, there can be moral reason to bring them into existence, since reasons of beneficence are not necessarily person-affecting reasons to do what benefits individuals (in the event sense).

It is easy to overlook the distinction between the impersonal and inclusive person-affecting view of reasons, since whenever the set of benefits is increased, someone is benefited according to the inclusive person-affecting view, and vice versa.[11] As noted, this means that impersonal reasons of beneficence are superfluous if you adopt an inclusive view of person-affecting reasons of beneficence. As also noted, it strikes me as implausible to hold that we should be morally concerned about sets of benefits in addition to being morally concerned about benefiting individuals, and that the existence of benefited individuals could be a mere means to generate sets of benefits. Our familiar dispositions of altruism, benevolence, sympathy, and compassion are dispositions to do what benefits individuals for their own sakes, not as a means to boosting the total aggregate of benefits.

In contrast, the view that there are impersonal reasons of beneficence could be a complement of a narrow person-affecting view of benefiting. The latter view restricts person-affecting reasons of beneficence to making independently existent individuals better off, that is, to benefiting individuals who already exist, or who will exist independently of the benefiting acts, claiming that individuals cannot be benefited by being caused to exist. I shall be arguing against this view in Chapter 2. But since it may seem implausible to claim that there is *no* moral reason to add individuals who are well off, that a greater number of such individuals does not make for a better outcome, it could be maintained that there are in addition to these person-affecting reasons, impersonal reasons to boost the total aggregate of benefits and, thus, to bring into existence new individuals with good lives. Impersonal reasons are then naturally understood as being weaker than person-affecting reasons to benefit to the same extent. Of course, my dissatisfaction with the notion of impersonal reasons of beneficence carries over to this mixed theory.

As will be seen in Chapter 2, there is a further view that is like this mixed view in important respects. This is Jeff McMahan's view (2013), which distinguishes between *comparative* and *non-comparative* benefiting (in the event sense) and claims that, while independently existing beings can be comparatively benefited, beings can only be non-comparatively benefited by actions which cause them to exist, and that this form of benefiting has less moral weight, like impersonal benefiting according to the mixed view. But I deny that the fact that an act benefits in McMahan's non-comparative sense can provide a reason for performing the action.

I hope that this has elucidated the distinctions between person-affecting and impersonal conceptions of reasons of beneficence and between inclusive (or wide) and narrow conceptions of benefiting and, hence, of the scope of person-affecting reasons of beneficence.

Some Troubles for the Inclusive View

On the inclusive view of benefiting, an outcome contains more benefits than another, as B and C do compared to A, if and only if the individuals contained in it all together

---

[11] Cf. Parfit's claim that a wide person-affecting view '*restates the Impersonal Principle in a person-affecting form*' (1987: 400), but this claim should not be taken to imply that there is only a trivial, verbal difference between these views.

benefit more by its existence. But this does not mean that, on the inclusive view, we can determine which of two alternative outcomes is the best by looking only at what these outcomes are intrinsically like. For one of these outcomes may be better for the individuals involved than the other, though they contain the same sum of benefits and burdens distributed according to the same pattern over the same individuals. This is because in the first outcome an amount of burdens is dispersed over a large number of individuals, each of whom is carrying a small portion, whereas in the other outcome this amount is concentrated among a few individuals, each of whom is carrying a larger portion. The former distribution is better according to what Temkin calls *the disperse additional burdens view* (2012: 67–8).

As will emerge in Chapter 4, the view that a dispersal of burdens over more individuals can reduce the moral badness of an outcome can be traced to the fact that benefits and burdens are not quantifiable in the sense that they can be assigned numerical values and be subjected to arithmetical operations. I shall contend that, due to the fact that values are *supervenient*, the relations of being better/worse than in some respects and all things considered are *non-transitive*, that is, although A is better (worse) than B, which is better (worse) than C, it is not *necessarily* true that A is better (worse) than C. This non-transitivity enables us to avoid the slide to what Parfit calls *the repugnant conclusion* even in its most compelling forms (1987: ch. 17). It also explains the disperse additional burdens view, how a great burden can be worse than many smaller burdens which seemingly add up to it. Since the series of numbers is transitive, the non-transitivity of values rules out the assignment of numbers and, thus, arithmetical operations with respect to values. (This is why I would rather talk about a 'set' or 'collection' of benefits than the more usual 'sum' or 'amount' of benefits, since the latter suggests an addition of benefits, but it strikes me as pedantic to adhere consistently to this terminology.)

The repugnant conclusion does not arise only if the inclusive person-affecting view is adopted. It can make do with the assumption that the impersonal value of an outcome in respect of benefits can be increased by the addition of individuals who possess benefits though—in accordance with (1) above—this does not benefit the newcomers. This can be achieved by denying (2) and claiming that there is an (impersonal) moral reason to increase the total set of benefits, even though this does not benefit anyone.

Chapter 3 discusses two other apparent difficulties for the inclusive view of benefiting. The first is that it makes beings *replaceable*, that it makes it possible at least in principle to counterbalance the harm done to one being by killing it by means of creating another being who would enjoy a life as good as the life that the one killed would have led had it lived on. It will however be seen that it is more dubious that the inclusive view is vulnerable to this objection than that the impersonal view is.

Secondly, common-sense morality features what McMahan has called *the Asymmetry*, the claim that whereas we have no strong moral reason to cause to exist those who will lead worthwhile lives, we do have a noticeably stronger moral reason not to cause to exist those whose lives will be worse than non-existence. However, by comprising *the act-omission doctrine*, common-sense morality is in general asymmetrical in the sense that it takes there to be stronger reasons against harming than in favour of benefiting. Furthermore, I suggest that there is *an asymmetry between abilities and disabilities* to the effect that, while disabilities, if grave enough, can make a worthwhile existence impossible, abilities can only make it possible, since other conditions, like opportunities to exercise them, are also necessary to make existence worthwhile. This means that by causing someone with (severe) congenital disabilities to exist, we can *ensure* that this individual will not lead a life worth living, but by causing the existence of someone with an ever so rich repertoire of congenital abilities we *cannot* ensure that their life will be worth living. Therefore, we can have greater responsibility for a life not being worth living than for a life being worth living and, so, have more reason to prevent the former than to promote the latter. If we look at examples of starting good and bad lives which do not involve such considerations that are not specific to procreation, it seems to me doubtful that there is anything left of the Asymmetry. Consequently, I believe that the Asymmetry supplies no evidence in favour of a denial that beings can be harmed by being prevented from starting a good existence just as they can be harmed by starting a bad existence.

A further reason against the inclusive person-affecting view might be that it seems to imply that it can be harder to justify morally the killing of a human embryo than an adult human being because the former is likely to have more of a worthwhile life ahead. However, one reason why this does not follow has already surfaced: the adult has a capacity for autonomy, the exercise of which there is moral reason to respect. Moreover, a good future life of an embryo requires a greater input of other (act-)events to be realized; as remarked, its potentiality and congenital abilities are far from sufficient to ensure this. This means that the extrinsic goodness of allowing an embryo to continue its life may be small in comparison to the value of its future life because the contribution of this allowing to the realization of this value is small and contingent on many other contributory factors kicking in.

The irreversible cessation of consciousness is a moral turning point at which reasons of beneficence by and large cease to apply. As I argue in 5.1, the irreversible cessation of consciousness should not be confused with *death* which is the irreversible cessation of *biological life processes*, like breathing, circulation, digestion, and so on. It is not logically impossible that consciousness continues after the death of its 'host' organism, but it is in all likelihood empirically impossible (as long as transplants of the higher areas of the brain, or keeping brains alive in a vat are not feasible). However, as will be seen in 5.2, it is not even logically possible that there be consciousness which is independent of everything physical. This yields a sketch of an explanation of why the existence of value presupposes minds by tying it to their essential function of representation. At the same time, by tying this function to the dependent mode of existence of the mental, it ensures that what is of value for other minds is in principle within the reach of moral action in virtue of their dependence on the physical.

Some view membership of the species *Homo sapiens* as a ground for an especially elevated moral status. They regard non-human animals as having no moral status, or a lower status than human beings, simply in virtue of their not being human. In Chapter 6 I argue that membership of a biological species is not anything that could enhance moral status, in particular that human beings cannot have a higher moral status than non-human animals simply in virtue of belonging to the human species. This argument appeals, among other things, to the phenomenon of a *ring species*, which shows that species membership cannot be an essential or intrinsic property of biological individuals, as the biological view of our nature and identity probably has to presuppose. At the end of Part II when justice as equality has been added as a second moral principle, it will be seen in outline that the resulting morality will diverge radically from common-sense morality, and some of the problems that this raises will be examined in the first chapter of Part III. In the actual world, this denial of anthropocentric speciesism is of considerably greater practical moment than the inclusion of possible beings within the ambit of morality, though philosophically it is less controversial.

Egalitarianism and Prioritarianism

Common-sense morality features negative (claim-)rights *not* to have our person and property interfered with, and corresponding negative obligations *not* to interfere with the person and property of others, but no positive rights to receive assistance (see Persson, 2013: ch. 1). According to common-sense morality, reasons against harming by violating rights are generally stronger than reasons for benefiting, though strong enough reasons of the latter sort could reasonably outweigh the reasons of the former sort. Also, it takes less of a personal cost to agents to make it permissible for them to omit acting on reasons of beneficence—and make it supererogatory to do so—than to omit acting on reasons of rights.

The space of permissible action left by our rights and obligations is the sphere of our autonomy. This space permits us to treat ourselves better than others, though it is also permissible—and supererogatory—to be more concerned about others. As remarked, since rights will be rejected in Chapter 7, another justification for the limits of permissible autonomy will have to be found—an enterprise which will not be carried out in this book.

In Part II the topic is *justice or fairness* in respect of distribution of benefits. It is my belief that there is a principle of justice to the effect that justice requires everyone to be equally well off unless there are rights or deserts which make it just that some are better off than others, or the worse-off autonomously choose to be worse off. The denial of rights and deserts supported in Chapter 7 in conjunction with this principle issues in a far-reaching or extreme *egalitarianism*: justice requiring everyone to be equally well off, unless some autonomously choose to be worse off. Since it is morally permissible to favour others at one's own expense, we should not expect justice to rule it out.

In Chapter 8 it will be spelt out what this welfare egalitarianism is tantamount to. An attempt will be made to specify when one instance of unjust inequality with respect to benefits is worse than another, and what the value of just equality is. Justice is an impersonal value in a stronger sense than an interpersonal aggregate of benefits is. This is manifested by the fact that an outcome can be better than another in virtue of its distribution of benefits approximating more closely to what just equality requires—and even be better all things considered—without being better for anyone. But, I shall contend, just equality is not anything that is good in itself; it consists merely of the absence of the intrinsic badness of unjust inequality. The badness of unjust inequality diminishes the impersonal value that an outcome has in virtue of its amount of benefits, and at least in cases in which individuals begin or cease to exist, it may outweigh the latter value. That is, in these circumstances an outcome can be better (or worse) all things considered than another, even though it is not better (or worse) for anyone.

For this reason, unjust inequality can make it true that individuals ought not to be brought into existence if their level of welfare will be too much lower than that of existing individuals, while justice as equality never provides any reason to bring individuals into existence rather than bestowing the same amount of welfare on already existing individuals. By contrast, a rival to egalitarianism, *prioritarianism* or *the priority view*, provides a reason to prefer in this situation the bringing into existence of individuals even if their welfare level is low. Indeed, as will be demonstrated in Chapter 9, prioritarianism implies, counterintuitively, that a diffusion of welfare over a greater number of individuals is preferable to concentrating it to a smaller number. Thus, prioritarianism is less attractive than the version of egalitarianism here advocated. But irrespective of whether we are egalitarians or prioritarians, a morally justifiable distribution of benefits must refer to impersonal values. However, the primacy of personal values reveals itself in the fact that an outcome cannot exemplify impersonal values of the moral kind without containing personal values.

Chapter 10 reviews some problems of finding a ground for a more selective egalitarianism than the extreme egalitarianism here proposed, in particular an egalitarianism which ranges over only human beings or persons. This chapter also argues against the idea that, alongside an equal distribution of welfare, the equal treatment demanded by justice should comprise equal inviolability, or protection against being treated as a (mere) means.

The Usefulness of the Principles of Inclusive Beneficence and Extreme Egalitarianism

Part III is dedicated to general reflections on philosophical thinking about how to live. Its first chapter, 11, explores the applicability of the two moral principles put forward in this book, the inclusive view of reasons of beneficence and justice consisting in equal distribution of benefits. It will be seen that these principles sometimes pull in opposite directions and will have to be balanced against each other in an altogether intuitive fashion. This is one reason why a morality composed of both of these principles will not issue in determinate precepts about what morally ought to done in practice. Another reason is that both the value of aggregates of benefits and the degree of unjustly unequal distributions of benefits are highly imprecise magnitudes. Benefits have an overwhelming complexity, comprising not only the two aspects of well-being and exercises of autonomy, but also higher and lower qualities of well-being. There is no objective or intersubjectively acceptable way of weighing these dimensions of benefits against each other, just as there is no such way of weighing them against the injustice of an unequal distribution of benefits. Thus, it will often be indeterminate which of two outcomes is best all things considered, and ought to be chosen. A third reason for the absence of definite precepts is the incompleteness of our knowledge of morally relevant facts, especially about the amounts of benefits that different lives contain, or will contain if certain actions are performed.

If, as I have argued elsewhere (2013), the act-omission doctrine and the doctrine of the double effect should be rejected—for the reason that they embody a defective conception responsibility as causally based as well as a theory of rights—the two principles of inclusive beneficence and justice should be put in a consequentialist framework. Moreover, since I hold that personal identity is of no significance, this morality will not feature any options to favour oneself for reasons of identity. The result will be a morality more demanding than common-sense morality for those of us who are affluent, in particular since modern technology has vastly increased our powers of action. This is enough to ensure that it will be hard for us to conform to it. Compliance will however be even harder because, unlike common-sense morality, the revised morality will not have the intuitive support that common-sense morality enjoys, nor the authority that norms acquire simply by having been followed for generations.

Commonsensical moral distinctions are typically based on perceptually salient differences, for instance between what exists and what does not exist, what is alive and dead, what is human and non-human, what is caused and what is allowed to happen, and what is done or used as a means and what is done as a side effect, between what is present or future and what is past, and between oneself and others. These differences are taken to be the grounds for differences as regards value, or responsibility and related features like deserts and rights. A morality, such as the one expounded here, according to which such salient distinctions are declared morally irrelevant, will appear to most of us as too abstract and general to be taken seriously. To be sure, it will harness some commonsensical moral attitudes, in particular an altruistic desire to benefit others for their own sakes, and a desire to do what is just, but the content of these desires will be much more capacious. Again, the altruistic desire should encompass possible sentient beings, regardless of species and, since rights and deserts are groundless, contrary to what common sense assumes, justice is mostly a matter of wide-ranging equality.

If those of us who have these desires go along with this explication of their content, we shall be guided in roughly the right direction, but we shall have to do without any clear-cut and readily applicable moral rules. Although it is not part of the objective of this book to demonstrate it, I take it that morality rests on no firmer ground than the fact that desires oriented at beneficence and justice are widespread among us. It seems to me unlikely that metaethicists will be able to inject additional authority into moral norms by supplying them with an objective or attitude-independent support that will be persuasive to any larger number of us.

The Point of Moral Philosophy and a Philosophy of Life

Chapter 11 ends up with the suggestion that there are two necessary conditions for morality having a point: (a) it must be possible for most people to follow it, and (b) it must promote the welfare of the collective endorsing it, for example by means of promoting peaceful cooperation within it. This chapter shows that the morality defended here does not meet condition (a). By contrast, common-sense morality is in a better position to meet this condition, but now the hitch is that in the contemporary globalized world the relevant moral collective has to be expanded to include not only all present inhabitants on earth but future generations as well. For the current moral mega-problems, like anthropogenic climate change, environmental overexploitation, global poverty, and overpopulation, cannot be solved unless international cooperation replaces competition between smaller, for example, national, collectives. However, it is not easy to understand how a morality could both aim to promote the welfare of this vast collective and meet condition (a). A chief reason for this lies in genetically based, hard-wired features of our moral psychology that were suitable in our evolutionary past in which our ancestors lived in small communities with primitive technology. Thus, it seems to me that morality can scarcely have any point today.

Chapter 12 starts out by distinguishing between morality and moral philosophy having any point. Even if it is true that morality cannot have any point, it does not follow that moral philosophy does not have any point, but Chapter 12 contends that it does not in the most important sense. The argument is that (doing) moral philosophy will achieve its primary point just in case it results in a rational consensus about what is morally right and wrong, and what the ground and meaning of this is. But such a result is unlikely, since it appears inevitable that moral philosophy will be stuck in deep inconclusiveness. This holds both for normative ethics, where for instance the opposition between consequentialism and deontology is liable to remain unresolved, and for metaethics, where the same is likely to be true, for instance, of the opposition between externalist and internalist accounts of moral norms. The inconclusiveness of moral philosophy could have a deleterious effect on the authority of morality in the eyes of the public were it not for the fact that contemporary moral philosophy is largely esoteric.

Chapter 13 turns to a kind of philosophical thinking about how to live which is not committed to the goal of producing a consensus, since its subject is not a code claiming universal validity, like morality, but a code for individuals with particular aims. This kind of thinking—which I call *a philosophy of life*—is entirely intrapersonal and concentrates exclusively on how we should act and react in view of such basic facts about our lives as that they are strongly dependent on luck, the fact that we are more easily harmed than benefited, our mortality, the transience of our existence in a cosmic perspective, and the unimportance of our identity. Contemplation on how it is best for us to act and react in the light of such existential facts was practised by ancient philosophers, like the Stoics, who honoured the ideal of *autarchy*, of detaching ourselves from the external world by controlling our desires. This could help us cope with the demandingness of morality by weakening self-regarding desires which oppose moral motivation. It does not help with the more epistemic problems of implementing the two principles of inclusive beneficence and extreme egalitarianism identified in Chapter 11, problems that have to do with these principles being difficult to apply to concrete situations because of their great generality, the inexhaustibility and elusiveness of relevant empirical facts, and the complexity and imprecision of values, which have to be balanced against each other in a wholly intuitive fashion. Nevertheless, my impression is that by advocating a transition from an extravagant to a more frugal lifestyle, an autarchic philosophy of life could mitigate moral mega-problems to the extent that they no longer constitute a threat to human survival.

PART I

The Inclusiveness of Benefiting and Reasons of Beneficence

1
Two Aspects of Things Being Intrinsically Valuable for Us
Well-Being and Autonomy

1.1 The 'Inner' Aspect of Well-Being

In this chapter I shall examine two aspects of the notion of things going well for us or being intrinsically valuable for us. The first and less contestable aspect is the 'inner' or experiential aspect. I stipulate that this is what constitutes our *well-being*. As will be clear, there is both a sensual and a non-sensual part of our well-being. Then there is also an 'outer' or non-experiential aspect of things going well for us. This consists in our successfully exercising our *autonomy*. We successfully exercise our autonomy when we make and successfully implement informed, rational, and free or unconstrained decisions about how to arrange things for ourselves in a future extending beyond the immediate continuation of our current experiences. Provided our decisions meet the conditions mentioned, we have a moral permission to exercise our autonomy, but it is limited by the harm that we might do to others (again, no attempt will be made to fix these limits because this cannot be done without a more complete moral theory). As remarked in the Introduction, in my terminology to be benefited, being made better off or having more welfare can consist in either having more well-being or getting autonomy more respected.

The experience of pleasure figures prominently in the experiential side of things being intrinsically valuable for us. It has been extensively discussed in the history of philosophy since ancient times. I shall argue that on the basis of being aware that we have a desire to feel a current pleasure for its own sake, we can know, or be certain beyond reasonable doubt, that feeling this pleasure is intrinsically desirable or good for us. Likewise, on the basis of being aware that we have a desire not to feel, or be rid of, a current sensation of pain for its own sake, we can be certain beyond reasonable doubt that it is intrinsically undesirable or bad for us, but I shall phrase my argument exclusively in terms of pleasure.[1]

---

[1] The account that follows is a heavily revised version of the one I give in Persson (2000).

The reasoning to be presented here is reminiscent of an (in)famous argument that J. S. Mill puts forward in his *Utilitarianism* (1861). There he argues that 'the sole evidence it is possible to produce that anything is desirable is that people do actually desire it' (1861: 4.3).[2] G. E. Moore's objection to this passage is just as familiar. He claims that this argument embodies a fallacy—the so-called naturalistic fallacy—'so obvious, that it is quite wonderful how Mill failed to see it' (1903: 67). More recent commentators have retorted that Moore's charge is uncharitable: Mill does not commit the naturalistic fallacy of trying to *deduce* that something is desirable from the fact that it is desired, since he does not intend to formulate a deductively valid argument.[3] In contrast to these commentators, I believe that Mill's argument is, or rather could be turned into, a deductive argument given the truth of a cognitivist account of desirability or goodness. I also believe that such an account of the goodness of pleasure is true, but shall not argue for it here; therefore, I shall state my main claim differently.

I claim that the nature of intrinsically desiring pleasure is such that on its basis you can be *certain* that pleasure is intrinsically desirable for you, but you cannot be certain of any non-natural or irreducible normative/evaluative fact such as there being a reason for you to desire pleasure intrinsically; therefore, no such fact can be entailed by pleasure being intrinsically desirable for you. This claim holds good even if non-cognitivism is true, and 'Pleasure is intrinsically desirable for me' *expresses* my intrinsic desire for pleasure rather than makes an assertion about it. Then the presence of this desire still guarantees that I could confidently and rightly assert 'Pleasure is intrinsically desirable for me', though this would not be because I can *infer* the truth of this claim from the fact that I have the desire in question.

Whereas Mill describes the relevant desire as the 'sole' evidence that you can produce for something's being good, I would rather describe it as the *best* evidence that you can have, and as evidence which is good enough for rational certainty. Mill talks about 'happiness' by which he means 'pleasure and the absence of pain' (1861: 2.2). But I shall be talking simply about the intrinsic desirability of pleasure, since the absence of pain is not desirable in itself. The state of feeling pain is bad or undesirable in itself, but of course it does not follow from this that *the absence* of pain is desirable in itself. It is *not un*desirable in itself, which is not the same as it being desirable in itself; this state may also be one of not feeling pleasure, and as such not desirable in itself. On the whole, my aim is not exegetical; I am more concerned with something that Mill could truly have said than with what he in fact said.

Let me begin by trying to clarify the notion of pleasure (for a fuller exposition, see Persson, 2005: ch. 2). We can broadly distinguish between *sensory pleasure*—the sort of pleasure that you could feel when you scratch where it itches, stretch your cramped legs, eat something sweet, smell freshly baked bread, and so on—and *propositional*

---

[2] Due to there being many editions of *Utilitarianism*, I shall follow the common practice of referring not to pages, but to chapter and paragraph.

[3] See Frankena (1963: 69–70); Norman (1983: 136); Skorupski (1989: 285–6); and Crisp (1997: 74).

pleasure, that is, being pleased that something is the case, for instance that you have spotted a rare bird. Propositional pleasure is dependent on a belief that could be false, though the construction 'being pleased that' is factive, that is, it implies that that about which one is pleased is actually the case. If you did not in fact spot a rare bird, we would have to say something like that you are pleased because you think that you spotted a rare bird. Sensory pleasure is not belief-dependent: for instance, the sort of sensation of pleasure that you have when you are tasting something sweet does not rest on any belief that you have about sweetness (or about anything else). Belief-independence is something that plausibly distinguishes sensations from emotions (see Persson, 2005: 61–2): in virtue of having so-called intentional objects—that is, when you are afraid, there is something that you are afraid *of*, when you are angry, there is something that you are angry *at*, and so on—emotions are dependent on certain beliefs about their objects. Sensations of pleasure do not have such objects, while propositional pleasure does and, thus, is an emotion.

If the belief involved in propositional pleasure is false, it is arguable that the state of feeling this pleasure is not *wholly* intrinsically good, since it may be held that it is bad for you to have a false belief (e.g. because you want your beliefs to be true). But the component of pleasure in propositional pleasure could still be good for you. To postpone this complication of the falsity of a belief tainting the state of feeling pleasure—which would take us beyond a purely experiential notion of well-being—I shall initially focus exclusively on sensory pleasure.

Some, for example Fred Feldman (2004: 57 and 79–81), claim that sensory pleasures can be understood as a sort of propositional pleasure. This has some plausibility if one assumes, as Feldman seems to do, that propositional pleasure includes not just being pleased that something is the case, but also *enjoying* something. It is more plausible, I believe, to hold that having a sensation of pleasure is having a sensation that you are enjoying having than that it is having a sensation that you are pleased that you are having. It is possible to have a sensation of pleasure not only without being pleased that you have it, but while being displeased that you have it, say, because you are of an ascetic or puritanical bent, or because this particular pleasure is a sign that something is awry with your body.

Enjoyment is, however, different from being pleased that something is the case. As Feldman himself notes (2004: 62n), enjoyment differs from being pleased about some fact in that, while we can be pleased about a past or future fact, it seems that we can enjoy only what is present. Moreover, enjoyment is not propositional and belief-dependent like being pleased that: we cannot enjoy *that* something is the case which we (truly) believe to be the case. The object of enjoyment is rather some *event* that we are currently experiencing, for instance some sensation that we are feeling. As I have already admitted, there is some plausibility in the view that having a sensation of pleasure is having a sensation that is enjoyed. Like the view that a sensation of pleasure is a sensation that you are pleased that you are having, it is a view of the kind that says that what makes a sensation a sensation of pleasure is not that it in itself has a special sensory quality, but that the subject feeling it takes up a certain attitude to it. In the case of enjoying, or liking, the sensation, this attitude is an attitude of wanting or desiring for its own sake that the sensation continues.[4]

Although I believe that as a matter of fact we almost always take up such an attitude towards sensations of pleasure, I have elsewhere (2005: ch. 2; cf. ch. 1 on sensations of pain) argued that the correct view is that a sensation is one of pleasure because it has an intrinsic sensory quality of being pleasant or pleasurable. I maintain that we intrinsically desire, like or enjoy such sensations *because* they are (in possession of this quality of being) pleasant; it is not the other way around, that they are pleasant because we intrinsically desire, like or enjoy them. However, we can here sidestep this controversy, since we shall only be considering sensations of pleasure that are intrinsically desired, liked, or enjoyed. This is because it is only such sensations of pleasure that are plausibly desirable or good for us.

Parfit's view is that liking is better not regarded as a desire (2011: vol. 1, 52–6). One of his reasons for this view is that liking is not future-oriented. Now it might seem that liking is not future-oriented when it is *elicited* by a current sensation of pleasure—this is, I believe, the situation in which we speak of enjoying the sensation—but the *object* of the liking is that this sensation should *go on*, and that is an (imminent) future state. More precisely, the liking of pleasure is a disposition to have such a desire which is elicited by a pleasant sensation that is currently felt. The satisfaction of the elicited occurrent desire by the continuation of the sensation is enjoying the sensation.[5] It is hard to see why evolution would have equipped us with a liking and disliking of sensations of pleasure and pain, respectively, if these were not reactions of seeking and avoiding these sensations (which tend to signalize conditions that are beneficial and harmful to our organisms).

Another reason that Parfit gives for not regarding liking as a desire is that it cannot be fulfilled or unfulfilled. But it *can* be fulfilled or unfulfilled, by the relevant sensation continuing or stopping.[6] A third (tacit) reason might be that, since Parfit grants that liking a pleasure makes it good, accepting that liking is a desire would have supported the view that having desires for things can make them good. But this is a reason for denying that liking is a desire only if one rejects the view that goodness can be desire-dependent, as he does.

My claim is that the state of feeling pleasure is intrinsically good *for the subject feeling it*.[7] As noted in the Introduction, this notion of what is personally good stands in

---

[4] As observed, in the case of Feldman's account the relevant attitude is that of taking pleasure in the sensation. Thus, in contrast to theories that appeal to the other attitudes mentioned, his account appeals to another kind of *pleasure*—propositional pleasure—in the analysans of sensory pleasure, and it does not answer the question of what this other kind of pleasure consists in. Consequently, Feldman cannot claim to have offered an analysis of all kinds of pleasure.

[5] So, the explanation of the fact just mentioned that enjoyment is restricted to the present is that it consists in the satisfaction of a desire which is elicited by a current experience.

[6] I spell out these two replies to Parfit a bit more fully in Persson (2013: 272–3).

[7] Sometimes when we employ the phrase 'good for you', we use it in the different sense of something being of *extrinsic* value for you, for example eating vegetables is good for you.

opposition to the notion of what is impersonally good, or good full stop. The things in an outcome that are (personally) good for individuals can together make an outcome impersonally good and—according to utilitarianism, for instance—the action of producing the outcome morally right. Other things than the sum of what is personally good can be impersonally good, for instance a just or fair distribution of what is personally good. But now I am not talking about what is impersonally good, or what is morally good which, as suggested in the Introduction, is a species of impersonal goodness that essentially involves what is personally good. By contrast, Mill moves swiftly from personal goodness to impersonal and moral goodness: 'each person's happiness is a good to that person, and the general happiness, therefore, a good to the aggregate of all persons' (1861: 4.3).

Few would deny that, in virtue of being an intrinsic, personal good, pleasure in whatever form—sensory pleasure, propositional pleasure, or enjoyment—is at least a part of our well-being; what is controversial is the hedonist claim that it is *all* of it. I am prepared to accept that our well-being is all a matter of our experiences, though I regard it as misleading to say that it is all a matter of pleasant (and painful or unpleasant) experiences. However, if we adopt such an experiential conception of well-being, I think that we should insist that there is more to the notion of things going well for us, or being intrinsically good for us, than well-being. To recycle an example used in the Introduction, consider people who are pleased with their lives only because they are thoroughly deceived: they think that they are loved and respected by family and friends and successful in their professions, whereas they are in fact secretly despised and ridiculed by family and friends, and complete failures professionally. These people desire to be loved and respected and professionally successful, and would be devastated if they were to find out the truth. I think that we should admit that things would have been better for them if this desire had been fulfilled, and they had in fact been loved, respected, and successful, though their experiential states would have been the same.

Feldman proposes to build this outer aspect into hedonism by launching the notion of *truth-adjusted* pleasure (2004: 112–14). Then hedonism could still be a full theory of well-being in the more encompassing sense of what makes things intrinsically valuable for you. Personally, I find it more natural to take 'well-being' to designate only things going experientially well for you—the experiential inside of things going well for you—and provide room also for an outer aspect of things actually going well for you as your successfully exercising your autonomy. This terminology clearly brings out that there are two separable elements here, one of which requires a more sophisticated mind that has a conception not only of things beyond present experiences, but also of itself as having such experiences at other times than the present.

Putting aside autonomy until the second section of this chapter, let me state the principal reason why I think that we should not characterize the experiential conception of well-being as hedonist, why the experiences that make up our well-being are not simply pleasant and painful experiences (for a fuller discussion of this point, see

Persson, 2005: ch. 3). Sensations of pleasure are good for us because we like them, that is, are disposed occurrently to enjoy them when we have them. Such instances of enjoyment may be labelled *sensual enjoyment* because what we enjoy is the having of certain types of sensation. Sometimes, however, what we enjoy is not the having of certain types of sensation; it is the doing of certain activities in which we take an *interest*, that is, want to engage in for their own sakes. These activities can be of many different kinds, some being predominantly intellectual, like doing mathematics or philosophy, while others are predominantly physical, like running or riding. I propose to call the enjoyment that we can obtain from the doing of such activities *interest-enjoyment*.

When we enjoy doing an activity, we necessarily have experiences of doing it, but our enjoyment of these experiences is different from sensual enjoyment. A way to tell these two kinds of enjoyment apart is by looking at their opposites: the opposite of sensual enjoyment is *suffering*, whereas the opposite of interest-enjoyment is rather *boredom*. Except when we are overwhelmed by some experience (such as an orgasm), we incessantly have desires to *do* one thing or another, to be *active*, but when we do not experience anything that gives us the opportunity to do anything that captures our interest, we are or feel bored. This is different from having experiences that we positively want to be rid of—for example, pains—which happens when we suffer. Sometimes, though, these two kinds of enjoyment are entangled. Take wine-tasting, for instance: here we may be both enjoying the having of certain pleasant sensations, and be interested in discriminating between kinds of flavours that give rise to them. Also, it seems that we can suffer from feeling bored, that is, the feeling of being bored can evoke an intrinsic desire to be rid of this feeling, a desire which is frustrated by our failing to get rid of the feeling.

It may sometimes seem quite strained to regard that in which we take an interest as something purely experiential. For instance, if we take an interest in conducting some scientific experiments, it is likely that we do so only because we believe that we shall thereby discover some truths. But there is nevertheless an experiential inside of enjoyment, and that is what makes up a contribution to our well-being. Although we would not take an interest in conducting the experiments if we did not have the belief that they would reveal truths, we might enjoy them as much even if they fail to do so.

Summing up what has been laid out thus far, the result is that positive well-being consists in experiences like sensual enjoyment, interest-enjoyment and propositional pleasure that something is the case. It should be added that propositional pleasure can assume different forms, not just being pleased, but also being glad, delighted, overjoyed, excited, and relieved, due to differences in the intensity of the feeling, or the kind of propositional object. Also, we should not forget that there are (positive) *moods* which differ from emotions in not having objects (see Persson, 2005: 63). Ill-being consists in suffering from painful or otherwise unpleasant sensations (itches, nausea, dizziness, etc.), being bored, having different kinds of propositional displeasure, or moods like depression. It does not matter for present purposes how complete these lists are; nor does it matter whether the view proposed is classified as a version of hedonism.

The positive experiences listed are all intrinsically good for the subject. It might be objected that goodness *for* a subject cannot be intrinsic because it involves a relation to the subject. But that would be a confusion. The fact that the goodness of something, X, is intrinsic implies that its goodness does not derive from the *goodness* of anything *external* to X. But the subject is not anything external to the state of feeling enjoyment, since this state is necessarily a state of a subject. Nor does the claim that enjoying pleasure is good for the subject imply that the goodness of this state of enjoyment derives from the goodness of the subject, or the relation to anything external to this state. It is the—relational, if you like—state of a subject feeling enjoyment which is good, and the goodness is intrinsic to this state, that is, the state is good in virtue of features intrinsic or internal to it.

This could be so, although the goodness of feeling enjoyment is open to an *analysis* in terms of this feeling standing in the relation of satisfying one of the subject's desires, and this relation is a relation to something external. For this analysis does not imply that the desire is the primary bearer of goodness and that the goodness of the feeling is derivative from its goodness. It is instead a *metaethical* claim about how goodness should be *analysed*, or what it consists in, and as such it is compatible with the *axiological* claim that the goodness of feeling enjoyment does not derive from the *goodness* of anything external to this state. By contrast, the distinction between intrinsic and extrinsic goodness, being axiological, is to the effect that the goodness of what is extrinsically good derives from the goodness of something external to it—goodness here being a primitive, undefined notion.

A metaethical theory could then provide room for something being intrinsically good by analysing it in terms of it satisfying some intrinsic desire, though the desire is something external to the good thing, which in the present case is a feeling of pleasure. This is because such an analysis does not imply that the goodness of the state of feeling pleasure derives from the goodness of the desire. This state must, however, satisfy such a desire in virtue of its intrinsic properties in order for its goodness to be intrinsic. Just as it should provide room for the axiological distinction between intrinsic and extrinsic goodness, a metaethical theory should provide room for the axiological distinction between goodness that is personal and impersonal. It can do so by laying down that what is (personally) good for you is so in virtue of satisfying some desire of yours which is in some suitable sense 'self-regarding'. I submit that a desire is self-regarding just in case its object contains an ineliminable reference to the subject having the desire, as your desire to feel pleasure does when it is a desire that *you* feel it (see Persson, 2005: 151). What is impersonally good would rather have to satisfy some desire which is impersonal or universal in the sense of containing no ineliminable reference to particular individuals.

The desire that we have as regards a sensation of pleasure when we are enjoying it is an intrinsic desire, that is, we desire to feel pleasure for its own sake, for what it is in itself, independently of its relations to anything external to it. Furthermore, I take it that the desire is *originally* intrinsic unlike, say, a miser's intrinsic desire for money. The intrinsicality of the latter desire is not original if money was originally desired by the miser for the sake of something external to it, such as the pleasure money can buy, and this association of having money with other pleasurable states of affairs has subsequently fallen into oblivion, while the desire for money persists.[8] On pain of an infinite regress, the intrinsicality of all intrinsic desires cannot be acquired or derivative in this fashion; in some cases it must be original.

I maintain that the originally intrinsic desire for pleasure is 'incorrigible' or immune to factual errors (cf. Persson, 2005: 144–8). An instrumental or, more broadly, an extrinsic, desire can obviously involve factual mistakes about its object: for instance, you desire to take a pill because you believe that it will make you happy or pain-free, but, in fact, it will cause you pain. The same goes for intrinsic desires which started their lives as extrinsic desires. But the intrinsic desire for pleasure started out as intrinsic; it is originally intrinsic and can involve no such mistakes.

In order to desire (or have any propositional attitude) with respect to X, you must have the concept of X. To qualify as having the concept of X, there are certain truths about X that you must know: for instance, you do not have the concept of a triangle unless you know that a triangle is a plane figure with three straight sides. But it is reasonable to claim that an originally intrinsic desire for X involves nothing about X other than knowledge of truths about X that you must know to qualify as having the concept of X. This is, I think, true of the originally intrinsic desire for experiencing pleasure. I take the concept of pleasure to be learnt largely ostensively, by having experiences of pleasure, and take an intrinsic desire for experiencing pleasure to involve nothing about pleasure other than the knowledge of the nature of pleasure that you then acquire. If this is so, it is logically guaranteed that an intrinsic desire for pleasure cannot be factually mistaken about its object. If it were to involve any such mistakes, the object of the desire would not really be pleasure because the subject would not possess the concept of pleasure.

Notice, however, that the desire that I am claiming is incorrigible is an intrinsic desire to the effect that a *current* pleasure continue. Desires that you have with respect to *future* pleasures are corrigible. For instance, you may be rather indifferent to a pleasure that you will have in the future because you do not fully realize how much you will like it when you are having it. This sort of mistake is not possible with respect to a desire which concerns a pleasure that you are currently feeling and which is elicited by this pleasure.

Now, like all desires, an originally intrinsic desire with respect to a particular thing arguably presupposes a factual belief that may be false. Mill appears to suggest that a desire presupposes a belief to the effect that the object of desire is 'attainable' (1861: 4.3; I make a similar claim, e.g. 2005: 48–9). But the falsity of such a belief about the attainability

---

[8] This is a distinction to which Mill, for one, draws attention (1861: 4.6).

of a particular object desired does not imply that the object is not of a general kind that would be good for the subject were it acquired, and the desire were satisfied. *Qua* being originally intrinsic, or with respect to the beliefs that make a desire for pleasure originally intrinsic, this desire cannot be mistaken.

Desires that are 'incorrigible', in the sense that I have proposed that the intrinsic desire for pleasure is, could be seen as the practical counterparts of the allegedly incorrigible beliefs about sense-experience that are a typical feature of foundationalist epistemology. But the different 'directions of fit' of beliefs and desires make the case for the incorrigibility of intrinsic desires in the present sense stronger. It is widely accepted that the 'direction of fit' of desires is opposite to that of beliefs.[9] The function of beliefs is to have a content that fits the facts, or is true; that is the function that beliefs have evolved to serve. By contrast, the function of desires is to make the facts fit their content or object; the function that desires have evolved to serve is to make us so act that they are fulfilled. So, when desires do not fit the facts, this does not imply that they are misdirected in the sense of having objects that would not be valuable were they realized. In contrast, if beliefs fail to fit the facts, they are misdirected and should be corrected.

If the purely factual correctness of the beliefs involved in an intrinsic desire is sufficient for it being intrinsically desirable for the subject that the object of desire obtains— that is, if this factual sense is the only sense in which an (originally) intrinsic desire can be misdirected—Moore's objection to Mill is met. This is not to say that 'pleasure is intrinsically desirable for me' is *entailed* by 'pleasure is intrinsically desired by me' (even if metaethical cognitivism is assumed). The argument goes through because the object desired, pleasure, is such that an (originally) intrinsic desire for it cannot be wrong or misdirected in the sense indicated. The deductive argument would then start from the fact that you have an originally intrinsic desire for pleasure, proceed via the additional premise that this desire cannot be relevantly misdirected, to the conclusion that pleasure is intrinsically desirable for you.

The crux is, however, that it is controversial whether the factual sense delineated is the only sense in which an originally intrinsic desire can be misdirected. Moore, for one, would deny it. When he writes (1903: 67) that the desirable is 'what *ought* to be desired', he means to exclude not only what would be wrongly desired because of mistakes about non-normative or non-evaluative facts. Moore believes that there are normative or evaluative facts that are not reducible to non-normative/evaluative facts. So does Parfit who believes that there is an irreducible or non-natural reason to desire pleasure for its own sake (2011: vol. 1, pt. 1).[10] Even if an intrinsic desire is impeccable as far as natural facts go, it may not be a proper response to this kind of reason.

---

[9] The term 'direction of fit' may have been coined by Platts (1979: 256–7). But the idea of contrasting beliefs and desires in this regard is older, going back at least to Anscombe (1957).

[10] Cf. also Feldman who believes that there are certain states of affairs that deserve to be objects of pleasure, or that it is fitting or appropriate to take pleasure in (2004: 119–22).

In reply, it could be noticed first that, due to their direction of fit, intrinsic desires do not call for supporting reasons to the same extent as beliefs do. This is because desires are not designed to fit the facts, or be true as beliefs are. If we know that each of p and not-p is attainable, we can go ahead and desire one rather than the other, being confident that we shall get the requisite fit. But knowing that p and not-p is each possible, we cannot go ahead and believe one rather than the other, being confident that we shall get the requisite fit. This fact that there is less of a need for a reason for having an (originally) intrinsic desire for pleasure seems fortunate because the idea of such a reason faces serious problems, as I shall now try to show.

(a) What could the content of this reason be? It cannot be that pleasure is pleasure. That is no reason to desire pleasure. If such a platitude were a reason, there would be a reason to desire anything, since anything is identical to itself. It might be thought that there cannot be any reason to desire something, X, for its own sake, since every reason must relate X to something else, and then the desire that one has for this reason will not be intrinsic, but extrinsic. However, this is not so because the relation to which the reason refers need not be a relation to anything *external* to X; it could be a relation that X has to a proper part of itself. Suppose, for instance, that being pleasant is only one of a number of properties that a sensation has in itself, for example the sensation is also cool or sweet. Then, if one desires this complex sensation for the reason that it is pleasant, the desire for it is intrinsic. We may, however, still deny that it is an originally intrinsic desire, since it is derived from an intrinsic desire for pleasure. But it seems that there cannot be a reason for the latter desire.

The reply to this might be that pleasure could be desired for the reason that it is intrinsically good. But then it would be intrinsic goodness, not pleasure, for which we had an originally intrinsic desire. Moreover, although Moore could give this reply, since he believes goodness to be a simple and indefinable property (1903: 6ff.), Parfit could not because he accepts the so-called buck-passing account of goodness which analyses the good in terms of what there is reason to desire (2011: vol. 1, 38–9). However, irrespective of whether the basic non-natural facts are taken to be normative or evaluative or both, the following problem arises (see also Persson, 2013: 275–81):

(b) According to the non-naturalist view under consideration, a normative truth such as that there is a reason to desire intrinsically a particular sensation is not *entailed* by the natural or empirical truth that it is a sensation of pleasure—this would be naturalism. But it is still supposed by Parfit to be *necessarily* true that if something is a sensation of pleasure, there is a reason to desire it for its own sake. Thus, although this truth cannot be shown to be a truth by conceptual analysis, it is supposed to be necessary. Granted, it seems that there are truths that are necessary, though they are not analytic or conceptual even in a broader sense, for instance identity statements such as that Hesperus is identical to Phosphorus. Notice, however, that such truths are known a posteriori, or on the basis of experience. Once we have established by astronomical observation that what the names 'Hesperus' and 'Phosphorus' refer to is the same planet, Venus, the necessity involved comes out as straightforward as any necessity can be: it is the necessity of something being identical to itself.

The necessity of the normative truths cannot be demystified by any similar means because they are supposed to be known a priori, not a posteriori or by observation. But how is such knowledge of these truths possible when they are not true on conceptual grounds which would give us naturalism? The medium of thinking is concepts; so, if a proposition is not true in virtue of the relations between its concepts, it is hard to see how it could be known to be true a priori, on the basis of pure thinking. It might be replied that I can know a priori that I exist, or that I am here, though these are not analytic or conceptual truths. However, since these examples are not necessary truths, but contingent truths about this world, there is room for the suspicion that they are after all known a posteriori on the basis of experiences that I cannot fail to have if I am thinking these thoughts, in particular, an introspectible experience of thinking these thoughts. Because this issue seems hard to resolve, it will be difficult to make a convincing case for there being synthetic truths a priori by adducing these examples. Further, even if there are contingent truths that are synthetic and a priori knowable, it does not follow that there are any *necessary* truths that are synthetic a priori knowable (for a more elaborate version of this argument, see Persson, 2013: 275–81). It seems mysterious how we could know by pure thinking that something is true in every possible world if this truth is not conceptually guaranteed: what could then be the ground of this knowledge?

(c) The considerations (a) and (b) might not suffice to refute the view that there are non-natural reasons to have intrinsic desires, including a non-natural reason to desire pleasure for its own sake, but they are surely enough to make it reasonable or rational to *doubt* that there are such reasons.[11] This gives rise to another difficulty for the view that there are non-natural reasons for intrinsic desires. Suppose that you are aware of the content of such a reason, for example that you are aware of feeling pleasure. Then, according to Parfit, you are rationally required to respond to this awareness by intrinsically desiring that the sensation you are having goes on. But we have just seen that you can rationally doubt that there is a reason for you to have an intrinsic desire for pleasure, a sensation of the sort you are feeling. It would seem that this rational doubt about the existence of this reason releases you from the (alleged) rational requirement to respond to what you are feeling by an intrinsic desire. For you are certainly not rationally required to respond to a fact in some way if you rationally doubt that it is a reason requiring you to respond in this way. However, it does not seem right that you could release yourself from the rational requirement that a reason that you are aware of having puts you under by rationally doubting that it is a reason.

---

[11] The mere fact that there is a metaethical debate about the existence of non-natural reasons supports the same point, for surely it cannot be seriously maintained that all those who deny or doubt the existence of such reasons do so irrationally.

For imagine that you are aware of a paradigmatic reason, such as if p then q and p. This is a reason that puts you under a rational requirement to respond to it by believing q. Surely, you cannot release yourself from this requirement by doubting that if p then q and p is a reason for believing q. If you were to entertain this doubt, it would show that you do not understand what a reason for belief is, what it means that the truth of some proposition counts in favour of the truth of some other proposition. Such a failure of understanding would undermine the rationality of your doubt. Thus, in the case of a bona fide reason of whose content we are aware, it appears that we cannot release ourselves from the rational requirement that it imposes on us by rationally doubting that it is a reason. But in the case of putative non-natural reasons for intrinsic desires, such as an intrinsic desire to feel pleasure, it would seem that we can release ourselves from the rational requirements that they supposedly impose on us by rationally doubting that they are such reasons. Therefore, they are spurious reasons (for a more elaborate exposition of this argument, see Persson, 2013: 281–8).

(d) There is another kind of epistemic argument which applies more specifically to alleged reasons to desire pleasure and to be averse to pain for their own sakes. If any sort of normative/evaluative fact can lay claim to being beyond reasonable doubt, it is surely such facts as that pleasure is intrinsically desirable for us (and pain intrinsically undesirable for us). The fact that we intrinsically desire pleasure plausibly gives us such good evidence for believing that pleasure is intrinsically desirable for us that this is beyond reasonable doubt. However, if we cannot reasonably or rationally doubt that p, while we can reasonably or rationally doubt q, we are rationally required to deny that p entails q. Therefore, since we can be rationally certain that pleasure is intrinsically desirable for us on the basis of intrinsically desiring it, while in view of (a), (b), and (c), we could rationally doubt that there is a non-natural reason to desire pleasure intrinsically, rationality requires us to deny that the fact that pleasure is intrinsically desirable for us entails that there is a non-natural reason to desire pleasure intrinsically.[12]

It might be remarked that it is only if you are absolutely certain that pleasure is intrinsically desirable for you that you are rationally required to take it as absolutely certain that this entailment does not hold. True, but I take it that you can be so certain that pleasure is intrinsically desirable for you that you cannot rationally doubt it. Since you have strong reasons to doubt that there is a non-natural reason to desire pleasure intrinsically—in the shape of (a), (b), and (c) above—you are rationally required to assign such a low probability to the claim that the former entails the latter that it is tantamount to a denial of this entailment claim. Anything but the lowest probability of this claim would mean that the doubtfulness of the existence of the reason undermines the certainty of the intrinsic desirability.

I conclude, then, that the fact that we intrinsically desire pleasure and the fact that this desire cannot go factually wrong guarantees that pleasure is intrinsically desirable

---

[12] In an attempt to rebut scepticism, some epistemologists question this sort of argument—that knowledge or rational certainty is closed under known implication—but this seems to me very far-fetched.

for us, since there is no question of any other kind of wrongness. Thus, the following claim is true:

(D) If I intrinsically desire pleasure, pleasure is intrinsically desirable for me because an (originally) intrinsic desire for pleasure is incorrigible (*qua* being intrinsic).

(D) is analogous to an incorrigibility claim traditionally made by epistemological foundationalists:

(B) If I believe that I am feeling pleasure, I *am* feeling pleasure because this belief is incorrigible.

However, I submit that (D) is harder to deny than (B) because desires, as opposed to beliefs, are not designed to fit the facts.

According to normative/evaluative non-naturalism, however, (D) is not true. To see why more precisely, let us split up (D) into two claims:

(D1) If I intrinsically desire pleasure, I have a desire which is not in any way corrigible.

(D2) If my intrinsic desire for pleasure is not in any way corrigible, pleasure is intrinsically desirable for me.

I believe that (D1) is true because an intrinsic desire could only be corrigible in a factual way, by involving a mistake about natural or non-normative/evaluative facts, and I have argued that an intrinsic desire for pleasure, *qua* being intrinsic, is incorrigible in this way. It follows that this is also how I understand the antecedent of (D2). Non-naturalists about reasons, however, must take 'is not in any way corrigible' in (D2) and, hence, in (D1), as implying something like being in accordance with an irreducible normative reason. But if this is so, (D1) is *not* true, since the natural fact of my intrinsically desiring pleasure cannot guarantee the existence of a non-natural reason to desire pleasure intrinsically to which my desire is a proper response.

To summarize, I have contended that, on the basis of being rationally certain that I intrinsically desire pleasure, I can be rationally certain that pleasure is intrinsically desirable for me because (D) is true. According to a non-naturalist construal of intrinsic desirability, however, I could rationally doubt that pleasure is intrinsically desirable for me, though I am rationally certain that I intrinsically desire it. This is because, as noted, there are ample grounds to doubt the existence of a reason to desire pleasure intrinsically—namely (a), (b), and (c)—which, according to this construal, is entailed by the intrinsic desirability of pleasure. If I can doubt the existence of such a reason, I can of course doubt that my intrinsic desire is in accordance with it.

However, this seems to me intuitively implausible. Rather, when I am rationally certain that I intrinsically desire pleasure, I cannot rationally doubt that pleasure is intrinsically desirable for me. I should conclude that I can be rationally certain of this, too, on the strength of (D). But then normative/evaluative non-naturalism is false in this instance: the existence of a non-natural reason for me to desire pleasure intrinsically is not necessary for pleasure being intrinsically desirable for me.

If the existence of such reasons is not necessary for something being intrinsically desirable for you and me, it is not plausible to hold it to be sufficient, either. This would have to mean that there were two very different kinds of sufficient conditions for something's being personally desirable. Moreover, it seems hard to believe that it could be intrinsically desirable for me to be in some experiential state—such as the one of feeling pleasure—if in fact I do not intrinsically desire to be in that state, though I am aware of being in it.

1.2 The 'Outer' Aspect of Successful Exercise of Autonomy

In my view there is, however, more to things going well or being intrinsically valuable for us than our well-being. Things could go well for us, even though they transcend the bounds not only of the immediate continuation of our current experiences, but all of our experiences as does, for instance, the purely factual satisfaction of our intrinsic desires to the effect that our friends do not secretly despise and backbite us, or that our last wills are respected. But, as remarked in the Introduction, if the factual satisfaction of such desires which are not at all about our having certain experiences can be a component of what makes things go well for us, the factual satisfaction of intrinsic desires which are at least partly about our having certain experiences, but go beyond the immediate continuation of our present experiences, can surely also be a component of what makes things go well for us. The goals that we have in life—including the hedonist goal to lead the life which maximizes the net sum of one's pleasurable experiences—are desires of this trans-experiential type. Consequently, I suggest that alongside the inner or experiential aspect of things going well for us—our well-being—there is an outer aspect of things going well for us which consists in our successfully exercising our autonomy or, in other words, in the factual satisfaction of our autonomous desires about things having to do with us, which extend beyond the immediate continuation of our current experiences.

While I argued in the foregoing section that our intrinsic desires oriented at our current experiences are incorrigible, our self-regarding, intrinsic desires which stretch beyond such experiences can be mistaken. Thus, in order for it to be plausibly claimed that the fulfilment of such desires is good for us, or benefits us, they must meet a condition of being rationally formed on the basis of relevant, comprehensive information. As indicated, to spell out more precisely what this condition involves is too complex a task to be undertaken here. The same goes for the condition that they be freely formed, that is, formed when the individual is not subject to factors like coercion or compulsion. These conditions partly overlap, because it is not unreasonable to take the condition of being rationally formed to exclude compulsion, as in the case of a kleptomaniac's desire to steal, which illustrates unfreedom due to internal circumstances.[13] I propose, then, that it is intrinsically good for us if our self-regarding, intrinsic desires that are autonomous in the sense of meeting such conditions are fulfilled.

Needless to say, it is only individuals with more sophisticated minds—persons—who are in possession of autonomy; it is only they who have a conception of themselves existing as psycho-physical beings in a future beyond the immediate continuation of present experiences. Simply to draw a distinction between how you experience things and how they actually are requires conceptual sophistication to a degree that is reasonably the privilege of persons. Thus, the capacity of forming trans-experiential desires which is a prerequisite for autonomy is a capacity which only persons can have.

To respect our (exercises of) autonomy is to let us pursue the fulfilment of our self-regarding and autonomous desires. Respect for our autonomy comprises some but not all autonomous future-oriented desires that we have had in the past, but no longer have; for instance, it comprises respecting last wills. There is a distinction between future-oriented desires that we have lost because we have autonomously changed our minds, and ones that we have lost because we have lost the capacity to form such desires, due to factors like death and dementia.[14] Respect for autonomy only requires that past desires of the latter sort are taken into account.

As remarked in the Introduction, the term 'autonomy' is ambiguous: it can designate either the capacity to form desires about ourselves in a more extensive future, or a moral permission to do this, provided that the desires formed meet the conditions of being autonomous. I have proposed that we take desires being 'about ourselves' to mean that they are self-regarding in the sense that their objects or contents involve ineliminable reference to ourselves.[15] However, their objects can involve such reference to ourselves and still seriously affect other sentient beings. This raises the problem of the limits of our permission to exercise our autonomy, which I have already announced that I shall largely shelve, along with the task of providing a more precise account of the conditions of being autonomous. I hope that this is an affordable omission in the context of the ambitions of this essay; nonetheless, some comments on these issues may be useful.

Mill's famous 'principle of liberty' affirms that 'the only purpose for which power can be rightfully exercised over any member of a civilized community, against his will, is to prevent harm to others' (1859: 9). But the problem is: what counts as 'harm to others'? My view is that common-sense morality incorporates a theory of negative (claim-)rights that answers this question (and that Mill may implicitly and illicitly

---

[13] The freedom that I take to be an ingredient in autonomy is freedom in a compatibilist sense which I explore most fully in Persson (2005: chs. 32 and 33), not the incompatibilist sort required by ultimate responsibility.

[14] If we have forgotten a desire, it may be unclear whether it belongs to the first or second class. This depends on whether we would endorse it were we reminded of it.

[15] As will be seen later in this section and in more detail in 3.1, it is strictly speaking too narrow to require ineliminable reference to *ourselves*. This requirement should be broadened to include 'successors' of ourselves whose existence would be as good for us as our own survival.

have relied on it). The idea would be that as long as you do not infringe the rights of others, you act within the boundaries of your autonomy even if what you do has other harmful consequences for others. For instance, since normally no shopkeepers have rights against you that you buy their merchandise rather than that of their rivals, you act within the bounds of your autonomy if you do your shopping from their rivals, though this harms their business. By contrast, they have rights that you do not rob or inflict physical harm on them, so this goes beyond your autonomy. Such an appeal to rights, however, will not do in the present context, since their existence is denied in Chapter 7 (see also Persson, 2013: ch. 2). But, to repeat, no attempt to replace it with a full-scale account of the limits of our autonomy will be made here, since this will take more of a moral theory than the principles of inclusive beneficence and justice as equality here offered.

Your successfully exercising your autonomy, then, consists in your forming autonomous and self-regarding desires with respect to a future beyond the immediate continuation of the present, and implementing these desires so that they are actually fulfilled. Although these self-regarding desires go beyond the immediate continuation of your current experiences, their objectives may have to do with your future experiences. An example of such an objective would be to maximize the well-being of your life in a sense which takes into account only the intensity and duration of enjoyment (and suffering).[16] But you could instead prefer some kinds of well-being to other kinds, for instance some kinds of intellectual enjoyment to sensual or physical kinds of enjoyment, on grounds other than such quantitative grounds (or rather, for reasons that will be expounded in Chapter 4, quasi-quantitative grounds). For instance, suppose that, like Socrates, you prefer to lead an 'examined' life, though you believe that such a life will be comparatively jejune in respect of sensual enjoyment. You would not prefer this life if you took no interest in and, consequently, got no enjoyment from, the intellectual activity of (philosophically) examining your life, but you need not think that the examined life contains more enjoyment—and thus is better for this reason—than any other life. Instead, you might prefer it because it is better designed to give you knowledge about your place in the world. This is something that has to do with the propositional content of enjoyment rather than its felt character. You may also want to remain a person with such interests, though you realize that this will make the amount of well-being in your life significantly smaller.

Due to such interests, you may further engage in certain long-term projects, such as trying to work out a philosophical system. You may then judge it to be devastating for you to be interrupted by a premature death in the pursuit of this project, so awful that you regard this as worse for you than dying earlier, before you were capable of framing such projects. It seems quite common to find it worse to be interrupted in the midst of a process of carrying out some worthwhile project than being interrupted before it is started, though you may have had valuable experiences in the course of working on it.

---

[16] And even if this means being on a Nozickean experience-machine which produces delusive pleasurable experiences (1974: 42–5).

Such a contravention of a long-term aim is something that could make death in, say, young adulthood worse for you than death in infancy, though the latter would deprive you of a greater amount of well-being.

Consider twins, Sophia and Sensia. Sophia prefers to lead an examined life, though she anticipates that such a life will contain less well-being than some other courses of life available to her. Sensia prefers a life ripe with sensual enjoyment because she thinks that this is the life that quantitatively maximizes the amount of well-being. Suppose that they are expected to be equally successful in realizing their aims, and to lead equally long lives. Then it would be implausible to claim that it is less bad that Sophia dies in the middle of her life-project than that Sensia dies at the same point for the reason that Sophia's future is likely to contain quantitatively less well-being. It is more reasonable to hold that death at this point would be equally bad for the twins because it would be equally disruptive of their autonomy.

This indicates that it is reasonable to assign more importance to successful exercises of autonomy than to the amount of well-being awaiting someone in the future, and grant permission to exercise autonomy in cases like this. We should respect as much Sophia's autonomous choice to lead an examined life, even though this life is expected to contain quantitatively less well-being, as we respect Sensia's autonomous choice. If this is right then, although prospects of future well-being start providing reasons against killing humans earlier in their development than respect for their autonomy, once the latter kicks in, it has the upper hand. When humans themselves become capable of forming a view of the value that their future lives could have for them, it is inescapable that this capacity largely determines the course of their lives. If it appears that this capacity is not exercised autonomously, it should be encouraged to do so. And if there occurs a conflict between their view and our view of what is best for them, it is in most cases reasonable to let their view carry the day, since they are likely to be more knowledgeable about what is of value for them, and more concerned about their future, since they are the ones who will experience it.

Your successfully exercising autonomy may then promote the maximization of your long-term well-being, or it may counteract it (or it may have no impact on it, as in the case when your last will is fulfilled). The same goes for the maximization of your successful exercises of autonomy over time. That is, you may autonomously aim to maximize both the inner and the outer aspects of your future welfare, or you may have an autonomous aim which runs counter to it. If other people interfere with your pursuit of the latter aim, they exhibit an impermissible disrespect of your autonomy. This is in line with Mill's principle of liberty which, over and above the positive clause already quoted to the effect that prevention of 'harm to others' is a legitimate ground for interference with somebody's conduct, states: 'His own good, either physical or moral, is not a sufficient warrant' (1859: 9). But Mill's principle 'is meant to apply only to human beings in the maturity of their faculties' (1859: 9), not to children, people who are mentally deranged, and so on. To put it in the present terminology, it is meant to apply only to human beings who meet the conditions of being autonomous.

However, your current life-projects may appear so obviously bad for you that they present evidence that you do not satisfy these conditions, but are irrational, misinformed, or unfree in some way—say, if you want to mutilate yourself, or sell yourself into slavery. Then others are permitted not only to try to persuade you to abandon your aims, but to restrain you forcibly if necessary. Consequently, there is a sense in which reasons having to do with your 'own good'—that is, what is intertemporally best for you—can justify what might in fact be a violation of your autonomy. But this is because your behaviour would be so outlandish that it appears doubtful whether you are autonomous and, thus, whether interference with your behaviour is after all tantamount to interference with your autonomy. In this manner, harm to yourself can justify coercive action, but this is so only in rather extreme cases when the harm would be both extensive and irreversible. In cases in which it is less clear whether you fail to meet the conditions of being autonomous, we may take the intermediate course of allowing you to go ahead, but not assisting you. Anyway, it should not be assumed that everyone who is autonomous must have the goal of maximizing the welfare of their life, that whenever an aim runs counter to such a maximization goal, it cannot be autonomously chosen.[17]

A particularly important case in practice is when people, at a time at which they are apparently fit to live up to the conditions of being autonomous, express wishes that their lives should be ended if they lose their capacity for autonomy because of severe dementia, brain injuries, and so forth. Now, there is an understandable reluctance to put to death severely demented patients, especially if they are seemingly satisfied with their current lives, for the reason that they earlier expressed an apparently autonomous wish to this effect by issuing advance directives. Nevertheless, along with many contemporary bioethicists, I believe that this is what we should do if the wishes are in character with how people led their lives when they were in possession of their full powers, for instance in cases in which these lives have been dominated by pursuits that grave dementia renders impossible.

Suppose that there were a pill, which, if taken in advance, would painlessly kill us were grave dementia to set in. Then, if people of the sort described wanted to take these pills, I think that it is clear that they should be given access to them. But if this is so, it is hard to see how in actual circumstances they could justifiably be refused euthanasia when they are severely demented. If on the brink of an outbreak of severe dementia, it would be justifiable to fulfil requests to be given these 'advance' pills, it seems that somewhat later it must be justifiable to grant these patients the death that these pills would have given them, though this may be psychologically harder as it is in conflict with their current attitudes. It is, however, not my ambition to show how all such

---

[17] In Persson (2005) I argued that the aim of living in the light of truth and reason is a permissible aim, though it is at odds with this maximizing aim. On the other hand, it should not be assumed that having this aim is *required* to be rational in the sense which is a condition of being autonomous. This is a point that should be kept in mind in the discussion of the philosophy of life in Chapter 13: complying with its instructions is not necessary for being autonomous.

conflicts between respect for autonomy and long-term good or interests should be resolved. My main point is merely that there are these two aspects of things being good for us to take into account, and to flesh out to some extent how they might interact.

In the case of 'harm to others', Mill suggests that interference with such a harmful activity is unjustifiable if the activity occurs 'with their free, voluntary, and undeceived consent and participation' (1859: 11). So, just as we grant people permissions to do things to themselves, we grant them permissions to do things to others. The condition for the permission is the same in both cases: the presence of autonomous consent. In other words, it makes no crucial difference whether the person undergoing the treatment is oneself or another (cf. Persson, 2006a). This makes a difference only to the extent that autonomous consent could be presumed if we autonomously inflict harm on ourselves, but not on others, with wills of their own, who could put up autonomous opposition.

The importance of the distinction between oneself and others will be further eroded in 3.1, where it will emerge that there are possible cases of being 'succeeded' by someone to whom you are not identical which are as good as (or even better than) ordinary survival. I suggest that the permission to exercise autonomy—without asking for consent—covers such individuals, too, because there is likely to be as little opposition from their will.[18] This means that it is strictly speaking incorrect to present autonomy as having to do with *self*-regarding desires, but because this term is good enough in practice, I shall continue to employ it in order to keep things simple.

It might be objected that if you propose to act in a way that affects your (or your successor's) more distant future, your future self may fail to 'consent' not because it lacks the capacity for autonomy, but because it autonomously embraces some contrary goal. I claim that even in the face of such 'opposition', you should be permitted to go ahead, provided it is reasonably certain that the decision on which you act is autonomous. Furthermore, since I also endorse the view that personal identity makes no relevant difference, I am committed to the view that, if there are no other relevant differences—like present dissent—it is permissible to act contrary to the future goals of another.[19]

What if there are several others? Let me sketch the outline of my answer which is that there is no *general* answer. I am assuming that the fact that things like pleasures and pains are good and bad for others, like the fact that they are good and bad for oneself, are things that make outcomes morally good or bad or, in other words, provide us with moral reasons (of beneficence). Now, since some of the grounds that I advanced in the preceding section for being sceptical of the existence of non-natural, externalist reasons to desire to feel pleasure for its own sake apply as well to moral reasons to desire that others feel pleasure for its own sake, I have little choice but to proceed on the assumption that these reasons are not non-natural, externalist reasons, either. Rather,

---

[18] Contrast DeGrazia who writes: 'if the advance directive's author is not the individual to whom it would apply, it lacks authority' (2005: 185). But later on (2005: 198n) he concedes that there 'may' be exceptions of the kind that I have in mind.

[19] These are claims that I argued for in (2005: pt. IV).

the fact that we have moral reasons to promote the welfare of others has to be taken to depend on our having altruistic desires to this effect. But the strength of these desires, relative to competing desires, will vary between individuals. This implies that there is no general answer to the question of the extent to which we may permissibly set aside the welfare of others. It will depend on the contingent orientation and strength of our individual desires, just like the extent to which we may permissibly set aside our own long-term welfare.

I am aware this sketch is not particularly illuminating, but it is meant merely as a hint to why I am shelving the topic of the extent to which we may permissibly harm others. It involves metaethical issues about the analysis of the concepts of reasons and goodness that transcend the scope of this book. Let me, however, make an observation that seems to me to weigh against the hypothesis that the universality or non-relativity that is commonly attributed to moral claims stems from a belief in non-natural, external moral reasons. Suppose that you were to know that *everyone* who *at any time* clear-headedly contemplates the fact that somebody about whom nothing is known is enjoying pleasure wants this state to continue for its own sake. Then it seems that you must agree that it is intrinsically desirable or good full stop that this state continues. But, if so, this fact's being intrinsically desirable full stop cannot entail any non-natural fact, since such a non-natural fact is not entailed by everyone's wanting this state to continue.

Likewise, suppose that you were to know that *nobody* who *at any time* clear-headedly contemplates some state—such as there being a certain number of toothpicks on this planet right now—wants it to obtain for its own sake; then it seems that you cannot deny that it cannot be intrinsically desirable full stop that it obtains. But, if so, there being an externalist or desire-independent non-naturalist reason to want something intrinsically cannot be sufficient for it being intrinsically desirable full stop. For such a reason can exist even if nobody who is aware of it responds to it. Thus, externalist non-naturalism seems to be neither a necessary nor a sufficient condition for impersonal desirability, or desirability full stop.

This argument suggests that the universality or non-relativity which is seemingly implied when we speak of something as being good *simpliciter* is due to an assumption not about there being any externalist non-naturalist reason or value, but about there being (something approximating to) a universal convergence of our attitudes. If such a convergence does not obtain *in fact*, this would necessitate a relativization of morality. However, this is a worry that I shall bracket here; I shall proceed on the commonsensical assumption that, for all of us, there are some things that are impersonally good, or good full stop. For instance, it is impersonally good that beings have more of what is intrinsically good for them and less of what is intrinsically bad for them, and that the amount of what is good and bad for them is distributed in a manner that is just or fair. These impersonally good outcomes of beings having a surplus of what is personally good for them which is justly distributed are also morally good, since moral goodness is, I submit, a species of impersonal goodness, namely, a species which essentially involves what is personally good for beings. There may be other species of impersonal goodness than the moral kind, such as the impersonal goodness of beautiful things, but they play no role in the context of this essay.

My view is, then, that moral goodness is dependent on our having other-regarding desires to the effect that outcomes involving the personal good of others obtain, despite the fact that this makes moral goodness dependent on desires, the strength of which may vary from person to person. I shall not make any further attempt to defend the truth of this metaethical view; I mention it only to make explicit a limitation of this book. It is a view that I am not content with, but I see no way of getting around it to something more solid.

2
Defence of an Inclusive View of Benefiting and Reasons of Beneficence

2.1 The Moral Importance of the Potentiality for Consciousness

The amount of well-being of the life of a sentient being—that is, a being who has desires directed at its current experiences, but no capacity for autonomy—is the amount of the well-being that it will experience at different times throughout its life. When it dies at some point, its death deprives it of the well-being that it would have experienced had it lived on beyond that point.[1] If the balance of its future well-being would have been positive, its death is *extrinsically* bad for it by depriving it of the net surplus of positive well-being lying ahead of it. It follows that its death *harms* it, since it makes it worse off than it would have been had it lived on.

Being dead cannot be *intrinsically* bad for sentient beings if, as I have argued, intrinsic badness for a subject presupposes consciousness, and being dead excludes being conscious. (Remember that sentient beings are incapable of having desires which are oriented at times after their death.) An event, such as their dying, can however be extrinsically bad for the beings who undergo it, since this is tantamount to the event being bad for them because in some ways it contributes to something that is at least partly external to this event and that is intrinsically worse for them than the state that they would otherwise be in. Thus, if the event of dying leads to the state of being dead, which is intrinsically neutral, but survival would overall have been intrinsically good for the beings who die, dying is extrinsically bad for them.

The notion of extrinsic badness is broader than that of instrumental or causal badness, since it also covers, for example, cases in which an event (or state) is bad because it is a part of a whole that is necessary for its intrinsic badness. Being conscious may be extrinsically bad when it is a non-redundant part of being conscious of pain which is intrinsically bad. When the badness of an event is instrumental or causal, it derives

---

[1] As remarked in the Introduction, when I discuss what death deprives us of, I am assuming that it involves a permanent loss of consciousness, as it usually but not necessarily does.

from the intrinsic badness of something that is wholly external to the event, as an effect of it must be. This is the most common kind of extrinsic badness. Being biologically alive is instrumentally bad if it is a necessary causal condition for consciousness which is consciousness of pain.

Our death could then be extrinsically bad for us even if we were to die in our sleep without being conscious of the fact that we are deprived of future benefits, though we would then be spared the horror of realizing that we are in for this loss. Death could be extrinsically bad for us even if we were to die in our infancy when we were incapable of forming a conception of our future (except perhaps the most imminent) and, thus, would possess no capacity for autonomy. There are however philosophers who deny the latter claim. For instance, Michael Tooley argues (1983: ch. 5) that an individual's possession of the concept of a self or subject of desires (and experiences) existing over time is a necessary condition for it to be in the individual's interest to exist over time, which in turn is necessary for it to have a right to life or, more precisely, a right to continue to exist as a self or subject of desires. Plausibly, having a concept or conception of oneself as existing in the future is necessary for having desires to exist in the future. But, although Tooley believes that the possession of such desires is sufficient for having an interest in continued existence and a right to such an existence, he does not believe it to be necessary. It is enough if the individual has desires at different times that belong to a single, continuing subject of desires.

However, if such a temporally extended subject can have an interest in its continued existence as such a subject, and a right to such an existence, it follows that having this interest and right requires having the concept of a subject having desires at different times only if having this concept of a subject of desires is necessary for *being* such a subject of desires (cf. Tooley, 1983: 120). But this seems implausible. Generally, it is the other way around: experiencing first person instances of a psychological concept is necessary for acquisition of this concept, for instance feeling pain is necessary for acquiring the concept of pain, and so on. So, it is not surprising that Tooley ends up failing to defend his claim and concludes that the unification of temporally dispersed desires into a single subject is 'deeply puzzling' (1983: 133).

It would not be more plausible to claim that having a desire to go on existing as a subject of desires in the future is a necessary condition for one's future life having value for one and death to be harmful.[2] For suppose that you want to go on living because

---

[2] This may be John Harris's view, but he seems to waver between saying that the lives of people have value because they *do* value them and saying that they have value because people have the *capacity* to value them. For instance, he writes 'it's wrong to kill them [people] because they *do* value life... The wrongness of killing another person is... chiefly the wrongness of permanently depriving her of whatever it is that makes it *possible* for her to value her own life' (1985: 17; my emphasis). The ambiguity may be due to the fact that Harris slides between talking about the value of *persons* and the value of *their lives*. Thus, he writes: 'When we ask what makes human *life* valuable we are trying to identify those features... which both incline us and entitle us to value *ourselves* and one another, and which licence our belief that *we* are more valuable... than animals, fish or plants' (1985: 9; my emphasis). His claim that 'it is the *capacity* to value one's own life that is crucial' (1985: 17) is more plausible if he is understood as talking about what is crucial for the value of persons, while it is more plausible to claim that their lives are valuable when they do value

you think that you will experience a lot of pleasure in the future. The fact that this is a reason for you to want to go on living implies that you think that it is good for you to experience this pleasure and that it would be bad for you to miss out on it. But then it is not the case that future life *becomes* valuable for you because you want it; it is instead the other way around: you want it because you think it *is* valuable for you. So, your wanting to go on living simply shows that you *take* it or *believe* that future life would be valuable for you and that it would be bad for you to be deprived of it; it does not *make* future life valuable for you.

Let us bracket Tooley's idiom of rights for the time being and conduct the discussion in terms of the notion of what is in our interest. Even beings with a rudimentary mental life, like neonates, can enjoy currently felt sensations of pleasure. This implies, according to the analysis of enjoyment in Chapter 1, that they can have intrinsic desires, elicited by these sensations, to the effect that they go on. They can have such desires because they can imagine their sensations continuing in the immediate future (whereas they cannot imagine themselves starting to have sensations after a break, since this would require a grasp of the contrast between what is experienced and what is real). As was seen in that chapter, the having of such desires makes it intrinsically good or desirable for them to continue to have these sensations. I take the latter evaluative claim to entail that it is in their interest that these sensations go on. Now, that these neonates continue to exist as subjects of desires and experiences is a necessary means or part of the continuation of the experience of the pleasures that they are currently experiencing. This means that it is also in their interest to continue to exist as such subjects. It is in their interest, since it is extrinsically good for them to continue to exist as such subjects because this is indispensable for the continuation of the pleasure that they are feeling, which is intrinsically good for them. What is extrinsically good or desirable for us is in our interest, just as what is intrinsically good or desirable for us.

Clearly, you can enjoy pleasures that you are feeling at the present moment without having the concept of a temporally extended subject of desires and experiences. Thus, it follows from the reasoning in the preceding paragraph that existence in the future as such a subject can be in your interest because it is extrinsically good for you, although you do not possess a conception of such an existence. Consequently, it can be extrinsically bad for you to be deprived of your future existence in spite of the fact that you are unable to form a conception of this future to the extent that this necessitates having a conception of yourself as a temporally extended subject. Nevertheless, we have not yet got very far, for what if a newborn is not currently having any enjoyable experiences, say, because it is asleep? We want to be in a position to say that it could still be in its interest to go on existing rather than being painlessly killed, even though it does not possess any desire to the effect that some of its current experiences continue.

---

them (positively). However, as remarked in the text, the latter view is not really plausible, and it will be seen in Chapter 6 that the former view is not plausible, either. Harris might have avoided this ambiguity had he talked about the value that the lives of persons have *for them* instead of their value *simpliciter*.

The problem here is unlikely to arise in the case of persons who, definitionally, have a conception of a future existence beyond what is imminent and normally have desires with respect to this existence. When they are asleep and lack *occurrent* desires with respect to their future, they are still likely to have *dispositional* desires to this effect, dispositions that are actualized by their forming occurrent desires when they are awake. We could claim that it is bad for such persons to be killed in their sleep because their dispositional desires—in virtue of which they possess autonomy—are contravened by being prevented from manifesting themselves in occurrent desires which can be satisfied. But neonates cannot have any dispositional desires to experience enjoyment in the further future, since they can form no conception of themselves existing in such a future. Therefore, it is more controversial that it can be extrinsically bad for them to be killed when unconscious than it is that it can be extrinsically bad for persons.

These neonates normally have, however, a *capacity* to experience enjoyment, a capacity that they have started to exercise. It is extrinsically good for them that this capacity continues to be exercised in the future in so far as this results in experiences that are intrinsically good for them. But their continued existence is a necessary means or part of the continued exercise of this capacity, so their continued existence is extrinsically good for them, or in their interest. Therefore, it is extrinsically bad for them to be deprived of a continuation of their existence.

Can we go further and claim that it can be bad to be killed even for a *pre-conscious* foetus who has not yet developed any consciousness? Compare a newborn, or a foetus just before birth, who has exercised its capacity for having enjoyable experiences on a few occasions, but is now asleep and unconscious, with a pre-conscious foetus who is just about to start exercising its capacity by having its first enjoyable experiences. The difference between these foetuses appears so small that it is reasonable to assume that, if it can be bad for the former foetus to be deprived of its existence, as I have argued, it can be bad for the latter, pre-conscious foetus as well.

The pre-conscious foetus does not yet have a capacity for having enjoyable experiences, but it has a *potential* to develop such capacity, a potential that will soon begin to be actualized. It is instrumentally good for the foetus that this potential is actualized if the upshot of this is a capacity the exercises of which can overall be intrinsically good for the foetus, since if the potentiality was not actualized, nothing would be either intrinsically good or bad for it. But the continued existence of the foetus is a necessary means or part of the actualization of this potential for enjoyment, so its continued existence, too, is extrinsically good for the pre-conscious foetus. Therefore, it is extrinsically bad for it to be deprived of its existence in the future if this existence will overall be for the better for it.

It might be objected that, although the difference between the pre-conscious foetus who is on the verge of having its first experiences or conscious episodes and the currently temporarily unconscious foetus who has had a few rudimentary experiences might prima facie seem negligible, it is in fact crucial. Imagine that we accept a psychological theory of our nature and identity according to which *we*, the kind of entity that we essentially are, begin to exist at the time at which our brains start sustaining our first experiences, that is, that personal pronouns, 'I', 'you', and so on, as used by us, refer to a kind of entity which is at least partly mental and which springs into existence when our first experiences emerge from our brains (see e.g. McMahan, 2002: ch. 1). Then the difference between the foetuses considered is that only the latter one is *one of us*. This might well be deemed to be morally significant.

For instance, Melinda Roberts advances a 'person-based consequentialism' which 'requires, for each person who ever exists, that agents maximize that person's well-being' (2002: 326), but according to which '*merely possible people*—those who could have existed...but who do not and never will exist—do *not* count for moral purposes' (2004: 101). She uses 'person' in a broad fashion to designate a being with some kind of consciousness. So, on Roberts's view, it is not until a foetus acquires consciousness that a being who morally counts pops into existence.

Notice, however, that even if it is true that a new kind of being pops into existence at this point—a being that is identical to one of us—there is still in the case of the pre-conscious foetus *something*—namely a human being, organism, or animal—which is equipped with the potential to develop a consciousness and, thereby, a capacity for having enjoyable experiences. Those who advocate a biological view of our nature and identity—the chief rival, viable alternative to psychological theories—identify us with such human organisms (see e.g. Olson, 1997). However, even if we grant that the biological view is erroneous, the human organism is undoubtedly there, as a bearer of a potential for consciousness. I have in effect argued that it can be extrinsically bad for this organism not to have this potential actualized. I shall later supplement this argument with a criticism of an account put forward by McMahan, according to which things can be good or bad only for beings in possession of (a capacity for) consciousness.

To be sure, if a psychological rather than a biological view of our nature and identity is true, the pre-conscious foetus, a human organism, for whom I have contended that it can be extrinsically bad to be deprived of future existence, is not one of us. But it would seem to be indefensibly discriminatory to hold it to be of less moral significance if this human organism is deprived of its future conscious existence if it is not identical to one of us than if it is. After all, this is just a matter of what the reference of our personal pronouns is. What is there, independently of this linguistic or conceptual issue, is a human organism with a potential to develop consciousness.

In response to this reasoning, the battleground might be shifted. It might instead be claimed that there is a morally significant difference between preventing a human organism—whether or not it is identical to one of us—from actualizing its potential for consciousness and preventing a human organism with the same potential *from coming into existence* and actualizing its potential. The former might be held to be worse than the latter on the ground that the latter is not extrinsically bad *for anyone who is in existence*. But this is a view that is also hard to uphold, amongst other things for the reason that the coming into existence of a human organism or being is a gradual process, as we shall now see.

This might seem like a surprising claim, since it is a familiar view that a human being begins to exist at conception which is thought to be a more or less momentary event. But in fact conception or fertilization is a process which takes around 24 hours. It starts when a spermatozoon begins to penetrate the outer boundary of an ovum or egg, the membrane called *zona pellucida*. Inside the egg, the sperm forms a male pronucleus which fuses with the female pronucleus to form a single cell—the zygote—which is genetically human, combining chromosomes from the sperm and the egg. This fusion process—*syngamy*—occurs in the interior of the ovum, which still exists at the end of fertilization. Its outer boundary is intact and the processes occurring inside it are 'controlled by substances produced before fertilization that were present in the egg' (Dawson, 1990: 4). Consequently, we must distinguish the egg from an entity that is formed inside it at syngamy, the zygote, a cell which is genetically human.

Those who maintain that a human being begins to exist at fertilization or conception should claim, more precisely, that the human being begins to exist at syngamy and is identical to the zygote rather than to the whole egg (as a bird would be identical to the zygote inside an egg rather than the egg). For the egg existed before fertilization, and it is reasonable to say that it ceases to exist a few days after fertilization when the *zona pellucida* begins to dissolve, and the processes inside it are no longer controlled by those substances that were present in the egg before fertilization.

However, although a human zygote is an organism which is genetically human, it would be absurd to regard this fact as sufficient for it to be a human being because it would then follow that each of us is constituted by countless human beings in virtue of being constituted by cells that are genetically human! Hence, if the zygote is to qualify as a human being, it must be in virtue of something over and above the fact that it is a cell or organism of the human genotype. It might then be proposed that it is a human cell with a *special potential* to develop consciousness and other capacities that a fully fledged or paradigmatic human being has.

There is however a problem with the idea that *the zygote* has this potential. When it is said that an entity has a potential to become F, it is usually implied that this entity persists until *it* acquires F. But it is not true of the zygote that it persists until it acquires consciousness: the single-cell zygote ceases to exist after a few hours, when it divides into two cells. These two cells are obviously numerically distinct from each other, so the zygote cannot be identical to both of them—since numerical identity is symmetrical and transitive, this would imply, absurdly, that they are identical to each other—and it would be gratuitous to identify it with one cell rather than the other. Hence, the zygote has ceased to exist by division. Rather than being something with a potential to develop consciousness, the zygote is something from which a distinct being or organism with this potential *originates*. In other words, rather than being identical to a human being in virtue of having a potential to develop consciousness (and other features of a mature human being), the zygote is the origin of a being with this potential (for further discussion of this point, see Persson, 2003a).

The (normal) zygote is *totipotent* in the sense that a (paradigmatic or full-blown) human being can originate from it. A couple of hours after syngamy, it divides into two cells or blastomeres which are totipotent as well. Each of them has more or less the same potentials and capacities as both of them together have, in particular the potential to produce a paradigmatic human being. Thus, just as such a human being could originate from them in conjunction, it could originate from each of them were they separated—as happens in the event of monozygotic twinning—or from either of them were the other removed. But if this is so, there is no reason to hold that the blastomeres together constitute a further organism over and above each of them; these cells are simply two largely independent and symmetrical organisms stuck together inside the *zona pellucida*. Even if there is some interaction between these organisms—largely controlled by substances present in the ovum before fertilization—this is not sufficient for them together to constitute a single, numerically distinct organism if they could easily be separated, and each could separately develop in virtually the same way as they could do together.

These facts undermine the view that a human being begins to exist at this early stage (for further elaboration, see Persson, 2009b). For the single-cell zygote ceases to exist after a few hours, when it divides into two cells. If it were a human being, it would have to be a very short-lived human being with a capacity to divide into two distinct human beings. It will not do to say that the human being that was the zygote continues to exist as the cluster of the two resulting cells since, as we have seen, these cells are so independent of each other that they do not together constitute a single organism. This cluster of cells is simply a set of cells which ceases to exist when each cell ceases to exist by dividing into two new cells—such are the identity conditions for sets.

The conclusion of this reasoning is that a human being has not formed until the integration within a cluster of cells is so extensive that we can truly say that a multicellular organism has formed, an organism which could outlive the exchange of its individual cells. Moreover, a human being cannot be said to have formed unless the embryoblast or inner cell mass, from which the foetus proper grows, has differentiated itself from the trophoblast, from which the extra-embryonic membranes, the placenta, the umbilical cord, the amniotic sac, and so on, grow. The reason for this is that the human being, who sheds these extra-embryonic structures at birth, is identical to the foetus (proper) and not to a whole which consists of the foetus plus these extra-embryonic features. The umbilical cord is a link between the foetus and its mother rather than a proper part of the foetus; monozygotic twins can share the same placenta, and they are enveloped by the same amniotic sac, so these entities are not parts of either of the twin foetuses. This process of the embryoblast differentiating itself, *compaction*, occurs some four or five days after fertilization.

As already remarked, a further necessary condition for the formation of a human being is that monozygotic twinning is ruled out, since otherwise we would have to say that a human being—rather than merely a human cell or cluster of human cells—ceases to exist by the twinning division.[3] This sort of division is not ruled out until a stage sometimes called *gastrulation* which occurs around two to three weeks after fertilization. The so-called primitive streak, the first sign of the spine, then appears, making monozygotic twinning impossible.

There is still the problem, however, that at this time conjoined (or Siamese) twins can make their entrance. Conjoined twins make up a spectrum of cases at the one end of which there are clearly two human beings, since there is only a small organic overlap, making the twins easily surgically separable, and at the other end of which there are presumably not two human organisms or beings, since the sharing of organs is too extensive (for further discussion of conjoined twins, see Savulescu and Persson, 2016). Plausible, but not uncontroversial, examples of the latter sort are those twins who have a head and a neck each, but share almost all other organs and limbs, including a heart. These twins are not surgically separable into two viable human organisms. But in these cases, they are two of our kind according to psychological theories, whereas this is not so in cases in which there are two faces on a single head (with a single brain) and the upper portion of the torso is fused, while the lower portion is divided. At least in such cases it is implausible to maintain that there are two of us.

By being instances of incomplete twinning, conjoined twins indicate that the possibility of twinning gradually peters out after the onset of the primitive streak rather than coming to an abrupt halt. It seems natural to hypothesize that the explanation of why some twinnings are incomplete, that is, do not produce separate twins or conjoined twins that definitely are two human beings, is that these twinnings occur so late that a human being has already partly formed, whereas the explanation of why other instances of conjoined twinning result in two separable human beings is that they occur before this point.

The upshot is that we cannot determine with any precision when a human being begins to exist. We can tell that it does not happen before gastrulation, and that it has certainly happened within a week or so after it.[4] Some time during this interval, the bearer of a potential to acquire consciousness enters existence. Prior to this period, when there is successively a spermatozoon and an ovum before fertilization, a zygote after syngamy, and a cluster of cells after a few divisions, there is not anything which is the bearer of this potential. Nothing can be extrinsically good or bad for these entities, since—in contrast to a multi-cellular organism which will later be formed—*they* will never acquire consciousness and be in conscious states that are intrinsically good or bad for them. But as soon as there is something with a potential to have consciousness

---

[3] Also to be excluded is the possibility of a *fusion* of two zygotes, resulting from two fertilizations, into a chimera. Otherwise, we would have to say that two human beings are fused into a third human being.

[4] A view of this sort is defended by Ford (1988: ch. 6). He writes more specifically that 'after gastrulation, by the end of the third week when the neural folds have been formed and the primitive cardiovascular system is functioning to enable nutrition and growth as a whole to take place, there are sufficient reasons to justify asserting that a living individual with a human nature has been formed' (1988: 170). I am prepared to agree with Ford's more precise claim that a human being exists by the end of the third week, but I do not need to insist on any such more precise claim.

later on, there is something for which events can be extrinsically good or bad and, thus, something that can be benefited and harmed.[5]

Sometimes people claim that a being cannot be benefited or harmed if it does not possess consciousness, probably because they wrongly assume that you cannot be benefited or harmed until something can be *intrinsically* good or bad for you, like pleasure and pain are. Peter Singer, for instance, claims that a foetus cannot be harmed until it acquires consciousness which he assumes does not happen before the 18th week after conception. But he realizes that he has to qualify this claim as follows:

> While the fetus prior to 18 weeks may, strictly speaking, be unable to be harmed, if the fetus is allowed to develop into a child, the future child could be very seriously harmed by an experiment that caused the child to be born in a disabled state.[6]

However, if 'the future child' could be 'very seriously harmed' by an experiment done to a pre-conscious foetus, then the foetus can 'strictly speaking' be harmed by this experiment, since the foetus and the child are the very same human being (for further elaboration of this argument, see Persson, 1999a). It is the pre-conscious foetus which has acquired consciousness and now is a child. Certainly, the pre-conscious foetus cannot *experience* any harmful effects, that is, nothing can be intrinsically bad for it. For this reason, it cannot be *hurt*, since to hurt someone is presumably to do something that directly causes this individual mental or physical pain or suffering. In contrast, you can *harm* somebody by performing an action whose harmful effect occurs much later.

Since Singer believes that the future child can be harmed, he makes an exception to his proposed rule that prior to 18 weeks the foetus needs no 'protection from harmful research' for the reason that it 'cannot be harmed'. This exception is to the effect that any research on a pre-conscious foetus is permissible *on condition* that it is not allowed to survive those 18 weeks: 'research that allows the fetus to survive beyond 18 weeks does not come under the permissive rule' (1993: 165). It is however dubious to hold that it is permissible to do things to a human being that would impoverish the quality of its life (if consciousness is acquired) *on condition* that it is killed (and the acquisition of consciousness is blocked). For if the impoverishment would fall short of making life not worth living, killing appears to be the greater wrong because it prevents *all* that is good in life.

It is a mistake to claim that an act can be permissible on condition that it is accompanied by another act, unless the second act is itself permissible. An act cannot be permissible on condition C unless C itself is permissible. Consequently, the idea behind Singer's caveat must be that the killing here is permissible, and that its

---

[5] I shall go on to claim that something can be extrinsically good or bad for *possible* conscious beings, but this does not gainsay the claim that nothing can be extrinsically good or bad for entities like zygotes, since possible conscious beings are of course not identical to these or any actual entities.

[6] Singer (1993: 165). This sentence does not occur in the third edition of the book (2011), but it is not clear to me that Singer is not still committed to something like it. Anyway, it is a view worth discussing.

permissibility has the effect of cancelling the wrongness that would inhere in the preceding act if it were to occur on its own. Presumably, this is because he believes that you cannot harm a being by preventing it from acquiring consciousness. This is probably because he assumes that something cannot be harmed, unless things can be intrinsically bad for it at the time of action, and that this is impossible in the absence of consciousness. As we have seen, however, in order for something to be harmed, it only takes that something can be extrinsically bad for it, can make it worse off than it otherwise would be, and this is compatible with it being in an intrinsically neutral state.

2.2 The Moral Importance of the Possibility of Consciousness

There remains a further step of my argument for the inclusive view that beings can be benefited and harmed by being caused to exist, or being prevented from doing so. I have contended that, at least a week or so after gastrulation, killing human beings can be extrinsically bad for them because it prevents their potential to acquire consciousness being actualized. This implies that they can be harmed by being killed on the assumption that their being dead is worse than the conscious existence that they would otherwise have had. We can assume that for them the value of the state of being dead is intrinsically neutral, that is, neither intrinsically good nor bad, since they never acquired the capacity to have future-oriented desires. Therefore, a life whose net sum of intrinsic, personal value is positive for them is better, in intrinsic respects, than being dead, and a life whose net sum of intrinsic, personal value is negative for them is worse than being dead. But can human beings also be harmed by being prevented from entering existence because fertilization, or the embryonic development prior to gastrulation, is obstructed? I have already suggested that the fact that the coming into existence of a human being is a gradual process makes it hard to defend a negative answer. I shall now offer further support for the view that preventing their existence could harm or benefit somebody.

The fact that humans who are prevented from entering existence forever remain non-existent and 'merely possible' has occasioned misgivings about the claim that blocking existence could be worse for a being. John Broome writes that 'if she had never lived at all, there would have been no her for it to be worse for, so it could not have been worse for her' (1999: 168). McMahan also claims that it cannot be worse for someone never to exist (e.g. 2013: 6), but he denies that this has to imply that individuals cannot be said to be benefited by being caused to exist. For he suggests that there is a *non-comparative* sense of the verb 'to benefit' in which we can be said to benefit individuals by causing them to exist:

It is coherent, and plausible, to claim that to cause a person to exist is *good* for the person when the intrinsically good elements of that person's life more than compensate for the intrinsically bad elements...If causing a person to exist is good for that person, it is convenient and perspicuous to say that causing that person to exist benefits him or her. (2013: 6–7; cf. 1981: 105)

To claim that a being has been benefited in the proposed non-comparative sense by being caused to exist does not imply, then, that it would have been harmed had it not been caused to exist, or that it would have been worse for it never to exist.[7]

Now, as mentioned in the Introduction, it is true that there is a non-comparative sense of 'benefit' in which the term designates something that is intrinsically good for someone. When someone enjoys a benefit or is given a benefit, they enjoy, or are given, something that benefits them in the sense of being intrinsically good for them. Although this is a non-comparative claim, it implies a comparative claim. This is not surprising, since the claim that something is good obviously implies that it is better that this thing is present than absent. But, clearly, this does not mean that the claim is reducible to, or is nothing but, the comparative claim implied. So, the fact that the claim that individuals enjoy benefits implies that things are intrinsically better for them than they would be without these benefits *if everything else remains the same* does not mean that this is a comparative claim.

By contrast, when individuals are benefited in the comparative sense, the comparison is to the effect that things are intrinsically better for these individuals than they were before they were benefited, or would have been had they not been benefited, *all things considered*—that is, taking into consideration all those facts that would in fact have been different had the benefits not been bestowed. Thus, if I provide you with a non-comparative benefit—for instance, a pleasure—which excludes your having or getting a bigger benefit that you would otherwise have or get, you are not comparatively benefited, better off considering other circumstances than your simply getting or not getting the non-comparative benefit provided. You are rather harmed in what I called the qualified sense in the Introduction, harmed by me bestowing a benefit on you.

It is this comparative sense, I maintain, that we need to express what we have moral reason to do. To have a reason to do an action is to have a reason to do it *rather than* not to do it. Thus, to find out whether you have a reason to perform an action, you need to compare the outcome—the *actual* outcome, not an outcome which is conditional on some facts being fixed though they may in fact change—of performing the action with the outcome of not performing it. To ascertain that an action would provide someone with a non-comparative benefit is therefore not sufficient to show that—as far as this individual is concerned—there is reason to perform the action. For it may be that the outcome of performing the action is not better, all things considered for the individual, than the outcome of not performing it because bestowing this benefit removes or prevents the individual's having or getting an even greater benefit. Thus, in order to determine that—as far as this being is concerned—you have reason to perform the action, you need to ascertain that it results in the being having *more* benefits (or less harm)

---

[7] Parfit has also denied that the claim that benefiting individuals by causing them to exist has to have the 'implausible' implication that it would have been worse for them not to exist (1987: 395; cf. Appendix G).

than it had or would otherwise have had. In other words, you need to ascertain that the action benefits the being in the comparative sense.

But, according to McMahan, you cannot benefit beings in the comparative sense by bringing them into existence. This has curious consequences. Suppose that you consider whether to bring a being into existence, and you find that this being will then have a life that is good for it. On the other hand, if you do not bring it into existence, somebody who exists or will exist independently of your action will benefit, but less than the non-existent individual would have. Then if you bring the being into existence, you would have done what most benefits the beings who morally count. But, on the other hand, if you do not bring this being into existence, you would *also* have done what most benefits the beings who morally count, since now the being that you could have brought into existence does not count morally because, being forever non-existent, it cannot be said to have been harmed by being denied existence. Therefore, you do not have a reason to bring a being into existence *rather than* not to bring it into existence if it can be benefited only in a non-comparative sense because if you do not act on the reason, it dissolves, and there is no reason to which you have acted contrary.[8]

It may sound plausible to claim, as does McMahan, that we have reason to cause a being to exist if its existence would be good for it in the sense of containing more of what is intrinsically good than bad, but I think that this is because we are tacitly assuming, as I shall argue below is true, that the alternative to existence, non-existence, is neither intrinsically good nor bad for anyone and, thus, that existence is *better* than non-existence for the being, so that the being would be harmed by not beginning to exist. Therefore, in order to express what we have moral reason to do, we need a comparative sense of 'benefiting' (and 'harming') but, as I shall now contend, such a sense is available with respect to starting to exist.

Returning to Broome's claim: in what, if any, sense does the claim that something would have been worse (or better) for someone imply that there *is* someone for whom this is worse (better)? Most of us agree that we can intelligibly and truly claim of someone who—even early in life—escaped being blown to pieces and went on to lead a good life, that it would have been worse for her to have been blown to pieces though, on any plausible account of her nature and identity, there would then no longer *be* anyone for whom this is worse. So, those who want to persuade us that someone cannot be harmed by not beginning to exist are ill advised to rest their case on the claim that it is necessary that someone exists at a time for things to be worse for her at that time.

The fact that someone has existed, if only for the briefest period, might be thought to make a difference. The idea might be that existence at some point is necessary in order for us to be able to identify and refer to particular or specific individuals and make true-or-false statements about them, for instance to the effect that something is better

---

[8] Although it does not feature the notion of non-comparative benefits, this is also an implication of Roberts's 'person-based consequentialism' (2002, 2004), since according to it only beings who exist at some point count morally.

or worse for them. It might be thought that things which might never exist are not bone fide particulars to which we can make fixed or rigid references. Suppose that I say 'My first-born child will inherit my estate.' If it takes some years before I beget a child, then, in making my statement, I did not refer to this child specifically, saying that *it* would be my heir. I was using the description 'my first-born child' in the so-called *de dicto* sense, speaking about *whoever* would be my first-born child. If the world had taken a different course, another child might have fitted the description. What might be doubted is whether I could use such a description in a *de re* sense to refer to a particular possible individual whose identity is fixed.

On reflection, however, it seems beyond doubt that we *can* refer in this fixed way to possible beings. We can bring off this sort of reference by referring to a particular (human) individual as the one who would come into existence if we fertilize a certain egg with a certain sperm, provided that we can foresee that fertilization will be successful and that monozygotic twinning will not occur.[9] This description is sufficient to secure reference to a definite human being because it can fit one and only one such being, though it does not imply that this being has begun to exist. If we have sufficient knowledge of the genetic properties of this human individual and the social environment in which it would be raised, we could make rough predictions about how good or bad life might be for this specific but still non-existent individual, although such predictions are of course hazardous. On the basis of such predictions, we could decide against fertilization. If so, this individual will never exist. Similarly, we can refer to a particular consciousness—and thus, according to psychological theories of our nature and identity, one of us—as the consciousness that will develop in a particular human organism (for further elaboration of this point, see Persson, 1995a).

Therefore, scruples about the possibility of fixed reference to non-existent beings can be laid to rest. Moreover, it should be noticed that to make *general* claims about possible individuals such as 'There are some (possible) individuals, who would have come into existence with severe congenital handicaps if some couples had not used contraceptives, for whom it is better not to exist', all we need is to speak about possible individuals in a *de dicto* sense. No reference to particular possible individuals is needed, since their numerical identity is unimportant for the truth of the claim.

It may be objected that it is paradoxical to claim that there *are* (merely) possible beings for whom it is better not to have begun to exist, for (merely) possible beings are beings who are non-existent, and it is self-contradictory to claim that there are or exist beings who do not exist. However, this is obviously so only if 'exist' has the same meaning in both of its occurrences, but I do not think that it has. In one sense of 'exist', it is true that there are merely possible beings because this follows from the clearly true claim that it is possible that some beings will begin to exist in the future. This is the

---

[9] Contrast DeGrazia who writes: 'prior to conception, it is radically indeterminate who the possible person might be; prior to conception, there are millions of possibilities about who might be conceived' (2012: 146). In an earlier work, he also writes: 'coming into existence cannot benefit an individual because there is no determinate being who could either exist or not exist' (2005: 263n).

sense in which I believe there to be merely possible and, thus, non-existent beings. I cannot provide a philosophically adequate explication of this sense, but there are many commonsensical claims to which we can permissibly help ourselves, though we cannot accurately expound their sense philosophically.

Consequently, scruples about claims about the comparative value of non-existence to existence cannot turn on the impossibility of reference to or talk about merely possible beings. It must rather have to do with the content of what is asserted of them, namely that non-existence could be worse (or better) for them than some state of existence (these two lines of resistance are also distinguished and discussed by me in 1995a and 2009a). Granted, this assertion will appear problematic if it is assumed that in order for something to be worse (or better) for a being something must be intrinsically *bad* (or good) for it—but that is a mistaken assumption. If it is a fact that nothing is either intrinsically good or bad for a being, this is worse for this being than the fact that things are overall intrinsically good for it (and better for it than the fact that things are overall intrinsically bad for it).[10] Thus, it follows that never having existed is worse for possible beings than an existence in which things are overall intrinsically good for them if it is true that:

(1) for a being who has never existed nothing is either intrinsically good or bad, and
(2) the fact that nothing is either intrinsically good or bad for a being is worse for it than the fact that things are overall intrinsically good for it.

If (1) and (2) hold good, it is worse for a being not to have been brought into existence to lead a life in which things are overall intrinsically good for it.

It seems to me that both (1) and (2) are incontestable. Plausibly, nothing can be intrinsically good or bad for a being before it acquires consciousness (and desires); in other words, everything is evaluatively neutral for a non-conscious being. Some existing beings do not have consciousness at any time, for instance, anencephalic infants; nothing in their existence can therefore be either intrinsically good or bad for them. Non-existent beings are like non-conscious beings in the respect that *they do not have consciousness*. In order for it to be true that a being does not have consciousness, it need not exist. A being can truly be said to be neither conscious nor existent—in fact, the latter implies the former. So, if it is true of non-conscious beings that nothing is either intrinsically good or bad for them because they have never had consciousness, it is also true of non-existent beings that nothing is either intrinsically good or bad for them for the same reason, namely that they have never had consciousness.[11] That is to say, (1) is true.

---

[10] Henceforth, I am going to leave out the parenthetical insertions.
[11] It is not necessary for this sort of argument that something's having consciousness is taken to be a necessary condition for things having value for it. Any other property—for instance, being alive or human—which is supposed to be a necessary condition for things being intrinsically good or bad for existing beings could be substituted for it. For non-existent beings will lack this property and, thus, nothing can

Of course, there is a way in which it can be true that nothing is either intrinsically good or bad for someone only if this individual exists at some point. Suppose that we start with an individual who has an experience that is good for it solely in virtue of being pleasant, and then gradually reduce the intensity of this quality of pleasantness. Eventually we might get an experience that is intrinsically *indifferent* to this individual. Now it may be that nothing is intrinsically good or bad for an individual because all of its experiences are intrinsically indifferent to it in this sense. Obviously, this way of nothing being intrinsically good or bad for somebody presupposes the existence of this being because it presupposes its having consciousness. Consequently, this is not why nothing is intrinsically good or bad for non-conscious or non-existent beings; for them there is not even anything—like an experience—that is qualitatively indifferent, so to speak. This is what I have in mind when I say that non-existence is of neutral value for those who do not exist.

Turning to (2), it seems to me as indisputable as (1). For instance, it seems indisputable that, given that existing without consciousness, like anencephalic infants do, is neither intrinsically good nor bad for them, this is worse for them than having consciousness and leading a life in which things are predominantly good for them. But we have seen that non-conscious beings are like non-existent beings in that nothing is either intrinsically good or bad (or indifferent) for them. Therefore, non-existence is worse for a being than a predominantly intrinsically good existence, just as its existence is worse for a non-conscious being than a good existence. Irrespective of whether nothing is ever intrinsically good or bad for a being because it exists without consciousness or is non-existent, this state of affairs is worse for it than a state of affairs in which things are overall intrinsically good for it (since we have already ruled out the possibility that in the case of non-existence there is a failure of reference). Non-conscious existence is neither better nor worse for a being than non-existence is.

It follows that if an (act-)event makes it true that a being gets an overall intrinsically good existence instead of remaining in non-existence—or in an existence that is intrinsically neutral for it—this event benefits the being, or makes it better off than it would have been had the event not happened. In other words, this (act-)event is *extrinsically* good for the being, good for it in virtue of the fact that it brings along consequences that, intrinsically, are better for it than what would otherwise have been the case. This is so regardless of whether the alternative would be non-existence, or existence which is intrinsically neutral.

When a human being begins to exist, it will first enter a state of existence which is intrinsically neutral for it because it has not yet acquired even the most rudimentary form of consciousness. This change of its ontological status will be neither intrinsically good nor bad for it and, thus, it will neither be benefited nor harmed by the change. However, when it subsequently acquires consciousness, it may be either benefited or

be good or bad for them for the same reason as that nothing can be good or bad for existing things which lack this property.

harmed by the change, depending on the intrinsic value of its states of consciousness. This brings out that the claim that a human being would be benefited by entering an intrinsically good existence can be broken down to two evaluative comparisons: one comparison of its being non-existent to its having non-conscious existence, and another comparison of its non-conscious existence to its conscious existence. It seems undeniable that no being is either benefited or harmed by a transition from non-existence to non-conscious existence, whilst a being can be benefited by the transition from non-conscious to conscious existence, since the latter state may be intrinsically good for it. Thus, when it is disputed that a being would be benefited by entering a good existence, or harmed by being prevented from doing so, one of these claims will have to be disputed, but it appears impossible to deny either.

The fact that when a human being is caused to have a good existence, there *is* someone who has become better off—namely, a human being who was non-conscious—when the benefit is bestowed is noteworthy also for the following reason. If this does not undercut the idea of non-comparative benefiting, by showing that in fact there always *is* someone who is benefited when benefits are bestowed, it at least shows that such benefits cannot provide less of a moral reason than some comparative benefits, since surely it makes no moral difference whether or not the starting of a non-conscious existence occurs along with the transition from non-conscious existence to conscious existence. On the other hand, if a human being is prevented from having a good existence, it *may* be that there *is* someone who is harmed, and left worse off in a non-conscious state, by this prevention. But if there is not—if no human being has entered non-conscious existence—it cannot reasonably be claimed that this is better from a moral point of view, since it is not worse or bad for any being to be caused to have a non-conscious existence which is neither intrinsically good nor bad for it than to remain existent. Thus, if there were non-comparative benefits, failures to allocate them could not provide less of a moral reason than failures to allocate corresponding comparative benefits to non-conscious beings.

Failure to realize that beings can be benefited or harmed by being brought into existence could also be nurtured by a mistaken model of these actions. Some of our actions are such that they involve contact with the object acted on, either by our own bodies or by some tool or instrument in contact with both our own bodies and the object. Cutting, stabbing, pushing, pulling, and squeezing are examples of this kind of action. The object of these actions must of course exist when these actions are performed. Benefiting and harming are not such 'contact' actions. They are more like killing and curing, which are 'result' actions, that is, actions which are described in terms of the result or effect that they produce, without alluding to the means used. But killing and curing presuppose that their objects exist *at some point* because what you kill has to be alive and what is cured has to be ill or injured. I have argued that benefiting and harming are unlike curing and killing in this regard: their result of someone becoming better or worse off than they would otherwise be does not presuppose that these individuals exist. This is because a possible state of existence can be compared to non-existence in terms of benefits and be found better or worse for somebody. Therefore, just as you can be harmed (or benefited) by an act of killing which deprives you of future existence, you could have been harmed (or benefited) by being deprived of your *entire* existence.

It might be objected that, if something's lacking consciousness and desires forever implied that everything is forever evaluatively neutral for it, there would be countless things—like numbers and (possible or real) inanimate things—for which everything is of neutral value. These things could crowd our moral calculations and force us to make absurdly irrelevant comparative judgments, such as that a beggar's life might be worse for him than existence is for his worn-out shoes, or for the number five. But there is no reason to include in our moral calculations such items as numbers and inanimate things, since there is nothing that we can do to make something better or worse for them because we cannot make them conscious. Furthermore, although it is normally absurd to bother to *make* such comparative judgments as the ones cited—because there is virtually no context in which the information that they impart is called for—it is not absurd to believe them to be *true* (indeed, so obviously true that it is pointless to assert their truth!). That this is the explanation of the apparent absurdity of making these statements comes out if they are expanded—if it is said, for instance, that the beggar's life is worse for him than existence is for his shoes, since nothing can be good or bad for them, but life is bad for the beggar. This expansion removes any misleading conversational implications about the value of existence for shoes. Moreover, it is hard to deny that we can claim to have stronger reasons against creating miserable beings than against creating inanimate objects because we can make such comparisons.

The assumption that we cannot be benefited or harmed by what happens before we begin to exist seems to be what has led John Harris to endorse what he (reluctantly) calls the 'Gametic Principle' (1992: 61), to the effect that 'an individual's life begins when one of the gametes from which that individual will develop is first formed' (1992: 59). As he realizes (1992: 57), it is only with 'the benefit of hindsight' that we could with any air of plausibility identify gametes with beings like us, since this would evidently not be correct if they are not later united to form a zygote, and so on. He does not see this as a difficulty for his principle, but that is a mistake (the argument below is extracted from Persson, 1999c).

According to the everyday *three-dimensional* view of bodies (whether animate or inanimate), they are *wholly* present at every time at which they are present. This is in contrast to the *four-dimensional* view, according to which bodies also have a temporal extension which corresponds to the period of time during which they exist on the three-dimensional view. Consequently, on the three-dimensional view the numerical identity of bodies does not hinge on what happens in the future. For instance, I could have died at the age of five; what in fact happened in the future to this five year old is irrelevant to his numerical identity: irrespective of whether he dies or survives, he is still me.

The Gametic Principle is at odds with our ordinary three-dimensional view of bodies, including ourselves, for according to it, whether a pair of gametes is identical to one of us will depend upon what happens to it in the future, whether the gametes are joined to form a zygote, and so on. This creates problems for the Gametic Principle. As Harris agrees, you and I begin to exist only if certain gametes merge to form a zygote at conception. But of course the merging gametes do not begin to exist only if they merge at conception. It follows that you and I are not identical to these gametes.

We must then reject the Gametic Principle. It is in fact so strained that Harris gets entangled in contradictions when expounding it. For instance, he writes that one of us 'starts to exist... when the gametes from which she will develop are first formed' (1992: 56). But if the gametes are something from which you or I *will develop*, we cannot start existing at the time when they start existing, but must start existing *later* than them. Nor can we be identical to that from which we shall develop.

What could have led Harris to adopt such a strange principle? He claims—truly— that someone can be 'favourably affected' by acts done to the gametes from which she develops (1992: 56). But he goes on to say that this is 'because in a real, though not unproblematic, sense they were acts done to her' (1992: 56–7). He adds:

It seems that persons are capable of benefiting from things done or not done *to them* at the gametes stage, and so it seems appropriate to say that an individual's life story begins, she starts to exist, when the gametes from which she will develop are first formed.

(1992: 56; my emphasis)

However, to assume that actions that benefit persons must be done 'to them' begs the question in favour of the view that persons must exist at the times at which acts which benefit them are executed. But, as Harris himself notes in one place (1992: 57–8), this view is false: you can be 'favourably affected' by acts which are done *to something or somebody else* because such acts can have *consequences* which are (extrinsically) good or bad *for you*. For instance, what was done to your mother—say, giving her a well-paid job—or what she did to herself—say, adopting a healthier lifestyle—some months before she became pregnant with you can be good for you if it has good effects for the development of the zygote from which you originate, or will provide her with means of giving you a good upbringing. Your being benefited by an act does not imply that you exist when the act is done: it only implies that the act has consequences that are better for you than would otherwise be the case, and this can be true of an act which ensures that you remain in the neutral state of non-existence, provided that existence would have been bad for you overall.

Therefore, if there is a possibility that an individual begins to exist and acquires consciousness which results in experiences that are intrinsically good or bad for it, then what actualizes this possibility, or prevents it from being actualized, can be extrinsically better or worse for—that is, can benefit or harm—this individual. It follows that merely possible conscious or sentient beings morally matter for their own sakes. In order to have intrinsic moral significance, it is not necessary that something exists, let alone that it has actualized its potential to acquire consciousness.

According to this *inclusive (or wide) view of benefiting* to the effect that individuals can be benefited and harmed by entering or not entering existence, it follows that if an outcome A contains a bigger set or sum of benefits than an outcome B, A will benefit individuals more, either by giving some individuals a better existence than they have in B, or by giving more individuals an existence better than non-existence. Since it is as uncontroversial as anything in ethics that there is a moral reason to benefit beings, an inclusive view of person-affecting reasons of beneficence also follows: there are reasons to benefit not only independently existing individuals, but individuals by having them exist as well, or preventing them from so doing. To deny that there is a moral reason to benefit some beings who can be benefited would seem to involve discrimination which is hard to justify.

It is rather uncontroversial that these reasons are stronger if individuals are benefited more, but it is important not to assume that if things will go very well for individuals, the reasons to have them exist are necessarily strong. The strength of these reasons also depends on what it means to 'have them exist'. One thing that you will ordinarily have to do to have individuals exist is to fertilize some eggs with sperm, but by itself this contributes very little to the creation of individuals who are in a position to enjoy even their first pleasurable experiences. Many other conditions—such as the fertilized eggs being implanted into uteruses and then being allowed to develop properly—must be present. In other words, whether events of fertilization benefit, or are extrinsically good for, individuals are conditional on how intrinsically good their existences will be overall, and thereby on a number of other factors that must be in place in order for there to be existences that are intrinsically good for them.

This means not only that there is less reason not to interfere with a process of fertilization than, say, with the development of a late term foetus because, as is normally true, it is less certain that the former process will result in a good existence. It also means that, even if we know that this happy result will occur in both cases, there will be less reason to refrain from interfering with the former process. This is because not interfering with the late term foetus will contribute more to something of intrinsic value—it might even be directly sufficient for the occurrence of the first pleasurable experiences. Thus, this non-action will be much more beneficial or extrinsically good for the individuals involved even if it is assumed that their existences be equally good.

If this point is not borne in mind, it might mistakenly be thought that—at least in a world significantly less populated than the actual one—the inclusive view of benefiting implies that we should spend a lot of our time conceiving new individuals. But, so far as I can see, even in a world with a much smaller population, we would have stronger reasons of beneficence to try to benefit those already in existence than to conceive new individuals in order to benefit them—at least as long as there is anything remotely like the level of suffering and hardships of the actual world.

2.3 Respect for the Autonomy of Persons

As long as we take into consideration only the well-being aspect of things being intrinsically valuable for us, the inclusive view implies that if human beings lead lives that are intrinsically good for them, death is extrinsically worse, or more harmful, the earlier it occurs in their existence. But, as argued in Chapter 1, there is also the aspect of autonomy to take into account. If you have a conception of your future conscious existence and informed, rational and free desires to spend it in certain ways, this constitutes another reason, a reason of respect for your autonomy, alongside reasons of beneficence, for holding that death is bad for you. It is bad for you not only because of the future well-being and the possibilities of future exercises of autonomy of which you are robbed, but also because your current exercise of autonomy is blocked. In my terminology, individuals who are in possession of a capacity for autonomy are persons.[12] For persons, then, we should adopt a 'double-aspect' account of things being of intrinsic value for them, whereas for sentient beings there is only the single aspect of well-being.[13]

Respect for the autonomy of people should be distinguished from a concern that they maximize their exercises of autonomy in their lives. This respect is expressed by permitting people to fulfil their *current* autonomous self-regarding desires. The fulfilment of these desires may conflict with the maximization of their lifetime exercises of autonomy and of their lifetime well-being, that is, with the maximization of the benefits or welfare that their lives contain (though the fulfilment of these desires could also have objects that require this maximization). For instance, persons may autonomously choose to sacrifice their lives to save the lives of others. Then respect for autonomy requires us to permit these people to go ahead and make this sacrifice, though this will almost certainly run counter to an aim of maximizing the amount of benefits that their lives contain. But people may also autonomously choose to act contrary to the goal of maximizing their lifetime benefits for other reasons than moral ones, for example in order to pull off some athletic, artistic, or scientific achievement. In either case, permitting the fulfilment of current autonomous desires implies that they are granted a moral significance which is out of proportion to their strength and the amount of fulfilment that they could yield, since this may easily be less than what future exercises of autonomy may yield. This greater significance is the justification for the permission that we grant people to act on the basis of these desires, though it may be at odds with the intertemporal maximization of their welfare (i.e. their faring well in the double aspects).

It seems reasonable to assign greater importance to successful exercises of autonomy than to an intertemporal maximization of welfare or benefits, and let people be directed

---

[12] I readily grant that the distinction between persons and other sentient beings must be vague, since all psychological capacities—rationality, self-consciousness, etc.—that could plausibly be definitive of personhood admit of degrees.

[13] I do not claim originality for this type of account which I designate by a label borrowed from the philosophy of mind. More or less similar accounts have been advanced by a number of writers.

by their own evaluations of their lives rather than by other people's evaluations of what is best for them, because they are likely to have the most intimate knowledge of the value of their lives, and they are the ones most affected by their lives because they will lead them. If respect for autonomy has this moral priority over estimates of future benefits, we have at hand a justification for letting a person rather than an infant or foetus survive, though the future life of the latter would in all probability have contained more benefits. Such respect for people's current autonomous desires about their lives does not manifest a bias towards them rather than the autonomous desires that they may have in the past or future, for people could not now be permitted to act on the latter; only their current desires could determine what these people will now do with their lives.

In other words, we have arrived at an account which explains why death is not necessarily worse for a human being, whose life is good, the earlier it occurs.[14] A later death can be worse than an earlier death because it is a greater contravention of autonomy—a greater loss incurred by not being allowed to act autonomously—though it deprives the victim of less intertemporal welfare. On the other hand, it should be noted that this priority of respect for autonomy can be overridden. This can happen, for instance, in the case of elderly people who stand to lose little by not being permitted to act autonomously, since they have only a short life left. Many of us would agree that death for us as infants could be worse for us than death as elders who still autonomously treasure life.

However, it is also reasonable to hold the view that death for us as fairly youngish people with many years of good life ahead could be less bad than death in infancy because, though still youngish, we have already lived long enough to have achieved a lot of what we regard as most important in life (as I have elsewhere argued, 2015: 421). For instance, towards the end of the 1975 Tour de France the Belgian star-cyclist Eddy Merckx had a bad crash. He broke his cheekbone, but completed the Tour, though he could take only liquid food. Suppose that he had instead died in that crash, aged 30. At that time, he had already accomplished more than enough to be recognized by most as the greatest cyclist of all time and, indeed, as one of the greatest athletes in all categories. For instance, he had more than twice as many victories in the grand tours and the one-day classics than all the other five-time winners of the Tour de France together (including Lance Armstrong, who has been disqualified, alongside Jacques Anquetil, Bernard Hinault, and Miguel Indurain). After the unhappy 1975 Tour, Merckx did not win much, and he quit cycling a few years later. A main reason for Merckx's astonishing winning record—525 wins in a little more than ten years—was that he loved cycling and racing, and did it virtually non-stop all year round.

It appears to me that, looking back on his life from the age of 70, Merckx could well hold that it would have been much worse for him to have died in infancy than in that 1975 crash. His reason could be that death in infancy would have eclipsed his

---

[14] Throughout this discussion it is assumed that the death of a human being—with consciousness—involves the irreversible cessation of consciousness, though this is not necessarily true, as will be seen in 5.1.

achievements in cycling which he could reasonably regard as the peak of his life. Death immediately after such a peak in life is plausibly less bad for you than death in infancy. Merckx had a similar, but worse crash in 1969. If he had died then, his death would surely have been a lot worse for him than the death in 1975. You might with good reason think that it would also be worse for him than dying as an infant. The reason could be because in 1969 he had just begun to actualize his enormous potential as a cyclist. Dying then, with a sense that there was a lot more left for him to accomplish as a cyclist, might reasonably count as worse than infant death when he had not yet acquired the ambition to be a top cyclist.

The bottom line is that when death is worst for us depends crucially on how much of what we want most to achieve in life would be left undone. For this reason, death in early adulthood is often worse for us than death in infancy before we have formed any life-projects. Perhaps for most of us death is worst if it occurs soon after we have begun to exercise full autonomy, say, in our late teens, but we can still look ahead to the decades of life when we shall be in our prime and have the best chance to accomplish what we place most value on.[15] Nonetheless, as the case of Merckx is meant to illustrate, death in relatively young adulthood can be less bad for us than death in infancy, provided that we have had enough time to complete the projects that we hold dearest in life.

It might be thought that if this had not been so, if death in early adulthood had always been worse for a person with a good life than death in infancy, it would have been paradoxical that we believe that we ought to save the lives of infants when we predict that they have a condition that will kill them after some 30 years of good life. For then we would save these individuals to face a death which is worse for them.[16] But the fact that a later death will be worse for them than an earlier death for the reason that it will contravene their autonomy (to a greater degree) is no reason to let them die now. If life will be good for them up to the point of the later death, they will benefit by being saved to countenance this death. For that death will be worse for them *when it occurs* because it will then contravene their autonomy, but that does not imply that it would have been better for them to have been prevented from acquiring autonomy by dying in infancy. People who possess autonomy might autonomously decide that it would be better for them to die now instead of dying later (say, in disgrace), even though life in the interim period would overall be good for them. Then there would be a reason—namely respect for their autonomy—to let them die now, but there is no such reason for individuals who do not (yet) possess autonomy. For them there are only reasons of beneficence which count in favour of letting them live.

---

[15] Incidentally, this is also likely to be when our reproductive value is greatest and, thus, the point at which death will be worst from an evolutionary point of view. Paradoxically, this also seems to be the period of life when we—at least those of us who are male—are most prone to do things that put our life at risk.

[16] As McMahan points out (1988: 58–61), this is a paradox that threatens his time-relative interest account to be discussed next.

The issue that we have been discussing—whether death before the acquisition of autonomy could be better than death after the acquisition of it—should be distinguished from the issue of whether death early on in the process of fulfilling autonomous life-projects is better or worse than death later on in this process. With respect to the latter issue both reasons of beneficence and autonomy are in play. One factor that tells against an earlier death being preferable is if engaging in a project has brought along more in the way of rewards than sacrifices. But even if engaging in a project has paid off handsomely, an earlier death might be preferable if the interruption meant a loss of competence and so on that has been acquired, but not much used. For then what Daniel Kahneman and Amos Tversky have called 'loss aversion' (2000: 46)—the phenomenon that we tend to be more averse to losing what we already possess than not gaining something that is dangling in front of our noses—might kick in. However, this is not an issue to which I need to give a general answer—if, indeed, such an answer can be given.

McMahan has put forward an alternative to the double-aspect account of the value that things have for us—a 'time-relative interest' account—to justify that the death of a person can be more harmful to this person than death to a foetus or infant, though the latter deprives the victim of more benefits (for a similar account, see DeGrazia, 2005: 189–97). According to McMahan, the loss or reduction of future benefits is bad for us at a time in proportion to the 'prudential unity relations' (2002: 79) in which we then stand to ourselves in the future when the benefits would have befallen us. The tenuousness of these relations creates a *discount rate* with respect to the value that future events would have for us consisting in

the value that future events would have within one's life at the time they would occur multiplied by a number... representing the strength of the prudential unity relations between oneself now and oneself at those times when the events would occur.   (2002: 80)

Roughly, there is some measure of prudential unity if there is enough identity of a brain to sustain some capacity of consciousness over time: 'sufficient physical and functional continuity of the areas of the brain in which consciousness is realized in order for those areas to retain the capacity to support consciousness' (2002: 79). According to McMahan, consciousness at different times need not be united at the psychological level by the existence of memories or future-oriented intentions stretching from one time to another, though if there is such a 'psychological unity' (2002: 74)—as there must be in the case of persons who have autonomy—this boosts the prudential unity. But in order for there to be *some* prudential unity, it suffices that there be 'islands' of conscious episodes at different times belonging to the same consciousness in virtue of the identity of their neural basis.

The prudential unity relations between a foetus and a postnatal individual in the future can only be non-existent or weak: non-existent if the foetus is pre-conscious, and weak if the foetus has just about gained consciousness, since this will only be an elementary form of consciousness, insufficient to generate psychological unity. The weakness of these prudential unity relations brings along a discounting of the value that its future life has for a foetus. Therefore, even if its future life would be of great intrinsic value because it would consist of many decades of a highly valuable existence, it might not be so bad for a conscious foetus to be deprived of it by being aborted that this badness cannot be outweighed by a significant setback of the pregnant woman's interests. It cannot be bad *at all* for a pre-conscious foetus to prevent the greatest amount of future benefits to the postnatal individual that it would have become because it is not prudentially united to this individual (though this act of prevention will make the world contain a smaller sum of benefits and, thereby, be impersonally worse).[17]

In the case of Merckx discussed above, the time-relative interest account seems to imply—implausibly, to my mind—that death in infancy would have been less bad for him than death in 1975. However, since its discount rate cannot be precisely determined, it might seem that proponents of this account could deny that it implies that dying in 1975 would have been worse for Merckx than dying as an infant (as does DeGrazia, 2015: 423). But suppose that we take 'in infancy' to be more precisely at birth when consciousness is quite rudimentary (especially if birth is premature). Then, if there is a discount rate proportional to psychological unity or connectedness, surely it must be steep at a point at which consciousness has been recently acquired and is consequently rudimentary. Assuming, reasonably, that this relation is at least less than half of what it is in the case of a normal adult and, with McMahan (2002: 80), that in the case of normal adults we should multiply by 1, we should in the case of the neonate multiply by less than 0.5. Suppose further that in 1975 Merckx still had half of the value of his life to look forward to, consisting in harvesting the fruits of his fame, and so on. Then this value should be multiplied by 1. If so, the time-relative interest account implies that dying as a neonate would have been less bad for Merckx than dying in 1975. For even if he had by 1975 reached the zenith of his life, it must be granted that at this point there could still remain ahead of him such a great portion of value that would have been reaped by a future self with whom he would be maximally psychologically connected that this would be a larger loss for him than the one incurred by infant death.

By contrast, the time-relative interest account could plausibly imply that if Merckx had died in 1969, this death would have been worse than infant death. Certainly, death in 1969 would have deprived him of more value than death in 1975, perhaps as much as three-quarters of the value of his life. Now, while it is quite plausible for adherents of this account to hold that the psychological unity or connectedness of a neonate is less than three-quarters of that of a normal person, it would seem implausible were they to hold that it is nonetheless more than half as strong as that of a normal person in order to heed the intuition that death in 1975 is less bad than infant death.

Another objection to the time-relative interest account than this one about death after an early peak in life being less bad than infant death is that it sometimes makes

---

[17] This is true according to McMahan's version of the account. DeGrazia is more ambivalent, allowing that 'bare' organic identity may be a basis for *some* prudential concern (2005: 288).

what benefits individuals more vary over time.[18] Imagine that a woman rightly concludes that the modest benefits that killing her newborn baby would bring her outweigh the heavily discounted benefits of the future life of her baby. Thus, in terms of a principle of beneficence she has more reason to kill her newborn than not to do so. However, she cannot bring herself to do so; it goes on to live a life whose value for it will not be discounted because it proceeds to acquire personal interests. Then this alternative will later come out as the one that most benefits the individuals affected (the woman and her child) because the discount rate will cease to apply to the neonate's benefits, since letting it live allows it to develop its interests fully. Hence, it later turns out that the woman did what she had more reason to do according to a principle of beneficence when she did not kill it. That is, the time-relative interest account implies that the alternative of letting the child live, which, at the time of action, did not most benefit the individuals affected, later benefited them most. This is because its discount rate will later cease to apply. To put it a bit paradoxically, the neonate will lose comparatively little if it is killed, but gain a lot if it is not, since then the value that life has for it will eventually cease to be discounted. But it is odd that acceptance of the time-relative interest account could have the consequence that by failing to do what we have more reason to do, according to a principle of beneficence, we have done what we *later* have more reason to have done, according to this principle.

For this reason the time-relative interest account can advise us to be unduly myopic in the domain of prudence rather than to do what is best for individuals over time. Imagine that a newborn is engaging in some activity that, if continued, will give it immense pleasure of considerable duration, but which will also damage it in a way that would substantially reduce the value of its future, perhaps by reducing its life-expectancy by some years. On the other hand, if the activity is immediately stopped, the newborn will not be damaged. Then the time-relative interest account may imply that, at the time, it is best for the newborn to allow it to continue to engage in the activity, since we have seen that it may have a strong desire that it continue and, thus, be strongly psychologically connected to the imminent self who will experience this pleasure, while the value of its more distant future is heavily discounted. But this value will no longer be discounted later in life when the former neonate is strongly connected to its once distant future; consequently, it may then turn out that it was *not* better for it to let it continue with the pleasurable activity. This would rather be analogous to letting a person succumb to the bias towards the near future, the tendency to exaggerate the positive or negative value of what happens to oneself in the nearer future (see Chapter 13 for a brief discussion of this bias). It follows that if continuation of the pleasurable activity had killed the neonate, it might have benefited most by being allowed to continue, but if we nevertheless stop it, this alternative will turn out to be most beneficial for it. That is, whatever we do, we have done what benefits it most.

---

[18] See Bradley (2009: 142) for another argument against this account which also concerns how it makes what benefits depend on what is done.

DeGrazia's reply to this objection that what is the most beneficial course could vary over time is that it is mistaken because it assumes that the time-relative interest account (TRIA)

> would retrospectively...evaluate the decision based on the non-discounted goods of the [neonate's] life; rather, TRIA would evaluate the harm of death *at the time of death* and would make the same judgment about it regardless of when the judgment is made. (2015: 423)

This reply appears to assume that combining a principle of beneficence with TRIA would be equivalent to a *time-indexed* principle of beneficence to the effect that there is more reason to do what benefits individuals more *at the time when the relevant action occurs*.[19] Such a principle would indeed imply that we do not have much reason to refrain from letting the 'pleasure-wallowing' neonate die, since at the time of death it would not have benefited much from being spared this death, and this judgment will stand forever. But this time-indexed principle is not plausible: surely, it is more plausible to claim that we have more reason to do what benefits individuals more *over time* than merely at the time of action. Furthermore, a time-indexed principle would allow us to ignore the interests of individuals who will begin to exist independently since, being non-existent at the time of action, they cannot benefit *then*. But, clearly, we should take into consideration how much they will benefit *later* when they come into existence.

The principle of beneficence should not be time-indexed, then. But when a non-indexed principle is conjugated with the time-relative interest account, the implication will be that we should concentrate on how individuals are benefited at the time of action in the case of *some* actions, such as killings, because then there is no question of how the victims will be benefited in the future. However, if they are not killed, and their psychological unity over time is strengthened, what benefits them most over time will not be constant. This is in effect conceded by McMahan when he writes: 'we must evaluate the act in terms of its effect on all those time-relative interests it affects, present *or future*' (2002: 283, my emphasis).

However, even in cases in which the time-relative interest account does not imply that what benefits individuals most varies over time in a contradictory fashion, the fact that time-relative interests change over time has consequences that seem counterintuitive. Modifying a case discussed by McMahan (2002: 280), suppose a woman could gain a benefit at the cost of either killing her newborn or causing it some disability that would reduce the value of its future life as a person to half of what it would otherwise be, though it would still have a life well worth living. Suppose further that the newborn's psychological connections to its future self are less than half as strong as those of an adult. Then, according to the time-relative interest account, to calculate how much its future life is worth to the neonate, we have to multiply its value by less than 0.5, as we

---

[19] If the question is whether killing someone benefits the beings affected most, the relevant action is the killing, not the actions by means of which you kill. If you use slow-working means, the actions by means of which you kill—giving the victim the poison—would occur long before the time at which you kill the victim which, I take it, does not occur until the victim dies.

have seen. This yields a value that is less than what the disability removes. It follows that reasons of beneficence could support securing the benefit to the woman at the cost of killing the neonate, but not at the cost of causing it the disability. But, as was remarked in the foregoing section in the context of a view of Singer's, this seems odd because killing it is depriving it of *all* of the value of future life, whereas causing it the disability only halves it. Intuitively, the former would seem harder to justify morally. Of course, this oddity is accentuated if, as seems realistic, we assume that the neonate is considerably less than half as well-connected to its future self than an adult person, so that the discount rate is much lower than 0.5.

Now, the double-aspect account also incorporates something of a time-relative ingredient. This was manifest when I explained why it may be justifiable to let an infant live, though its death at 30 would be worse for it *then*—when it seriously infringes its autonomy—than dying now. But my account differs from the time-relative interest account in that, while a new type of moral reason kicks in with the possession of autonomy, there is no discount rate operating on the value that existence has for individuals on account of the welfare that it contains. This value does not change when individuals acquire autonomy: the reason that death at 30 would be worse is not that the victim would be deprived of a future that is of greater value to it than the future that it would be deprived of were it to die as an infant. It is that death at 30 would contravene the autonomy that the individual then has. Autonomy cannot be respected or contravened before it is acquired, albeit things can be done in advance to satisfy an autonomous desire when it comes into existence. There is a reason of beneficence to do the latter thing, but there can be no reason to respect an autonomous desire until it has been formed.

A third objection to the time-relative interest account is that there are also reasons to deny that the weakness of the prudential unity relations that a foetus or neonate has to itself in the future must always mean reduced prudential concern. Granted, a weakening of our prudential unity relations that signifies a *deterioration or loss* of valuable psychological features—as in the case of dementia—might well make it reasonable for us to be prudentially less concerned about our future fate, with the result that death then would become less bad for us. But as regards a foetus or neonate, there is a *growth or improvement* in respect of valuable psychological features. To the extent that we could imagine something similar happening to persons—for instance, by their taking a drug that will speedily amplify the power of their brains to a superhuman degree of rationality and virtue and sever the future high-flying beliefs and desires from their current partly irrational beliefs and base desires—it is far from obvious that it would be rational for them now to be less prudentially concerned about themselves after such a transformation (despite McMahan's suspicions to the contrary, 2002: 81). Surely, people could autonomously choose to be subjected to such an enhancement, to bring themselves closer to an ideal, without this making the prospect of death in the further future less bad for them. If they could autonomously make this choice, there is a ground which makes this choice rational. This ground is present in the case of normal foetus or neonate as well, though it cannot recognize its presence. Such a ground consisting in that there is improvement or enhancement rather than deterioration or degeneration is something that plausibly offsets the tenuousness of the psychological connections.

Although humans are unlikely to undergo enhancements that bring along a significant loosening of connectedness, they do undergo deterioration processes that carry with them a loosening when they are afflicted by severe dementia. DeGrazia thinks that, in spite of such a loosening, it is rationally permissible to be greatly prudentially concerned about our demented selves, to prefer that our existence be pleasant rather than painful, more rather than less dignified and so forth. In contrast to McMahan, he proposes that, while the discount rate of the time-relative interest account is mandatory in the case of non-autonomous individuals, it should be optional in the case of autonomous individuals (2005: 200–1). This is in order to make it rationally permissible for us to care deeply about our severely demented selves, presumably simply on the basis of being identical to them. I propose that it is a permissible option for autonomous persons to be at least as much concerned about weakly connected future selves if the weaker connectedness is due to improvement as if there had not been any improvement and weakening, but they had persisted largely intact. In fact, I am prepared to go further and in Chapter 3 argue that psychological connectedness and identity in themselves are no proper grounds of prudential concern. Meanwhile, I suggest that it is permissible for persons to regard improvement as something that at least *offsets or counteracts* weak connectedness.

I conclude that the double-aspect account of the value of life provides a more plausible justification than the time-relative interest account for the badness of death and the view that, if the life of a human being is good for it, death is not necessarily worse for it the earlier it occurs. According to the double-aspect account, the basic variable determining the value that (future) life has for a being is the amount of well-being (i.e. intrinsically valuable experiences) that it will contain. But if the beings are persons, there is also a variable consisting in the strength of the autonomous desires that the beings might have with respect to their future. These desires are based on the value that the future life is estimated to contain, which in the case of persons will also include exercises of autonomy. However, it is not based on so-called prudential unity relations, nor on our identity (as will transpire in 3.1). Nonetheless, it is important that there be some sort of connections between ourselves at present and in the future that give us some measure of control over our future, such that the match between our present desires and our future is not purely coincidental. This is a part of the exercise of autonomy.

Although on the double-aspect account death is not rendered worse the earlier it occurs, death for human beings at the beginning of their existence is quite bad for them if they would otherwise had gone on to lead good lives. But this means that if we were to conjugate this account with a denial of the claim of inclusive beneficence that it is bad for these humans to enter existence, we obtain a rather incredible combination of views (cf. Kagan, 2012: 224). For, as was seen in 2.2, the coming into existence of a human being is a gradual process; so it will be implausible to claim that if we stop this process a few days after gastrulation—or at whatever point we think that human beings begin to exist—this would be quite bad for the beings just formed, whereas it would not be bad for them if we stop it a couple of days before gastrulation, before their existence commenced. Therefore, I believe that the double-aspect account is best accompanied by the inclusive view.

Because it implies that early death can be quite harmful for the individuals who die, it should be admitted that the double-aspect account makes abortion harder to justify morally than it is on some common liberal views (and harder to justify than an omission to conceive, for reasons indicated in the preceding section). But this implication does not seem counterintuitive to me: I would say that it *is* in fact harder than many believe to justify abortion *morally*. Such a justification takes serious medical reasons, such as a threat to the pregnant woman's life, or grave defects of the foetus, or serious social reasons, like the pregnancy being the result of rape, or the woman being under age. It may be unpleasant for pregnant women requesting abortion to have to admit this truth, and for that reason it is liable to be suppressed in societies with strong feminist movements, but it is still the truth. Morality is frequently quite demanding.

However, although the circumstances in which abortion can be *morally* justified are comparatively few, the *law* should probably be as liberal as it is in most Western countries. That is, the law should grant a general right to abortion until the foetus becomes close to viable. Generally speaking, the law should not be as demanding as morality. For instance, although parents may be morally required to donate kidneys to their children if they will otherwise die, the law should not require this. Likewise, the law should not require a woman to let a foetus use her body for several months in all situations in which morality requires it. Viability of the foetus might seem to be a suitable endpoint for a society to terminate a woman's legal right to 'evict' her foetus, since after the point at which the foetus becomes viable outside the womb, society will incur an obligation to sustain its life if it allows it to be evicted from the womb (given that it shoulders a general obligation to sustain human life). Also, the longer a pregnancy has lasted, the more complicated it is to have the foetus removed, and the smaller the cost to the woman to carry it to term and then have it adopted.

This is not the place for an extensive discussion of abortion. I hope, however, that enough has been said to show how combining the inclusive view of benefiting with the double-aspect view of what makes things go well for us removes the counterintuitive implication that the earlier death comes to a human being who leads a good life, the worse it is for it. But it might seem that the most counterintuitive implications of the inclusive view flow from the fact that it implies that beings can be benefited by being caused to exist, and it is such implications that will be explored in Chapter 3.

3

Three Problems of Procreation
Replaceability, the Asymmetry, and the Non-Identity Problem

3.1 The Replaceability of Sentient Beings and Persons

It might be thought that the inclusive view of benefiting faces a problem that has troubled, for instance, Singer for a couple of decades, namely the problem that sentient beings, including infants, are *replaceable* (1979: 100; 1993: 121). The problem is that, while disposing of sentient beings, say, infants with good lives in store, is bad for them, the inclusive view seems to imply that this loss of value can be made up for by creating in their place new infants with lives as good for them as survival would be for those disposed of. So it seems that, according to the inclusive view, this disposal would not be wrong if it is followed up by this sort of replacement. But this corollary seems counterintuitive.

Notice, however, that on the view that reasons of beneficence are person-affecting this implies that it is morally permissible to carry out such replacements instead of letting the same beings continue their existence only if, were the latter alternative realized, the would-be replacements would be as much harmed as the beings who would be replaced would be if they were replaced. If the harm befalling the would-be replacements is less than the harm done to the replaced would be, there would be less negative value to subtract from the value of the lives of the non-replaced survivors than from the value of the lives of the replacements. Thus, the value of non-replacement would come out ahead, and would be what a principle of beneficence bids us to bring about.

Now normally the beings who would enter existence if there were to be replacement cannot be identified. Rather, there are countless beings who could be made to exist by the methods of reproduction used, whether natural or artificial; so there are countless possible beings, each having only a minuscule chance of entering existence. Thus, the harm done to possible beings if there is not replacement consists in robbing each of them of this minimal chance of a valuable existence. However, it is arguable that it is less bad to rob a huge number of possible beings of a minimal chance of a good existence than certainly robbing one particular being of an equally good (continuation of) existence. For instance, it seems reasonable to choose an action which exposes each of a billion individuals to a one-in-a-billion risk of dying rather than an action which will certainly kill a particular individual. It seems that each one of this billion ought to take on a one-in-a-billion risk of dying rather than exposing a particular individual to certain death. This judgment squares with the disperse additional burdens view, defended in Chapter 4. If this is right, there is less harm done if existent beings are allowed to carry on their existence than if they are replaced.

It follows that replacement is not morally permissible according to the inclusive view, since it regards reasons of beneficence as person-affecting. But according to the view that the reasons of beneficence are impersonal and support the boosting of sums of benefits rather than the benefiting of individuals, replacement would be as good as letting existing individuals continue to exist and have the same benefits as the newcomers would have, since the sum of benefits would be the same whichever alternative is chosen.

Furthermore, as will be clear in Part II, there are other moral considerations that will tend to block replacement for, alongside a principle of inclusive beneficence, morality includes a principle of justice demanding an equal distribution of benefits. This means that, unless replacement is practised universally for all sentient beings—which is evidently impracticable—there would still be a moral objection to replacement even if there were no objection from the point of view of beneficence. The objection is that replacement is bound to be unjust or unfair by giving some shorter lives—and thereby a smaller amount of benefits—than others.[1] Consequently, there are two reasons why sentient beings are not replaceable according to the morality put forward in this book which consists of an inclusive view of beneficence and a view of justice as requiring equality of welfare. Replaceability is first and foremost a problem for a utilitarianism which sets up a single impersonal goal of maximizing the sum of benefits, like the 'total' utilitarianism that Singer had in mind.[2] But even for this view it would only be a theoretical problem, since *in practice* we can hardly carry out replacements without a serious loss of benefits.

This brings us to a point made at the end of 2.2. It is misleading to set having beings start good lives against having them cease leading such lives, for while the latter could be done by means of a single act, the former cannot. One thing that we shall have to do to have beings start good lives is to fertilize some eggs with sperm, but by itself this contributes very little to the creation of beings who begin to enjoy pleasurable experiences. This act will benefit, or be extrinsically good for, some beings only if many other factors come into operation, factors such as the fertilized eggs being implanted into uteruses and then being allowed to develop properly. We cannot in fact perform any act that would benefit beings who will have good lives as much as an act of killing beings who

---

[1] But does not causing beings to have a good existence contribute to equality of welfare by lifting them from a lower, neutral level? No, for reasons given in 9.3.

[2] Singer presents a dichotomy between a 'total' utilitarianism—which is the impersonal view indicated in the text—and a 'prior existence' utilitarianism which corresponds to the narrow view of reasons of beneficence (1979: 87; 1993: 103–4). But this dichotomy omits the view here espoused, the inclusive or wide person-affecting view.

have equally good lives would harm them, for the harmfulness of the latter act is not conditional on many other factors subsequently kicking in. Therefore, in practice we shall never be in situations in which we have as much reason to perform an act contributing to the commencement of existence as we have against performing an act of killing; thus, we cannot make up for performing the latter by performing the former.

Singer exempts persons from the replaceability that he sees as endangering sentient beings.[3] In my view, it is rather the other way around: persons are in theory replaceable by numerically distinct persons whose lives are equally valuable for them because they have the capacity to consent to being replaced. If they consent to being replaced, they are not harmed by it, since they would be compensated for their loss by benefits to their 'successors'; thus, there would be no injustice involved in replacing them. The centrepiece of the defence of this position is the claim that it is irrational to care about one's identity over time. Having elsewhere argued this point at length (2005: pt. IV), I shall now limit myself to sketching the argument in broad strokes.

As remarked in the Introduction, there are two main types of theory of our identity: psychological theories, according to which we are identical to something possessing some psychological properties, and biological theories, according to which we are identical to our human organisms. To illustrate the clash between these two types of theory, consider taking out those areas of your brain which underpin your mental states and transplanting them into another human organism or body in which those brain-parts are missing (this body may in other respects be a perfect replica of your body). Imagine that the operation is successful, and results in there being someone with your mind or psychology in the latter body, that is, someone with your memories, interests, personality traits, psychological capacities, and so on. Then, on standard psychological theories, the person in this body will be you; you will have accompanied the mind-supporting segments of your brain and will have received a new body. This will be an extreme case of organ-donation: you will have received not merely a new heart, new kidneys, and so on, but a whole new body (apart from those areas of your brain that are the seat of your psychology).

According to biological theories, this will not be so because they declare you to be identical to your human body or organism, and this body or organism would seem to be the one which is now bereft of its mind-supporting brain-parts. This claim might appear implausible, since we do have a strong intuition that we go with our brains in suchlike brain-transplant cases.[4] Yet, we also have intuitions that tell in favour of biological theories.

---

[3] His reasons for adopting this position are different in (1979) and (1993): in (1979) he takes the prior existence view to apply to persons, whereas in (1993) he believes that the total view applies to persons as well as sentient beings, but that persons are saved from replaceability by having future-oriented desires. For a critical discussion of the latter position, see Persson (1995b). His position in (2011) is different still, but also to the effect that persons are not replaceable.

[4] Another problem for the biological view is that it would seem to presuppose that it is an essential property of ours that we belong to a certain species, *Homo sapiens*. The argument of Chapter 6 implies that this must be false.

Suppose that, when the mind-supporting segments of your brains are taken out, what is left behind is a human organism which is still biologically alive, that is, an organism which breathes, digests food, whose heart beats, whose blood is circulated, etc. This is possible because the regions of your brain which regulate those functions are different from the mind-supporting ones, and could remain in your (original) body when the latter are removed. The result would be a human organism in a permanently unconscious or persistent vegetative state, PVS. If we encounter such a body without realizing that its mind-supporting brain-parts have been transplanted and kept alive, it is natural to say, as biological theories of our identity imply, that *you* are in PVS. For instance, it was said of the former Israeli prime minister, Ariel Sharon, that *he* was in PVS for some six years, and we would say things like 'I don't want to be kept alive if *I* were to enter into PVS'. Such claims would be false on psychological theories.

We cannot have it both ways, however, asserting both that you are now an organism in PVS and that you are the person in the body which has received your mind-supporting brain-parts. So, we face a dilemma: psychological theories maintain that we could lose all of our bodies, except perhaps the parts of our brain which are the seat of our psychology, while biological theories maintain that we could lose all of our psychology and, thus, all of the brain-parts that are the seat of our psychology. Clearly, both cannot be right, since then we could still be around, though nothing is left of our minds and organisms!

My hypothesis is that we come up against this dilemma because we pre-reflectively identify ourselves with our bodies or organisms *on the erroneous assumption that they are non-derivatively the subjects or owners of our consciousnesses or minds*.[5] The possibility of brain-transplants brings out the error of the assumption that our consciousnesses or minds *non-derivatively* belong to our bodies by showing that they belong only *derivatively* to them *in virtue of belonging more precisely to certain proper parts of our bodies*, namely certain areas of our brains. This is why these states would accompany the transplanted brain-parts to the new body rather than staying attached to the old body.

To ascribe a property derivatively to (the whole of) our bodies when it more precisely is a property of a proper part of them is in fact standard practice (as I argue in 1999b). For instance, my body—or, indeed, I—can be said to be in contact with the floor when, strictly speaking, only the soles of my feet are. Notice, however, that when I say this, I am *aware* of the fact that my body is only derivatively in contact with the floor, that, strictly speaking, it is only the soles of my feet that are in contact with the floor, and that my body is in contact with it *because* the soles of my feet are a part of it. We may put this by saying that what is *ontically* the non-derivative subject of predication is also *epistemically* the non-derivative subject of predication.

Not so when we attribute mental states to our bodies in everyday life: then we are not inescapably aware of the fact that these attributions must be understood as derivative,

---

[5] I have earlier advanced this hypothesis in (2005: pt. IV), and have recently restated it in (2016).

nor of any proper parts of our bodies that are their non-derivative subjects. The epistemic subject of non-derivative predication is then the body—it is what we ordinarily take ourselves as ascribing our mental states to—but it is not ontically the non-derivative subject of predication when what is predicated is mental states. Brain-transplants bring out that it is rather (certain areas of) our brains than our bodies that are the ontically non-derivative subjects of our mental states. But since brain-transplants, or any other events that make this point plain, do not occur in everyday life, it is not surprising that common sense could feature the belief that it is our bodies that are these subjects.

However, once it is brought to our attention that it is rather certain areas of our brains that are the ontically non-derivative owners of our mental states, could we not simply identify ourselves with these brain-parts rather than our (whole) bodies? A problem with this proposal is that these brain-parts are not epistemically the non-derivative subjects, as the soles of my feet are in the example above. They are not such subjects because they do not have what one might call *phenomenal accessibility*. I claim that this is a further condition that our selves—that is, the referent of 'I' as used by us—must fulfil alongside the condition of being the non-derivative subject or owner of our minds or mental states. That is to say, our selves must be something that we are able to pick out in everyday circumstances in order to attribute our mental states to it. Such attributions are what we engage in when we say, for instance, that we perceive or think this or that. Our bodies meet this accessibility condition because we perceive them whenever we are conscious. Moreover, we are able to recognize our bodies from one day to another because they do not change dramatically during shorter periods of time. This ensures that we can attribute our mental states to the same subject from one day to another and, thus, that our selves can have numerical identity over time.

To summarize, I propose an 'error-theory' of our commonsensical conception of our identity to the effect that we take ourselves to be identical to our bodies because (1) they have a phenomenal accessibility which enables us to attribute our mental states to them on an everyday basis, and (2) it does not occur to us that these attributions must be understood as derivative to be true, whereas our selves must be the non-derivative subjects of our mental states. The latter, erroneous assumption is reasonable because in everyday life nothing brings out that our attributions of mental states to our bodies must be construed as derivative, but this assumption is nevertheless false, as the possibility of brain-transplants brings out. However, it is also erroneous to identify ourselves with those areas of our brains which support our consciousnesses because they do not meet the first condition of phenomenal accessibility. In fact, nothing meets both of the conditions of phenomenal accessibility and non-derivative ownership, so we are not identical to anything.

All the same, we are undeniably strongly inclined to identify ourselves with those areas of our brains which sustain our psychological states, as evidenced by our intuition that we go with these areas when they are transplanted. Why do we have this inclination if it is mistaken? I hypothesize that this is because we have a tendency to identify ourselves with the features of ourselves *that matter most to us*. We have a general tendency to narrow down the applicability of terms to the most important features of the things to which these terms are literally applicable. For instance, we sometimes take 'human being' to designate the features of human beings that matter most to us, such as their moral qualities or high intelligence; we say that somebody who exhibits such qualities is 'a real human being'. Analogously, I suggest, we are prone to narrow down the reference of 'ourselves' to the features of us that matter most to us, namely our minds, to identify ourselves simply with that part of ourselves that is the non-derivative owner of our minds, and ignoring less important parts of our bodies. I shall later argue, following Parfit (1987: ch. 12), that this urge to make our identity matter is doomed to frustration, but first I want to argue that, even apart from the fact that our identity, so construed, cannot matter, this construal of it cannot be satisfactory.

Granted that nothing could be both the non-derivative owner of our mental states and be phenomenally accessible to us, could the conception that we have of ourselves be satisfactory if it were revised to satisfy one condition or the other? If we want to hold on to the firm intuition that we go with our brains when they are transplanted (without division), we have to sacrifice the phenomenal accessibility of our selves and conceive of them as what meets solely a requirement of being the non-derivative owners of our minds. As I shall now argue, this course will not yield a satisfactory conception of our selves. My argument draws on an elusiveness of both possible psychological and physical ingredients of our identity. The problem about the physical ingredient is that once we are forced to surrender the idea that, non-derivatively, our bodies are the subjects of our minds or consciousnesses, we shall be hard put to pinpoint these subjects.

As regards the psychological element, we saw in the preceding chapter that McMahan's account of our identity does not require any intertemporal psychological connections, like memory at one time of what happened at an earlier time. This is in contrast to Parfit, who defines our identity in terms of psychological continuity conceived as 'the holding of overlapping chains of *strong* connectedness' (1987: 206). Psychological connectedness is *strong* on his conception 'if the number of direct connections, over any day, is *at least half* the number that hold, over every day, in the lives of nearly every actual person' (1987: 206). It has to be psychological continuity rather than psychological connectedness which figures in a plausible criterion of personal identity, since we would like adults to be identical to toddlers, say, though there are no psychological connections between them, for example the adults do not remember anything from the time when they were toddlers. Still, even this is too strong. We definitely want to claim that we are identical to foetuses just before birth and neonates—surely, we were once born!—and, yet, there is certainly not from one day to another in the lives of these individuals at least half the number of psychological connections that hold 'in the lives of nearly every actual person' (taking a person to be a self-conscious being). The same sort of difficulty also arises at the other end of life, with individuals who are gravely demented.

Thus, there is a good case for taking it that only a very weak psychological ingredient can be necessary for our identity. Indeed, it can be so weak that some find appealing the biological view that no psychology at all is requisite for our identity, but let us grant that that would be going too far. Nonetheless, it seems undeniable that the psychological ingredient could shrink to the point that what is left is not anything that is *distinctive* of our personality. Parfit discusses (1987: 229–30) an imaginary case designed by Bernard Williams in which a nefarious neuro-surgeon removes more or less at one go all of his personal memories, character traits, interests—in short all psychological dispositions that are distinctive of him as a person, while he undergoes severe pain. Because the pain absorbs all of his attention, he does not notice that he loses his memories, his philosophical capacity, his fascination with Venice, and so on. Parfit apparently agrees with Williams that it is still plausible to assert that the individual who emerges at the end of this surgery is him. This is true even if he were to lose consciousness for a while at the end of the surgery.

Now suppose that, while unconscious, the regions of his brain that sustain the remaining basic, non-distinctive psychological capacities to feel, to perceive and perhaps to make simple sensory and perceptual classifications are transplanted and properly connected to a body quite dissimilar to Parfit's body, perhaps a body like Greta Garbo's as he envisages at one point (1987: 237). Would it be plausible to judge the resulting individual who has neither any physical nor any psychological features distinctive of Parfit to be identical to him? Not to my mind. I conjecture that the fact that we normally rely on the fact the subjects of our minds must satisfy the phenomenal accessibility requirement and, thus, be identical to our bodies and, thereby, have a lot of physical features distinctive of us, allows an attenuation of the requisite psychological element to the point at which nothing distinctive of our psychology remains, only basic perceptual and sensory capacities. But then we cannot let go of the phenomenal accessibility constraint as well and accept that we accompany our brains in the case of transplants of our brains when their capacity has been so reduced that they carry no psychology distinctive of us, since this would allow us to persist when *nothing* distinctive of us is left. If only my basic capacities of perceiving the environment and feeling physical pleasure and pain survive in a body qualitatively and numerically distinct from mine, it seems clear that *I* do not survive.

So much for the problem about the psychological element. The problem about the physical element concerns what, if anything, physical must be retained for us to persist. We are assuming that brain-transplant cases show that bodily identity is not necessary, but we should ask whether even identity of *any* brain-parts is necessary. The following thought-experiment suggests that they are not. Suppose that, as in Parfit's division case to be discussed below, each of the hemispheres of our brains is capable of upholding all of our psychological capacities, our memories, personality traits and so on, and that they work in shift. When we are asleep, the neural processes underlying our mental dispositions are transmitted from one hemisphere to the other. Suppose further that just before such a transmission occurs, your active hemisphere is taken out and transplanted into another body which is a replica of yours, but which has only one inactive or mentally 'empty' hemisphere. Later in the night the neural processes underlying your mental dispositions migrate to the empty hemisphere. When this migration is completed, the hemisphere that comes from your body and that is now empty is removed and replaced by an empty replica.

The mental dispositions of the person resulting from these transplants will then no longer be realized by *any* parts of your brain. But it still seems plausible to hold that what they realize is *your* mental dispositions, *your* mind. If this is right, it follows that the identity of *no* brain-parts is necessary for the persistence of your mind, or for your identity if we take the persistence of your mind to be sufficient for your persistence. McMahan's requirement of 'physical and functional continuity of the areas of the brain in which consciousness is realized' (2002: 79) must be then abandoned. It seems that it is not necessary that there be identity as regards *anything* physical that realizes your psychology or mind throughout its existence.

Summing up, the possibility of such 'migration' of mental states shows that, once we surrender the phenomenal accessibility constraint, we risk ending up empty-handed in our search for the owners of our consciousnesses. It would seem that there has to be something that could qualify as such and that persists when we are unconscious—otherwise, we would cease to exist then—but what is this? Moreover, surrendering the phenomenal accessiblity constraint risks emptying our identity of everything distinctive of us, since this constraint has made us accept weakenings of the psychological ingredient in identity to the point of non-existence. Therefore, we should not give up the phenomenal accessibility constraint. But the non-derivative ownership constraint also has great plausibility: surely, we are something from which our minds cannot part ways. However, if we endorse both of these constraints as necessary conditions for our selves or the referents of 'I', nothing could fill the role of such selves or referents. It is not that it is logically impossible that there be something that fulfils these two conditions—conceivably, the seat of our minds could be inseparably spread out all over our bodies—but as a matter of fact there is not.

It may seem paradoxical to claim that there is not anything to which we are identical because this may appear to entail that we do not exist! However, it should be borne in mind that there *are* human bodies or organisms which are in various psychological states in virtue of some of their proper parts. Their existence *suffices* for our existence, even if we cannot specify precisely what it is in them to which we are identical. These bodies with their physical and psychological properties constitute us, as a chunk of marble could constitute a statue, though the statue is not identical to this chunk, since most of it could conceivably be replaced without the statue going out of existence, say, by the chunk being hollowed out.

If there is not anything to which we are identical, it cannot be rational for us to be especially concerned about some individuals going on existing and having things going well for them for the reason that we are identical to them. Moreover, even if it had been possible to identify us with our minds, or some non-derivative owners of our minds, Parfit has argued—convincingly, in my view—that identity is not what rationally matters (1987: ch. 12). His argument appeals to the conceivability of our minds dividing. Suppose that there is a redundancy in your brain such that each of your two hemispheres is sufficient to sustain all of your mental attributes, that is, your memories, personality traits, and so on. Suppose further that these hemispheres are separated by the connection between them, the *corpus callosum*, being cut, and that each hemisphere is successfully transplanted to a living body, which is a replica of your current body (except for the fact that the hemispheres of its brain have been removed). The result is two persons, each with a mind like the one you had just before the transplant.

It would be arbitrary to identify you with one rather than the other post-transplant individual, and you cannot be identical to both of them, since they are evidently distinct from each other. The most plausible conclusion is therefore that you have ceased to exist. So has *your* mind, that is, the mind that *you* had before the division. It has ceased to exist by division, not by ceasing to function, as normally happens when you die. But the chief point for now is that such a division of your mind can be just as good for you as your mind continuing without division in a single organism, as in the original transplant case. You do not seem to have any reason to be less concerned that things go well rather than badly for the two post-transplant persons than for the person resulting from a transplant of your undivided brain. If so, what matters to you cannot be your identity, that it is *you* who persist.

What matters is, Parfit suggests, 'psychological connectedness and/or psychological continuity with the right kind of cause', where the 'right kind of cause could be any cause' (1987: 262). To constitute our identity, psychological continuity cannot branch, as it does in his division case, but it should not matter for us whether or not it branches. Nor should it matter whether its cause is the normal one, the continuous existence of certain neural structures. The cause could be what it is in his imagined case of teletransportation in which a scanner records the state of all the cells of your body, destroys your body and transmits the recorded information to a receiver which creates a replica of you (1987: 284–7). I am prepared to go further. If *any* cause would do, why not *no* cause at all, provided that the outcome is the same? Consider a final thought-experiment (which I first put forward in 1985b).

The micro-particles composing your brain and body are in a constant state of flux, being successively replaced by other micro-particles. Imagine that this replacement of the micro-particles constituting your brain and body at present were instead to occur at one go, such that there was an interval in between the moment at which the particles composing your brain and body were dispersed and the moment at which other, qualitatively identical particles are joined together to constitute a qualitatively identical brain and body. This interval might be so short that it cannot be registered by our consciousness, and it might occur when you are deeply asleep. Then the person existing after the interval of non-existence would not be *numerically* but *qualitatively* identical to you. There cannot be numerical identity here because there is nothing in this situation that rules out that another copy of you simultaneously pops into existence somewhere else in the universe, perhaps even due to a reunion of the very same micro-particles that originally composed your brain and body. And this would create a dilemma similar to the one in Parfit's division case: you cannot be numerically identical to both of these copies, and there is not sufficient reason to select one for identification.

But, plausibly, it would not be any worse for you to be succeeded in this way by someone qualitatively identical to you than to survive as numerically identical. Suppose that you are informed that this sort of replacement has happened many times in what you have falsely thought to be the lifetime of a single person with whom you have identified yourself. You are now told that tonight it will happen again. It is essential that we imagine that this has happened many times in the past and that, looking back, you cannot find any experiential difference between the occasions when there has been persistence and when there has been replacement; otherwise replacement is likely to appear scary and unreliable—perhaps the replica will not crop up. It would not then seem rational for you to be less concerned about the person who will soon pop into existence than you would be about yourself were you to continue to exist without any gap. If so, what matters to you cannot be any kind of continuity, be it physical or psychological. It would be as good for you if you were succeeded by somebody who is just qualitatively identical to you.

Spontaneously, this conclusion strikes most of us as too radical. I think that this is because, spontaneously, we attach a significance to bodily or physical continuity that we can be led to surrender on reflection. Consider a modification of Parfit's division case: imagine that after the separation of the two hemispheres of your brain, only one hemisphere is transplanted to another body; the other hemisphere remains connected to your body and continues to sustain your psychological capacities there. In this case I think that we would intuitively identify you with the person who has your body and one of your hemispheres. We would treat this as a case in which you have lost one of your hemispheres. So the fact that psychological continuity branches here would *not* make us withhold a judgment of personal identity. I take this intuition to be evidence supporting my error-theory's claim that common sense identifies us with our bodies as the subjects of our minds. I have already argued that this identification is untenable, so my reason for calling attention to this thought-experiment is another, namely that you would also be spontaneously inclined to care more about the fate of the person who has both one of your hemispheres and your body than about the person who consists of one of your hemispheres in a new body.

However, I suggest that you can be led stepwise to give up this spontaneous attitude on reflection. In a standard brain-transplant case in which the whole of your brain is transplanted to a body which is a replica of your body, you would be as much concerned about the post-transplant person as about yourself had you lived on in the ordinary way. So, bodily identity is not really essential for concern. If you then suppose that your brain functions as it did in the above example in which your mental states migrate from one hemisphere to other, and there is the envisaged replacement of them, with the result that your mental states end up being supported by hemispheres numerically distinct from your original hemispheres, I think that you will agree that you should be as much concerned about the resulting person as about your ordinary self. But the step from this case to the last replacement case is a very short one, so I think you will have to agree that you should be as much concerned about the resulting person in this case as well.

That is to say, in order to be rational—which is a condition of being autonomous—your future-oriented desires must be to the effect not that you, but that *somebody like you*, be around in the future to lead a good life. If, however, you would rationally consent to being replaced by such a replica, this replacement would not violate your autonomy. Against this backdrop, one of the reasons that I adduced in the foregoing chapter for doubting the time-relative interest account can be stated more accurately.

To begin with, notice that McMahan's prudential unity relations would not hold between you and a replica who is succeeding you after a brief interval of non-existence, since these relations presuppose numerical identity at the neural level. But it has been seen that it is just the qualitative similarity that matters, not whether it is underpinned by the sort of continuity which is requisite for identity or psychological connectedness. Furthermore, although I have so far considered only a successor who is qualitatively similar to you, I believe that your prudential concern should rationally be greater rather than smaller if your successor is *superior* rather than similar to you in respects that you value. For it is rational to strive for self-improvement, and if personal identity is rationally insignificant, this improvement can take the shape of being replaced by a superior numerically distinct successor without any loss of what rationally matters. Imagine that you have certain traits that you want to discard, for instance your tendency to procrastinate, your irascibility, disorderliness, or nicotine addiction. Imagine further that you face the following choice: either the successor of you cropping up after the dispersal of your micro-particles is exactly like you, or like you apart from lacking these undesirable features. Then it would seem rational for you to prefer to be succeeded by the latter, enhanced version of yourself because you would then be rid of characteristics that you have striven to erase. Nonetheless, the enhancement cannot be so radical that you cannot recognize any of your individuality in the enhanced person; this person must be recognizable as an enhancement of *you*.

Now if people rationally consent to being replaced by qualitatively identical or enhanced successors of themselves, there would be no moral objection to their replacement: it would respect their autonomy and offer full compensation for the loss of benefits to the people being replaced, so it would not be unjust. Therefore, in contrast to sentient beings, persons are in theory replaceable, since they can autonomously consent to being replaced whereas sentient beings obviously cannot. The objection from justice is then silenced. In practice, however, persons are even harder to replace effectively than sentient beings; adequate replacement will be impossible until we have a medical technology to create mature persons 'from scratch'. The replacement of foetuses, infants, and other more developed sentient beings raises almost as many practical problems in addition to theoretical objections.

3.2 The Asymmetry between Starting Good and Bad Lives

What McMahan calls *the Asymmetry* seems to pose another problem for the inclusive view of benefiting and person-affecting reasons of beneficence. The Asymmetry is to the effect that, according to common-sense morality,

> while the fact that a person's life would be worse than no life at all (or 'worth not living') constitutes a strong moral reason for not bringing him into existence, the fact that a person's life would be worth living provides no (or only a relatively weak) moral reason for bringing him into existence. (1981: 100; cf. 2002: 300)

If an implication of the Asymmetry is that there is a strong moral person-affecting reason not to make an unfortunate being enter the world because this would harm it, while there is no such reason to make a fortunate being enter it because this would not benefit it, then there is a clash with the inclusive view. For this view is to the effect that just as there is a person-affecting moral reason against causing a life that is worse than no life for a being, since this would harm it, there is also a person-affecting moral reason in favour of causing a life that would be better than no life for a being, since this would benefit it.

We should however not be too quick to conclude that the Asymmetry clashes with the inclusive view. In general, common-sense morality takes there to be a stronger reason not to harm than to benefit, or not to omit benefiting, for instance a stronger reason not to kill than to save life, or not omitting to save life. The fact that the reason against omitting to save life is weaker surely does not show that common-sense morality does not regard saving life as benefiting the individual saved. This is because, as already remarked, this morality features *the act-omission doctrine*, the doctrine that there is a stronger reason against harming in such ways as by killing than against omitting to benefit by saving life. Consequently, it might be that the fact that, intuitively, the reason to bring somebody into the world to a good life is weaker is not evidence that this is not an act of benefiting the individual, but rather evidence of the influence of the act-omission doctrine. To neutralize the effect of this doctrine, we must consider a case in which an *act* of bringing an unfortunate individual into existence is not compared to an *omission* to bring a fortunate individual into existence.

Consider a human zygote or an embryo before the point at which monozygotic twinning becomes impossible (around two to three weeks after conception) and, thus, before the point at which a human being begins to exist—consider, say, a zygote just after conception.[6] Let us assume that we have caused this zygote to exist by fertilizing an egg with a sperm, without expecting anything out of the ordinary. Suppose that we then find out that the embryo will soon divide into a pair of twins, one of

---

[6] If, in spite of the argument in 2.1, you continue to believe that human beings begin to exist at conception—or, more precisely, at syngamy—you have to concede at least that, albeit it may be *ordinarily* true of human beings that they begin to exist at this point, it cannot be true of human beings who are monozygotic twins.

which will have a life as great as the life of the other will be miserable. To inject more determinate sense into this, first conjure up a day that is clearly so unpleasant that you would rather have spent that day deeply asleep than experiencing it. Then conjure up another day that is pleasant to the degree that you are indifferent between having it along with the unpleasant day or having neither, being deeply asleep for two days instead. Suppose that the fortunate twin will have a life entirely consisting of as many such pleasant days as the unfortunate twin's life will contain such unpleasant days. It seems to make sense to hold that the former life is as much better than non-existence as the latter life is worse than it.

Now imagine that we cannot prevent only the latter twin from beginning to exist: we either have to prevent the existence of both of the twins, by putting an end to the zygote, or neither of them, by leaving the zygote alone. If there is an Asymmetry independent of the act-omission doctrine and specific to procreation, we should intuitively feel that we ought to prevent the existence of both twins because we have strong reason to prevent the existence of the unfortunate twin, and little, if any, reason not to prevent the existence of the fortunate one. But it seems to me that in these circumstances the difference between the reason not to prevent the existence of the fortunate twin and the reason to prevent the existence of the unfortunate twin is felt to be noticeably smaller, perhaps even non-existent. There is more of a dilemma than an asymmetry in this case.

If this impression is correct, it indicates that McMahan's Asymmetry is propelled at least in part by the act-omission doctrine which is not in operation in the twin case. This doctrine is not in operation here because, I suggest, whatever we decide with respect to the zygote, we shall have *harmed* one of the would-be twins. If we omit ending the existence of the zygote, we shall have harmed the twin who will lead the bad life, since we caused the fertilization to occur. On the other hand, if we end the zygote's existence, we shall have harmed the twin who would have led the good life rather than omitted to benefit it because we *make* this twin worse off than it would otherwise be by blocking benefits to it in the pipeline. Consequently, in this case the act-omission doctrine does not imply that we have stronger reason to choose one alternative rather than the other, that is, its asymmetry-creating influence is smothered. Now if there had been an asymmetry springing from the circumstances of procreation rather than from this doctrine, it should still be felt undiminished, but my impression is that it has been muffled at least. However, to the extent that the Asymmetry highlighted by McMahan is due to the act-omission doctrine, it gives no support for a doubt that having a fortunate individual exist is (comparatively) benefiting it.

I argued elsewhere (2013: ch. 3) that the act-omission doctrine combines two doctrines: a conception of responsibility as based on causation and a doctrine of negative rights. This conception of responsibility implies that we feel more responsible for what we cause by acting than for what we let happen by omitting to act; for instance, we feel less responsible for the violation of a right if we let someone else violate it than if we violate it ourselves. The twin-example eliminates the influence of this factor, since even if we omit taking (preventive) action as regards twins, we shall have caused their existence. But to explain fully McMahan's Asymmetry and why it is smothered in the twin-example, we need to explore how rights are involved in common-sense morality.[7]

According to common-sense morality, we have *general negative* rights holding against *all* others who are capable of recognizing rights to the effect that they do *not* interfere with our person or property, but we do not have general positive rights that they assist or aid us with respect to our person or property. The other side of these negative rights are negative duties or obligations of others to abstain from such interference, for instance not to kill, mutilate, rape, imprison, or steal. In addition to these general, negative rights, common-sense morality postulates *special* rights, which may be positive, and which correspond to special duties or obligations on the part of others (the distinction between general and special rights was introduced by Hart, 1955). People impose these special duties on themselves by their acts towards (general) rights-holders (an obvious example being the act of promising). These duties are special in the sense that they are owed only to the patients of the relevant acts; thus, the corresponding rights of the patients are special in virtue of holding only against the agents in question. Special rights could well include rights to receive positive help to preserve life, limb, and property, for instance, against agents who have endangered them.

Common-sense morality also recognizes reasons of beneficence, but these are weaker than reasons not to infringe general rights. This is what makes it wrong, for instance, to kill one innocent in order to save the lives of some smaller number; unless one is under a special obligation to save the latter, one is under no obligation at all to save them, since there is no general (positive) right to be saved. Nevertheless, it seems reasonable to hold that reasons of beneficence can at least in extraordinary circumstances outweigh reasons of rights, so that it can be permissible, and even obligatory, to kill one if this is necessary to save millions of lives.

Now rights theorists could at most assert that beings acquire certain rights *if or when they begin to exist*; they could not plausibly claim that non-existent beings have rights, for example rights to enter existence. It might be asked why this is so if rights have the function of protecting interests, as many hold, and I am correct in my argument that it could be in the interest of a being to begin to exist. The reason is, I surmise, that it is not the function of rights to protect any old interest; it has to be an interest to use something that you have 'occupied' and are in a position to use, like your body and its psycho-physical capacities, or your property (more will be said about this condition in Part II). But, obviously, the non-existent are not in a position to use anything.

Tooley suggests: 'Every individual has a right to a life that is worth living' (1983: 272) that is acquired when the individual begins to exist. Your causing a gravely deformed or handicapped individual to exist might then be wrong because it imposes on you a

---

[7] See Persson (2013: ch. 1) for a fuller account of rights. It should be stressed that I appeal to rights only to *explain* why the Asymmetry is an element of common-sense morality. As will be clear in Chapter 7, I reject the theory of rights in question.

special duty that you cannot discharge, namely, to make the life of this unfortunate individual worth living. As remarked, according to common-sense morality, our acts could put us under special duties, or endow the patients of these acts with special rights against us.

Against Tooley it could be pointed out, *ad hominem*, that it is hard to see how he could consistently make adequate use of such a right as he argues at length that only persons—that is, in his terminology, beings with a conception of themselves as persisting conscious subjects—can have rights to life. Since, as Tooley would admit, no biological being is a person in this sense when it begins to exist, it cannot then have a right to a life that is worth living, since surely only a being with a right to life can have a right to a life that is worth living. Nor will a human being ever acquire such a right if it is sufficiently gravely mentally retarded never to become a person, but this is precisely a type of case in which it could be most gravely wrong to cause a human being to begin to exist.[8]

Tooley is prepared to admit, however, that sentient beings who do not qualify as persons can have other rights, for instance a right not to be tortured, or be caused gratuitous pain—a right which derives from their interest or desire not to feel pain (1983: 100). If a being has any rights at all, such a right not to have pain and suffering inflicted, without good reason, is plausibly a right that it acquires as soon as it becomes sentient. Nonetheless, it is not obvious how such a negative right not to have pain and suffering inflicted on you could be violated by causing miserable beings to exist. For the progenitors of such beings do not literally inflict pain and suffering on their offspring as, say, torturers inflict it on their victims. Consequently, it is not clear that they violate these rights of their offspring and, so, not clear how a theory of negative rights could explain why it can be wrong to cause miserable beings to exist.

We would have a more promising start if we could find a basis for claiming that human beings acquire rights to life and limb as soon as they become sentient. For we could then argue that, by causing their offspring to exist and be sentient, progenitors shoulder a special obligation to help them exercise their rights, by helping them to remain alive and in use of their faculties in ways that put the value of their lives at least on a par with the neutral value of non-existence. But this is an obligation that cannot be discharged if the offspring caused to exist is sufficiently disabled. This idea could explain how their progenitors could act wrongly without relegating them to the same category as, say, torturers who violate general rights to life and limb. They would instead act wrongly by violating a special right that they incur by their acts of procreation.

---

[8] It might also be asked how every individual could have a right to a life worth living if rights are held against people who shoulder corresponding obligations. For it would seem that some individuals are so deformed and handicapped that it is *impossible* to make their lives worth living, and could we have duties to do what is impossible? We avoid this awkwardness if we instead go along with Velleman's claim that 'we are obligated to have those children to whom we can give the best start' (2008: 276), and hence that children have a right to be given this start. But I would rather say that this is what we ought to do on the basis of reasons of beneficence.

I think that we can plausibly hypothesize that, according to the doctrine of negative rights, infants do acquire rights to their life and limbs as soon as they become sentient. Consider again an infant who is currently having some pleasurable experience. Imagine that it has the right not to have this experience interfered with, a right which Tooley invokes. Then it is quite plausible to think that the infant must also have a right not to have its life and limbs interfered with to the extent that this interferes with the pleasure it is experiencing. If so, it has a negative right to life and limb, though it is not a person in Tooley's sense. This could be the kind of right that parents have a special obligation to help their infants to benefit from.

People who have children are then analogous to agents who cause (general) rights-holders to be in situations in which they can no longer (as easily and effectively) retain things to which they have rights. Suppose, for instance, you endanger a victim Vic's life by pushing him into the sea. According to the commonsensical rights theory, even if the push is accidental, this puts you under a special obligation to try to save him, an obligation that you would not have had had you not caused his fall (cf. McMahan, 2002: 376). It should be emphasized, however, that the positive obligation to save Vic presupposes that he has a (negative) right to life. It is because Vic has such a right and is dispatched by your act from a state in which he could maintain his life to a state in which he cannot that you are put under a positive obligation to try to save him.

It might be objected that the case of causing beings to exist differs crucially from the case of causing Vic to fall into the sea in that in the former case you do not transfer rights-holders from a state in which they are capable of retaining things to which they have rights to a state in which they are incapable of this. For, as remarked, merely possible beings cannot be rights-holders (or, for that matter, have any capacities). However, by causing these beings to exist, you may transfer them from a state in which it is *not* the case that they are incapable of retaining things to which they have rights—since when non-existent they have no rights—to a state in which this is the case. For instance, when they begin to exist, they may be incapable of maintaining their life because they are insufficiently developed to obtain food and drink and to fend off external threats. This may reasonably be held to be enough to put you under a positive obligation to help them do so since, it might be claimed, the state of being incapable of sustaining one's life is often worse than the state of having no life to sustain. For in the former state the subject often positively suffers, as Vic is likely to do when he has been pushed into the sea.

In the case of a drowning person, the content of the obligation incurred is to restore, as well as you can, the safer situation that you have eliminated, by pulling the person ashore. It might be thought that the counterpart to this in the case of causing somebody to exist would be euthanasia, since the state of being dead is the closest possible equivalent to that of not having begun to exist. Then, if you are able to euthanize an individual before it acquires any rights against you and begins to suffer, it may seem that you have not done anything wrong to it by causing its existence, though its disabilities are so severe that, with all available assistance, its life would have to be worse than non-existence. However, you have still needlessly exposed this individual to some *risk* of being harmed, since there is always some risk that you will fail to euthanize it painlessly before it is harmed. And it is wrong to expose an individual to a risk of being harmed without any justification.

It is now time to introduce a second source of McMahan's Asymmetry, alongside the act-omission doctrine and the attendant theory of rights:[9] an asymmetry between abilities and disabilities which consists in that, while congenital disabilities, if grave enough, can make a worthwhile existence *impossible*, even the most extensive repertoire of congenital abilities can only make a worthwhile existence *possible*. Other conditions than the most well-endowed bodily constitution are obviously necessary to provide an individual with a worthwhile existence, whereas sufficiently grave congenital disabilities can by themselves exclude an individual from a worthwhile existence. So, when we cause the existence of individuals with a range of congenital abilities even on a par with what the most fortunate ones of us possess, we do merely something to enable them to benefit from their existence, since being congenitally well equipped is far from a sufficient condition for having a good life. Life might still turn out to be not worth living due to lack of opportunities to exercise the abilities for various reasons, but the presence of these opportunities is not part of what we cause when we cause someone with abilities to exist. The same goes for protection against accidents that may cut a life short. By contrast, when we cause the existence of individuals with sufficiently extensive congenital disabilities, we may make them unable to lead worthwhile lives. This means that we can be more responsible for their lives not being worth living than we can be for the fact that fortunate individuals whose existence we cause have lives worth living, and that we have more of a reason to avoid creating individuals with congenital disabilities than to create congenitally well-equipped individuals.

Consequently, reasons of beneficence to create even such fortunate individuals can only be quite weak. Moreover, according to common-sense morality, it generally takes smaller costs to ourselves to justify omitting to act on reasons of beneficence than to act against reasons of rights. This may add to the impression that there is no reason to cause even well-endowed individuals to exist.

However, even though it takes less of a cost to ourselves to justify setting aside reasons of beneficence than reasons of rights, it may be permissible to benefit somebody in need by infringing a right, though the cost to us necessary to make permissible omitting this benefit is smaller than the cost necessary to make permissible infringement of the right. For instance, I might be permitted to take some of your medicine without your consent in order to cure Vic, although the cost to myself of helping Vic by giving him is this medicine is so great that I would be permitted to refrain, but not so great that I would be permitted to infringe your right to escape a similar cost.

---

[9] The appeal to this 'second source' as well as consideration of the twin-example constitute additions to how I explained the Asymmetry in (2009a: 29–33).

This may seem paradoxical, for could I then not first permissibly take your medicine in order to cure Vic and later give myself permission not to help Vic by appealing to the cost for me, though escaping this cost would not permit me to infringe your right in the first place? No, because I am permitted to take your medicine only on condition that I shall help Vic; so, having taken the medicine I am no longer permitted to omit helping him. Thus, I do not think that there is anything paradoxical about the relations between these reasons, but, since reasons of beneficence to procreate are so weak, it would in any case have little bearing on them.

Now, by altering the twin case we could attempt to gauge whether we have been on the right track in trying to account for the Asymmetry by other factors than the virtual non-existence of a reason of beneficence to create life. We can imagine that we are offered, as an alternative to the prevention of the existence of both twins, the prevention of the existence of only the unfortunate twin as soon as the twinning process begins to occur. Then, if there were a specific procreative Asymmetry, which had its source in there being next to no reason of beneficence to have fortunate individuals exist, we would have next to no reason to wait and prevent only the existence of the unfortunate twin instead of preventing the existence of both twins before the twinning starts. But it seems to me clear that we would be inclined to think that we have a stronger reason than this to spare the life of the fortunate twin. Plausibly, this reason is provided by the fact that we believe that its existence would benefit this twin.

If we prevent the existence of a being whose life would have been good for it, the extrinsic badness for this being of this act of prevention will be as great as the life ahead of it would have been good for it, since this act makes its having this (or any) life impossible. That is a high price to pay. On the other hand, if we prevent the existence of the unfortunate twin, the extrinsic goodness for this being of this act of prevention will be equally great, since its life would be as bad for it as the fortunate twin's life would be good for it. That would be an equally great gain; thus, we are confronted with a dilemma. The opportunity to prevent only the unfortunate twin's existence seems to be a welcome way out of this dilemma.

My hypothesis is, then, that McMahan's Asymmetry has two sources: the act-omission doctrine, including a theory of rights, and the asymmetry between abilities and disabilities. The latter asymmetry is easily fitted into the theory of rights. If we cause individuals with grave congenital deficiencies to exist then, if such deficiencies make individuals unable to lead good lives, we would incur obligations that we cannot discharge—at best it may be that we can rid ourselves of them before we harm the right-holders by resorting to euthanasia, but we have still put someone at a risk of being harmed. On the other hand, if we refrain from causing well-endowed individuals, we eschew undertaking obligations that we normally cannot be sure to be able to fulfil. There is no moral reason to undertake such obligations, while we have moral reason not to undertake, or risk undertaking, obligations that we cannot discharge. Hence, something like the Asymmetry results.

These two explanatory factors do not have any essential connection to the commencement of existence; both factors apply as much to the continuation as to the commencement of existence. Since I shall in Chapter 7 reject rights—and appeal to them in this section only to explain the intuitive force of the Asymmetry—it is important to point out that their rejection is compatible with the asymmetry between abilities and disabilities still standing and affecting the strength of reasons for benefiting. But before we go on comparing the strength of these reasons with respect to the distinction between commencement and continuation of existence, I would like to mention that there is a set of moral considerations that I am putting to the side in the present discussion.

It may be felt that considerations of justice provide us with more of a moral reason to prevent the existence of both twins than to let it start. For if we let their existence start, we create an inequality as regards welfare between the twins—one is better off and the other is worse off than non-existence—and it appears that this inequality is unjust or unfair for reasons that will be explored in Part II. There are two reasons why these considerations can be put aside now. First, notice that even if it is true that having the twins exist gives rise to an unjust welfare inequality between them, this fact does not undermine my claim that there is a reason of beneficence to have the fortunate twin exist. Secondly, we can alleviate the worry about injustice by imagining that it is not determined which of the twins will have the good and the bad life, respectively, but that for each of them there is a 50 per cent probability both that they will be the fortunate twin and the unfortunate one. Then it seems that there is no injustice or unfairness involved in having the twins exist.

Now the central issue is whether there is a moral reason to let the fortunate twin exist because this would benefit it just as there is a moral reason to prevent the existence of the unfortunate twin because this would harm it. My claim that there is can be strengthened by an argument that McMahan himself puts forward (1981: 120n), following Richard Sikora (1978). This argument turns on the observation that if what would be bad for individuals in life is a reason against having them exist, but what would be good for them in life is no reason in favour of having them exist, then, as far as those individuals are concerned, it would be wrong to have them exist, however much good their lives will contain, provided that they will also contain something that is bad for the individuals. This is patently absurd.

(A variation of this argument appeals to the fact that there is always some probability, however slight, that were you to have a child, it would be miserable, owing to some congenital disability or later misfortune. If this is a moral reason against having a child, and the probability, however great, that its life will be overall good for it is no reason in favour of having a child, then, as far as we take into account just the interests of the child, we would only have a moral reason against having a child exist, and no reason in favour of this. But that is patently absurd. So, it is plausible to think that, if the fact that its life risks being miserable is a reason not to have a being exist, the fact that its life has a chance of being worth living is a reason to have it exist.)

McMahan has recently responded to this argument by suggesting that

> while goods have a canceling function in procreative choices, they have no reason-giving function...they weigh against and cancel out corresponding bads, but they do not otherwise count in favor of causing a person to exist, no matter how greatly they may outweigh the bads.
> (2009: 53)

In a later paper (2013: 20ff), however, he accords *some* reason-giving weight to—non-comparative—benefits in procreative choices, though less weight than to—comparative—benefits to individuals who exist or will exist independently of the action taken. The former benefits are, according to a view of his discussed in 2.2, non-comparative, while the latter are comparative benefits. This concession appears to be necessary, since non-comparative harms must have such a weight because we feel that there is reason not to bring a being into existence if its life will be miserable; as McMahan puts it, harms in life 'count against causing people to exist' (2013: 20). But if non-comparative benefits had no reason-giving weight, it would be mysterious how they could weigh against and cancel such reasons and make it permissible to cause someone to enter a life which contains more benefits than harms. However, if the balance of benefits over harms can be such that it is *permissible* to cause a being to exist, one wonders why the surplus of benefits could not be so great that it counts or gives reason in favour of causing existence to the extent that this act becomes *obligatory*.

I do not believe, then, that McMahan can be right when he maintains that the 'reason-giving and canceling weight are quite distinct and independent ways in which benefits might matter' (2013: 21). It seems to me that benefits cannot have cancelling weight without having reason-giving weight: they cannot weigh against and cancel the reasons that harms give without giving opposing reasons. It should be noted, though, that this claim is compatible with the idea that non-comparative benefits—or, as they would be on my account, comparative benefits bestowed on beings caused to exist—have less reason-giving weight than corresponding benefits bestowed on independently existing beings (and perhaps than non-comparative harms).

But there are problems even with this weaker view that non-comparative benefits have less moral weight than comparative benefits. It could morally justify our bestowing a much smaller amount of benefits on human beings who are brought into existence by our action than on humans who will exist independently of it. The upshot could be a large inequality in respect of benefits between the dependent and independent humans under circumstances which, according to the account of Chapter 7, would make this inequality unjust. But if we then could do something to reduce this inequality, the fact that it is unjust provides us with a good reason to do so. Since the former dependent humans are no longer dependent on our act, benefits to them will be comparative. All together this puts us in a situation in which we are morally justified in creating an inequality that we predict we shall later be morally justified in alleviating. Surely, this is a rather curious situation. A more plausible view would imply that already at the outset, when we performed the action that brought the dependent humans into existence, we ought to effect a more equal distribution of benefits. It would be easier to justify such a distribution if benefits to the dependent individuals had as much moral weight as benefits to the independent individuals.

Returning to the twins, I want to claim that, as far as benefiting and harming are concerned, the choice between either having both of them *start* existing, or precluding the *whole* of their existence intuitively strikes us as being morally on a par with the choice between either having a pair of pre-conscious twin foetuses—who are indisputably human beings—*continue* existing when they have just begun to do so, and preventing this. Let us suppose, then, that the monozygotic twinning of the embryo has occurred, and that two foetuses have emerged but have not yet developed consciousness. I think that we would be ill at ease to kill the fortunate foetus, thereby depriving it of future benefits, even if this was part and parcel of killing the unfortunate twin to save it from harm. Just as in the above case of blocking the twins' entrance into the world, we would welcome the alternative of being able to put an end to the existence of only the unfortunate twin.

In the case of beings without consciousness, like pre-conscious foetuses, the reasons to benefit them by having their existence continue do not seem noticeably stronger (or weaker) than the reasons to benefit them by having their existence commence. In view of the fact that, as surfaced in 2.1, the formation of a human being (and other multicellular organisms), and the subsequent development of a human being, is a gradual process, making it indeterminate when a human being commences its existence and is transformed from an embryo to a foetus, this is what we would expect. In the case of beings with consciousness—and especially a consciousness sophisticated enough to feature a capacity to have future-oriented desires or plans—we have however seen in previous chapters that the reasons to benefit them by having their existence continue are stronger than the reasons to benefit them by having their existence commence. What I would like to stress now is that this increase in strength is due, not to a transition from non-existence to existence of some kind of being, but to the kinds of properties that begin being instantiated, namely properties related to consciousness.

This point can be illustrated by McMahan's time-relative interest account, according to which it makes a difference as regards benefiting whether we consider the beginning or the continuation of the existence of a being with rudimentary consciousness: only when there is at least rudimentary consciousness can there be the morally more weighty comparative benefiting, according to McMahan. I have rejected this account in 2.3, but on my own view, too, it morally matters whether we consider the beginning or the continuation of the existence of something with the consciousness of a person, since reasons of respect for autonomy could kick in when there is such a consciousness.

For my own part, however, I am not assuming that when consciousness becomes personal—or, for that matter, when consciousness first emerges—a new sort of entity pops into existence with distinctive conditions of identity; instead, this can be treated as a case of an already existing kind of entity acquiring a set of new properties. But McMahan (2002: ch. 1) couples his time-relative interest account with a doctrine of our nature and identity which declares that we begin to exist when foetuses acquire consciousness and which takes the psychological relations to which the time-relative interest account refers to be a component of our identity over time. Consequently, a new kind of being—who is one of us—would come into existence when existence acquires a greater moral significance. This may create the false impression that the new moral significance has to do with this ontological change in itself.

However, the time-relative interest account could consistently be accompanied by a biological account of our identity,[10] according to which we are identical to human beings or organisms that come into existence earlier than the emergence of consciousness, most plausibly when the cells composing human embryos become so integrated with each other that twinning is excluded. The time-relative interest account might then imply that when a human organism acquires consciousness, the continuation of its existence takes on a moral significance that it did not earlier have. On this view of our identity, this change of moral significance would not be accompanied by the coming into existence of a new kind of being with distinctive identity conditions, as on McMahan's view, but would simply be the continuation of the existence of a human being with new properties. Thus, it would be obvious that the change in respect of moral significance does not turn on whether anyone comes into existence.

Moreover, it may seem that this biological view sits better than McMahan's own view of our identity with his suggestion that benefits to those caused to exist are non-comparative and that they have less reason-giving weight than comparative benefits to independently existing individuals (2013: e.g. 21 and 30). For McMahan's view implies that when a human being—who undoubtedly exists irrespective of whether or not it is identical to one of us—is comparatively benefited by being made conscious, one of us is non-comparatively benefited by being caused to exist. However, it may seem odd that one and the same instance of benefiting can be both non-comparative and comparative, but even if we allow that to pass, this case supplies a ground for thinking that the reason-giving weight of non-comparative benefits cannot be less (or greater) than that of some corresponding comparative benefits. This is what we should expect if, as I have suggested, a difference in respect of the ontological status of the beings under consideration, whether they are possible or existent, and whether what is considered is their beginning or continuing to exist, does not matter morally.

These speculations about the emergence of consciousness inspire the construction of a parallel to the Asymmetry. Suppose that we have two pre-conscious foetuses who need a certain drug in order to develop consciousness. Suppose further that we know that the life of one of them will be as bad as the life of the other will be good. Then, just as we intuitively take ourselves to have more of a reason not to conceive an individual who would lead a life not worth living than we have to conceive an individual whose

---

[10] As DeGrazia, who combines the time-relative interest account with the biological view, points out (2005: 192n). But then the reason why psychological relations ground interest could not be that they are identity-constituting.

life will be worth living, it seems that we would take ourselves to have more of a reason not to give the drug to the unfortunate foetus than we have in favour of giving the drug to the fortunate foetus. But the latter asymmetry cannot have anything to do with the beings in question being non-existent, since they evidently exist. As we have seen, even if we go along with McMahan's view that beings like us spring into existence with the emergence of consciousness, there still exist human beings who could be (comparatively) benefited or harmed in this situation. This provides a further reason for thinking, as I have argued, that the Asymmetry does not turn on the fact that the beings in question are non-existent.

To sum up the rather long and winding discussion of this section. I have argued that McMahan's Asymmetry is not due to our thinking that a being is not harmed by being prevented from entering the world to lead a life that is good for it as it is harmed by entering the world to lead a life that is bad for it. Rather, it is due to the fact that common-sense morality features the act-omission doctrine, according to which there is stronger moral reason not to harm in some ways than there is against omitting to benefit. These are ways of harming that involve the violation of rights, and we do not in general violate any rights by omitting to benefit. If we cause someone severely disabled to exist, we may put ourselves in a position in which we cannot avoid violating this individual's rights (assuming the existence of rights). By contrast, if we omit causing someone with an abundant repertoire of abilities to exist, we omit undertaking obligations—to the effect of providing this individual with a worthwhile life—which we might reasonably expect that we shall be capable of discharging. While we have moral reason not to undertake obligations that we cannot help failing to discharge, we have no such reason to undertake obligations even if we can be fairly confident that we shall be capable of discharging them, let alone if we are more doubtful that we shall be capable of this.

If this is the source of the Asymmetry, it is compatible with the view that a being is harmed by being prevented from entering the world to lead a life that will be good for it just as it is harmed by entering the world to lead a life that will be bad for it and, thus, that there is a person-affecting reason of beneficence against the former act as well as against the latter act. Furthermore, we have seen that there is a positive argument to accept this view: otherwise, concern for beings would advise us not to conceive them, since their lives are bound to contain something that is bad for them. Also, there could be as much reason to benefit a being by starting its existence as there could be to prolong it, though in the case of beings with consciousness and, in particular, personal consciousness, the reasons to prolong existence are usually stronger.

3.3 The Non-Identity Problem

Turning more briefly to another familiar problem in population ethics, Parfit's *non-identity problem* (1987: ch. 16), it should be clear that it is no problem for the inclusive view of person-affecting reasons of beneficence. To simplify an example that Parfit uses to illustrate this problem (1987: 367), suppose that there is a disease that will make children mildly handicapped if their mothers have it when pregnant, but the disease is easily cured if the pregnant women imbibe some harmless drug. Suppose further that a pregnant woman is diagnosed with this disease. Intuitively, we would think that she acts wrongly if she does not undergo the harmless treatment, and as a result gives birth to a child who is handicapped. For her child is made worse off by her refraining from undergoing a treatment which would not have harmed her, but which would have made the life of her child significantly better.

But what if, instead of waiting until she has been cured of the disease, a woman gets pregnant, though she knows that if she had instead taken the drug and postponed her pregnancy for a couple of months until she had recovered, she would have had a healthier, but numerically distinct child (since it would have grown from a different egg and sperm)? Intuitively, it seems that the second woman has acted more or less as wrongly as the first one, by not waiting to have a numerically distinct child after she has been cured. However, we cannot justify this judgment by claiming that the second woman acted wrongly by making the child that she in fact had worse off—as the first woman did—since the disability is so slight that her child leads a life better than non-existence, and it would not have existed had she postponed her pregnancy.

Notice, however, that although we cannot maintain that the second woman has acted wrongly towards her child, and that the child has a complaint *against her*—in view of the limits of her powers of action—it does not follow that it does not have a complaint, or that there is no moral reason to compensate it for its disability and make it better off. For this child could have originated—that is, a particular egg could have been fertilized by the same sperm—in more fortunate circumstances than the actual ones. This is especially true nowadays when IVF-techniques are available, which enable us to collect the egg and sperm, carry out fertilization by these techniques, and insert the fertilized egg into the woman's uterus when she has recovered. So, it could be claimed that this child was *unlucky* to be conceived in the actual, disadvantageous circumstances, and that the egalitarian concerns to be expounded in Chapter 7 provide us with a moral reason to make it better off, though its existence is in fact dependent on conditions which make it worse off. This could be true, even though it was beyond the power of the second woman to conceive this child in the more fortunate circumstances, which is a necessary condition for her acting wrongly by not conceiving it in those circumstances.

More to the present point, however, we have a justification for judging that this woman has acted wrongly if we are allowed to say that, if she had waited to get pregnant until she was cured, she would have benefited *another* healthy child *more* by bringing it into existence than she benefits the disabled child that she in fact has had. On the inclusive view, this is true: the alternative child would benefit as much as would the child who would be cured in the first case, and it counts as much morally, though it may never exist.

Boonin objects that, on an inclusive view, for a woman to choose to cause the existence of the healthy child rather than the disabled child is like for a mother to choose to save the life of a healthy child rather than a mildly disabled child, and that the latter is not anything that she is morally required to do (2014: 107). But, at least on the proviso that the children are not old enough to possess autonomy, I believe that this is indeed something that is morally required of us if the life of the healthy child would be more fulfilling for it. Suppose that the disabled child were so severely disabled that its life would be barely worth living; then I believe many would agree that it would be wrong to save it rather than the healthy child. But it seems to me natural to think that there is only a slight difference between these cases in the sense that, while the reason to save the healthy child is *much* stronger if the disabled child is gravely disabled, it is only *slightly* stronger if this child is mildly disabled and, thus, it is only a little wrong to save this child. That is why people might overlook that there *is* a stronger reason even in the latter case and that, therefore, it is wrong to save even the mildly disabled child rather than the healthy child.

Another objection that Boonin hurls at the inclusive view is that it makes it wrong to fail to conceive a healthy child whenever we could have done so (2014: 106).[11] But, as was noted at the end of 2.2 and again in the preceding section, to claim without qualification that, according to the inclusive view, someone could be benefited by being caused to exist is to overstate the view: what is true is that by executing any of the acts involved in causing someone's existence—acts like fertilization, etc.—we do something that is beneficial or extrinsically good for the individual only *on condition* that many other factors come into operation. We merely do one of many things that are necessary for this individual to be benefited, so our contribution to him or her being benefited is slight. Now in a world in which there are plenty of individuals who are already in a state of being ready to be benefited, causing further individuals to be in this state is something that we rarely if ever have most reason to do if our goal is to see to it that individuals are more benefited. It is in general more productive to this end to spend resources directly on benefiting those who are already in a state fit to be benefited than to first add to the stock of these individuals and then set about benefiting the expanded stock of existing individuals. For this reason, I do not think that the inclusive view of benefiting has any practical implications in the actual world that are disturbing. What has disturbing practical implications in this world is the claim—rejected by advocates of the act-omission doctrine—that there is as strong a moral reason to see to it that individuals are benefited as that they are not harmed, even if it is interpreted as it is on a narrow person-affecting view.

One of the few types of situation in which the inclusive person-affecting view of reasons for benefiting becomes crucial is when the choice is between conceiving individuals with different life prospects due to their congenital features. If we accept this view, we are likely to conclude that it would be wrong not to conceive the individuals with the better life prospects, but if we do not accept this view—either because we

---

[11] In addition, Boonin protests that 'harm requires a subject' (2014: 105), but we saw in 2.2 that this claim is not true in any sense that undermines the inclusive view.

endorse a narrow person-affecting view, or because we think that reasons of beneficence are weak—we are likely to conclude that it would be permissible to conceive individuals with less bright life prospects, or not to conceive at all. Thus, I am not surprised that Boonin, who assumes that it is not wrong 'to add nothing at all to the total amount of human well-being in the world' (2014: 199), could reach such conclusions.

The inclusive reading of a person-affecting principle to the effect that an outcome can be better (or worse) in respect of its benefits only if it is better (worse) *for someone* then disposes of the non-identity problem.[12] As noted earlier, even if the inclusive view is rejected, it could be held that the outcome which would result if the second woman defers her pregnancy is *impersonally* better in respect of benefits because it contains a greater amount or set of benefits than the outcome which results if she does not postpone her pregnancy. This is the view that one gets if one believes that, although there is no person-affecting moral reason for her to postpone her pregnancy, since this benefits nobody (in the event sense), the fact that postponing it will produce a greater set or sum of benefits provides an impersonal moral reason to postpone it. But, as remarked in the Introduction, this view strikes me as sitting ill with the nature of our moral disposition of altruism or benevolence.

To be sure, it is psychologically hard—perhaps well nigh impossible—to extend this disposition to possible individuals, and this may be a reason why many people find the inclusive person-affecting view counterintuitive. But on this view this disposition still has the right kind of object: it is oriented at what is good and bad for individuals rather than sums or sets of such goodness and badness. The person-affecting view also sits better with the concern about the badness of unjust inequality in respect of welfare that is the topic of Part II, for although the badness of this relation is impersonal, I do not think that the concern about it can be understood, unless it is seen as a concern about what the unjustly worse-off lose by inequality and, thus, as presupposing a sympathy with them rather than with the better-off who gain as much.

---

[12] It will be seen in 9.3 that we should not claim that an outcome cannot be better in *any* respect, or all things considered, unless it is better for someone in this respect, or all things considered. For it can be better in respect of just equality without being better for anyone, and for this reason better all things considered.

4

The Repugnant Conclusion and the Non-Transitivity of Value Relations

4.1 The Problem and Some Attempted Solutions

It is clarifying to keep the distinction between person-affecting and impersonal reasons of beneficence in mind when we move onto another of Parfit's problems of population ethics: *the repugnant conclusion* (1987: ch. 17). This is so, even though it would be a mistake to think that this problem arises only if we endorse the inclusive view that bringing individuals into existence can be better or worse for them. For it arises also on the view that additional individuals can make outcomes impersonally better or worse simply in virtue of increasing or decreasing their sums of benefits. This is enough to make possible the repugnant conclusion that an outcome, which consists in a huge population of beings all leading lives barely worth living, could be better in virtue of containing a greater sum of benefits than an outcome in which a much smaller population of beings all are leading lives of the same very high quality. However, having given vent to my discomfort with the impersonal view, I shall now proceed on the assumption that reasons of beneficence are always person-affecting, so that increasing the sum of benefits, whether by making independently existing individuals better off, or by seeing to it that individuals begin to lead worthwhile lives, always benefits someone.

Here is one of Parfit's formulations of the repugnant conclusion:

Compared with the existence of very many people—say, ten billion—all of whom have a very high quality of life, there must be some much larger number of people whose existence, if other things are equal, would be *better*, even though these people would have lives that are barely worth living. (1986: 150)

Parfit arrives at the repugnant conclusion by considering a series of outcomes in which different numbers of individuals exist. Compare an outcome A in which there are, say, ten billion individuals 'all of whom have a very high quality of life' to an outcome B in which there are many times more individuals all of whom enjoy a quality of life which is just minimally lower than the quality of life in A. It seems plausible to say that, other things being equal (such as, for instance, the quality of life enjoyed in B not being more or less deserved and just than it is in A), B must be better than A because the total quantity of what makes life worth living in B is larger if the population in B is sufficiently greater. According to the inclusive view of benefiting, B would be better because it benefits individuals more, by benefiting a much greater number of individuals, and each only slightly less than in A.

If B is then compared to an outcome C which is related to B as B is to A, the verdict will be the same. And so on until we reach an outcome Z in which there is an enormous population with members having lives that are barely worth living. If the relation of *being better than* is transitive, Z will be better than A for the same reason: that it contains a larger quantity of what makes life worth living and, thus, benefits individuals more. Now, since by hypothesis there is no other morally relevant aspect which is opposed to the aspect of benefiting, it follows that Z is better all things considered than A. But this conclusion strikes most of us as repugnant since, for the many individuals in Z, life is barely worth living.

However, as Parfit notes, there is something that could make the repugnant conclusion less repugnant, or not repugnant at all.[1] Consider what he calls:

the best things in life. These are the best kinds of creative activity and aesthetic experience, the best relationships between different people, and the other things which do most to make life worth living. (1986: 161)

Suppose, he writes, that the deterioration in quality of life in the series from A to Z is due not to the best things in life being entirely lost, but to these things being gradually more 'thinly spread' (1986: 162), without being wholly lost even in Z. We may imagine, along with Parfit, that in the category of the best things in life are such things as the enjoyment of Mozart's music, of visits to Venice, of performances of Shakespeare's plays, and so on and so forth. Consider a 'Century of Ecstasy' filled to the brim with such things. Parfit contrasts this with a 'Drab Eternity' in which life is barely worth living because, though 'there would be nothing bad in this life, the only good things would be muzak and potatoes' (1986: 160). It is hard not to share his view that of these two futures, the Century of Ecstasy would be more valuable, though the total quantity of value that it contains would be finite as opposed to the infinite quantity of the Drab Eternity.

But consider an alternative eternity, Diluted Eternity, which contains more of the best things in life than the Century of Ecstasy. On average, however, this eternity is barely worth living just like the Drab Eternity, since these peak experiences are separated by very long periods of deep sleep or unconsciousness of neutral value. To my mind, there is no reason to prefer the Century of Ecstasy to Diluted Eternity because the latter contains more of the best things in life, and the neutral periods in between them need not detract from their value.

Similarly, suppose that the quality of life in Z is not barely above the neutral level because life monotonously consists in nothing but muzak and potatoes, but because in

---

[1] The discussion of Parfit (1986) which follows largely reproduces Persson (2004). See also Persson (1997), in which I first suggested non-transitivity as a solution to the repugnant conclusion.

it each life consists of protracted periods of deep sleep or unconsciousness sprinkled with merely a few moments of the best things in life. Then it is not clear to me that it would be repugnant to have to conclude that, all things considered, Z is better than A. For then it may contain more of the best things in life, and it is not clear that Z is made worse by the fact that these best things are dispersed over a greater number of individuals instead of concentrated to a smaller number.

To avoid this difficulty, the repugnant conclusion could be formulated in terms of a comparison of stretches of life the quality of which is, definitionally, constant. By 'an instance of well-being being of a certain intensity', I mean an instance that is of the *same* intensity for a certain period of time. The duration of this period may vary from seconds to hours, but an instance of well-being of a certain intensity lasts only as long as its intensity is constant. At least as regards the more valuable kinds of experience such as enjoying some of the music of Mozart or reading some Shakespeare, the duration will have to be longer than an instant. It can be as long as several hours if the degree of well-being can be the same throughout such a comparatively long period of time. What an instance of well-being of a certain intensity cannot have, however, is a value that is an average of higher and lower values, due to changes in respect of intensity.

With the help of these tools, we can formulate a proposition at the root of the repugnant conclusion which is not vulnerable to the above objection:

Root: For every intensity of (positive) well-being, however low, there is an instance (or set of instances) of it of sufficient (aggregate) duration for this instance (set of instances) to be better in respect of well-being than a (minimal) instance of a higher intensity of well-being, however high it may be.

Since *Root* speaks of the value of shorter stretches of time than whole lives, it is applicable intrapersonally no less than interpersonally. With respect to the case of one life, *Root* implies, for instance, that the Drab Eternity would be better in respect of well-being than the Century of Ecstasy. With respect to an interpersonal case, it implies that an outcome with a sufficient number of lives like the Drab Eternity, but of finite duration, could be better in respect of well-being than an outcome with fewer lives like the Century of Ecstasy. Furthermore, although *Root* is phrased in terms of positive well-being, it could be rephrased in terms of 'ill-being'. It would then imply that it could be less bad to inflict excruciating pain of comparatively short duration on a few individuals than mild discomfort of much longer duration on them, or such discomfort of shorter duration on a huge crowd. This is another repugnant conclusion, perhaps even more repugnant.

One way of blocking the repugnant conclusion would be by inserting in the progression from A to Z various dividing lines such that whatever the (finite) duration of an instance of well-being of an intensity below the line, this instance cannot be as good in respect of well-being as an instance of well-being of an intensity above it of shorter duration—that is, the latter would be 'lexically' better. Parfit reviews and rejects some such dividing lines (1987: § 139–40). In (1986) he tentatively proposes an alternative: the *perfectionist* view that 'what is best has more value – or does more to make the outcome better – than any amount of what is nearly as good' (1986: 164). Suppose, to take one of Parfit's examples, that the best music is exemplified by the music of Mozart and that Haydn's music is in the category of the second best music. Then the perfectionist view has it that no amount of enjoyment of Haydn's music could be as good for us as a sufficient amount of enjoyment of Mozart's music.

This does not seem plausible to me. The continuum between what is best, second best, third best, and so on, can be made out as so smooth that the differences between what is best and second best, between what is second best and third best, and so on, are minimal. For instance, the enjoyment derived from Mozart's music might be only slightly more intense, or qualitatively better, than the enjoyment derived from Haydn's music. The difference in quality might be so small that we could barely tell that Mozart's music is better than Haydn's. But great differences as regards the quantity of things that we find enjoyable make us put a higher value on the greater quantity of the qualitatively lower enjoyment. Thus, we would value higher a greater quantity of what is, qualitatively, minimally less good than a much smaller quantity of what is, qualitatively, minimally better. It would seem that it must take a decisive difference in quality to keep a great difference as regards quantity in check.

Secondly, although Parfit states the repugnant conclusion in terms of populations that are leading lives better than non-existence, as already remarked, there are also negative versions of it according to which we reach the repugnant conclusion that an outcome, Z-, in which there is an enormous population having a life quality just below the neutral level is worse than an outcome A- in which a population of ten billion lead lives that are horrendously bad, say, by being exposed to the most gruesome torture. But it seems perverse to appeal to a perfectionist view as regards negative value and assert that the worst things in life are so bad that they should be kept out however much of the second worst thing you let in.

The negative repugnant conclusion brings out that there is a distinction to be drawn with respect to what could be meant by the 'quality' of episodes of well-being. I have talked about the different *intensities* of such episodes. Now it seems plausible to hold that, say, a week of excruciating physical pain can be worse than decades of mild physical pain or discomfort, even though the difference between these pains is one of intensity. This fact may make us inclined to say that the difference between these pains is not *merely* one of intensity, but that if the difference in intensity is large enough, it turns into a difference of quality (which it never does when duration is stretched out). If it were purely a matter of quantity, it might seem that the mild pain would be worse because it is so much longer. However, this is a different sense of quality than the one in operation when we say that the enjoyment to be got from listening to Mozart's music is of a higher quality than the enjoyment to be got from listening to muzak. The former enjoyment need not be more intense than the latter. This difference in quality rather has to do with a difference in the quality of *the object of enjoyment*, what you derive enjoyment from, instead of the *felt* intensity of the enjoyment derived from the object.

To keep things simple, in the following section (4.2) I shall confine myself to cases in which differences in quality are due to large differences in intensity, as in the case of physical pain. In such situations it might seem that the intrinsic value of an instance of well-being, like physical pleasure or pain, must be quantifiable, since it is a function of two quantifiable aspects: duration and intensity. We shall however see that this is not so. It follows that the value of individual lives in virtue of the number of such instances that they contain, and the value of outcomes in virtue of the number of such lives that they contain, are not quantifiable, either. This enables us to block the regress to the repugnant conclusion, even though the discussion proceeds on assumptions that seemingly make the value of well-being quantifiable, by bracketing the complication of qualitative differences that derive from the objects of the experiences of well-being.

4.2 The Supervenience of Value and Consequent Non-Transitivity

Ideally, we should try to escape the repugnant conclusion not by accepting claims that we would be loath to accept were it not for the fact that they allow us to escape this conclusion, but on the strength of claims that are independently plausible. Parfit's perfectionist view strikes me as an attempt of the former sort, and so do other attempts to detect lexical differences in the series from A to Z. What we should instead do is, I believe, to deny that the relation of being better/worse than in an respect like well-being and all things considered is transitive. For, as will transpire, there is an independent ground for this denial in the fact that values are *supervenient*. If this relation is non-transitive, we can consistently hold that Z is not better than A in respect of well-being—and all things considered, if there is no difference in any other respect— albeit B is better than A in this respect, C is better than B, and so on all the way to Z. Furthermore, we can hold this without being saddled with the awkward view that there is some *definite* point in the series at which transitivity gives out. As we approach the midpoint of the series, it may be *indeterminate* whether transitivity still holds and, say, K or L is better than A. But if we continue further along the series, we shall eventually exit from the grey zone of indeterminacy, and find that, say, R or S is definitely worse than A in respect of well-being and, consequently, worse all things considered.

However, denying the transitivity of the relation of being better/worse than is a radical move with far-reaching consequences for the ranking of outcomes. So we should not resort to it merely for the reason that we want to block the repugnant conclusion. I shall now present a general ground for denying the transitivity of this relation which is inferable from the widely accepted observation that value is a supervenient property. It will be shown that the relation of *sameness* or *perfect similarity* with respect to value is non-transitive, which in its turn implies that the relation of being better/worse than is also non-transitive.[2]

---

[2] For a fuller exposition of this argument, with more replies to objections, see Persson (2013: ch. 9); see also Persson (2014).

According to an informal understanding of the notion of supervenience, to say that S is a supervenient property of X means that there have to be other properties of X, basic or subvenient properties, B, *in virtue* or *because of* which X has S, properties that *determine* or *explain* X's having S. This implies that X's possession of B is not determined or explained by X's having S. Thus, the notion of supervenience is asymmetrical. I shall say no more about this notion than that I take it to imply that supervenient properties are not logically entailed by or identical to their subvenient properties.[3]

To give a few illustrations of what I take this to exclude, X's having some less specific or more determinable property such as the disjunctive property of being yellow or green, or being coloured, is not supervenient on X's being yellow because the former properties are obviously entailed by the latter. They do not seem to be genuinely supervenient on X's being yellow, since X's having them is not ontologically anything *additional* to X's being yellow. Similarly, the weight and spatial properties of a thing do not supervene on the weight and spatial properties of its proper parts, since if you know the weight and spatial properties of all parts, you could deduce or calculate the weight and spatial properties of the thing that they constitute. Thus, the property of the whole is not in these instances anything over and above the sum of the properties of the parts. Nor is a dispositional property like X's being brittle supervenient on X's having a certain molecular structure if being brittle *is* having this structure (identified in terms of how it responds to certain causes).

Alongside the properties of being of positive or negative (but not neutral) value, or being good or bad, so-called secondary qualities, such as having a particular colour or taste, are often cited as examples of supervenient properties. However, as has been pointed out, for instance by Simon Blackburn (1988: 66ff.), it appears to be a matter of *linguistic competence* to know that value properties are dependent on other properties. You show that you are not in command of the terms 'good' and 'bad' if you think that something can be good or bad without being so in virtue of some other properties that it has.[4] In contrast, knowing how to apply colour terms apparently does not entail knowledge that if something has some colour, it is in virtue of some other properties. But this fact does not make it uncontroversial that values are supervenient in the sense that I have adopted, which implies that they are ontologically distinct from subvenient properties. Still, in 1.1 I sketched an account of personal intrinsic value which enables it to supervene on the pleasantness of a sensation.

It follows from the informal notion of the supervenience of a property that if there is something, Y, that is perfectly similar to X in respect of the base B, X and Y are also perfectly similar in respect of a property S that is supervenient on B. In other words, if there is a difference between X and Y with respect to S—if X has S but Y lacks it,

---

[3] In terms of Kim's distinction between strong and weak supervenience (see e.g. 'Concepts of supervenience', reprinted in Kim, 1993), the essential point is that the dependence must not be so strong that it jeopardizes the distinctness or irreducibility of the supervenient properties.

[4] Perhaps this is the reason why the notion of supervenience was first introduced into value theory by Moore (1922: 261). The term 'supervenience' was probably introduced by Hare (1952: 145).

or if X has S to a greater or smaller degree than Y—there must be a difference in respect of B between X and Y. Otherwise, the difference in respect of S cannot be explained in terms of B.

By contrast, supervenience does not imply that, if there is no difference, or perfect similarity, between X and Y with respect to S, there is no difference between them with respect to B. Differences in respect of B which are insufficient to generate differences in respect of S may well exist. As a matter of contingent fact, it may be the case that whenever there is a difference as regards B, there is also a difference as regards S (though this is presumably not so in fact). But if we were to *require* this of the notion defined, we would be defining a stronger notion than supervenience.

For the purposes of my argument, I need not plunge any deeper than this into the notion of supervenience, since I have already secured the simple implication of supervenience which forms the first premise of my argument:

Simp: If S is a property of objects that supervenes on their having B, then, for all objects X, Y and Z, even if both X and Y, and Y and Z, are perfectly similar or the same with respect to S, it is logically possible that there are differences with respect to B between both X and Y, and Y and Z.

To illustrate: even if the physical stimulations X and Y are felt to be equally painful and bad for (some) humans, and the same is true of Y and Z, it may be that there are differences between X and Y and Y and Z that are too minute to be registered and transmitted by the human nervous system to the brain.[5]

This is an example of the very simplest kind of value judgment. As already indicated, there is reason to focus on such simple examples. But although this example is as simple as they come, it is controversial how it should be properly understood. There are three things whose precise relations to each other are debatable: the painfulness of a sensation for the subject, the intrinsic dislike of or aversion to it that the subject has, and the intrinsic badness of it for the subject. According to the account in 1.1, a pain is intrinsically bad for the subject because it is disliked for its own sake by the subject, and so disliked because it is painful. The first 'because' is conceptual, and the second is empirical and contingent, although this claim is not crucial for present purposes.

The next step in the argument is a claim about the possible differences as regards B between X and Y, and Y and Z, of which *Simp* speaks:

Add: Even if there are differences in respect of B between X and Y, and between Y and Z, neither of which are sufficient for differences in respect of S between X and Y, or between Y and Z, but X is perfectly similar to Y, and Y to Z, with respect to S, it is *logically possible* that there are differences in respect of B between X and Z that are sufficient for a difference with respect to S between X and Z.

---

[5] I take a 'stimulation' to have both a physical aspect (a cut, burn, etc.) and a psychological aspect (a sensation). These aspects are distinct, but both can be said to be painful, the physical aspect in virtue of giving rise to the psychological aspect.

The fact that the differences with respect to B neither between X and Y nor between Y and Z are sufficient for there to be a difference with respect to S between X and Y, or between Y and Z, must be compatible with there being *another* difference in respect of B between X and Z which *is* sufficient to manifest itself in a difference with respect to S between X and Z. Since B and S are distinct properties, the sufficiency in question is contingent, for instance causal. But, evidently, the fact that neither the difference in respect of B between X and Y nor between Y and Z is contingently sufficient for a difference in respect of S between them cannot *logically entail* that the difference in respect of B between X and Z—which may be twice as big as either of the two other differences—is not contingently sufficient for a difference as regards S between X and Z. For instance, the following is clearly logically possible: the difference between X and Y and between Y and Z with respect to B (the pain-producing properties) is one unit each, but the difference in this respect between X and Z is two units, and a difference of two units is minimally sufficient to give rise to a difference as regards S (pain) for the subjects in question.

This additive possibility is one reason for the name of the second step of the argument. Another reason is that it is an additional premise, supplying the link between supervenience and transitivity. This link comes out in the third step:

Trans: If *Add* is true, it must be false that the relation of perfect similarity or sameness with respect to S is transitive, that is to say, it must be false that it is a *logically necessary* truth that if X and Y, and Y and Z, are perfectly similar or the same with respect to S, then X and Z are perfectly similar or the same with respect to S.

If *Add* is true, it must be logically possible that there be a difference with respect to S between X and Z, even though there is no such a difference between X and Y, or Y and Z, for, as observed, the latter perfect similarities are compatible with there being a difference with respect to B between X and Z which is *sufficient* to manifest itself in a difference as regards S. If it is logically possible that there is a difference which is sufficient for the manifestation of another difference, it must be logically possible that the second difference obtains.

Now, from *Add* and *Trans* we may infer by means of *modus ponens*:

Conclusion: The relation of perfect similarity or sameness with respect to a supervenient property S is not transitive.

According to *Simp*, this is true of S because of something that follows from the fact that S is supervenient, namely that there might be differences in the subvenient properties, though there is no difference in the supervenient ones. So, that there is no transitivity of perfect similarity or sameness as regards these properties follows from their supervenience.

It might *in fact* be true of some, or even all, objects X, Y, and Z that if X and Y, and Y and Z, are perfectly similar with respect to S, X and Z will also be perfectly similar in this respect. This might be because it is in fact not only the case, as the notion of supervenience implies, that if two things are perfectly similar in respect of B, they are also perfectly similar in respect of S but, conversely, that if they are perfectly similar in respect of S, they are perfectly similar in respect of B. This possibility refutes the (implausible) claim that the relation of perfect similarity as regards supervenient properties is *in*transitive, not my claim that it is *not* transitive, or non-transitive. The fact that in all cases it is in fact true that, if X and Y, and Y and Z, are perfectly similar as regards S, then X and Z are perfectly similar as regards S, does not establish that this is so as a matter of *logical necessity*, which is what the denial of the transitivity of the relation of perfect similarity is tantamount to. This fact only establishes that it cannot follow that X and Z are not perfectly similar as regards S, which would follow if the relation was intransitive.

It is, then, logically possible that, even though the difference with respect to B between X and Y, B_{xy}, is insufficient to create a difference in respect of S between X and Y, and another difference with respect to B between Y and Z, B_{yz}, is insufficient to create a difference with respect to S between Y and Z, a third difference with respect to B between X and Z, B_{xz}, *is* sufficient to create a difference in respect of S between X and Z. The heart of my argument is that, since this possibility statement is incompatible with the necessity statement which expresses transitivity as regards sameness with respect to S—that it is necessary that if X and Y, and Y and Z, are the same with respect to S, so are X and Z—the latter statement cannot be true when the former is.

Notice that it is not possible to argue 'top-down' that since X and Y, and Y and Z, are identical as regards S, and identity is a transitive relation, there cannot be differences as regards subvenient properties which are sufficient for a difference between X and Z as regards S. Since it is subvenient properties that determine the supervenient properties, and not the other way around, the argument has instead to be 'bottom-up': because it is possible that the difference B_{xz} is sufficient for a difference between X and Z in respect of S, transitivity breaks down.

It might be objected that it is impossible that one and the same thing, Y's S-ness, can be perfectly similar to both X's and Z's S-ness, when X and Z are different with respect to S. But this is in fact not impossible if S is a supervenient property, and how something intrinsically is with respect to S can remain the same, though the stimulation which is its cause varies within a certain range. For then the stimulation Y may lie within the same range as the stimulation X and within the same range as stimulation Z—at a point at which these ranges overlap—though X and Z do not lie in the same range.

Imagine, again, that it takes a difference of two units of physical stimulation for there to be any difference in respect of S (painfulness, say) and that X consists in one unit of stimulation, Y in two units and Z in three units. X is then S-in-virtue-of-one-unit, Y is S-in-virtue-of-two-units, and Z is S-in-virtue-of-three-units. By hypothesis (since a one-unit difference in stimulation is insufficient to give rise to a difference as regards S), X and Y are qualitatively identical as regards S-ness, and so are Y and Z. Hence, being S-in-virtue-of-one-unit-*or*-two-units expresses one kind of S-ness, and so does being S-in-virtue-of-two-units-*or*-three-units. But being S-in-virtue-of-one-unit-or-two-units and being S-in-virtue-of-two-units-or-three-units do not express one kind of S-ness, since X which is S-in-virtue-of-one-unit and Z which is S-in-virtue-of-three-units differ in respect of S. Nevertheless, since Y is S-in-virtue-of-two-units, and this is a common element of the two disjunctive properties, Y is both S-in-virtue-of-one-unit-or-two-units and S-in-virtue-of-two-units-or-three-units. So, Y can after all exhibit just one kind of intrinsic S-ness and still be perfectly similar in respect of intrinsic S-ness to both X and Z, though X and Z are distinct from each other as regards intrinsic S-ness.

This highlights another condition of the non-transitivity of perfect similarity as regards supervenient properties, namely that supervenient properties are less precise than their subvenient bases. It is the possibility of there being differences in respect of the subvenient bases, while there is perfect similarity or no difference in respect of the supervenient properties, which implies that perfect similarity in the latter respect cannot be transitive.

Nonetheless, Temkin professes (2014) that he cannot understand how both X and Y, and Y and Z can be the same in respect of S-ness, when X and Z are not. This is indeed incomprehensible if one does not keep two points in mind. The first point is that a supervenient property can remain the same, though there is variation with respect to the subvenient properties. If you keep this point in mind, it is not difficult to understand how the S-ness of Y can be the same as the S-ness of both X and Z, though X and Z differ in S-ness: the subvenient properties of Y can lie within the same relevant ranges as the subvenient properties of both X and Z, though their subvenient properties do not lie within the same ranges as each other. This was simply illustrated by taking the subvenient properties of X, Y, and Z's S-ness to be one, two and three units of stimulation, respectively, and taking the relevant ranges to be one-two units, and two-three units. Y's S-ness will then be in the same range as both X's S-ness and Z's S-ness—that is, it will be the same as them—though the latter are in different ranges.

The second point to be borne in mind is that the fact that there are differences in respect of subvenient properties between one unit and two units of stimulation, and between two and three units, does not imply that there are (undetected) differences *in respect of the properties that supervene on them*. A failure to grasp this point seems to come to expression in Temkin's 'main' reaction to my argument which is that it involves being 'caught in the equivalent of a normative optical illusion' (2014: 156). His idea seems to be that X and Y and Y and Z are judged to be the same in respect of S-ness because some inconspicuous differences between them are overlooked. But the differences might not be differences in respect of the supervenient properties, but simply in respect of the subvenient properties. In opposition to what Temkin suggests (2014: 152–3), it is not the case that there *have* to be differences *in painfulness* between X and Y, and Y and Z that are too minute to be noticed.[6] Nor is it the case that there are

---

[6] In the cases in which quality of well-being depends on the objects of well-being, as when Mozart's music is enjoyed—cases that I set aside at the end of the preceding section—it is quite plausible to claim

subvenient aspects that we fail to 'focus' (2014: 154) with the result that the values of X, Y, and Z are misjudged. Since the subvenient properties are distinct from and more precise than the properties that supervene on them, they can account for how X and Z differ in painfulness, though X and Y, and Y and Z do not. These subvenient properties are not objects of our awareness, or properties that we *could* 'focus'. It seems to me that Temkin's inability to understand my argument is largely a result of his failure to take in the full significance of the supervenience of a property, of its distinctness from subvenient properties.

For, by contrast, properties that do not supervene on other properties—let us call them *primary* properties—perfect similarity or identity must be transitive. Imagine that we observe a difference in length (or weight) between X and Z, though according to our most accurate measurements of X and Y, and of Y and Z, the members of these pairs are equally long. Then, provided that the comparison of X and Z is correct, we are forced to conclude that there *must* be unobserved or unmeasurable differences in *length* between X and Y or Y and Z (or the particles constituting them and the spaces in between these particles). Since the length of these objects does not supervene on any other kind of property that they have, a difference in length between X and Z cannot be explained in terms of differences between X and Y and Y and Z as regards such an underlying property. It must be explained in terms of differences in length. In the case of supervenient properties, however, there are perforce subvenient properties in terms of which they can be explained. Since it might be that greater precision is possible as regards these underlying properties, it might be that there is perfect similarity with respect to the supervenient properties—that is, *no* difference whatsoever with respect to *them*—though there are differences with respect to the underlying properties. This implies that perfect similarity or identity with respect to supervenient properties is not transitive.

A possible objection is that this goes to show that the relation perfect similarity or identity is not really applicable to supervenient properties, since this relation is by definition transitive. This objection cannot be refuted: anyone who so wishes can so define this relation that it becomes a definitional truth that it is transitive (rather than something that is necessary only when this relation holds at a primary level). My argument then implies that this relation is not applicable to pairwise comparisons of supervenient intrinsic properties, such as the comparisons of X and Y, and Y and Z, with respect to S. If we use a relation of perfect similarity which is applicable to such comparisons, it will have to be non-transitive.

It might, however, be thought that this cannot be the relation that you are applying when you are feeling the sensations X, Y, and Z *simultaneously* (cf. Temkin, 2014: 154). The idea is that you cannot simultaneously compare X and Y, Y and Z, and find them

that they can only *roughly* be of equal value, and that the relation of being of roughly equal value is non-transitive. But this is too uncontroversial to be worth much discussion. I mention it only to make it explicit that I believe that there are different ways to respond to different kinds of regresses to a repugnant conclusion.

the same in respect of painfulness, and X and Z and find them different in this respect. Suppose that this is true. The explanation might be that the most accurate comparison between two sensations requires *undivided* attention to them, so that when you try to execute three comparisons at the same time, none of them gets undivided attention. This makes it likely that a difference between X and Z, which is bound to be minute, will escape notice. So, all three sensations could erroneously be judged equally painful. But suppose instead that we do notice a difference as regards painfulness between X and Z, but none between X and Y, or Y and Z. Then what Temkin maintains about their value in virtue of painfulness is this: 'we will have good reason to be confident that Y's value is *not perfectly similar* to, or the *same* as, X and Z's values, since...those values *are* clearly distinguishable from each other' (2014: 154). However, I take myself to have already illustrated how Y *can* be perfectly similar to both X and Z in respect of painfulness, though the latter differ in this respect. So, we do not have 'good reason to be confident' that this is impossible.

Now, it is easy to see how my argument can be extended to an argument against the transitivity of the relations of being better/worse than in some particular respect and, thus, being better/worse all things considered which are the relations at work in the repugnant conclusion. Imagine, for instance, that the painful stimulation Y is noticeably slightly shorter than X, though there is no difference in the felt intensity of the pain. Then Y is better than X all things considered (assuming that intensity and duration are the only relevant factors). If Z is slightly shorter than Y, but they are felt to be equally painful, Z will be better than Y all things considered. Still, it might be that Z is not better than X as regards painfulness and all things considered because Z is felt to be more intense than X, and this difference is judged to outweigh the longer duration of X.

To turn to some simple outcomes that are more similar to the one in the repugnant conclusion, imagine instead that X is minimally more painful than Y, but that Y is markedly longer than X. The same goes for Y and Z. Then Y may be worse than X all things considered, and Z may be worse than Y all things considered because the greater difference in duration outweighs the smaller difference in intensity. Yet, Z may be better than X all things considered because, due to unmanifested differences in the subvenient properties, the difference in intensity between X and Z may exceed the sum of the differences in this respect between X and Y, and Y and Z. Therefore, it is possible that the difference in intensity between X and Z in favour of X's worseness overpowers the difference in duration in Z's favour. In the case of both examples, non-transitivity may come out as more plausible if the series are made longer, as in the case of the repugnant conclusion.[7]

In a monumental book (2012) Temkin proposes another way of grounding the non-transitivity of being better/worse than all things considered. He defends what he terms an 'essentially comparative view' of the value of outcomes, according to which there are some ideals such that how good an outcome is with respect to those ideals depends

---

[7] Stuart Rachels has also presented such arguments (1998) and (2001).

not only on its internal features, but also on its relations to other outcomes to which it is compared. Thus, how good an outcome is all things considered will depend not only on its internal or intrinsic features—as is true on the rival 'internal aspect view'—but also on its external relations.

To illustrate the essentially comparative view, consider three outcomes: A: a large number of people at a very high level of welfare; A+: this population plus an equally large number of individuals at a significantly lower level of well-being, but still well above the neutral level; and B: these two populations at the same level which is significantly higher than halfway between the levels of A and the extra population. Now suppose that inequality in respect of well-being is not a bad feature that detracts from the value of an outcome if it comes about by bringing individuals into existence. Then it is not a respect in which A+ is worse than A. However, it *is* a respect in which A+ is worse than B, since these outcomes contain only individuals who exist in both outcomes. Therefore, B would be better than A+ with respect to equality, but A+ would not be worse than A in this respect. So, if A+ is better than A with respect to the ideal of well-being, because its sum of well-being is greater, A+ will plausibly be better than A all things considered. B might be better than A+ all things considered because it is better both in respect of equality and sum of well-being. True, it is worse in one respect because nobody in B is as well off as the better-off individuals in A+; so, some of the better things in life may be lost. But we might feel that this aspect is outweighed by the other two aspects in which B is better. Nonetheless, we might also feel that B is not better all things considered than A because its greater sum of well-being alone—without any difference as regards equality—does not outweigh the qualitative loss.

Now, if we also endorse the transitivity of the relation of being better than all things considered, we face a paradox, what Parfit calls *the mere addition paradox* (1987: ch. 19). But by adopting an essentially comparative view of the ideal of equality and taking it to be relevant for the comparison between A+ and B, but not for the comparison between A and A+, we remove the paradox by denying the transitivity of 'all-things-considered better than'.

When applying the essentially comparative view to the spectrum of outcomes which leads to the repugnant conclusion, Temkin asserts that 'the relevant factors, or the significance of those factors, for comparing "distant" alternatives A and Y, may differ from the relevant factors, or the significance of those factors, for comparing intervening "adjacent" alternatives' (2012: 224). Therefore, he claims that the value of Y might vary when Y is compared to adjacent X and to distant A (cf. 2012: 229). This is supposed to be parallel to the variation of the value of A+ when it is compared to A and B, respectively, and an essentially comparative view is taken of the ideal of equality. Then the value of A+ will be higher when it is compared to A than when it is compared to B because it is only in the latter case that the badness of its inequality detracts from its value. Since one factor, the factor of equality, which is relevant for the comparison of A+ and B, is irrelevant for the comparison of A+ and A, it is not surprising that the transitivity of 'better/worse than all things considered' breaks down.

However, the relation between the 'factor' that kicks in when A and distant Y are compared and the factors that are involved in the comparison of adjacent outcomes, like A and B, B and C, and so on, seems quite unlike the relation between equality and the other factors involved in the comparisons between A, A+ and B, factors like quantity and quality of well-being. While equality is obviously a separate factor from these, the corresponding separateness of the factor that allegedly kicks in when distant outcomes are compared is far from obvious. In the series leading to the repugnant conclusion, the factors are basically *the same*, irrespective of whether we compare the value of adjacent outcomes, like A and B, or distant outcomes like A and Y, namely the intensity and duration of well-being. The difference between A and the distant Y apparently *consists* in a number of the adjacent differences between A and B, B and C, and so on. And it seems to me that the value of Y is the same regardless of whether it is compared to adjacent X or distant A. Nevertheless, Temkin believes that, while we adopt an 'additive-aggregationist' approach to the comparisons of the value of adjacent outcomes, when distant outcomes are compared, it is replaced by an 'anti-additive-aggregationist' approach which flouts transitivity. But, so far as I can see, he provides no justification for the soundness of the anti-additive-aggregationist approach, no explanation of how the value difference between Y and A could be anything but the sum of the adjacent value differences between A and B, B and C, and so on, *unless transitivity breaks down*. Thus, his account is in danger of being circular: in order to account for a putative non-transitivity in the repugnant conclusion series he appeals to an approach which presupposes non-transitivity.

I have offered an explanation of how non-transitivity is possible here, which refers to the greater imprecision inherent in supervenient properties than in their subvenient bases. This explains why values are not quantifiable in a sense that makes them amenable to mathematical operations like addition. So, it readily justifies the adoption of an anti-additive-aggregationist approach in the series, or an approach that need not yield judgments in accordance with an additive-aggregationist approach. It explains why we could find the repugnant conclusion repugnant, but would not find repugnant a similar conclusion with respect to properties which are not supervenient: for instance, there is nothing repugnant in the conclusion that a huge number of minuscule weights can together weigh more than a small number of big weights. In his reply (2014) to an earlier presentation of this account (Persson, 2014), Temkin rejects it for reasons indicated above, but he does not offer anything else in its place. This leaves a suspicious lacuna in his explanation of how there can be non-transitivity, or a switch from additive aggregationism to anti-additive aggregationism in the spectrum leading to the repugnant conclusion.

All the same, I believe that Temkin is right that we should accept the essentially comparative view—that is, that sometimes their external relations are relevant to the value of outcomes—and that this is a source of non-transitivity, though a source that should not be tapped to respond to the repugnant conclusion in the sort of examples considered here. The need for the comparative view can be brought out by an example which involves what Temkin calls *the disperse additional burdens* view on which the denial of transitivity also bears. He provides the following illustration (2012: 441–2, which is said to derive from Alex Voorhoeve).

Suppose that an island is ringed with 100 villages, in each of which a single individual has contracted a progressive disease. It can only be cured by a medicine that has to be flown to the island, but the aircraft can only land in two villages, villages 1 and 2. The medicine then has to be distributed by car to the other villages, but owing to the condition of the roads, the car has to travel clockwise. It will take one hour to fly the drug to either village 1 or 2 and then one hour to drive from one village to the next. Every hour of delay will mean that the symptoms of the disease get worse. If the drug is flown to village 1, the victims in the 99 other villages will have to wait an extra hour for treatment, compared to what would be the case if it were flown to village 2. Their symptoms will thus be slightly worse than they otherwise would be. On the other hand, flying it to village 2 will mean that the patient in village 1 will have to wait for an extra 99 hours for treatment, until the medicine has been driven clockwise around the island. The symptoms of this patient will consequently be much worse.

But, although the outcomes of flying to village 1 and of flying to village 2 contain the same burdens, distributed according to the same pattern—one person having to wait one hour for treatment, and a second two hours, and so on—many of us are inclined to think that the outcome of flying it to village 1 is better. The reason is that we feel that one person's burden of having to wait for an extra 99 hours for the medicine—which is the fate of the person in village 1 if we fly it to village 2—is worse than 99 people each having to wait an extra hour—which is the lot of people in all other villages if we fly the medicine to village 1 instead of 2—though additively their sum is the same. This judgment is underwritten by the disperse additional burdens view: a dispersal of a sum of burdens over many individuals is better than concentrating it to a few individuals. The denial of transitivity defended in this chapter can account for this, that is, it can account for how a single individual's wait for an extra 99 hours can be worse than 99 individuals each waiting for an additional hour: the badness of a single wait for an extra 99 hours does not necessarily equal the badness of the sum of 99 waits for an extra hour because a sufficiently great increase in the intensity of suffering does not increase its badness merely additively.

Notice, however, that this view implies that when we decide which of the outcomes to bring about, we have to consult how these outcomes benefit individuals in the event sense rather than simply look at the benefits that the outcomes intrinsically contain. In other words, the appeal to the disperse additional burdens view presupposes that we adopt a person-affecting view rather than the impersonal view of reasons of beneficence. It also presupposes that we accept the essentially comparative view to the effect that to determine the value of outcomes all told, it is sometimes not enough to look at their intrinsic value; their relations to other outcomes have to be brought in.

By means of a denial of the transitivity of perfect similarity of value and what follows from it, then, the repugnant conclusion can be blocked, and the disperse additional burdens view can be accounted for. But this denial comes at a considerable systematic cost: if we find Z better than Y all things considered, we can no longer infer that Z must be better all things considered than everything that Y is better than, for instance X. We must take the trouble to compare Z to everything to which Y has been compared and found better than. Otherwise, we risk being 'money-pumped', or tricked into paying to get Y in place of X, and Z in place of Y, only to end up with something that is inferior to what we started with, Z in place of X. We can protect ourselves against such exploitation, but not without the inconvenience of executing extra comparisons. However, that the non-transitivity of 'better/worse than all things considered' is thus inconvenient is no objection to it being *true*.

To repeat, this non-transitivity implies that values are not quantifiable in the sense that they can be assigned numbers and subjected to arithmetical operations, since the series of numbers is transitive. But this is something that strikes me as intuitively right anyway: intuitively, there seems to me to be this difference between what I have called primary properties and properties that are supervenient in my sense, like values and secondary qualities.

5
The End of Life and of Consciousness

5.1 The Definitional and Moral Meaning of Death

I have talked a lot about death, in particular about it being something that is extrinsically bad for us to the extent that it deprives us of future benefits. But what *is* the death of a human being, definitionally? As will transpire, there are reasons why a more precise definition eludes us, but fortunately this is not crucial for a moral inquiry, like the present, since death in itself is not of moral importance. This is because the death of an organism with consciousness neither consists in nor entails an irreversible loss of consciousness (though when I have discussed the badness of death, I have assumed that it is accompanied by an irreversible loss of consciousness, since this is normally the case).

To begin with, we must distinguish the death of an organism from *the end of its existence*. The death of an organism is the end of the *life* of an organism rather than the end of the organism itself. 'Life' should here be taken in a purely biological sense. I shall not attempt to determine precisely what this sense is, but in order to infuse some measure of concreteness into the notion of biological life, let me suggest that an organism's being alive is tantamount to something like it being engaged in processes of acquiring energy from the environment in order to maintain its internal organization. These processes consist in such things as the uptake of oxygen and having it circulated, as well as feeding and digestion. This is rough, but precise enough to set life-processes apart from conscious processes.

Life in the biological sense can be distinguished from life in a 'biographical' sense (to borrow James Rachel's term, 1986: 5–6, 24–7): 'your life' or 'the life you lead' in the biographical sense is, I suggest, something like the sum of events which happen while you are biologically alive and which make some difference to how you act or react. These events include both events that involve nothing external to you, such as your feeling pain somewhere in your body, and events which do involve something external to you, such as your becoming famous for some feat. The phrase 'make some difference to how you act and react' is of course awfully vague, but is meant to require more than that you are conscious of something. For instance, if you are just passively aware of the civil war in Syria, this is not enough to make it a part of your life; to be a part of your life, consciousness of something must have some impact on your emotions or motivation. Still less do events which occur while you have a capacity for consciousness, but of which you are not conscious, qualify as parts of your life; this includes many micro-events going on in your body, for instance. However, in the present context nothing much hangs on the demarcation of our biographical lives since, as remarked already in the Introduction, the notion of the value of our lives for us is too narrow for present purposes, as it cannot without strain include such things as the value of having our last wills fulfilled, or our getting posthumous fame for something that we have accomplished. Even if we were to have beliefs about such future events, they—like events that occurred before our lives began—do not satisfy the other condition of being co-temporal with our being alive. In such cases, it is only the beliefs about the events, not the events themselves, that could be parts of our lives.

Now consider some reasons for distinguishing the death of an organism from the end of its existence: first, it is plausible to think that organisms often go on existing for some time after their dying, that there are many dead organisms. This is however denied, for instance by Eric Olson who holds that 'an animal necessarily ceases to exist when it dies' (1997: 136).[1] In my opinion, this claim is strongly counterintuitive. Intuitively, the death of an animal is the termination of the *life-processes* of the animal, and this seems evidently to be something distinct from the *animal itself* ceasing to exist: a dead organism is still an existing organism that to our unaided senses may be well nigh indistinguishable from the living organism. So, to all appearances, an organism may outlast its death—if it is not blown to pieces, consumed by fire and so on. Life-processes, having created an organism, could desert it without causing it immediately to cease to exist. It does not cease to exist until decomposition has done its work fairly thoroughly (this degree of course being vague). In other words, we must distinguish the end of the life-processes of an organism—that is, its death—from the end of the existence of the organism undergoing these processes.[2]

Conversely, an organism may plausibly cease to exist without dying. For instance, if an amoeba, A, at t divides into two amoebas, B and C, then A goes out of existence at t because, as at least theorists who are not four-dimensionalists would admit, A is identical neither to both of B and C—these being distinct from each other—nor to any one

---

[1] This view is traceable back to Locke who wrote that the identity of a human organism is 'nothing but a participation of the same continued Life' (1689: II. xxvii. 6). In contrast, Feldman takes the view here adopted (1992: 94–5, 104). A number of the points here surveyed stem from Feldman and have been stated by me before (1995c).

[2] DeGrazia inclines towards the same view (2005: 55–6). In his case, however, this inclination is hemmed in by his adherence to the biological view of our identity and a reluctance to say that *we* can survive our death. But we do naturally suppose that *we* can be buried, or cremated, after our death; so, I do not see why this corollary of the biological view would be counterintuitive. DeGrazia also claims: 'I can't have properties when I am dead...because at that time there will be no thing that is me' (2005: 185). But when I die, I need not lose my height and weight—and I acquire the property of being dead! More generally, I do not understand his idea that properties have to be properties of something that exists. For instance, Leonardo da Vinci still has the property of being the artist who painted *Mona Lisa*, though nothing may remain of him.

of them, for that would be arbitrary. Since A has ceased to exist, it must have ceased to be alive in the sense that it has ceased to be true of it that it is alive. Still, it does not seem to me right to say that A has *died* at t.

However, if the separation of an organism into parts is very radical, we may be uncertain whether it has died. Feldman imagines (1992: 69) there being a 'cell separator' that grinds down animals and emits all their cells alive, as a purée. At t a mouse is put into the machine, and out comes a purée of living mouse cells. He is inclined to hold that this process causes the death of the mouse. I do not share his intuition: in the case of the mouse, *nothing has died* at the basic, cellular level. What has happened is rather that the organization of the living cells into a mouse organism has dissolved. In other words, the mouse has ceased to exist.

Imagine that the cells of the mouse could be put together to form a mouse again. Or, less radically, imagine, as Feldman does (1992: 69), that the organs composing a mouse or some other organism are separated, kept alive, and then joined together to form the same kind of organism. Then it may seem natural to claim that the resulting organism is numerically identical to the original organism. This is what we would say in the case of artefacts: we dismantle them in order to examine, clean or transport them, and then put them together to the same kind of thing. It is natural to say that the resulting thing is not merely qualitatively, but numerically identical to the original thing.[3] But then it is rather odd to hold that the organ separation *kills* the original organism and that the putting together of its living organs brings it back from the *dead*. After all, it has never been a *dead mouse*; it has rather temporarily ceased to be a mouse. Perhaps this is what a really thorough medical examination will be like in the distant future.

Such cases of temporarily going out of existence (as a certain kind of thing) are analogous to other sorts of problem cases, also discussed by Feldman (1992: 60–6): cases of suspended animation in which life processes are temporarily stopped. Living micro-organisms can be immersed in glycerol and frozen to the point at which their life-processes stop. When it is needed, the organisms can be warmed up until they resume the business of living. Since these micro-organisms were not *dead* when they were in the state of suspended animation, we cannot say that they are dead just in case their life-processes stop.

It will not do to have the definition demand that life-processes are stopped *forever*, rather than being merely temporarily interrupted. For suppose that in some cases the micro-organisms are never thawed out; then they surely do not die at the time at which they are frozen, although they forever stop living at that time. Nor will it do to say that A's death consists in A's ceasing to be alive, and it being *impossible* that A begins to live again. For imagine that reanimation of frozen organisms becomes impossible because the technique of doing it is lost; then, if the frozen organisms are preserved intact,

---

[3] However, this judgment can lead to quandaries, as the legendary ship of Theseus illustrates (see Persson, 2005: 302–6).

it would not be true to say that they die just because the technique of thawing them out is lost. Surely, a change in the world *external* to the organisms cannot mean that they change from being alive to being dead.

In other words, due to the fact their *internal state* remains the same, they are still alive; in so far as *it* is concerned, it is still possible that they will return to life. The claim must then be that an organism dies just in case internal changes of it cause its life-processes to cease irreversibly, or to make their continuation nomologically impossible. As Feldman remarks (1992: 65–6), the internal/external distinction and the notion of (im)possibility involved are far from clear, but these are snags of a general sort that we cannot try to sort out here. There are other problems more specific to the concept of death in more urgent need of attention.

Many readers will have missed reference to familiar definitions of the death of a human being or organism in terms of the death of *the brain* of this organism. It might seem that such definitions are more informative than an organismic definition in terms of an (internally caused) irreversible cessation of the life-processes of the entire organism. I shall now explain why these definitions are inadequate (cf. Persson, 2002).

There are both definitions which refer to the death of the *whole* human brain, the cessation of functioning of *all* of the parts of the brain, and definitions which refer to the cessation of functioning of merely those parts of the brain that underlie its capacity for consciousness, so that death essentially consists in the irreversible loss of the capacity for consciousness. Having a capacity for consciousness is, however, more closely connected to having a biographical life than to being biologically alive—as my characterization of biographical life is designed to bring out (though it should be conceded that there might be a tendency to stretch biographical life to incorporate what happens to humans when they are irreversibly unconscious). For it seems clear that there are human beings who are alive, though they permanently lack the brain parts that are the seat of consciousness, for instance anencephalic infants. Being alive, these infants can obviously die, but their death cannot consist in the death of brain parts that they lack. These beings do not have biographical lives.

Definitions of death which refer to the irreversible cessation of functioning of the whole brain are more plausible. Activity in certain areas of the brain is crucial for the integration of vital processes like breathing, circulation, heartbeat, and digestion in a highly complex organism like the human, but such activity is not necessary for the life of a human organism at every stage of its development. This is indicated by the fact that at the beginning of their existence, at gastrulation a couple of weeks after conception (see 2.1), human beings have *no* brains at all. Human embryos have no brains, or any other organs, that control their life-processes like the circulation of oxygenated blood. Yet, being alive, they can obviously die, that is, lose their life, but their death cannot possibly consist in the death of their brains, since they have no brains. Consequently, the death of a brain cannot be a logically necessary condition for the death of a human being (or of other animal organisms). Nor does the death of the brain appear to be a sufficient condition for the death of the human organism, since some residual life-processes seem to go on after the whole brain has ceased to function.[4]

Even if there were to be some brain-death definition that could deal with the last point, it would be ad hoc to maintain that death for humans who have acquired brains *means* something different than it does for human embryos. For if the human organisms without brains are numerically the same (human) organisms as those that later are equipped with brains, and these organisms are continuously alive up to, and beyond, the stage at which they acquire brains, what reason—other than the desire to preserve a brain-death definition for brain owners—could there be to deny that there is a single sense in which these organisms are alive and, thus, in which they can die, or lose their life?

The picture that I am outlining is this. When a brain develops in a human organism, this brain assumes an overarching role of controlling and coordinating life-processes, like the circulation of oxygenated blood and digestion. But in a simpler organism, as a human being in the earliest period of its life, these processes can go on with some degree of integration without the supervision of a brain. Thus, it is possible for an organism to be alive without having a brain, as is demonstrated by plants and simpler animal organisms. Naturally, it is then possible to lose life, that is, to die, without having a brain. Therefore, the death of a brain is not a logically necessary condition for the death of such organisms.

But then it is not surprising that this condition is not logically sufficient, either. For if the life-processes of an organism can go on prior to the acquisition of a brain, it should cause no surprise if they can in principle go on after the demise of the brain which was acquired by the organism at some later stage of its development. In fact, this is what happens when artificial life-support is in operation, and performs a function analogous to that of a pregnant woman's body in the case of an embryo. Hence, the death of a brain is neither a logically necessary nor logically sufficient condition for the death of a human being or organism.

It may be objected that this argument substantially rests on the contentious assumption that human beings begin to exist and live before they develop brains. However, the claim neither needs to rest on this assumption, nor is it easily disputed. Suppose, first, that human beings are not numerically the same organisms as human embryos without brains; instead, human beings are distinct entities that develop out of these embryos, say, when brains are formed by them. Then it would still appear reasonable to claim that human beings live and die in the same sense as the embryos out of which they grow by means of a continuous process. In view of the continuity of the development from one to the other, it would be gratuitous to hold that life and death mean one thing for organisms with brains and another thing for organisms without brains. Granted, life-processes may *as a matter of fact* assume somewhat different forms if there is a brain governing them, but this does not imply that the *meaning* of 'being

---

[4] See DeGrazia for evidence to this effect (2005: 142-7).

alive' is different. If this meaning must change whenever the life-processes of a species of organism assume a more or less different form, we could not meaningfully use the term 'life' without having biological expertise.

Secondly, I would like to insist on what was argued in 2.1, that it does seem plausible to trace a living human being or organism back to a point at least shortly after the appearance of the first sign of the spine, the so-called primitive streak, in the third week after fertilization. That is, it is plausible to say that it is *one and the same* living—human— organism which first has the primitive streak and then, growing out of it, a brain and backbone (and, as a result of that, a mind). But if a human organism can be alive without having a brain, its death or loss of life cannot be the same as its brain discontinuing its functioning. Moreover, assigning this pivotal role to the brain would also be implausible at the stage at which it has barely begun to develop, and its development is still too rudimentary for it to have assumed any overarching role of regulating vital processes.

Although simple, this argument 'from the beginning' appears to have been widely overlooked in the debate over how to define human death. Apparently, it has been thought possible to define human death without taking into consideration when a human being begins to exist. But this is not possible because a human being undergoes radical changes in the course of its development, and to *define* the death of a human being is to supply conditions that, by necessity, apply to *all* human beings. The *definiens* supplied must apply not only to a sub-class of humans, for instance postnatal humans, but to prenatal humans as well.

More remarkably, even when the issues of the beginning and death of a human being are brought together, the implications of the former issue are not consistently drawn out for the latter issue. For instance, Olson adopts a view in line with the view here espoused, namely that a human being comes into existence around the time of gastrulation (1997: 140). Yet, he also writes

> As soon as your brainstem is destroyed, you lose the capacity to direct your vital functions. Your individual cells and organs can no longer work together as a unit in the manner characteristic of a living organism. What we have is a corpse that merely appears to be alive because it is so freshly dead, and not a living animal. (1997: 140)

That is, a human organism dies when its brainstem dies or is destroyed. But if a human organism once was alive without having a brainstem, the fact that the brainstem that it has grown is destroyed cannot be *logically* sufficient for its death: the notion of a living human organism without a functioning brainstem cannot be incoherent. True, when its brainstem is destroyed, a human organism will *as a matter of fact* die (shortly)—if it does not receive artificial life-support. But the need for life-support external to the organism is no proof that it is not truly alive, since a living human embryo/foetus is also dependent on life-support from its mother. A (human) organism may be alive without being independently viable.

Clearer still, a non-functioning brainstem cannot be a logically *necessary* condition for human death if a human being can live and die before it acquires this organ.

Nonetheless, this is asserted by Olson when he writes that 'your brainstem, as the organ that is chiefly responsible for directing your life-sustaining functions, is essential to you' (1997: 140). To be sure, he does not write that a functioning brainstem is essential for a human organism being alive, but this is implied if we add two other claims of his. First, as already remarked, he holds that 'an animal necessarily ceases to exist when it dies' (1997: 136). Secondly, he adopts the biological view of our identity to the effect that we are identical to our human organisms.

For present purposes, I can afford to set aside the latter metaphysical problem of our identity, since irrespective of whether or not we are identical to them, there plainly exist human organisms that are alive and eventually die. This is the death that I am seeking to define. Further, even if we are not identical to these organisms, their death may be the only literal death that we can undergo, just as a rise in their blood pressure is the only rise in blood pressure that we can undergo. For it may be that the concept of death, like that of blood pressure, is literally applicable to us only because we are biologically embodied.

To sum up, the death of a human being cannot be the same as the death of its brain, or certain parts of it, like the brainstem, since a human being can die before it comes into possession of these organs. Notice also that this argument tells not only against brain-death definitions, but equally against their 'heart-death', or cardio-pulmonary, rivals. For it is no less true that at some stages of its development a human being is alive, and can die, though it has not yet a heart or lungs.

The death of a human organism, then, cannot definitionally consist in the irreversible cessation of functioning of some of its organs. Do we then have to rest content with a vague definition of a human organism's death as the irreversible cessation of the life-processes of the whole organism, or can we make the relevant life-processes more specific or precise? A logically sufficient condition is certainly the irreversible cessation of *all* of the life-processes of a human organism. But this condition is not necessary, since we surely want to say that a human being can be dead, even though some of its life-processes still continue, just as we say, for instance, that a machine is out of order, even though some parts of it may function. As it is enough that *most* of the parts of the machine are out of order, it is enough that *most* of the life-processes of an organism have ceased for good for it to be dead. But I am afraid that a definition of human death cannot be more precise and specific than this, just as a definition of when a machine has ceased to function cannot (cf. Persson, 1995c).

For, first, as already observed, since at different developmental stages of a human organism, the biological structures or organs responsible for life-processes vary, none of them can be specified in a definition of death which perforce must state conditions that are necessary and sufficient for every conceivable case of human death. So, this avenue to greater specification is blocked. Secondly, it is hazardous to specify the relevant life-processes. DeGrazia defends a 'circulatory-respiratory standard', which asserts that 'human death is *the permanent cessation of circulatory-respiratory function*' (2005: 149). This seems too specific to be true of the death of all life-forms, e.g. amoebas. It even seems doubtful that it captures the death of humans in the beginning of their existence at gastrulation if we accept DeGrazia's concession that 'arguably, we should allow that the human organism emerges earlier, perhaps when differentiation *begins* at the sixteen-cell stage' (2005: 251). If so, DeGrazia's standard would force us to countenance different concepts of death, which I find less plausible than leaving the life-processes in the *analysans* of the definition of death unspecified.

Empirical criteria for human death can sidestep these hurdles to greater specificity, since they need only be contingently true of humans of a certain category. Hence, a criterion for the death of postnatal human beings may refer, for instance, to the cessation of all activity in their brains, or brainstems. But such a criterion still has to grapple with a second source of vagueness: the fact that the cessation of the relevant activities, whatever they may be, is a gradual process. For instance, it has been found that there is some activity in brains at the time at which they are declared dead by standard methods (see DeGrazia, 2005: 143–4). Is this residual activity important enough to call for a revision of the criterion of brain-death? This is likely to be a matter of dispute.

Suppose that we instead adopt a criterion which allows that the life of a human being can be sustained even after the cessation of *all* of its brain-activities, by a heart-lung machine that keeps its circulatory, respiratory, and metabolic functions going. Then, if we turn off the machine, at what precise point in time have these functions ceased to the degree that we should declare the organism dead? Again, this is question which does not appear to admit of a non-arbitrary answer because the cessation of these life-processes in a complex organism is a gradual process, and it would be absurd to go to the extreme of claiming that it has not died until there are absolutely *no* life-processes going on anywhere in it.

This indeterminacy or vagueness may seem alarming because death is often assumed to be an event of the greatest moment to us, marking the end of a life which is thought to be of value for human beings and during which they have rights. For instance, Robert Veatch writes: 'When humans are living, full moral and legal human rights accrue. Saying people are alive is simply shorthand for saying that they are bearers of such rights' (1993: 21). In the same spirit, Daniel Wikler characterizes death as 'an absence of everything for which people value existence' (1988: 47). These writers take death to have to do with something like the irreversible cessation of consciousness, which I think is necessary for casting death as the great loss of moral status or personal value.

We have however seen that this kind of definition of death faces the objection that humans without consciousness—say, young foetuses and anencephalic infants—are alive and can die. To this it might be replied that there are *two* concepts of death: alongside a biological concept, like for example the holistic or organismic one here advocated, there is another that refers to the irreversible loss of the capacity for consciousness. While the first applies to all humans, the second applies only to those with consciousness, but it is the morally important concept. This two-concepts approach has perhaps been most impressively articulated by McMahan (1995; 2002: 423–6).

He attempts to motivate the introduction of the second concept of death by adopting, as already mentioned, a psychological view of our nature and identity to the effect that we are subjects of mental states who are distinct from our human organisms. On such a psychological approach to our nature and identity, irreversible loss of the capacity for consciousness marks the end of our existence, and 'when I cease to exist I die', as McMahan puts it (1995: 101). In sum, there are two distinguishable entities, an organism and a mental subject embodied in it, and each has its own death, a biological and a mental death, respectively.

Grant, for the sake of the argument, that we are identical to mental subjects, the non-derivative owners of our mental states, as I phrased it in 3.1. We should still keep in mind a point already made about the death of an organism: its death seems to be the permanent end of its life-processes rather than the end of its existence. Analogously, the death of a subject of conscious episodes could be conceived as consisting in the permanent end of its conscious episodes rather than in the end of its existence. It might be thought that this is a distinction without a difference, since the end of (the existence of) such a subject is equivalent to the permanent end of its conscious episodes. This would be a mistake, however. As was seen in 3.1, someone's mind may conceivably divide, bringing about the end of the existence of this subject, though its conscious processes run on in two distinct 'branches' (cf. Parfit, 1987: ch. 12). So, let us rather take it that the proposal is that the death of a mental subject amounts to the irreversible cessation of its mental processes, which entails the end of (the existence of) the subject.

There is still the objection, however, that mental processes seem so different from biological life-processes that it is confusing to use the same term 'death' to designate their respective terminations. Against this, it might be insisted that, in everyday discourse, we already have a biographical concept of life alongside the biological one, and that the biographical notion of 'having or leading a life' presupposes a capacity for consciousness. But even so, it does not follow that this notion of life *means* having a capacity for consciousness. Your biographical life is rather *the series of events* that you are aware of yourself to some extent participating in—your growing up, going to school, forming personal relationships, travelling around, and so on—than your stream of consciousness itself. For instance, the biographical life that you are leading might be described as rich or dull because the series of events that you might be aware of yourself participating in are rich or dull, whereas your stream of consciousness itself cannot be described thus. A series of events could certainly have an end, but this end is not properly called a 'death': whatever its medium, the series of events that constitutes a biography does not 'die'. So, the linguistic data do not support speaking of consciousness as life and of its termination as death.

I think, then, that we should resist the idea that there are for human beings who have consciousness two deaths to die, one consisting in the irreversible termination of biological life-processes and the other in the irreversible termination of conscious processes. The second concept of death does not have an established use and to introduce it would be to risk blurring over the important distinction between life-processes and conscious processes. But we could still adopt the irreversible cessation of its consciousness as the point at which a human being can no longer be in states which enable things to be intrinsically valuable for it and at which it loses its rights to life, freedom, property, etc.—that is, as a point at which it suffers loss of moral status or standing.[5] However, we must not conflate the question 'When does a human being lose its moral status?' with the question of when it dies. The loss of moral status is due to irreversible loss of consciousness, but this is not what defines death.

A corollary of adopting this view of the basis of moral status and its relation to death is that it is not of crucial moral importance to be able to determine precisely the moment of death of a human being. We have seen that there are at least three reasons why the concept of the death of a human being is vague. (1) We should separate the death of a human being from its ceasing to exist, but ultimately this distinction is fuzzy. (2) The notion of life-processes ceasing irreversibly, or resuscitation becoming impossible because of internal factors, is not sharp. (3) We are hard put to specify the functioning of any organs, or processes, and a more precise point at which they have irreversibly ceased to a sufficient degree for a human being to be dead.

It does not matter, however, that the concept of our death is indeterminate, since death is not the moral turning point at which we lose our moral status, and it becomes morally permissible to do things to humans that were hitherto forbidden. For instance, we could reasonably maintain that it is permissible to remove organs for the purpose of transplantation from irreparably unconscious humans even though they are alive. This is because it is not death, but the irreparable absence of consciousness, that makes this permissible on the present view of moral status.[6]

It is presumably the assumption that 'human life' is of intrinsic value and, thus, that a human donor of vital organs must be dead, that makes people forge definitions, or criteria, of human death that allow them to declare dead brain-dead—or even irreparably unconscious—humans. But we have seen such conceptions of human death to be erroneous, and if we take it that it is not life but consciousness that supplies humans with moral status, by enabling things to have intrinsic value for them, we are no longer tempted by these conceptions. We can calmly accept a definition of death that, like the vague organismic one here delineated, implies that humans in these circumstances are alive, since this is no longer seen to carry the further implication that they have a moral standing which makes them unavailable as donors.

---

[5] As indicated in the Introduction, I distinguish the narrower class of what has moral status or standing from the wider class of what has (intrinsic) moral importance or significance. The latter class includes deceased persons who had moral status in the past and individuals who could get moral status in the future.

[6] I here bracket the possibility that these humans may earlier in their lives have had wishes concerning how they should be treated in this condition. The claim is only that such a state of non-consciousness does not *in itself* provide a ground for moral standing.

It is no cause for alarm if this definition has to be imprecise and, consequently, that no precise criterion for the death of a human being can be devised. There is as little need to define precisely the death of a human being as to define precisely the end of its existence, which, as we have seen, does not necessarily coincide with its death. *Prima facie*, it might seem of utmost importance when a human being dies. Equally, it might also seem of great importance when a human being ceases to exist. Both of these impressions are illusions, probably created by confusing an organism's death and its ceasing to exist with an event in their wake that undoubtedly matters, namely the irrevocable cessation of its capacity for consciousness. This event matters morally in itself, since it means that there is no longer any possibility of intrinsic value for the individual who has suffered the loss.

It should be added that the disappearance of the capacity for consciousness is not an all-or-nothing matter. In the case of many of us, the capacity deteriorates, due to ageing or injuries, before it is eventually entirely lost. This results in a reduction of the intrinsically valuable experiences that we can savour. However, this is a topic which will not be pursued in this book.[7]

Many believe in immortal souls or spirits that can persist when our organisms have died and ceased to exist. If there were such mental substances, and we were identical to them, our death or organic non-existence would not necessarily be tantamount to our no longer being in states in which things can have intrinsic value for us. I am prepared to grant that, *logically*, our consciousness could continue in the absence of *living* and *organic* bodies and brains. But, according to all empirical evidence, the laws of nature do not permit this, that is, it is nomologically impossible. However, I shall in the next section argue that it is not even logically possible that our consciousnesses persist, though they are no longer consciousnesses which are physically embodied or realized in some piece of organic or inorganic matter. Consciousness must have a *physical* subject or owner. Thus, it is in the deepest sense impossible that there be disembodied consciousnesses for which things can have intrinsic value. Nonetheless, the consciousness of an organism could in fact persist, though its organism dies, if the parts of its brain which are the seat of its consciousness are transplanted to another living organism, or kept alive in a vat. So, although disembodied existence is strictly impossible, the popular belief that our minds can survive the death of our bodies is not entirely off the mark.

5.2 The Necessity of a Physical Subject of Consciousness

I believe that there are two forms of consciousness: perceptual/sensory consciousness and conceptual/cognitive consciousness. Examples of the first form of consciousness are seeing something red, tasting something sweet, feeling a smooth surface, or a

---

[7] See McMahan (1995) for a refinement of the notion of irreversible loss of the capacity for consciousness.

pleasure or pain somewhere in your body. Examples of the second form are thinking of something like an upcoming meeting, thinking that something is the case—for instance, that you see something red, that you are sitting down—or making a decision to get up. There is a dispositional sense of being conscious in which you can be conscious of the accelerating loss of biodiversity even when you are asleep. But you can be dispositionally conscious or aware of something only if you have at least once been occurrently conscious of it. It is this primary, occurrent form of consciousness that I shall here focus on.

Some conscious states are mixtures of perceptual/sensory and conceptual/cognitive consciousness. For instance, fearing that you will be late is thinking that you might be late, and as the result of this undergoing some bodily changes, such as faster heartbeat, dryness of throat, trembling, and so on, of which you have sensations (for my account of emotions, see 2005: ch. 5). But I shall not try to establish that all states of (occurrent) consciousness are either perceptual/sensory, conceptual/cognitive, or combinations of these two.

Consciousness is always consciousness *of* something: it has an object or content. The claim that consciousness is either perceptual/sensory or conceptual/cognitive is tantamount to this object or content being either perceptual/sensory or conceptual/cognitive. Since, as I shall argue, conceptual/cognitive objects are derived from perceptual/sensory objects, I shall start by examining the latter.

A central claim of mine is what might be called the *object account of consciousness* (see Persson, 1985a: 162–80):

(OC) A full description of what a momentary state of perceiving or feeling some objects is *intrinsically* like is a description of these objects, of there being such and such objects in such and such spatial relations to each other.

(OC) implies that no mental 'act' or relation of perceiving or feeling is an intrinsic feature of a state of perceiving or feeling. Furthermore, the subject doing the perceiving or feeling is present only as another object perceived and felt; more specifically, it is present as a body standing in spatial relations to other objects perceived or felt. The subject's body is however perceived or felt in a special way, 'from the inside', since the body is innervated through and through: it is felt as a three-dimensional thing that fills a volume of space. Every other object of the subject's consciousness is spatially related to this 3-D thing: bodily sensations are located inside it, what is tactually felt is located on its surface, and visual objects and sounds are outside it. These different modes of perception are distinguished by the qualities of their objects, for example in the case of visual perception the objects are coloured, in the case of tactile perception, they feature thermal qualities, and so on. Intrinsically, your seeing a red circle in front of you and feeling a pain in your knee consist in there being a red circle in front of your 3-D body and a pain in its knee-part.

Now, what can we say about the notion of existence used in saying, for instance, that there *is* a red circle in front of you when you see one there? The crucial claim is that this sense is *neutral* between the mental and the physical, that it is implied neither that the red circle is something *merely* perceived, nor that it is 'really' there, independently of being perceived. That is why I originally characterized my position as a *neutral* monism (1985a).[8] Furthermore, thanks to this neutrality, it can be employed to define both mental and physical existence. This is the rationale for the characterization of my position as a monism. It follows from (OC) that these definitions cannot refer to anything that is intrinsic or internal to the objects experienced. The notion of existence in itself must be taken as primitive and indefinable, and as acquired by experiencing it, just like manifold properties experienced, colours, thermal qualities, smells, pains, and so on, that are also indefinable and learnt by experience.

But if the distinction between the mental and physical is not part of what we experience, what is it and how do we acquire it? We notice that perceptual objects are *dependent on our bodies*: for instance, visual objects disappear when we close our eyes, they change as we move about, and so on. Thus, my proposal is that, for instance, your seeing a red circle in front of you consists in there being a red circle in front of you whose existence is dependent on your body. So, perceptual or sensory existence is existence which is dependent on a body, the body of the perceiver.

Your body is a constant element in your perceptual world, that is, you perceive it whenever you perceive anything, and anything that you perceive is spatially related to it.[9] I submit that your perception of your own body from inside, in proprioception, also supplies you with your concept of a 3-D thing. Since our bodies are invariably perceived whenever we perceive anything, and they reappear after a period of unconscious sleep in roughly the same condition and surroundings as they were when our perception of them was discontinued, it is natural to assume that they have been there even when not perceived, that is, that they have an existence which is not dependent on the existence of anything else, that they exist in their own right, so to speak. This idea of an independent existence is, I hypothesize, the idea of *physical* existence. When you take the existence of your perceptual objects to be dependent on your body, you take it for granted that your body has this independent, physical existence.

Although no other objects are perceived invariably as our own body is, many of these other objects often reappear in a similar state when perception of them is resumed after shorter breaks. Therefore, it is natural to assume that, apart from being dependent on our bodies, externally located perceptual objects are also dependent on there being something externally located that has independent existence, just like our bodies. Our commonsensical, default position is that these independent external things are pretty much as we perceive them, that is, that the dependency of our perceptual objects on our bodies does not significantly affect their character. But the progress

---

[8] The picture I here paint in broad strokes is basically a summary of the view I put forward in this book. I summarize this view in (2006b).

[9] Except in extraordinary circumstances, like Oliver Sacks's 'disembodied lady' (1985: ch. 3).

of science has thrown this assumption into doubt. However, this issue of how far our perceptions correspond to physical reality is not one that need detain us now.

Nor should the precise details of the dependence of perceptual objects on states of our bodies detain us now. There are two issues here: the issue of what features of perceptual objects depend on what bodily, or more precisely, neural states; and also the issue of the precise nature of this dependence relation. I take it to be a kind of symmetrical correlation, but why some perceptual objects are correlated with certain neural events rather than others is, so far as I can see, likely to a be brute, inexplicable fact. In other words, we are capable of finding out what perceptual qualities are correlated with what neural states, but ultimately we cannot explain why these particular correlations rather than other conceivable correlations, or no correlations, hold. A corollary of this inexplicability is that we cannot tell whether mental states can be correlated only with organic matter, or with some kind of inorganic matter as well.

The important point in the present context is the following. According to my account, the concepts of mental and physical existence are *complementary and interdependent concepts*; we cannot have one without the other. However, this does not mean that there cannot *be* one form of existence without the other. Their interdependence is *conceptual*, not *ontological*. (Compare: we cannot have the concept of unmarried people unless we have the concept of married people, but of course there can be unmarried people in the absence of married ones.) The physical world can exist—and in all likelihood has existed—without there being anything mental. It seems reasonable to take realism with respect to the physical world to consist in this world's existing independently of minds and their states. If so, my neutral monism is a realist view of the physical world, in spite of the fact that the concept of it as physical requires a contrast with the psychological. On the other hand, psychological states of perceiving cannot exist without there *being* something physical, since the psychological is a dependent form of existence which presupposes an independent form of existence. I believe that this account gets our intuitive ontological priorities right.

It also concords with the widely accepted point that mental states can only be individuated, numerically distinguished from qualitatively indistinguishable ones, by reference to something physical (cf. Strawson, 1959). Otherwise put, mental states are, by necessity, states of physical subjects, as their definitional dependency entails. This rules out substance dualism and renders property or attribute dualism the only viable dualist alternative. Initially, it might seem puzzling how it can be metaphysically necessary that, if distinct in kind and irreducible to physical states, conscious states have a physical subject or owner, but this is explained by the fact that the conscious is a dependent form of existence, and the physical an independent.

The view here proposed gives us a conceptual guarantee that there is a physical reality of *some* kind. It cannot be that whenever something exists, that is, some properties are instantiated, this is dependent on something else existing; the existence of something must be 'self-supporting', that is, physical. What this is—whether it is just the elementary entities of physics or the macroscopic objects of common sense as well—is an empirical matter and, so far as I can understand, it is *conceivable* that we are seriously mistaken in thinking that there is a physical world that conforms to the conception of either common sense or science. Conceivably, my mental states could be dependent on nothing but my body, which in its turn might be utterly different from how I perceive it (think of brain-in-a-vat thought-experiments), though there is no good reason to think that this is the case. However, this issue of the character of the physical world is one that has to be put aside for now.

Let us instead turn to the other mode of consciousness, the conceptual/cognitive. It is an essential or definitional feature of the objects or contents of this mode of consciousness that they are capable of *representing, designating*, or *referring to* something, for instance the objects of perceptual/sensory consciousness. What is it about them that enables them to perform this function? My proposal is that the first representations that we acquire in the course of our development succeed in referring to the perceptual objects from which they are derived because they *resemble* or *are isomorphic* with them. I cannot see how our *original* representations—the first representations that each of us has—could succeed in representing something in virtue of relations that are wholly extrinsic or external to the nature of the relata, as linguistic conventions are. There must be some similarity in respect of intrinsic features, as there is in the case of images and what they are images of.

But resemblance cannot be sufficient for representation, since representation is an asymmetrical relation, whereas resemblance is symmetrical. What creates the asymmetry is that images are *derived from*, or *dependent on*, that of which they are images. Thus, to take the simplest sort of example, representations of perceptual qualities, like colours, sounds, tastes, and so on, represent the perceptual qualities from which they are derived because they resemble them. This is in essence the traditional empiricist doctrine, championed by Locke, Berkeley, Hume, and their followers—a doctrine that has fallen into disrepute in the last century.

Laurence BonJour puts well the chief objection to a linguistic or conventional symbolic conception of representation:

According to that conception, *all* that is present in my mind (or brain) when I think contentful thoughts is symbols of the appropriate sorts; these symbols are meaningful or contentful by virtue of standing in relations of some sort to something lying outside the mind in which they stand, but this meaning or content is represented in the mind only by the symbols themselves, not by any further content-bearing element or feature. Thus, merely having such thought-symbols present in my mind (or brain) in itself gives me no awareness of their content, and there is apparently nothing else that the symbolic theory can appeal to in order to account in general for such awareness. Therefore the acceptance of the symbolic conception seems to lead inexorably to the conclusion that I have no awareness of the content of my thought, no internal grasp or understanding at all of what I am thinking. But this is surely an absurd result... (1998: 169)

BonJour concludes:

> Instead, at least some of the elements of thought must be *intrinsically* meaningful or contentful, must have the particular content that they do simply by virtue of their intrinsic, non-relational character. (1998: 180)

There seems to be only one means by which we can achieve this: by taking the representation itself to instantiate the property that it represents, that is, by there being resemblance in an intrinsic respect. This move would abolish the 'distance' between the representation and the property represented, and so the need for the mind to 'reach out' for the latter. But it might seem to do so at the cost of making it hard to tell them apart. BonJour distinguishes between two ways of discriminating between the representation and the thing represented: 'make sense of two distinct instantiation relations' and postulate two 'distinct, though presumably intimately related universals' (1998: 183). BonJour favours the second alternative, whereas I favour the first one.

I would like to suggest a revival of the traditional empiricist idea which BonJour spurns, that of a representative medium of images (to use a term which is really only apt in the case of visual representation). Plausibly, images of redness, triangularity, and so on, themselves instantiate redness, triangularity, and so on. So, images seem to fulfil one requirement of being capable of representing something in virtue of their intrinsic nature, by sharing a feature with what is represented. But BonJour denies that they meet another requirement: 'an image does not represent anything by itself, but rather needs at least to be supplemented by a content directing that it be interpreted in the right way' (1998: 182n).

That is, we are confronted with the question of what it is about an image of red that could make it represent redness. It is not enough to reply: the fact that it instantiates redness. For a perceptual object which is red also instantiates redness, yet it does not represent (or designate) redness. My answer, which is implicit in the empiricist tradition, is that an image of red represents the redness of perceptual objects for the reason that it belongs to a class of entities whose members are in general *derived* from perceptual objects of the appropriate colour. Put in a nutshell, my claim is that images are representative of perceptual objects because their existence is derivative from or dependent on these objects, and they represent those kinds of objects from which they could be derived by virtue of the fact that they are (most) similar to them (and they belong to a class of entities whose existence is derivative). It is the second feature that makes the representativeness of images partly intrinsic to their nature because they represent something to which they are similar in an intrinsic respect.

(OC) with respect to representative or conceptual/cognitive consciousness can now be stated: it consists in the existence of objects that stand in a similarity-preserving dependence relation to the objects of perceptual/sensory consciousness which, as we have seen, themselves are dependent. It is this order of dependence rather than any difference as regards some intrinsic feature—like the comparative faintness of which Hume speaks (1739: I. i. 1)—that distinguishes images from perceptual objects. It is dependency that accounts for the asymmetry of the relation of representation, in contrast to the symmetry of the relation of similarity which is a characteristic of perceptual objects no less than the images that represent them. If perceptual objects are regarded as similar to the physical objects to which they are dependent, it is natural to describe perceptual objects as representing these objects, as a traditional theory of perception, the representational theory, does.

As is all too well known, the idea of thinking in a medium of images faces many challenges: for instance, how can thinking in such a medium be propositional (that is, of a subject–predicate structure) and be about abstract states of affairs? I do not pretend to have the answer to all these vexing questions, but sometimes the difficulties seem to me to be exaggerated. For instance, it has been said that an image must be too specific or determinate to represent unequivocally cats rather than black cats, striped cats, etc. But a drawing can be very sketchy and indeterminate and can as a result be seen as a drawing of a cat rather than as a drawing of a black cat, and so on. Moreover, if this is correct, we can see the beginnings of an account of how propositional thinking in terms of images could be possible. For thinking that a cat is black could then be something like having an indeterminate image of a cat and superimposing an image of blackness on it. All the same, it must be admitted that it is a daunting task to make it comprehensible how we acquire the knack of thinking abstract thoughts by means of learning a complex language.

It is however a task that need not be undertaken here. What I have tried to do is to suggest an answer to an ontological question: what the distinction between the mental and the physical amounts to. In particular, I have tried to answer this question in a way that brings out the essential dependence of what is paradigmatically mental—namely, occurrent consciousness—on the physical. This answer implies that, though conscious states are distinct in kind from physical states, they must perforce have a physical subject or owner. It follows that we can identify an individual consciousness by, and only by, the fact that it is the consciousness dependent on a particular physical entity.

I have not tried to argue in favour of the truth of the claim that conscious states are distinct in kind and irreducible to physical states. It is however a claim that, intuitively, we are strongly inclined to embrace, and not surprisingly half a century or so of eager philosophical attempts to identify or reduce consciousness to something physical have proved unsuccessful. If consciousness is distinct in kind from physical states, it is easier to understand how it can bring with it new phenomena. It brings with it such phenomena as representation and truth but, I submit, also something of greater relevance in the present context, namely *value*. As suggested in Chapter 1, value for us consists in the satisfaction of certain desires. In other words, value consists in a fit between representations and facts that is opposite to that of truth, a fit of the facts to representations rather than of representations to the facts. Since being conscious is necessary for being in a state in which things can have intrinsic value for somebody, and consciousness requires a physical subject, we can conclude that things can have intrinsic value only for physical subjects, that is, only such subjects can have moral status.

This yields an—admittedly somewhat speculative—explanation of why the existence of value (like truth) presupposes the presence of mind as something which is distinct in kind from the physical: value presupposes representation—since it consists in facts fitting something that is represented as the object of desire—and a nonconventional representation must have a dependent existence which is precisely the nature of the mental. Further, we have a guarantee that, in principle, what is of value to other minds is within the reach of moral action because the mental is dependent on the physical, which in principle can be affected by our actions. It is only via this indirect route that we can affect the minds of others. Thus, as inclusive as the ethics of this book is, it does not include, even in principle, disembodied minds.

6

The Inclusion of Non-Human Animals

So far I have been discussing things being of intrinsic value mostly for human beings. But will it make any moral difference whether the subject for which something has intrinsic value is human or a non-human? Many animals are sentient and capable of having, for instance, sensations of pain that they dislike. Having these sensations is intrinsically bad for them, just as it is intrinsically bad for human beings. It will not be as bad if their dislike is less intense, but it is still bad for them to feel pain to the degree that it is disliked. It has however been claimed, or tacitly assumed, that it is morally (and thus impersonally) less bad—or even not bad at all—that they feel pain even if it is as (personally) bad for them as for human beings. That is to say, the idea might be that the fact that a pain is felt by a human being bestows on it a special moral significance, so that it adds more to the moral (dis)value of an outcome. Those who deny this claim regard it as an anthropocentric form of *speciesism*, a form of discrimination based on species membership analogous to racism and sexism. I shall in the present chapter support this denial.

The idea that human beings count for more morally seems cut out to have originated in Christianity, in its idea that humans—and they alone of all earthly creatures—are made in the image of God and have immortal souls.[1] Since an immortal soul is presumably of higher impersonal value than anything else found in other earthly creatures, the attribution of a soul to humans could explain why humans have a higher impersonal value than other creatures in virtue of which they may deserve or have a right to be better off. If we reject such supernatural ideas as the idea of an immortal soul—in line with the conclusion of 5.2—it is however difficult to find any property that could play the roles requisite to vindicate this idea of an elevated moral status of all humans. What underpins this status has to be a property which (1) is of especially great moral value, and which, since the value is supposed to be intrinsic, (2) is an intrinsic property of all humans, and only humans (among earthlings).[2]

---

[1] This origin has been suggested by, for instance, Veatch (1986), Singer (1993: 88–9), Pojman (1997), and Waldron (2002).

[2] Standardly, it is further claimed by anthropocentric speciesists that all human beings have *the same* or *equal* value, and then a third requirement is necessary: that the property belongs to all humans to the same degree. An immortal soul could meet this requirement, too. But human equality is not our present

The point has often been made (e.g. by Singer, 1993: 117–18; Tooley, 1983: 67; McMahan, 2002: 209–17) that it is hard to see how the property of being a member of the biological species *Homo sapiens*, which apparently satisfies (2), could be thought to satisfy (1) as well, unless this property is conflated with some other property like that of having an immortal soul. Consider two individuals, Alpha and Beta, who have the same mental faculties; they are equally capable of being self-conscious, of acting rationally and morally, of understanding scientific theories, of creating art, of participating in complex social relations and enterprises, and so on. We could even imagine Alpha and Beta to be morphologically alike, to the extent that in everyday circumstances they are indistinguishable. It then seems preposterous to hold that their moral importance or worth could differ, so that, for instance, it might be permissible to kill or enslave one in circumstances in which it would not be permissible to do so to the other. However, this could be true if only one of them is a member of the human species, and this is a ground for special moral worth.

On the most common type of view, species membership is based upon genetic properties, so that for species that reproduce sexually, two populations belong to the same species if and only if members of them are *interfertile*, that is, adult individuals of different sexes of the two populations are capable of mating and producing fertile offspring. According to some of these accounts, there are further necessary conditions for sameness of species, such as this genetic similarity having its source in a common evolutionary origin, but for present purposes we may bracket such conditions.

Now imagine finding out, by means of a genetic test, that only one of Alpha and Beta, who might both be among your friends or acquaintances, is a member of the human species. Surely, it would be unacceptable to propose that, therefore, the other one of the pair does not have the same high moral worth or status as the first one. If so, the property of belonging to the human species does not meet condition (1).

To amplify this conclusion, let us look closer at the property of being a human being. In 2.1 a distinction was drawn between being genetically human and being a human being: a human being is a multi-cellular organism formed out of genetically human cells two to three weeks after conception. It would be implausible to maintain that a cell which is genetically human thereby has a higher value than a cell of a chimpanzee, say. So, it must rather be the case that this value arises when a human being is formed out of such cells. But since, as we saw, this is a gradual process, this is also hard to believe. Thus, the reasonable conclusion is that the fact that an organism is a human being or is a member of the species *Homo sapiens* is not anything that confers value on the organism.

A closer look at the property of being a member of a species also brings out that being a member of the human species fails to meet condition (2) of being an intrinsic

---

topic—it is the topic of Chapter 10; the present topic is whether humans have a higher moral status than non-humans. This is compatible with there being some evaluative variation within the class of humans. I am now concerned with what McMahan has called 'the separation problem' as opposed to 'the equality problem' (2008: 84).

property of humans (cf. Persson and Savulescu, 2010, for an earlier statement of this argument). On the one hand, it seems plausible to think that the relation of belonging to the same species has to be *transitive*: suppose that A (which may be an individual organism or a group of organisms) belongs to the same species as B, and B belongs to the same species as C; then it apparently follows that A belongs to the same species as C. For if A belongs to the species S, so must B, which belongs to the same species as A, and if B belongs to S, so must C, if C belongs to the same species as B. On the other hand, however, it seems that the relation of belonging to the same species *cannot* be transitive, since a reasonable criterion of species membership—such as interfertility—is *not* transitive: if A and B are interfertile, and the same goes for B and C, it does not follow that A and C are interfertile. There may be genetic differences between A and B, and between B and C, each of which are insufficient to block interfertility, but which together build up to block it.

The phenomenon of a *ring species* illustrates this quandary. Consider, for instance, the greater white-headed gulls whose range extends around the northern coasts of the Earth. The herring gull (*Larus argentatus*) and the lesser black-backed gull (*Larus fuscus*), both found in Western Europe, qualify as distinct species, since they are not interfertile and do not interbreed. They are also morphologically and phenotypically quite distinct. But, as we trace populations of lesser black-backed gulls eastwards, along the Siberian coast to North America, they become more and more genotypically and phenotypically similar to herring gulls. Now, if interfertility is a sufficient condition for sameness of species, each of these intermediate forms up to and including the end form would be linked by the relation of belonging to the same species. Consequently, if the relation of being a member of the same species were transitive, the end form must be lesser black-backed gulls, not herring gulls. But this is not only counterintuitive; it is contradictory if interfertility is also necessary for sameness of species, since the gulls at the 'end' of the ring are not interfertile with the lesser black-backs at the 'beginning' of the ring. Hence, we have a paradox on our hands: some gulls both being and not being lesser black-backed. The paradox arises because we have reason to hold both that the relation of being a member of the same biological species is transitive, and that it is not transitive, since interfertility is necessary for it.

In fact, the paradox is not confined to the case of ring species. If the Darwinian theory of evolution is right, and no form of organisms in the evolution from species A to species Z had become extinct, the transitivity of the relation of being members of the same species would lead to the absurd conclusion that all organisms from A to Z would be members of the same species. This is so because this theory holds that they have developed out of each other, and so there will be chains of interfertility linking A to Z, via linking A to B, B to C, and so on all the way to Z. Hence, if the relation of being a member of the same species were transitive, A and Z would belong to the same species, however dissimilar and incapable of interfertility they may be. All organisms that have a common evolutionary origin would belong to the same species—a patent absurdity.

But how can we deny the transitivity of the relation of sameness of species? My proposal is that we should give up the essentialist idea that species membership is a component of the nature or essence of an organism.[3] This idea implies that an organism can belong to one and only one species during its existence, but we should instead accept that it can belong to different species not only at different times of its existence, but even *at the same time*. If we accept this idea, we can explain how B could belong to the same species as both A and C, though A and C belong to different species, S and S*, respectively, by hypothesizing that the intermediate population B belongs to *both* S and S*. If A had been extinct, but everything else was the same, we would classify B as belonging to S* only. Likewise, if C had been extinct, we would classify B as belonging to S only. Thus, what species we classify B as belonging to depends not only on its nature or intrinsic properties, but also on its relations to what other beings there happen to be. In some circumstances, these relations force us to classify B as a member of two species, S and S*.

Thus, the property of being a member of a species fails to satisfy condition (2) of being an intrinsic property of an organism. In themselves individual organisms are not cut out to belong to the same species as some rather than other genetically closely related organisms; how they are grouped depends on what gaps the evolutionary selection conditions have created. Certainly, species classification also depends on genetic properties of individuals that are internal, but these are not sufficient for classification. And it is beyond dispute that they are not all essential properties of the individuals, since a fair number of them might be lost while identity is retained; still less is it essential for the identity of these individuals that the organisms to which they are genetically most similar do not change, or continue to exist. Therefore, species membership is not an essential property of organisms.

We probably have the concept of species because, when we observe biological organisms 'in the field', they come in seemingly distinct 'packages' of similar organisms

---

[3] Often proponents of the biological view of our nature and identity take the position that species membership is essential to an organism. For instance, Michael Ayers writes that 'biological individuals do not change kinds' (1991: vol. II, 87), e.g. one and the same organism cannot undergo a metamorphosis from being a horse to a deer. On the other hand, another proponent of the biological view, DeGrazia, writes: 'Perhaps with enough genetic manipulations I could become a member of another hominid species... What's crucial is that we are essentially animals of *some* kind' (2005: 48–9). It seems to me certain that most of us would be inclined to think that, as long as there is psychological continuity, we could change genetically and morphologically from being animals of one species to another. We could readily imagine ourselves going through the evolution of our species backwards, ceasing to be first humans, then hominids, then primates, then mammals, and so forth. But it seems more questionable whether we could imagine this happening to us when we are in PVS or dead, that it would then be intelligible that numerically the same individual passes through all the transformations indicated. However, the concept of an animal or organism—like the concept of an inorganic thing—would appear to be too general for it to be usable for the purpose of making judgments of numerical identity over time. But it is hard to see what more plausible way there is to obtain greater specificity than by taking the 'kinds' that animals or organisms must belong to as some species, thus making their species membership essential. We have however just seen that this is problematic. I am not sure what is the way out of this impasse, if indeed there is one. I concluded in 3.1 that our conception of our own identity is erroneous; the same might be true of our conception of the identity of biological organisms.

which noticeably differ from other such groups because of the gaps left by organisms who have gone extinct. But such an 'all-or-nothing' concept as that of a species fits the underlying biological reality badly. What we need to capture it is some graded concept, such as degree of genetic relatedness, a scale of diminishing genetic relatedness starting with monozygotic twins who are maximally related.

The conclusion that the property of being a member of the species *Homo sapiens* is not an intrinsic property of us wreaks havoc on the idea that it could be the ground of an intrinsic value of us. Imagine that A is a population of human beings. Imagine, again, that B is interfertile with A and with C, but that A is not interfertile with C. As long as A exists, B is classifiable as a human population, and its members would on the view under consideration have the higher value of humans. But if A goes out of existence, B is only classifiable as being of the same species as C which is not the human species, since C was not interfertile with A. Consequently, B would no longer have the high value of the human species. This goes to show that any value that B might have in virtue of its species membership would not be intrinsic. Moreover, since this property is not an essential property of us, but an accidental property that we could conceivably lose in the course of our existence, the eagerness to hold that it invests us with value is likely to subside.

The conclusion that species membership is not an intrinsic property also undercuts the proposal that membership of the human species could justify why all human individuals should be treated in ways that befit human individuals who have properties that are *characteristic or distinctive* of members of this species, even if they in fact happen to lack these properties. Apart from the fact that it is at best unclear why individuals should be treated in accordance with some properties that are characteristic of some kind to which they belong rather than in accordance with properties that they in fact have, this proposal is a non-starter if membership is not an essential property of biological organisms. For the rationale of the proposal must be that these individuals have some intrinsic—presumably genetic—properties which both (a) make them members of the human species and rule out their being members of some other species, and (b) are somehow the source or origin of the characteristic features. However, we have just seen that there are no intrinsic properties that satisfy condition (a). Granted, there are intrinsic properties that make them members of the human species, but these do not satisfy condition (b) because these beings lack the characteristic features in question. The intrinsic properties which make these individuals human, however, do not rule out their being members of some other species, and this might be a species of which the features characteristic of humans are not characteristic. On the proposal under consideration, this would have the contradictory implication that they need not be treated in accordance with the characteristically human features that they in fact lack.[4]

---

[4] McMahan also argues at length that this proposal is fraught with difficulties (2008: 84–93).

The idea that membership of the human species is a ground for (high) intrinsic value is then indefensible. Nonetheless, this speciesist view is doubtless a part of common-sense morality; so much is evident from our remarkably inconsiderate treatment of non-human animals for the purposes of research and food production. These practices and the doctrine that humans have a higher moral status should be repudiated as an expression of an unjustifiable evaluative elevation of membership of our species, but they are so firmly entrenched in common-sense morality that a morality rectified in this regard is likely to strike most of us as counterintuitive.

I have construed the (fictitious) moral value of being a human being as something that makes what has personal value for human beings add more to the moral value of outcomes than the same personal values for other subjects. This construal fits in with my view that moral values are impersonal values that are dependent on personal values, but other construals which provide impersonal values with a more independent role are also possible (see the quotation from McMahan below). As remarked, many elements of the biographical lives of humans have intrinsic value for them, but normally some elements of their lives also have extrinsic value for the lives of other conscious beings. On my construal of speciesism, this extrinsic value will also be higher if these other beings are human. The central point is however that, on anthropocentric speciesism, the moral value of outcomes would not entirely derive from the amount of personal value that they harbour, but would derive to some extent from the human 'frame' within which those values are embedded. All the same, this speciesism can assume a stronger and even less plausible form to the effect that the fact that a human being is preserved alive in an outcome is in itself—without there being any consciousness and personal value—enough to give it moral value.

At the beginning of this chapter, I hypothesized that the claim that human beings have a special moral status might at bottom be a claim not that membership of the species *Homo sapiens* in itself supplies the basis of this status, but that it is supplied by some other property—like having an immortal soul—which is thought to be correlated with this property. Furthermore, it is a linguistic fact that the term 'human being' hovers between designating *all* members of a certain biological species and designating *paradigmatic* members of this species, members who are paradigmatic in virtue of having characteristically human psychological capacities and dispositions. These capacities and dispositions may then be the real basis of the moral status ascribed to human beings when they are assigned an elevated moral status.

McMahan suggests an account of this type, the 'Intrinsic Worth Account', which states with respect to persons that

> killing is wrong because it involves a failure of respect for the worth of the victim, where the worth of the victim is entirely independent of the value—be it personal value (that is, value to him), instrumental value (value to others), or impersonal value—of the contents of his possible life in the future. (2002: 243)[5]

---

[5] In McMahan (2008: 94ff.) he abandons this view for reasons similar to those that will surface in 10.1.

He is anxious to 'remain agnostic about the basis of the worth that demands respect' (2002: 260), except for the claim that it has to do with properties which make somebody a person. I accept the idea that, as a rule, it is harder to justify morally the killing of a person than of a sentient being, even though the possible future life of the sentient being will harbour more benefits. Also, I accept that often the fact that one person's possible future will harbour less benefits than another person's possible future does not justify killing the former person rather than the latter if the autonomy of the former demands the same degree of respect as the autonomy of the latter, that is, if these people have projects of equal importance to them that could be realized to an equal degree in the futures at their disposal (see e.g. 1.2). But such respect for the autonomy of persons does not imply that a person has a worth that 'is entirely independent of the value...of the contents of his possible life in the future'; and it is a far cry from accepting the thesis that the killing of all innocent, non-consenting persons is equally wrong. For the successful exercise of your autonomy is not independent of the contents of your life: for instance, if future life is bound to be short, there is little space for the exercise of autonomy.

By proclaiming this independence of the worth of persons of the value of their lives, it sounds as though the Intrinsic Worth Account postulates that the basis of the relevant worth is the *possession* of personal capacities rather than their exercise. A capacity for example to exercise autonomy may be an intrinsic feature of a human being, but hardly its *exercise* which is something that is manifested in the biographical life of a human being and usually involves relations to other entities (compare the ambiguity in Harris's view noted in 2.1). According to the accounts of well-being and autonomy that I have proposed, it is however the exercise of psychological capacities rather than the capacities themselves that generates intrinsic personal value. It is various kinds of pleasant experiences and the successful carrying out of life-projects that have intrinsic value for us, and they are features of our lives rather than of us. Our capacity to experience pleasure and to exercise autonomy are features of us, but they have only extrinsic or instrumental value for us. If this was not so, why bother to exercise them rather than being content with simply possessing them, which we can do in a state of dreamless sleep?

Suppose that, due to some change of external circumstances, some people unavoidably drop into a state of dreamless sleep for the rest of their lives. Then, I maintain, death does not harm these people more than it harms human beings who lack these psychological capacities, say, anencephalic infants. The fact that the former are in possession of the relevant capacities makes no evaluative difference if it is guaranteed that they will never more be exercised (and have not been exercised in the past to form future-oriented desires which would be contravened by death). Thus, the value of these capacities is purely instrumental, and it is lost if they can no longer be exercised. This is true even of the capacity to perform morally good actions. Thus, the search for some property, whether biological or psychological, that could endow some beings, as opposed to their biographical lives, with intrinsic value has still left us empty-handed.

Rights theorists could propose that human beings have certain *rights* in virtue of having certain characteristically human capacities. Or the claim might be that human beings *deserve* certain things in virtue of such capacities. Both rights and deserts are (allegedly) features of human beings (or persons) rather than their lives and, thereby, would appear to rest on properties of their subjects. Deserts may seem to have a more intimate connection to value or worth than rights, since it is quite natural to speak of people who deserve rewards as being worth, or worthy of, these rewards. However, these expressions are more apt when people deserve something that is good for them than when what they deserve is bad for them, like blame and punishment. Besides, there is also a link between what we have rights to and what is intrinsically valuable for us, since we are only described as having rights to things from which we are expected to be able to extract something of intrinsic value for us (for example, we are not described as having rights to the waste products that we excrete). Thus, rights are conceptually linked to value just like deserts.

In Part II it will emerge that it is plausible to think that the psychological capacities that are necessary for having rights and deserts are *agential* capacities to perform actions, to acquire things and make use of them, and so on. This is in contrast to the *experiential* capacities, like sentience, required for well-being. But as regards some rights, like the right to the use of your own body, it may be hard to distinguish the relevant agential capacities from experiential capacities. For instance, there is a close relation between the activity of feeling something with some part of your body and the experiential capacity of having feelings and sensations. In the case of the right to your own body, you may intelligibly be equipped with this right without having exercised the relevant agential capacities, but this is not so in the case of the right to property external to your body. Such property must be appropriated by exercises of your agential capacities. Likewise, attributions of desert are frequently made on the basis of actions.

In this chapter I have argued that there is no feature of us, whether we are conceived as humans or persons, that could plausibly be regarded as endowing us with intrinsic moral value. What gives us moral status is that things can have intrinsic value for us. Some, but far from all, of this personal value presupposes the exercise of psychological faculties that organisms of few species other than the human species have, but on the other hand no humans have these faculties—definitional of personhood—throughout their lives, and some humans never have them.

However, the notion of desert brings out that there is another way in which we can have moral worth, a moral worth that is generally higher than that of members of other species (though it is certainly not a worth which all humans or persons would have to the same degree). To be deserving of something is apparently a feature that can be attributed to us, perhaps at least partly on the basis of some intrinsic property of us. But, as will transpire in Chapter 7, although the bases of desert must be of value, their value is typically not intrinsic. The extra intrinsic value that a state of something being valuable for us could derive from desert rather comes from a 'fit' between this value and the value of the desert basis. Thus, we have the following two models of how a state of something being valuable for us can possess extra intrinsic moral value: a 'fit' model, according to which the personal value has to fit in with another, not necessarily intrinsic, value that we have, and a 'frame' model, according to which we have to have an intrinsic value which is simply added to the personal value. The difference between these models manifests itself in the fact that, according to the fit model, the extra moral value obtains only if there is a certain fit or proportion between the degree of personal value and the value, whereas according to the frame model *any* degree of personal value for us will have the extra moral value. I have tried to repudiate the frame model in this chapter, and shall try to do the same with the fit model in Chapter 7.

In this part of the book my chief objective has been to defend and develop an inclusive view of benefiting and reasons of beneficence. Something can be benefited only if it is possible that it acquires consciousness, but it need not have begun to actualize this possibility, or even begun to exist. There are reasons to benefit everything which can be conscious, regardless of whether it has begun to be conscious, whether it exists, or what its species membership is. Such perceptually salient distinctions as between existing and being non-existent, being a member of one species or another, or being alive or dead are both less clear than they appear, and morally insignificant. The topic of Part II is the morally proper distribution of the benefits that the inclusive view doles out. It will attempt to undermine the moral importance of some other perceptually salient distinctions.

PART II
Extreme Egalitarianism

7
The Ground for the Justice of Equality

7.1 A Principle of Just Equality

My objective in this part is to defend *an egalitarian theory of justice or fairness*.[1] In the process of doing so, I shall reject theories to the effect that justice consists in getting what you deserve or what you have a moral right to, by arguing that the concepts of desert and moral rights have no application. This leaves standing *the priority view* or *prioritarianism* as an alternative distributive theory, but in Chapter 9 I shall go on to contend that it is less plausible than egalitarianism.[2] I shall deal with these theories only in their teleological as opposed to deontological form, which roughly concerns the moral value of distributions of benefits in outcomes, regardless of whether they are due to the actions of moral agents.[3]

I shall discuss three aspects of egalitarianism with respect to the distribution of benefits: (1) *the ground or justification* for just equality, (2) *the value* of just equality, and (3) *the degree* of inequality. (1) is the topic of the present chapter, while (2) and (3) are the topics of Chapter 8. The ground or justification here proposed yields an egalitarianism whose extension—that is, the class of beings to which it is applicable—is extreme.[4]

Extreme egalitarians claim:

(E) Justice requires that everyone—who is capable of being well or badly off—be equally well off, unless some autonomously choose to be worse off (thereby creating inequality).

---

[1] I sense a difference in meaning between the terms 'justice' and 'fairness', but I am not sure precisely what it is and shall use them as interchangeable.

[2] There are alternative theories of the distribution of welfare which I shall not examine, for example 'sufficientarian' views which stipulate that distributive concerns apply only up to a threshold at which individuals have 'enough' welfare. See, for example, Crisp (2003) for such a view, and an egalitarian reply by Temkin (2003). I do not see how any such threshold can be other than arbitrary and artificial.

[3] For a detailed discussion of this distinction, see Lippert-Rasmussen (2016: ch. 5).

[4] An alternative label would be 'radical egalitarianism', but it has been used for a different kind of egalitarianism; see Nielsen (1985).

Extreme egalitarians make this claim because they believe in a principle of justice to this effect:

(J) Justice requires that everyone be equally well off, unless there is something that makes it just that some are worse off than others, or some autonomously choose to be worse off.

And they make this negative claim:

(N) There is nothing that can make it just that some are worse or better off than others.

To clarify the role of autonomous choice in (J), consider:

(A) The fact that some autonomously choose to be worse off than others is not anything that makes it just that they are worse off; it makes it *neither just nor unjust* that they are worse off—that is, it makes the concept of justice inapplicable.

The main crux of this argument is premise (N), though (A) needs a good deal of explaining. Apart from implying (A), (J) is a formal principle which is hard to deny. I shall take *restrictive* egalitarians to agree with (J) and differ from extreme egalitarians by denying (N), affirming instead that there *is* something—for instance, a difference as regards deserts or rights—that sometimes makes it just that some are worse or better off than others. Thus, restrictive egalitarians hold that the scope of equality is restricted to those domains in which these just-making factors do not apply to make it just that some are worse or better off than others. How much restrictive egalitarians differ from extreme egalitarians in practice will depend on the size of the area outside the operation of these factors.

There are some shared features of the propositions (E)–(A) that I would like briefly to comment on before I focus on (A) and (N). First, there is the much-discussed problem of the *equalisandum* of equality, of what it is that egalitarians should make individuals equal as regards. Equality between individuals matters only if it is equality in respect of something that *matters to them*. For instance, it does not matter whether we are all equals with respect to having spent an equal amount of time at a certain distance from some fly or other because there is not anything good or bad for us about this. So, it would be misguided to maintain that justice demands equality in this respect.

Furthermore, in the end equality between individuals must be in respect of something that matters to them *for its own sake* or *in itself*. In Chapter 1 I argued that this is well-being and successful exercise of autonomy. This is what I have in mind when I speak of the *equalisandum* as being the amounts or sets of benefits or welfare that individuals get, or how well off they are (welfare being faring well in these two respects). In the end, this is what justice demands that there be equality as regards. It is true that we cannot distribute benefits directly, but have to do so indirectly by distributing resources—money, food, medicine, and so on—which generate benefits and, thus, are extrinsically or instrumentally good. However, equality with respect to such resources matters only so long as they are extrinsically good, or can produce what is of intrinsic value. For instance, the fact some have more money than others does not matter in circumstances in which the currency has lost its validity and the money cannot be used to make anyone better off in intrinsic respects.[5]

To bring out that it is equality with respect to intrinsic rather than extrinsic value that matters in the end, suppose that we live in an indeterminist world such that equality with respect to what is of extrinsic value—whether psycho-physical capacities or external equipment—does not guarantee equality with respect to what has intrinsic value for us. Suppose further that individuals can be provided with an equal amount of either what has extrinsic value for them or what has intrinsic value for them. Then we should surely do the latter and not run the risk that some end up worse in respect of intrinsic value through random events beyond their control when they use what has extrinsic value.

Secondly, there is the problem of the range of just equality of benefits, the extension of the class of beings whose relative levels of benefits can be just or unjust. I have provisionally specified it to be beings who are 'capable of being well or badly off'. It follows from what I just said that these are beings who have, or are capable of having, at least well-being and perhaps also autonomy. So, it is not unjust that cars and carrots are worse off than a lot of human beings because existence can be neither good nor bad for cars and carrots while it is good for these humans. This is not unjust because there is no possibility of cars and carrots being better off than they actually are. For, as they are incapable of consciousness, existence for them can only be of neutral value, neither intrinsically good nor bad.

However, it might also seem true of anencephalic infants that there is no possibility of them being better off than they are since, like cars and carrots, they lack not only consciousness, but even the potential to develop it. Yet, I am inclined to view it as a tragic instance of natural injustice that anencephalic infants, like other disabled humans, are in general worse off than normal humans (contrast McMahan, 2002: 147). It seems possible that in the not too distant future we shall acquire forms of genetic therapy by means of which we shall be able to modify embryos that would otherwise result in anencephalic infants so that they develop an actualizable potential for consciousness. Since these infants belong to a kind of entity for which consciousness is normal, such a genetic modification need not change their nature and identity.

A more general problem about the range of unjust inequality is whether it extends to possible conscious beings that we could bring into existence and, thus, lift above the neutral level of non-existence. In 9.3 I shall give my reasons for a negative answer to this question. It has to do with there being problems concerning how this affects the ratio between the better- and worse-off.

---

[5] For a recent critical survey of such-like alternative *equalisanda*, see Lippert-Rasmussen (2016: ch. 4). His positive proposal is somewhat different from mine, being more suitable for an egalitarianism for persons.

Thirdly, it should be borne in mind that there are other moral considerations alongside justice as equality. In particular, there are (person-affecting) reasons of beneficence exhorting us to see to it that individuals benefit more rather than less. If egalitarians could not appeal to reasons of beneficence, they would not be able to say that it is morally better if beings are equally well off at a higher level of welfare than at a lower level. Now egalitarians could—and should—agree that reasons of beneficence could morally justify that some are better off than others, although this is unjust. This could be because, were a small inequality to reign, everyone would be much better off than they would be were they all equally well off (say, for the reason that everyone benefits from the gifted being stimulated to greater activity by being rewarded). But to say that this outcome would be morally justified is not to say that it would be *just* (or fair), that it is morally justified because it is just.[6] It is instead morally justified because it contains so many more benefits that this outweighs its injustice. I shall later say a bit more about such weighings of considerations of just equality and beneficence. For the present, the point is only that the egalitarian claim that a state is just or fair if and only if everyone is equally well off in it should not be taken to imply that the state is *morally justified* if and only if everyone in it is equally well off.

Let me now turn to (A). The relation between autonomy and the justice of being equally well off is tricky. As I contended in Chapter 1, your successfully exercising autonomy by acting out rational, informed, and free choices is part of what makes things go intrinsically well for you, alongside well-being. Even so, you can make things go less well for you over time by successfully exercising autonomy: you can give away resources that generate well-being, or do things that curtail or relinquish your future capacity for autonomy, for instance cause damage to your brain, or sell yourself into slavery.

Suppose that, in a state in which, justly, everyone is equally well off, some individuals out of love, generosity, and so forth, autonomously transfer some of their benefits to others, friends or loved ones. They effect this transfer because they are concerned about the welfare of these others for its own sake, and more concerned about it than they are concerned about their own welfare (without this being due to their being misinformed or deceived about any relevant facts). The result would be a state in which some are worse off than others but, to my mind, this inequality is not unjust.[7] To say that it is unjust would imply that there was something morally wrong about bringing it about, but there is not. On the other hand, it is not the case that this state of inequality is made *just* by the fact that it arises through an autonomous transfer. Rather, an autonomous transfer has the force of making considerations of justice inapplicable

---

[6] Contrast Rawls's 'general conception of justice' (1971: 62).

[7] Contrast Nozick who writes: 'Patterned distributional principles...do not give the right to choose what to do with what one has; they do not give the right to choose to pursue an end involving (intrinsically, or as a means) the enhancement of another's position' (1974: 167). A plausible principle of equality *does* permit people to enhance the positions of others, though not on such morally illegitimate grounds as that they allegedly deserve or have rights to more, grounds that Nozick endorses.

to its upshot, just as they are inapplicable to autonomous distributions of welfare over one's own life. It follows that a state of equality, though just or in accordance with justice, cannot be said to be *required* by justice in the sense that a deviation from it is perforce unjust.

Imagine that our motivation had been perfectly altruist or benevolent, that is, that we had cared for its own sake at least as much about the welfare of others as about our own. Then I hypothesize that we would have had as little use for the concept of justice in interpersonal distributions of benefits as we now have in the intertemporal distribution of benefits over our own lives. The fact that we would undergo hardships for the greater benefit of others as readily as we now undergo hardships to gain greater benefits in the future would render this concept superfluous. The benefits of others could make up or compensate for our hardships, just as our own future benefits now do (and as many parents regard benefits to their children as doing). In other words, the application of the terminology of justice in its customary morally loaded sense presupposes an application to beings who as a rule do not autonomously choose to be worse off because they are more concerned about the welfare of others than about their own.

Contrariwise, suppose that we were unable to identify with ourselves at future times to the great extent that we now are; suppose that the psychological changes that we were undergoing in the course of a normal life were so drastic that were we to forecast how we shall be in the more distant future, we would confront people who appeared alien to us, with ideals and interests opposed to those that we now cherish. Then we might no longer be willing to regard benefits to them as compensating us for present burdens. If so, there would be a case for bringing the principle of just equality to bear on our intratemporal distribution of benefits within our own lives to see to it that we do not discriminate against our future selves. Thus, this principle is not *by necessity* inapplicable to the intrapersonal distributions of welfare, just as it is not necessarily applicable to interpersonal distributions. Rather, its applicability hinges on contingent psychological facts about identification and benevolence.

The demand for just equality between the welfare of one and the same individuals at different times of their lives independently of such psychological facts runs into obvious difficulties. Either the periods of time chosen are long enough for variations of welfare to be possible, and then it is long enough for demands of just equality to arise within them, or they are so short—'momentary'—that such variations are impossible, and then demands for just equality between them become implausibly excessive. This difficulty carries over to the demand for just equality of welfare between different individuals at various times of their lives, as opposed to with respect to their whole life spans.[8]

Considerations of autonomy, then, are not related to considerations of justice in the same way as considerations of beneficence were above described to be. The latter can

---

[8] Cf. McKerlie (2013: 83–6). Apart from McKerlie (2013: ch. 4), the topic of applying equality to temporal stages of individuals is discussed by Temkin (1993: ch. 8) and Lippert-Rasmussen (2016: 6.2).

make it morally permissible to bring about an unjustly unequal distribution of benefits—not merely by giving away benefits that you could permissibly keep for yourself—when this would significantly increase the sum of benefits. But then considerations of beneficence would *outweigh* considerations of justice, leaving the outcome unjust, though morally justified. By contrast, individuals are morally permitted *from the point of view of justice* to give away to others what is justly theirs, provided the conditions of autonomy are met. So, considerations of autonomy do not outweigh considerations of justice, leaving the outcome unjust. They rather render considerations of justice *inapplicable*, so that an unequal outcome which arises out of exercises of autonomy might be morally permissible because it is not unjust, without it following that it is just.

Autonomy has a similar relation to beneficence. It does not seem wrong from the point of view of beneficence to benefit another, although the benefit to this person is smaller than the damage that you yourself incur in the process. For instance, it does not seem *morally* wrong to sacrifice your own life to save the leg of another. If this decision is criticizable, it is because it fails to be autonomous—through being irrational or misinformed, say—not because it is morally wrong. Morality does not forbid you to favour others at your own expense. It rather sets lowest levels of self-sacrifice below which you are not allowed to fall (exactly where is moot), but no highest level. Such a highest level could easily be counter-productive from the point of view of beneficence, since people often get fewer benefits out of things that they want to give away. Thus, your autonomy permits you to deviate from both the maximization of benefits and the pursuit of justice.

Principles of just distribution must provide some room for autonomy. For instance, employees cannot be paid for their work at every moment. They must be paid at longer intervals, such as every day, week, or month. It is up to the employees themselves to distribute autonomously their money within these periods, since it is assumed that they are concerned about themselves at every point of time. In contexts in which it can be assumed that people care at least as much about others as themselves, such as, for example, the context of parents and their children, benefits may similarly be given to some representatives, with the expectation that they will be spread over the group in a way that best serves the interests of all members of the group.

If, in a state of equality, Alpha transfers some of his benefits to Beta, Beta might become better off not only than Alpha, but also than a third individual, Gamma. Arguably, Gamma cannot then protest that it is unjust that Beta is better off than her if Alpha and Beta together do not possess more than twice as much welfare as her, and Beta has more than Gamma only because Alpha out of love or generosity has autonomously transferred some of his benefits to Beta, who could be supposed to be his spouse. The equality exception in (E) 'unless some autonomously choose to be worse off' could plausibly be taken to cover this situation in which Gamma is worse off than Beta because of Alpha's autonomous choice to be worse off. But at least it should cover this situation if it is supposed that Gamma consents to it, which she should do since it is not based on any morally illegitimate grounds such as desert or rights.

The exception should not just apply to Alpha who is worse off than Beta and Gamma *through his own* autonomous choice.

This three people situation could be compared to the situation in which the lives of two individuals contain an equal number of benefits, but one is better or worse off than the other at the present moment because he has autonomously chosen to distribute his benefits over his life unequally and the other has chosen to distribute her benefits equally. Just as such unequal intrapersonal distributions of justly possessed welfare are morally permitted, so unequal interpersonal distributions of justly possessed welfare between lovers and friends who sympathize or identify with each other could reasonably be permitted.

For similar reasons individuals in a state of just equality are morally permitted to redistribute their welfare by autonomously engaging in a fair *gamble* which will result in some being better off than others. The resulting inequality is not unjust because the participants autonomously choose to do something that will inevitably result in an inequality. Notice that the situation would be different were people offered a lottery which would not, like the one mentioned, merely redistribute the *same* sum of welfare, but which would increase it as well as distribute it unequally. This case brings into play a further reason to undertake the gamble that might make it immoral not to undertake it—if the increase of welfare was big enough and the distribution not too unequal—which I believe a fair gamble among people who equally share a constant sum in itself cannot be.

Suppose, however, that you autonomously decide to try to save someone, though you realize that you risk being injured. (You may even be certain that you will be harmed, like a soldier who throws himself onto an exploding grenade to save his buddies.) Sure enough, you are injured, although you are successful in the rescue operation. If your injury leaves you worse off than others, this is unjust, and you should ideally be compensated for the injury, even though you autonomously accepted the risk of it just as gamblers autonomously accept a risk of losing.

For there is a relevant difference between the rescuer and the gamblers: the rescuer is forced to risk his own welfare to prevent that somebody else suffers a—probably larger—loss of welfare, whereas the gamblers choose to give up their present level of welfare in order to have a small chance of *increasing* it greatly, although they know that this will most probably make them somewhat less well off. It is unjust if the rescuer becomes worse off because he was unlucky enough to find himself in a situation in which he was forced to choose between either himself or someone else becoming (unjustly) worse off. It is not unjust if (most of) the gamblers become worse off because they could have avoided this without anyone becoming worse off. Thus, although the rescuer autonomously chooses to risk making himself worse off, he does not autonomously choose to risk making *someone* worse off: this is a choice that he is *forced* to make, since each available alternative involves such a high probability of somebody becoming worse off that he would not choose it for its own sake.

Such is my defence of (A). Due to (A), my vindication of (N), the claim that there is nothing to make it just that some are better or worse off than others should not lead us to expect that if some are better or worse off than others, this is necessarily unjust. For it may be neither just nor unjust because some have autonomously chosen to be worse off. There are other states that are neither just nor unjust. Consider, for instance, a wholly inanimate universe in which nothing can be good or bad for anything. The fact that this state cannot be called just does not imply that it is unjust; it is neither just nor unjust. However, this is an example of a state of equality—everything being at the neutral level—rather than a state of inequality being neither just nor unjust. Anyway, my claim that there are morally permissible states of inequality of benefits beyond the pale of justice implies that what egalitarians should strive for, strictly speaking, is not just equality, but the absence of unjust inequality.[9]

7.2 Two Just-Making Conditions: Desert and Rights

It is now time to examine (N). I suggest that there are two candidates for factors that could make unequal distributions of benefits just: *deserts* and *rights*. What someone deserves is clearly a consideration of justice: if some deserve to be better off than others, this speaks in favour of it being just or fair that they are better off. Likewise, if some are better off than others due to the fact that they have rights to healthier and better-equipped bodies or more property, this speaks in favour of it being just or fair that they are better off. Furthermore, it would be unjust if somebody capable of recognizing rights were to rob them of their property even if this were the only means by which some who have less than they deserve could be made better off. Thus, intuitively, rights 'trump' desert as, in Ronald Dworkin's well-known phrase, they trump considerations of beneficence.

That rights—more precisely, 'claim' rights, not 'liberty' rights which are mere permissions—have this characteristic follows from the fact that they are correlated with duties or obligations. Every right is had against other people who are capable of recognizing rights. To make intelligible this relation to others, we have to interpret a right to something, such as life or property, as having a reference to others. If your right to these things is construed as negative, it will come out as a right against others that they do *not* interfere with your life or property. The correlative duty is the duty of others not to interfere with your life or property.[10] It would be wrong to put aside this duty in order to give someone what they deserve, just as it would be wrong to put it aside in order to maximize welfare (at least if the gain in welfare is not very great).

Although I cannot prove that there are no further factors, alongside deserts and rights, that are designed to make it just that somebody is better or worse off than somebody

---

[9] This is in line with a claim that I shall make in Chapter 8, namely that just equality as regards welfare is not good in itself, but is merely the absence of the intrinsic badness of unjust inequality (see also Persson, 2003b: 111–13).

[10] A liberty right to X is equivalent to your not being under any duty not to use X. The ground of such a right is simply that nobody (else) has legitimately occupied X. For a fuller account of rights, see Persson (2013: ch. 1).

else, I shall now attempt to show in brief outline that deserts and rights fit together in a way that apparently leaves no space for any further just-making factors. The task that I then set myself in 7.3 is to argue that (N) is true because differences neither in respect of what individuals deserve nor in respect of what they have rights to can make it just that some are better or worse off than others.

When individuals deserve something, they do so in virtue of some features that they have. This has been called *the basis* of desert by Feinberg (1970: 59). A basis of desert is what is supposed to make it just that individuals get what they are said to deserve. I call the latter *the return* (deserved). The return consists in a benefit or burden or, in other words, something that is intrinsically good or bad for the recipient. An obvious example of a basis of someone's desert is the responsible actions that they have performed. Thus, the fact that individuals have responsibly performed good deeds is thought to make it just that they receive something that is good for them in return, and the fact that they have responsibly performed bad deeds is thought to make it just that they receive something that is bad for them. Presumably, there has to be a certain balance or equivalence between the value of the desert basis and the value of the return (where the value of the latter is a value for the recipient, but the value of the former is rather a value for others or an impersonal value). This balance is another complicated matter that I shall not explore here. It is of no great importance if I am right in my argument that the concept of desert has no application.

It might be thought that in order for a desert basis to make the receipt of a return just, the basis must itself be something that the subject *deserves*.[11] For if the basis is not deserved, but is due to fortuitous circumstances or luck, it would seem that an appeal to the (undeserved) basis could make a distribution just as little as a direct appeal to lucky circumstances. If the premise of this argument were correct, advocates of desert would be caught up in a regress which has all the appearance of being vicious. Nozick, however, replies to this objection by claiming that the basis of desert could be something to which you have a *right*—or are entitled—instead of being something deserved. It could consist in things you 'just may *have*, not illegitimately. It needn't be that the foundations underlying desert are themselves deserved, *all the way down*' (1974: 225).

Your own body and its psychological and physical capacities are things to which you could credibly be believed to have a right. John Locke famously writes:

every man has a property in his own person. This nobody has any right to but himself. The labour of his body and the work of his hands, we may say, are properly his. (1690: II. v. 27)[12]

It has been suggested by some rights-theorists that each of us has a right to their own body by being the first one to 'occupy' or make use of it (for instance, see Kamm, 1992: 101). As a consequence of this right to our bodies and their capacities, we might be

---

[11] Rawls (1971: 103–4) opposes such a view.
[12] Locke does not here seem to think it necessary to treat the person and the body separately—he switches from claiming that we have a 'property' in the *person* to implying that the *body* is ours—though he is celebrated for his distinction between them in his *An Essay Concerning Human Understanding* (1689).

thought to have a right to what, thanks to these factors, we make out of unowned natural resources. By this means we extend our rights, so to speak, to our own bodies into the physical world external to them. In Locke's own words:

> Whatsoever, then, he removes out of the state that Nature hath provided and left it in, he hath mixed his labour with it, and joined to it something that is his own, and thereby makes it his property. (1690: II. v. 27)

We can now see the difference between the basis of rights, consisting in first occupancy or appropriation, and the basis of desert.[13] The basis of rights is supposed to make it just that you continue to enjoy or make use of something that it implies that you have put yourself in a position to enjoy or make use of, or that it be returned to you if you have been deprived of it. In contrast, the basis of desert is supposed to make it just that you be in a position to enjoy or make use of something that it does not imply that you are already—or have been—in a position to enjoy or make use of, but that you may have to be given by others. To illustrate, suppose a farmer single-handedly cultivates his own land. Then he has a right to the crop that he in fact gets. But it may be smaller or greater than the crop he deserves—smaller if, despite his great efforts and expenses, the crop is non-proportionally small owing to circumstances beyond his control, such as bad weather. Justice then requires that the farmer receives a greater crop to make up for the hardship that he has incurred by these efforts. In light of such examples, I think that we can discern how deserts supplement rights, leaving no conspicuous room for any further just-making factors.

This comparison of deserts and rights also makes it comprehensible why it is tempting to adopt Nozick's strategy of appealing to rights to stop the regress of desert. If you deserve a return R in virtue of the basis B, R and B are distinct in the sense that you may possess B without possessing R. So, if your possession of B is to be justified as deserved, this may be in terms of the possession of something distinct from B, a basis B*, and so the question arises what justifies your possession of B*. But this question does not arise in the case of rights, since the basis of your right to B consists in something that gives you possession of *B* (before anyone else), and not in something distinct from it. So, the question what gives you the right to the possession of this distinct thing does not arise.

7.3 The 'Demolition' Argument against Just Inequality

The appeal to a right to that which constitutes desert bases is, however, of no avail because the regress argument can be restated in terms of *responsibility* instead of desert (as I have earlier done in 2005: ch. 34, and 2007). While the basis in virtue of which you deserve a return need not be deserved, it must be something for which you are responsible. Otherwise, your getting the return cannot be just. For example, it would not be

---

[13] The distinctive basis of rights makes them vulnerable to arguments which I give in (2013: ch. 2).

deserved and just to punish some infants because they cause their mothers a lot of pain while being born, and reward other infants who cause their mothers little pain. This is surely because these infants are not responsible for the amount of pain that they cause their mothers while being born. Therefore, if it is claimed that it is just that some are better off than others because they deserve more on account of something (e.g. bodily assets) to which they have a right, they must have this right in virtue of something—say, an act of occupancy—for which they are responsible.

Imagine, for instance, that it is claimed that it is just because deserved that some are better off because of the good deeds that they have responsibly performed by making use of psycho-physical capacities to which they have a right in virtue of their being the first occupants of their bodies. Then this can be just only if they are responsible for being the first occupants of these bodies rather than of other bodies or no bodies at all. If it is a matter of circumstances beyond your responsibility whether you find yourself in a well or poorly equipped body, it cannot be just to reward you if you are bodily well-equipped and consequently perform good deeds, and punish you if you are poorly bodily equipped and consequently perform badly. For this is to reward and punish you on the basis of features which are in the end a matter of luck.

It might be objected that the natural distribution of psycho-physical resources can be held to be just if it is viewed as the upshot as a sort of lottery. But this requires that the lottery itself can be regarded as just or fair. A natural lottery cannot, however, be regarded as just or fair because everyone has an equal chance of getting good resources and runs an equal risk of having bad ones. For this presupposes that individuals are 'bare selves' who could be identified independently of all their empirical features, and assigned equal chances of acquiring any possible set of these features.

Another possible objection is to the effect that the distribution of bodies and their psycho-physical capacities, since they are the upshot of non-moral, natural processes, cannot be said to be either just or unjust. It is of course true that this distribution cannot be *motivated* by considerations of justice. But even though a distribution cannot be motivated by justice, it can still be just or in accordance with justice in the sense that it *coincides* with a distribution that would be thus motivated. We have however seen that there can be nothing to make it just or in accordance with justice that some are better off than others—e.g. by getting better bodies—unless this is something for which they are responsible (to which this difference is somehow proportionate). So we arrive at the following claim:

(1) There is nothing that can make it just that some are better off than others, unless this is something for which they are responsible.

For instance, it is just that some are better or worse off than others only if this is proportionate to the greater goodness or badness of deeds for which they are responsible. As the example of the newborns illustrates, it is not just to make individuals better or worse off, to reward or punish them, because they benefit or harm others without being responsible for it.

But when you are responsible for a fact F, you must be so in virtue of certain facts—call them 'responsibility-giving facts'. These facts need not include every fact that is causally necessary for your being responsible for F, through being necessary for the existence of the world or life—for example, such general conditions as the occurrence of the Big Bang, or the presence of oxygen—but could be taken to include only facts which are causally necessary and sufficient to determine, specifically, that the world includes you with the properties that make you responsible for F.

Suppose that you are responsible for F because this is something that you have intentionally brought about. To bring it about that F intentionally, you must have a certain body of information, a character which inclines you to intend to bring it about that F in the light of this information, and abilities that allow you to execute this intention, and so on. It is possible that you are responsible also for these particular responsibility-giving facts, G. But if so, this must be in virtue of certain other responsibility-giving facts, H, which make you responsible for G. Evidently, this regress of responsibility cannot be infinite, as we are temporally finite beings. Instead,

(2) The responsibility-giving facts in virtue of which individuals are responsible are ultimately ones for which they are not responsible, that is, there is nothing for which they are *ultimately* responsible.

In other words, suppose that you are—*directly*, as we may put it—responsible for F, in virtue of your intentions, abilities and so forth. Then you still cannot be ultimately responsible for F, since when we trace backwards in time the responsibility-giving facts in virtue of which you are (directly) responsible for F, we eventually arrive at facts for which you are not (directly) responsible.

It should be stressed that ultimate responsibility cannot be saved by the introduction of an element of indeterminism. For suppose, for instance, that the responsibility-giving facts G do not fully determine the state of your being responsible for F, but that this state is partially undetermined, a matter of chance. Then to that extent you are not responsible for being responsible for F, since you cannot control what is a matter of chance. On the other hand, to the extent that your being responsible for F is determined, it will in the end be determined by facts for which you are not responsible. Again, you would not be ultimately responsible.

If the idea of our being ultimately responsible for anything is incompatible with both determinism and indeterminism, it might seem so manifestly impossible that it might be wondered how it could have become embedded in commonsensical thinking. My answer is that it is ultimate responsibility in an *epistemic* rather than in an ontic sense that is so embedded (cf. Persson, 2005: e.g. 443). That is to say, the causal origin of some facts about us is so obscure that in our commonsensical frame of mind we do not try to probe it. We simply posit these facts as starting points of causal chains. Thus, the ultimacy of a causal fact about us consists in an *absence of speculation* about its causal origin, not in a belief that it is causally determined by ourselves in some mysterious fashion. It follows that ultimate responsibility in the sense at issue is doomed to evaporate as soon as we begin to pry into the causal background of things.

However, some think that ultimate responsibility in a pertinent sense can be salvaged. Susan Hurley writes: 'If responsibility for X requires A's hypothetical choice rather than A's choice or control of X, then regressive responsibility is not impossible' (2003: 29). In other words, Hurley claims that if it were sufficient for one's being responsible for responsibility-giving facts that one *would* choose them to obtain *if* one had a choice in the matter, then regressive—or, in my terminology, ultimate—responsibility would be possible. But, as she realizes (2003: 28–30), hypothetical choice cannot be sufficient for responsibility. For instance, the fact that you would choose to be born in the country in which you in fact happen to be born does not show that you are responsible for being born in it. It follows that Hurley does not after all succeed in showing regressive or ultimate responsibility to be possible (though she claims to have shown it to be possible in a sense I do not understand).

Hurley makes a related claim about luck. Suppose that

> an agent did not choose and does not control the religious beliefs he was brought up with, and their associated burden of guilt. He would, however, have chosen them had he been able to, and would not choose to be without them. Thus, they are not plausibly regarded as matters of luck for him. (2003: 26; cf. 92)

If, through circumstances beyond his control, the agent in this respect turns out to be the way that he would choose to be, though he could easily have turned out in a way that he would choose not to be, I think, *pace* Hurley, that he could count himself *lucky* (for this is something for which he is not responsible), even if he is worse off than others through his feelings of guilt. This indicates that his hypothetical choice might make it the case that it is not unjust that he is worse off than others. If so, it shows that we could construe the justice-excluding condition of the autonomous choice in (E) hypothetically.[14]

Now, it follows from (1) and (2) that

(3) There is nothing that can make it just that some are better off than others for which they are ultimately responsible.

However, in the absence of ultimate responsibility-giving facts, making individuals ultimately responsible, somebody's being better off on the basis of what they are

---

[14] This is Jerry Cohen's view (1989: 935–9). There is much that I find congenial in Cohen's claim that the purpose of egalitarianism 'is to eliminate *involuntary disadvantage*, by which I (stipulatively) mean disadvantage for which the sufferer cannot be held responsible, since it does not appropriately reflect choices that he has made or is making or would make' (1989: 916). But if the condition of (autonomous) choice is widened to actual *or* hypothetical choice then, as I have argued, it is no longer sufficient for responsibility for the object of choice. That Cohen overlooks this is indicated also when he maintains, falsely, that hypothetical choice 'is strictly inconsistent with luck' (1989: 938). It seems that he mistakenly assumes that hypothetical choice is inconsistent with luck because it implies responsibility. However, even if the widened choice condition does not rule out luck (by ensuring responsibility), it could still rule out injustice, for reasons implied by my argument above.

directly responsible for can be just as little as it can be just that some infants are made better off than others because they cause their mothers little pain while being born. In neither case can this be just because that which is supposed to make just the differences in well-being are differences that are in the end due to factors beyond the subject's responsibility:

> (4) If there is nothing that can make it just that some are better off than others for which they are ultimately responsible, nothing for which they are directly responsible can make this just, since ultimately there is no responsibility for the facts in virtue of which they are directly responsible.

For this would mean that they are in the end better off because of properties on the basis of which it is agreed that it cannot be just that they are better off. It cannot be just that some are better off than others, on the basis of properties that they are guaranteed to have by properties that they are not responsible for having and that the others are prevented from having through lacking properties beyond their responsibility.

Imagine that a return R is held to be justly yours in terms of your being directly responsible for F, and it turns out that you are directly responsible for F in virtue of certain responsibility-giving facts, G, for which you are directly responsible in virtue of H, for which you are not directly responsible. Then, since you are not ultimately responsible for F, it is after all not just that you receive R on the basis of your (direct) responsibility for F. The rationale of the idea that it is just to give you R, whose value for you is equivalent to the value of F, only if you are responsible for F is that the value of F then is due to what flows from what is within your responsibility, and nothing else. But this rationale is undercut if F in the end turns out to flow from something external to your responsibility, just as it would be undercut if it had been false that you are directly responsible for F (like, for instance, the newborns for the pain that they cause their mothers). There is no plausibility in the idea that justice consists in an equivalence between the value of the return for *you* and the value of a contribution to the world which is only mediately within your responsibility. For then the value of this contribution in the end comes from something other than from what you are responsible for, and this does not make it just that *you* enjoy the value of the return.[15]

From (3) and (4) it follows that

> (5) There is nothing that can make it just that some are better off than others for which they are responsible.

More fully, there is nothing that can make it just that some are better off than others for which they are responsible in a sense required to make this inequality just, namely the sense of ultimate responsibility. Finally, (1) and (5) yield

---

[15] This is how I would reply to Victor Tadros who objects that proponents of this argument 'offer no real argument to those who deny that desert could only be true if contra-causal or ultimate responsibility is true' (2013: 62).

(6) There is nothing that can make it just that some are better off than others.[16]

That is, we have derived (N). But (N) in conjunction with the principle (J) establishes the extreme egalitarian view (E), that justice requires everyone to be equally well off, unless some autonomously choose—or would choose—to be worse off (which places an unequal outcome beyond the pale of justice).

This argument is consistent with—indeed, it presupposes—that there is responsibility in the direct sense. Direct responsibility is sufficient for a 'forward-looking' moral justification of the practice of rewarding and punishing, in terms of the future beneficial consequences of this practice. For if you are directly responsible for your actions in virtue of acting on the basis of certain intentions you have, rewards and punishments can change your future behaviour—to the benefit of all—by providing you with reasons to form different intentions in the future.

In the present context, it is important for at least two reasons to realize that we *are* responsible in some sense. First, if we were not responsible for anything, it would seem that there could not be anything that we morally or rationally *ought* to do, such as to benefit beings and reduce unjust inequality as regards the distribution of their benefits. For if we ought to do something, we must be responsible for whether or not we do it.[17] Secondly, it is a link to some conception of responsibility that renders it comprehensible why autonomously choosing to be worse off fails to make an outcome unjust. But the responsibility here involved is direct, not ultimate, responsibility. It need not be ultimate because autonomous choice does not make an unequal outcome just.

Ultimate responsibility is required by the 'backward-looking' justification of responsibility which is in play when it is held that rewarding or punishing you could be just, because deserved, in view of what you have done or are, that is, your contribution to the value of the world. Here the claim is that the fact that there is an equivalence or proportion between the value of this return for you and the value of a contribution that you are ultimately responsible for makes your receiving the return just. If there is nothing for which you are ultimately responsible, but everything that is valuable about you stems from factors outside your responsibility—as surely must be the case since you are a finite being—it cannot be just that you receive something whose value for you is equivalent to the value of any of your contributions that in the end do not flow from you. We do not have, then, an ultimate responsibility that could prevent inequality in respect of benefits from being unjust, by making it just, whereas we do have a direct

---

[16] This sort of argument is presaged by Sidgwick, albeit he remarks that it leads to 'such a precipice of paradox that Common Sense is likely to abandon it' (1907: 284). Similar arguments have been advanced by Nagel (1979) and Galen Strawson (1999). In reply to Strawson, Mele claims that freedom might be conceived as an 'emergent' property rather than a 'transmitted' property (1995: 224–5). As regards the notion that I have been focusing on, responsibility, I concede that direct responsibility is 'emergent', but it is self-contradictory to construe ultimate responsibility as emergent.

[17] In this respect, I agree with Hurley, who argues that egalitarianism cannot survive the rejection of all responsibility (2003: 175). But I believe that an egalitarianism worth its salt should reject deserts and rights along with ultimate responsibility.

responsibility that could prevent this inequality from being unjust—by making it autonomously chosen—without, however, making it just.

To sum up. The state in which some individuals are better off than others can be just only if it is based on some fact F concerning them (say, their having done certain good deeds) for which they are responsible. But since we are always responsible for something, such as F, in virtue of other facts, G (for instance, the formation of a certain intention and the possession of certain abilities), the question arises why G is a fact. If we are not responsible for G, it seems that it cannot after all be just for us to be better (or worse) off on the basis of F, for which we are (directly) responsible, than it would be if we were not responsible for F, since indirectly this is to be better off on the basis of properties for which we are not responsible. If we are responsible for G due to some other fact about us, H, the same question of responsibility arises as regards H. But eventually, since we are temporally finite beings, we are bound to arrive at responsibility-giving facts for which we are not responsible; the regress of responsibility cannot be infinite. So, we cannot possess the ultimate responsibility which is requisite to make it just that some are better off than others. But such an unequal distribution of welfare can be morally justified in other terms, such as those of beneficence or autonomy, since these forms of justification require only direct responsibility.

This constitutes my defence of (N), which along with (J) yields extreme egalitarianism, (E). It may be called *the demolition defence* of egalitarianism because it demolishes grounds which are designed to make inequality just. Compare its conclusion, (E), with the familiar view called *luck-egalitarianism*, roughly, the view that inequality is unjust or unfair if and only if the fact that some are worse off than others is due to their bad luck.[18] What this is tantamount to, more precisely, depends on what is put down to bad luck. On one kind of account it is unjust or unfair and, thus, bad in itself, just in case some are worse off than others through no fault or voluntary choice of their own (see e.g. Temkin, 1993: 13). This claim assumes that it is not unjust if it is the worse-off's own fault that they are worse off because then it is not due to bad luck. The worse-off may then be thought to deserve or have a right to no more than they have, while the better-off deserve or have a right to more. If so, this claim is evidently compatible with just-making factors like deserts and rights being in operation. Since the applicability of these factors is so elastic, due to the grounds for their applicability being so elusive and contestable, the risk is that, if they are allowed any application at all, they will spread and restrict the range of just equality so much that an egalitarianism worth its salt no

---

[18] Lippert-Rasmussen takes 'the core luck egalitarian claim' to state only a sufficient condition (2016: 1–2), but that cannot be right. The claim that it is unjust if some are worse than others through their bad luck is compatible with the claim that it is also unjust if they are worse off through factors that negate bad luck, such as voluntary choice. In fact, the claim that it is unjust if some are worse off than others, *irrespective of the explanation of this*, is compatible with the 'core' claim, but not with luck egalitarianism. So, the 'core' claim needs to be strengthened. It may be argued that the strengthening would have to be more complex than what I have suggested, but my statement will do for present purposes. It can be seen as expressing *pure* luck egalitarianism, unmixed by elements of other views.

longer remains. (As remarked earlier, it is also too narrow to talk about being worse off *through one's own* choices.)

On the other hand, extreme egalitarianism is in one way less extreme than utilitarianism, since the latter rejects justice along with desert and rights. Therefore, utilitarians do not acknowledge a principle like (J) which I find no reason to contest. Utilitarian principles of equality, like Singer's principle of equal consideration of interests, is another kind of egalitarianism which is not worth its salt. Singer's principle is to the effect that 'we give equal weight in our moral deliberations to the like interests of all those affected by our actions' (1993: 21). According to his reading of it, this principle is utilitarian because he takes 'like' to mean like *in respect of strength*, disregarding—controversially—differences in respect of other intrinsic properties of interests, such as their objectives. Following this principle, thus read, can lead to widening the gap between the better-off and the worse-off when the interests of the better-off happen to be stronger than the interests of the worse-off. For true egalitarians, this is an unacceptable result; there is for them a moral reason to benefit the worse-off rather than the better-off, even if the benefits then bestowed are smaller.

7.4 Self-Defence and Responsibility as Causally Based

I have contended that underlying the conceptual scheme of deserts and rights there is a conception of responsibility that is untenable because it assumes that responsibility can be ultimate. However, common sense seems to deem us responsible in a morally potent sense simply because we are the cause of something, even though we are not seen as an (epistemically) ultimate cause. The meaning of 'being responsible for' then appears indistinguishable from 'being a cause of', just as it is when we say things like 'The flooding is responsible for many deaths'.

I take this to be so in some situations in which, according to common-sense morality, we seem permitted to enforce our right to life and limb, even if this means that the equally stringent rights of others are infringed. Consider situations in which someone innocently—that is, in such a way that they cannot reasonably be thought to have forfeited their right to life—poses a threat to your life. Many hold that you are permitted to kill such an innocent threat if this is necessary to protect your own life. To use Nozick's well-known illustration of an innocent threat (1974: 34): if somebody forces you to fall down on me at the bottom of a well, many would say that I would be permitted to use my ray gun to make your body disintegrate in order to prevent myself from being crushed to death by its impact.

In this case it is however evident that you would not be the ultimate cause of my death, since it is readily seen that your fall is an effect of somebody else's push. I think that for this reason we would be reluctant to say that you *deserve* to be killed, or have a *duty* to let yourself be killed, though we believe I would be permitted to kill you. It is simply the fact that you would otherwise be the cause of my death that is thought to justify this permission. But this fact is not sufficient to justify your deserving or having a duty to undergo harm.[19] To see this, imagine that you and I are sitting in a forest, waiting for game. As I am about to doze off, a deer appears. To make me wake up, you push my gun in the direction of the deer. I startle and fire a shot that kills it. In these circumstances, I think that intuition tells us that it is you rather than me who deserves or has a right to the deer, even though I killed it. Nevertheless, simply because I would be the killer, Vic would arguably be permitted to kill me would my gunshot hit him instead of the deer, and killing me were necessary to preserve his own life. It is in the present context important to see that this view about the permissibility of self-defence is dubious because it might well result in someone being worse off through bad luck and, thus, be at odds with what justice (as well as inclusive beneficence) requires.

Tadros, however, proposes a defence of the permission of killing innocent threats to our lives along the following lines (2013: 251–6). It strikes him as 'highly intuitive' that 'a person has special responsibility to ensure that her body is not the source of a threat' (2013: 252). He is aware of the objection that this idea is hard to buy in situations in which 'it is a matter of luck whether my body rather than the bodies of others poses a threat' (2013: 253). His most important response to this objection is that a 'person's body is so intimately bound up with the person that failing to prevent one's body harming' is failing 'to *prevent myself from harming you* rather than failing to rescue you from a threat that has nothing to do with me' (2013: 255). In other words,

> It is the fact that I am responsible for what my body does, even when that is not a product of my agency, that gives rise to the permission to harm innocent attackers and threats. And I bear that responsibility because my body *is me*. (2013: 255)

But, granting at least for the sake of the argument that we are our bodies, we still need an account of how it could follow from this claim that we have a special *moral responsibility* for our (bodies) doing harm even when this is not a product of our (intentional) agency, and is beyond our control. The latter reasonably implies that we are *not* responsible in a morally potent sense, such that we can be held to have forfeited any rights. Tadros does not offer any such account, but although he fails to justify it, he has expressed the commonsensical sentiment that to some measure we bear moral responsibility for something simply because we/our bodies are the causes of it.

---

[19] Fiona Woollard claims that the protection against imposition on us offered by the act-omission doctrine's constraint on harming 'is necessary if anything is to genuinely belong to anyone' (2014: 105). But I think that the commonsensical permission that we possess to defend ourselves against innocent threats shows that this claim is not true, for this permission seems to allow us to defend ourselves even if this involves *causing* somewhat *greater* harm to the threats than this act saves us from (see e.g. Kamm, 1992: 47). And does not this fact that the harm that we could permissibly cause could be somewhat greater than the harm that we are thereby saved from—which is contrary to the act-omission doctrine—show that we have a special relation to ourselves/our bodies, a relation that could be called belonging? I have argued elsewhere (2013: chs. 3 and 4) that the act-omission doctrine involves a theory of negative rights in addition to causally based responsibility. It is the latter that makes it impermissible to violate one right in order to prevent the violation of a larger number of rights.

It may however be wondered whether, contrary to his proposal, the common-sensical permission to kill innocent threats to our lives does not extend to situations in which it is not our bodies that directly pose the threats to the lives of others, but other things that we have innocently causally affected with our bodies. For instance, if you have innocently set in motion a boulder that will crush me if I do not drag you in its path, it seems that I am as much permitted to do so as I would be permitted to protect myself by interposing some object with the result that you die instead of me if you were innocently falling down on me.

McMahan, however, wants to enter a qualification. Within the class of innocent threats, he draws a distinction between those who are responsible for the threats they pose and those who are not (2002: 10.1). His view is that it is only permissible to kill the former in self-defence. He writes of a driver who 'always exercises reasonable caution in driving and maintaining the safety of his vehicle', but who because of 'an improbable mechanical failure' loses control of his vehicle and veers towards a pedestrian that

> he *is* morally responsible for the threat he poses. He chose to drive knowing that there was a small risk that he would lose control of his vehicle and imperil the lives of others. This, I believe, constitutes a sufficient asymmetry between him and and the pedestrian to make it permissible, as a matter of justice, for the pedestrian to kill him in self-defense. (2002: 403)

To my mind, however, this driver seems no more morally responsible for posing a threat to the pedestrian than the latter is morally responsible for being threatened. The pedestrian also knew—or could reasonably be expected to know—that there was a small risk that, if he set out for a walk, his life would be imperilled by some car that went out of control, even if he were to exercise all reasonable precaution. Certainly, the risk was so small that the pedestrian is not at fault, or blameable for his action but, as McMahan grants, the same is true of the driver. Therefore, I cannot see that there is any asymmetry between the driver and pedestrian which could make it just that the former rather than the latter dies. If we feel that the driver dies, this is, I conjecture, because we are in the grip of a conception of responsibility as causally based on which (what we select as) the cause of harm comes out as responsible for it.

I shall then take it that there is no morally relevant difference between this driver and an innocent threat who McMahan would regard as non-responsible, for example you when you fall down on me because of a totally unpredictable gust of wind or earth tremor. In this case, the probability of this happening might be smaller than the probability of a mechanical failure of a car, but the pertinent point is that in both cases the probability is so small that the agent is not at fault. On my view, innocent (life) threats do not forfeit their right to life because they are not morally responsible for the threats they pose. Some writers, however, who take a more permissive stance on the killing of such threats in self-defence than McMahan, differ from him (2002: 405) in regarding it as impermissible to kill innocent *bystanders*—who have played no causal role in the creation of a threat—in order to save our skins. This is the view that I would now like to discuss because it, too, seems to rest on a conception of responsibility as causally based.

For example, Tadros (2013: 247) claims that it is not permissible for me to deflect a threat—like a falling boulder—from myself if, as a side-effect, it instead kills you who are innocently standing next to me. Contrast this with his view that if the wind has forced you off a height, and you are falling down on me, I *would* be permitted to deflect you, with the result that instead of my body cushioning your landing so that you will escape unscathed, you will land on the hard ground and be killed. The most conspicuous difference between these cases is that in the latter case it is you and not a boulder who are threatening to cause my death. Thus, the intuitive contrast between these cases is evidence of the commonsensical sentiment that responsibility attaches to those who are seen as (proximate) causes of harm. But we are left with the question how this sentiment could be justified: how could the fact that it is you who are threatening to cause my death justify my killing you if the causing is not responsible, but you are as innocent with respect to my death in this situation as when you are a (causally inactive) bystander who I am not permitted to kill in order to save myself?

To make the force of this question clearer, suppose that another person is swept from the height simultaneously with you, but that this person happens to fall towards a mattress which is lying next to me, so that he would survive unscathed. Suppose further that if I deflect you away from me, I have to deflect you towards the mattress, but then your body will collide with the body of your 'by-faller', with the result that he will land outside the mattress and die. Since it is just a matter of luck where the wind causes the two of you to fall, it is hard to understand how I could be permitted to deflect you, an innocent threat to me, in a direction that will kill you—as we saw in the preceding paragraph—but not in a direction that will turn you into an innocent threat to your innocent by-faller and kill him. After all, what I would be doing to you in the latter case is something that (a) you would be permitted to do yourself could you steer you fall, and have no reason to object to, and (b) your by-faller would have no *moral* reason (though a reason of self-interest) to object to were you to do it, since you are hardly morally obliged to be an innocent threat to me rather than to him. This is surely a matter that you would be allowed to let a flip of a coin determine. Analogously, I would be allowed to deflect you if I cannot tell whether the outcome will be that you or your by-faller will end up outside the mattress.

Returning to the scenario without a by-faller, it might be pointed out that another difference between you and the boulder falling is that, when you are falling, you would be taking advantage of my body to cushion your landing if I do not deflect you. Since you have no right to that advantage, I am permitted to deflect you. We can however modify the case of the falling boulder, so that it, too, would involve your taking advantage of my body. Imagine that my crushed body would make the boulder stick to the ground, and if it had not, the boulder would have rolled on and killed you. Then, if I do not deflect the boulder, I would be letting you take advantage of my body, and this is certainly nothing that you have a right to demand of me. But it would be odd if this fact was necessary to make it permissible for me to deflect the boulder on to you. If it is not, we come back to the view that the morally crucial difference between the cases of you and the boulder falling must be thought to lie in what would be the physical cause of my death, and we have seen no reason to accept that this could make up a moral difference.

To make things more complicated, it is, intuitively, also of moral relevance when you are an innocent bystander what I would be doing to escape a threat to my life, whether I would be killing you/*causing* your death, or enabling it to be caused. For it seems clear that I would be permitted to step aside with the result that the falling boulder instead hits the ground, even though I foresee that it will then start rolling and kill you instead. In this case, I do not *kill* you, or cause your death, by causing the boulder to hit you; I rather *enable* it to do so, by causing *something else*, namely a movement of my body. This is like a case in which by ducking I enable a lethal projectile instead to hit you who are standing behind me in that I enable something to be caused by removing an obstacle to an ongoing causal process. Intuitively, this is something that I am permitted to do, as long as the obstacle is something to which I have at least as much right as you.

But then it seems that I must also be permitted to *deflect* the boulder so that it lands on the ground, but on a spot where I foresee that it will roll and kill you. For how could it make a moral difference whether I bring about the rolling of the boulder by changing the trajectory of its fall or the position of my body, if the boulder is an object that I have at least as much right to manipulate as anyone else? But if I am allowed this act of deflection, why am I not allowed to deflect it *directly* at you? How could it make any moral difference that a sequence of rolling is interposed in one case when I can predict your death with the same certainty in both cases? Your death is in both cases a side-effect of the act of deflection which saves me, the difference being that in one case this side-effect occurs more directly.

Thus, consideration of this series of cases makes it hard to understand how I can be allowed to step out of the way of the boulder, but not deflect it at you. However, if I am allowed to deflect the boulder at you, I am allowed to kill you when you are a bystander just as when you are an innocent threat. Consequently, the fact that you are the cause that is threatening me again turns out to be morally irrelevant on closer inspection.

Suppose again that in the situation in which I am stepping out of the way of the boulder, it is also true that if my crushed body were not present to glue the boulder to the ground, it would have rolled on and killed you. Then my stepping aside makes this case similar to another case discussed by Tadros in which you and I are chased by a hungry bear. He asserts that in this case I am permitted to outrun you, though I foresee that as a consequence you will be killed by the bear. In other words, I am not required to refrain from outrunning you as a means of saving myself from the jaws of the bear—for this would involve letting myself be 'available as a means to save you' (2013: 211). But, then, I surely cannot be required to refrain from stepping out of the way of the boulder when this act would involve, as a foreseen side-effect, its rolling on to kill you because this would also involve letting myself be 'available as a means to save you'. These cases are also similar in that, by avoiding a threat to my life, I am enabling it to kill you.

In the bear case, I may be said to be using you as a means to my survival, since the fact that the bear could satiate its hunger by eating you plausibly makes it stop chasing me. We can however modify the boulder case to incorporate this feature as well: imagine that if your body had not been there to be crushed by the rolling boulder, it would have rolled on towards me and killed me instead. If I am permitted to outrun you in the bear case, I must be permitted to step out of the way of the boulder in this case, foreseeing that this would involve, as a side-effect, my using you as a means to my survival. It might be thought that my using your smashed body as a means should make it harder for me to justify avoiding the boulder but, at least according to my intuition, it does not make any moral difference. Perhaps the reason for this is that, although it amounts to my using you as a means, my stepping aside does not in itself involve any *additional* harm to you, over and above what you would have suffered if your crushed body had not done me the favour of serving as a glue. Nor does the fact that my smashed body would serve as a means to your survival make my stepping aside more justifiable. To my mind, it rather provides something of a reason against stepping aside, since something good would have come out of my refraining from it, though this is not to say that my stepping aside would be impermissible.

These considerations suggest that it is not harder morally to justify harming as a means than as a side-effect. For I have suggested that it is not harder to justify my stepping out of the way of the falling boulder when this involves, as a side-effect, using you harmfully as a means to my survival than when you are harmed to the same extent merely as a side-effect. This is not the place to engage in any fuller discussion of doctrines that propose restrictions on harming as means, like the doctrine of the double effect. I have elsewhere (2013: ch. 6) tried to show at length how this doctrine is underpinned by causally based responsibility and should be rejected along with it. In 10.2 I shall have occasion to supplement this argument.

In the same work (2013: ch. 4), I also argue that the other main deontological doctrine, the act-omission doctrine, is another manifestation of the fact that the commonsensical conception of responsibility is causally based in a way that is hard to justify. When we let something happen by omitting or refraining from acting, we do not cause it to happen; so, it is to be expected that, on the basis of a conception of responsibility as causally based, we shall bear little, if any, responsibility for what happens. In the process I argue against accounts which construe instances of removing obstacles that in some sense belong to the removers as instances of letting happen (2013: ch. 3). Always when we remove obstacles, we cause something, but for this reason I would say that it is *acting*, not letting something happen. Notwithstanding this—to highlight a fact which the view that I am opposing is hard put to make sense of—when we remove an obstacle to an ongoing process, we may be letting something happen *as well*: for instance, if we are in a position to return the obstacle to its original place, but refrain from so doing, we may thereby be allowing the process to run its course. Thereby, we might enable something to be caused. But when we remove an obstacle, we are *never just* letting something happen. We might also introduce a new cause of death, for example the removal of a life-protecting shield could cause a victim to die of shock. Then we would not just enable something to kill, but rather kill or cause death.

Suppose that causally based responsibility goes by the board along with rights and deserts. Then it follows that what is morally right in cases like the ones examined in this section, as well as in others, should be settled by what remains of morality after the rejection, which I suggest is an inclusive principle of beneficence according to which we have reason to do what makes as many as well off as possible, and a principle of justice according to which we have reason to make lives as equal as regards welfare as possible, unless some autonomously choose to be worse off.

Tadros remarks that

we have good reason to object to the idea that those who have more power are permitted to use that power against those who have less... The weak will convincingly complain that it is unfair that their bad luck in being physically weaker has this impact on their prospects of surviving.

(2013: 208; cf. 259)

I agree, and in this section I have attempted to show that commonsense morality in virtue of the fact that it features causally based responsibility, even without the accompaniment of ultimate responsibility, permits those who are lucky enough to 'have more power... to use that power against those who have less', for instance when they are innocent threats, and even if it means inflicting a bit more harm than they themselves would have suffered (see e.g. Kamm, 1992: 47). My proposal is that who will have to die is rather to be determined by the two principles mentioned. Earlier in this chapter, I argued that an appeal to rights and deserts, which does involve ultimate responsibility, also allows good and bad luck to infect moral deliberation with injustice.

8
The Badness of Unjust Inequality

There is not necessarily anything bad about an inequality in respect of benefits that is not just. This is because, as I argued in 7.1, it does not follow that such an inequality is unjust, since some individuals might autonomously have chosen to be worse off. By contrast, there is necessarily something bad about an unjust inequality of welfare. But I shall now go on to argue that there is not anything intrinsically good about just equality of welfare over and above the goodness of its welfare; the value of just equality consists merely in the exclusion of the intrinsic badness of unjust inequality. Thus, the justice of equality is not analogous to pleasure which is intrinsically good, but rather to the absence of pain (though injustice is impersonally bad, not personally bad like pain). I refer to this view as *anti-inegalitarianism*.[1] I shall then move on to consider the question of when one outcome is worse than another in respect of inequality of welfare, and suggest that this is so (a) the greater the number of those worse off than the average is, and/or (b) the more each of them must obtain from the better-off in order for them to be on the average level.

To see the plausibility of anti-inegalitarianism, imagine first that, contrary to the demolition defence, the concept of desert were applicable to individuals, and that justice consisted in individuals getting what they deserve. Then there would be a rationale for holding justice, that is, the 'fit' or 'match' between the desert and receipt levels of individuals, to be something intrinsically good which makes the value of a just outcome exceed the value of the sum of the benefits it contains (see, for instance, Feldman, 1995: 197). Likewise, if there were rights, and justice consisted in receiving that to which you are entitled or have a right. It could plausibly be held that there is something good about individuals having things to which they have rights over and above the degree to which they are benefited by the use of these things. Such instances of justice would be an *intra*personal matter, consisting in a relation between features of a single person.

If, in accordance with the demolition defence, the notions of desert and rights are denied application, justice will be an entirely *inter*personal matter, demanding that all be at the *same* level, whatever it may be. Is this equality intrinsically good? This does

[1] Cf. Parfit's remark that 'the heart' of telic egalitarianism is the claim that '*in*equality has *dis*value', but he adds that it is 'pedantic' to insist on this formulation rather than the more familiar one that 'equality has value' (1995: 5). I have earlier stated anti-inegalitarianism in (2003b), and this chapter largely derives from that paper.

not seem to be an attractive view. For instance, imagine that we all became equally well off at the neutral level by being robbed of everything that is intrinsically good or bad for us, perhaps by entering a persistent vegetative state. Surely, there is nothing intrinsically good about this state, though there is just equality in respect of benefits. On the demolition defence, we are free to endorse this view, since there is nothing in this defence that suggests that the feature of being a just equality in respect of benefits is something that adds positively to the value of the benefits. If there were some such extra value, it would follow that an autonomous choice which disrupts the equality would make the outcome worse in one respect, but that seems implausible.

As a matter of fact, there is something intrinsically good about a state of just equality in respect of welfare if and only if the individuals being equally well-off lead lives that are overall intrinsically good for them. So, if they lead lives that are overall intrinsically bad for them, their being in a state of just equality does not prevent the outcome from being *wholly* bad, whereas if they lead lives that are indifferent to them, it might be perfectly neutral. This is implied by my claim that the fact that an outcome exemplifies just equality in respect of benefits is not anything that adds to the impersonal or moral value that the outcome has in virtue of the sum of benefits that it contains; its total value equals the value of the sum of the benefits that it contains.

In contrast, the fact that an outcome exemplifies unjust inequality in respect of benefits is something that *detracts* from the value that it has in virtue of its sum of benefits, making it less than this value. Thus, unjust inequality is something that is intrinsically bad. It is my view that those who hold unjust inequality to be intrinsically bad should do so because they sympathize with the worse-off and regret what the worse-off unjustly lose due to the existing sum of benefits not being equally distributed. Accordingly, these anti-inegalitarians think that a state of unjust inequality is morally bad in itself to the extent that from the value of its sum of benefits a value should be subtracted that equals the amount of benefits that needs to be transferred from those better off than the average to those worse off than it for the total sum to be equally distributed.

This brand of egalitarianism is aptly called 'anti-inegalitarianism' because of its affirmation of the intrinsic badness of unjust inequality and its denial of the intrinsic goodness of just equality. It should be stressed that the intrinsic badness of injustice is impersonal. Perhaps this is most easily seen if, for the sake of illustration, we assume that justice consists in getting what you deserve. Suppose that you are a sinner and deserve to suffer, but that you are instead blissfully happy. Since it is, by hypothesis, unjust that you enjoy this happiness, there is something intrinsically bad about your enjoying it. However, it clearly is not bad *for* you to enjoy it; nor need it be bad for anyone else. It is rather *impersonally* bad, or bad *simpliciter*.

My claim is, then, that a state of unjust inequality (in respect of the distribution of benefits) is impersonally bad in itself. More precisely, it is that this state of inequality is impersonally bad in itself *in virtue of exemplifying the property of being unjust*. Thus, it is the exemplification of this property that makes the state impersonally bad in itself, not its exemplification of the property of being an inequality (in respect of benefits). As a consequence, the impersonal badness in itself of a state of unjust inequality should be compared not to the personal badness in itself of a sensation of pain but, say, to a painfully hot sensation, which is personally bad in itself in virtue of exemplifying the property of pain, not heat. The impersonal value of a state of just equality is then analogous to the personal value of a sensation, which, in virtue of its more moderate thermal quality, lacks any property that is personally bad in itself rather than possessing a property that is personally good in itself.

I now turn to the question of how my anti-inegalitarianism ranks the badness of different unjust inequalities in respect of benefits. This is a question that Larry Temkin (1993) has penetratingly and exhaustively explored: what are the conditions for one state of unjust inequality as regards welfare being in itself worse than another in respect of inequality? I shall merely put forward an answer that I think is at least as plausible as any other—rather than definitely the most plausible—to this question, referring readers who want a fuller discussion to Temkin's magisterial book.

If the badness of unjust inequality as regards benefits consists in the badness of some individuals being unjustly worse off than they would have been if there had been an equal distribution of the benefits contained in this outcome, an outcome seems worse in respect of inequality if either *more* individuals are worse off than the average, or some of them are worse off to a *greater degree*. In other words, we have a *general formula* for the ranking of the badness of unjust inequalities along these lines:

(GF) An outcome of unjust inequality as regards welfare is worse in respect of inequality (a) the greater the number of those worse off than the average is, and/or (b) the more each of them needs to have from the better-off in order for them to be on the average level or, in other words, for the benefits of the outcome to be equally divided by everyone existing in it.

We are asking how bad an unjustly unequal distribution of a certain quantity of welfare over certain individuals is in respect of inequality. The answer that (GF) returns is that this is determined by how far this distribution diverges from a distribution that spreads this quantity equally over these individuals, that is, by the amount of welfare that has to be transferred from the better-off to the worse-off to achieve this. Let me now try to develop and defend this answer.

Suppose that an unequal distribution of a certain quantity of benefits, Q, over certain individuals is due to an unequal distribution of resources. Suppose further that if these resources were equally divided among these individuals, Q would increase to Q+. Then it might seem that egalitarians should demand that all those worse off than the average that Q+ would yield—not just those worse off than the average that Q yields—when distributed over these individuals should be lifted to the average of the Q+ distribution, not just to the average of the Q distribution, as (GF) would have it.

Egalitarians should indeed demand this—by reference, however, not to their principle of equality on its own, but to this principle in conjunction with a principle of beneficence to the effect that it is morally better if individuals are better off. As already remarked, egalitarians need a principle of beneficence as well; otherwise, they would be committed to saying that just equality at lower welfare level would be as good as at a higher level. This distinction is liable to be obscured if one talks about equality of resources instead of equality of benefits because, owing to so-called diminishing marginal utility, resources as a rule generate more benefits in the hands of the worse-off. But resources are only of instrumental value for individuals, as means to the production of that which is intrinsically valuable for them, benefits. Therefore, what should be required as regards resources is the distribution—be it equal or not—which is justifiable in terms of both the maximization and equalization of benefits, balanced against each other. In real life, since welfare is usually distributable only by distributing resources, and this is likely to change the quantity of welfare, this is the issue that will preoccupy egalitarians.

We are however trying to isolate what they should demand solely by reference to their ideal of equality. (GF) specifies what would have to be done to a particular (unequal) distribution of benefits, that is, a distribution of a certain sum of benefits over certain individuals, to transform it *merely in respect of equality of benefits*, from being unequal to being equal. Hence, we are contemplating a situation in which the sum of benefits is fixed and is imagined to be directly redistributable. This reply must not be confused with what egalitarians would demand in more realistic settings in which the redistribution of benefits must proceed via redistribution of resources and so is likely to invoke their principle of beneficence as well.

For partly similar reasons, the worse-off cannot be understood as all those worse off than *the very best-off*, and what they should have in the name of equality cannot be to be raised to the high level of the very best-off. For, again, satisfying such a standard would take a boost of the total amount of welfare, and so could not be demanded simply in the name of equality of welfare. Certainly, in virtue of their endorsement of the principle of beneficence, egalitarians will want to raise the worse-off to the level of the very best-off. And not only that: they will want to raise all to the highest possible level at which equality is attainable. But, to repeat, this is not part of their campaign against unjust inequality of welfare.

Moreover, the worse-off than the best-off specification would have counterintuitive consequences, if the number of worse-off counts. Consider an instance of inequality, (1), in which one person, Odd, is at the welfare level of 11, but everyone else—99 individuals—is at 10.[2] Then, on my view, what these 99 persons each can claim in the name of equality is 1/99th of the extra unit that Odd has,[3] not one unit each, since this would necessitate a considerable increment of the total sum of welfare. This becomes

---

[2] For reasons of ease of exposition, I adopt the fiction of assigning numerical values to benefits, despite my argument in Chapter 4.

[3] When I talk about what the worse-off can 'claim' in the name of equality, this should be understood as a convenient way of talking about what justice requires that they have, and not as a reference to any rights of theirs.

crucial when (1) is compared to another inequality (2) in which Odd is at 9, and the 99 others are at 10. Here what the worse-off Odd can claim in the name of equality of welfare is 0.01 from each better-off person, that is, altogether 0.99. If we forget about scruples generated by the disperse additional burdens view, this is the same as what 99 persons each claiming 0.01 adds up to in (1). Consequently, in respect of inequality of welfare (1) and (2) are equally bad.

By contrast, if each of the 99 worse-off individuals in (1), and Odd in (2), could have claimed the one unit that it takes to be raised to the best-off level, the former state would have been much worse in respect of inequality. So, since (1) is only slightly better in respect of benefits, it would follow that (2) would be much better all things considered. This awkward consequence is avoided on the view here adopted. It reasonably implies that (1) is slightly better all told because it is slightly better as regards sum of benefits and not worse as regards equality.[4]

In the light of (GF), consider also Temkin's 'Sequence' (1993: 2.2). It is composed of a series of cases in which the ratio of the better-off to the worse-off is gradually altered, but their respective levels of welfare are constant. In the first case, 999 are better off and 1 is worse off, in the second case, 998 are better off and 2 are worse off, and so on, until we reach a last case which is the reverse of the first one: 1 is better off and 999 are worse off.

At first blush, it might appear that (GF) implies that, as we move along the Sequence, the situation *gets worse and worse* in respect of inequality, since more and more people are worse off. But, to repeat, (GF) does not harbour this implication, for as the group of the worse-off grows, the size of what each is entitled to in the name of equality diminishes, as the total sum redistributable shrinks. In fact, (GF) implies that the inequality first gets worse, and then better (cf. Temkin, 1993: 44).

This agrees with Temkin's 'final judgment' (1993: 297).[5] However, he believes it to be contrary to 'the common view' that 'we may, for a time, be *worsening* inequality even as our programs to benefit the worse-off *succeed*' (1993: 298–9), as when our programmes bring an inequality at the farther end of the Sequence closer to the midpoint. *Prima facie*, this consequence may indeed strike us as peculiar but, I think, this impression fades on closer inspection. The Sequence is bounded by two equalities, one at a higher level and one at a lower level. When the welfare of a single individual is increased, one step is taken away from the lower equality, when the welfare of a second individual is increased, another step is taken, and so on, with the result that the distance to the closest equality successively increases. Consequently, the inequality successively becomes greater. This continues to the midpoint, at which the distance to the closest equality is

---

[4] In addition, the disperse additional burdens view gives us more of a reason to rectify (2), since the loss of the 99 would be negligible, but the gain of Odd more substantial, whereas the gain of the 99 would be negligible in (1), and the loss of Odd more substantial. But notice that the loser Odd in the latter case is unjustly better off, which supplies a reason to disperse his extra benefit over the others.

[5] Although he also thinks that, for instance, the first case of the Sequence (with the biggest better-off population) is worse regarding inequality than the last, whereas I hold them to be on a par. I take up considerations bearing on this disagreement later.

maximal. Thus, at this point the inequality is the greatest. Thereafter the closest equality approaches, so the inequality again decreases. The lesson is that our programmes benefiting the worse-off may not reduce inequality if they benefit them *unequally*: if they benefit only a minority of them instead of spreading the benefits more evenly over a larger portion of them.

The mere *addition* of new worse-off individuals (leaving existing individuals intact) would make a situation worse as regards inequality, on my view. By contrast, some (e.g. Parfit, 1986: 156) have suggested that we could improve a situation in respect of equality by such an addition of new worse-off individuals, since this is a way of making the divergence from all being on the same level proportionally smaller. Accordingly, it might not be implied that in this respect this programme is inferior to one that evenly spreads the same amount of benefits over the existing worse-off. This seems to me unpalatable.

Suppose that we also believe, as adherents of the inclusive view of benefiting do, that creating new individuals with lives worth living is a way of benefiting them and making an outcome better. Then neither an appeal to beneficence nor to equality might recommend the policy of improving the conditions of existing worse-off individuals—which definitely reduces inequality—in favour of letting the number of individuals on a low welfare level grow by procreation. We might therefore be forced to conclude that, all things considered, the latter kind of policy is as good as the former. This consequence strikes me as counterintuitive, and I take it as a merit of my approach that it avoids it (cf. an argument against prioritarianism in 9.2).

My approach presupposes an answer to another question that Temkin discusses at length (1993: ch. 6): in determining badness in respect of inequality, is the relevant variable the *absolute* size of the claims of the worse-off, or their size *relative* to their level of welfare? Suppose that we face two alternatives in which the difference in how well off two equally big pairs of populations are is 20 units of benefits, but that in (1) their respective levels are 60 and 40 and in (2) 40 and 20. On the first alternative, the claims of each of the worse-off will be the same in both (1) and (2), namely (on my account) 10 units; so, these states will come out as equally bad regarding inequality. On the second alternative, (2) is worse, since the 10 units that the worse-off can claim amount to a 50 per cent rise for them, whereas in (1) it only amounts to a 25 per cent rise. Relatively speaking, the claims of the worse-off are then bigger in (2).

As opposed to Temkin, I have come down in favour of the view that it is the absolute size of the worse-off claims that counts, though this size must not be confused with the absolute size of the gap between the better- and worse-off. For instance, in (1) and (2) the worse-off can each claim only another 10 units, whereas the gap is 20 units. But the size of claims is a function only of the magnitude of this gap and the size of the worse-off class in relation to the better-off class, and not also of the absolute level of the worse-off. This size of claims is 'absolute' in the sense of not being relative to the absolute level of benefits of the worse-off (or the better-off). It should be noticed that if this variable of the absolute level were added to my approach (which also operates with the number of the worse-off), we could not rank states in respect of equality without implying a ranking of them in respect of sum of benefits. But I think that these respects are separate to the extent that this should be possible.

In support of leaving out the absolute level, notice also that if we were to change a situation from being like (2) to being like (1), that is, if we were to increase the welfare of the best-off and the worse-off to the same (absolute) degree, it seems reasonable to say that we have done nothing to remove the inequality, since we still have to do *as much* to remove it, for example to transfer from the better-off to the worse-off 10 units. But if the inequality is no closer to being removed, it seems to follow that it is as *big* and, provided that it is an inequality that is unjust, as intrinsically *bad*.

It may be objected that, surely, it is more urgent to remove the inequality in (2) than in (1) by improving the conditions for the worse-off; therefore, this inequality is worse. I accept the premise, but deny that the conclusion is true in the relevant sense: the inequality in (2) is indeed worse, but not in respect of *inequality*, only in respect of *sum of benefits*. When a relation of inequality is instantiated by a pair of populations, this *set of instances* or *state* of inequality can be called 'an inequality'. This state can be evaluated in respect of the inequality it instantiates, but it can also be evaluated in other respects, in particular in respect of how well off its subjects are in absolute terms. In the latter respect, the (state of) inequality in (2) is worse than the one in (1), for both groups here are at lower absolute levels. (Because it is assumed that the sizes of the populations in (1) and (2) are the same, it follows from this that the total sum of benefits in (2) is smaller.)

Since, on my view, the inequalities (1) and (2) are equal as regards inequality, but (2) is worse as regards sum of benefits, the inequality in (2) is worse *all things considered*. But we must not confuse the judgment that a (state of) inequality is worse all things considered with the judgment that this inequality is worse *with respect to the inequality that it exemplifies*. That is, we must not confuse a fuller evaluation of a state that exemplifies inequality with an evaluation of this state solely in respect of its inequality. The former involves evaluation of the state in other respects as well. Hence, this judgment is the morally more important one, but it is not of prime concern here.

The same question that we have discussed with respect to the magnitude of the claims of the worse-off arises with respect to their *number*: is what counts the *absolute* number of those who are worse off than the average or their number *relative* to the number of those better off than the average, their percentage of the total population? Again, I have adopted an absolutist answer: the absolute number of those worse off than the average is an independent variable determining the badness of an inequality, and its proportion to the number of the better-off is relevant only to the extent that it affects the size of the claims that the worse-off can legitimately make.

However, this relevance will make a state of inequality *worse* rather than better in respect of its inequality as the number of the better-off increases. Assuming that there is no difference as regards absolute levels, an inequality (3) in which one out of ten is one unit worse off might seem worse than one (4) in which only one out of a million is one unit worse off. Yet, on the view that I have adopted it is slightly *better* in respect of inequality, since what the worse-off individual should have from the point of view of equality is slightly greater in (4).

Against this verdict it may be urged that if we let the better-off population of (3) grow a hundred thousand times, so that this outcome changes to (4), we may appear to have done nothing to affect what makes the situation one of inequality: there is still one person one unit below the rest. On the other hand, the worse-off individual appears so much more unlucky in (4) than in (3), being the only one to be worse off among so many. The fact that we now have to transfer more from the better-off to remove the inequality lines up with that impression in support of the judgment that in respect of inequality (4) is worse than (3).

We have distinguished fuller evaluations of an instance of inequality of welfare from evaluations of such an instance solely in respect of the inequality that it instantiates. It has been seen that an instance of inequality gets worse in respect of benefits if the levels of both the better-off and worse-off sink in step, but that it remains the same in respect of inequality if it does not change in other respects. I have suggested that a conflation of the fuller evaluation of an instance of inequality with an evaluation of it only in respect of its inequality can help explain why it might seem that absolute levels are relevant to the latter evaluation. The same conflation might help to explain why the inequality in (3) could be thought worse than the inequality in (4): the outcome (3) is much worse as regards sum of benefits than outcome (4), since in (4) the better-off are 100,000 times as many (and the levels of the better- and the worse-off are the same). Thus, even if (3) is slightly better in other relevant respects, such as inequality, the inequality (4) will come out as better all told. But this judgment, though the morally most important, must not be confused with the one of primary interest in the present context: how inequalities rank solely in respect of their inequality.

There is however another factor that may contribute more to the illusion that (4) is better in this aspect. It might seem that if we take the number of the members of the worse-off group as being one variable determining badness in respect of inequality, we do not separate this respect as cleanly as possible from the sum of benefits respect. True, but if we insist on this radical separation, we end up with a view according to which the magnitude of an inequality is simply a matter of the absolute size of the gap between the better- and worse-off and the ratio between their numbers.

This would however be at odds with interpreting the badness of inequality in terms of the benefits of which it deprives the worse-off. It has also a counterintuitive consequence brought out by an argument of Temkin's to the effect that proportional population variations affect the badness of inequality (1993: 204–5). Consider two pairs of populations in which there is inequality, A_1 & A_2 and B_1 & B_2. The members of B_1 are twice as many as the members of A_1, and the same goes for A_2 and B_2. The levels of the better- and worse-off are the same in both pairs. Imagine that you figure out a way of establishing equality between A_1 and A_2 such that the loss in respect of benefits is barely outweighed by the gain in equality (that is, it is such that, although the better-off A_1 lose more benefits than the worse-off A_2 gain, this loss is just about outweighed by the gain in equality). Then contemplate establishing equality in the same way between B_1 and B_2, by letting each of the better-off B_1 lose the same amount as those in A_1 lose, and letting each of the worse-off B_2 gain as much as those in A_2 gain. Surely, it is reasonable to hold that if the gain as regards equality outweighs the loss of benefits in the case of A_1 and A_2, it does so in the case of B_1 and B_2 as well. But then the gain as regards equality must be greater in the latter case, since the loss as regards benefits is greater. Therefore, the fact that the number of individuals involved in the inequality between B_1 and B_2 is higher makes it greater and worse.

My view captures this by acknowledging the number of the worse-off as a variable determining the magnitude of an inequality (here the size of their claims will not diminish as the better-off class expands in step). Intuitively, it seems right that if it is bad that there is *one* individual unjustly worse off to a certain degree, it is worse if there are *two* individuals unjustly worse off to this degree, and so on (cf. Temkin's 'additive principle', 1993: 40). It could also be captured by counting the number of the better-off. However, if we believe in a principle of beneficence as well, we must prefer that equality be established by the worse-off being better off rather than by the better-off being worse off. This concern for the worse-off is expressed by counting the number of their claims alongside the size of their claims as determined by the size of the gap and the ratio between the respective numbers of the better- and worse-off. Recognition of merely the latter implies that badness as regards inequality is a function of the degree of deviation from perfect equality which then appears to be represented as something that is good in itself.

I have contended that, as expressed by (GF), the intrinsic badness of an inequality of welfare in respect of its inequality is a function of two variables. The first one is:

(a) how much each of those worse off than the average can claim of the greater sum of benefits of those better off than them in order to be equally well off at the average level.

This is in turn a function of the absolute gap between the better- and worse-off and the proportional size of these classes. The second variable is:

(b) the (absolute) number of those worse off than the average.

When the variables (a) and (b) pull in opposite directions, as they evidently can do, making a comparative judgment about badness in respect of inequality requires balancing them against each other. If the difference in welfare between the better- and worse-off is slightly bigger in one outcome than in another, it is reasonable to hold that it can be outweighed by the number of the better- and worse-off being somewhat bigger in the second case. This might create the impression that it is *always* true that a bigger gap between the better- and the worse-off can be offset by these groups being sufficiently numerous when the gap between them is smaller. But then we are up against a difficulty—analogous to Parfit's repugnant conclusion—that Temkin calls *the repellant conclusion*:

For any world F, let F's population be as large (though finite) as one likes, and let the gaps between F's better- and worse-off be as extreme as one likes, there will be some unequal world, G, whose population is 'sufficiently' large such that no matter how small G's gaps between the better- and worse-off might be G's inequality will be worse than F's (even if everyone in G is better off than everyone in F). (1993: 218)

The repellant conclusion is, then, that G's inequality will be worse than F's. If we find this conclusion repellant, it is because we find it repellant that, if they are numerous enough, the number of claims, (b), can outweigh their size, (a), so that G is overall worse in respect of inequality, just as in the case of the repugnant conclusion we find it repugnant that, if those who lives are barely worth living are sufficiently many, this can make the outcome better than an outcome in which many fewer individuals are at a much higher level. My way out of the repellant conclusion is the same as out of the repugnant conclusion, namely by a denial of the transitivity of 'better (worse) than in some respect' on the strength of the argument in 4.2. (So, to repeat, the assignment of numbers to amounts of benefits should be viewed merely as an expository device.)

Weighing the values of the two variables of inequality, (a) and (b), against each other—in order to assess badness in respect of inequality—is one thing. Weighing the value of outcomes in this respect against their value as regards sum of benefits is another thing. Both are intuitive procedures for which we cannot lay down objective or intersubjective standards. However, there is one general principle for the weighing of inequality and sums of benefits against each other that some might find attractive.

This is a version of egalitarianism that Parfit calls *moderate* (1995: 30ff.), though I shall instead call it *recessive* because it is awkward to have an egalitarianism that is both extreme and moderate. Recessive egalitarianism is the belief that gains (losses) in respect of benefits of *existent* individuals always outweigh losses (gains) in respect of equality. Increases of benefits of some existent individuals, when others are not affected, always make the outcome morally better all things considered, and decreases of benefits of some existent individuals, when others are not affected, always make the outcome morally worse all things considered, though less so in proportion to the degree to which those affected are unjustly better off than others. So, for instance, if an unjust inequality is reduced simply by the better-off becoming worse off then, all things considered, the outcome always changes for the worse. In order for the outcome to be better all things considered, the worse-off must gain *something* in respect of well-being, though they need not gain as much as the better-off lose. Thus, recessive egalitarians can claim that a change is for the better all told, though the sum of well-being has decreased. Therefore, it does not collapse into utilitarianism.

However, when we consider outcomes in which some individuals enter existence, we shall see in 9.3 that, contrary to recessive egalitarianism, gains (losses) in respect of sums of benefits do not always outweigh losses (gains) in respect of equality and, for this reason, that an outcome can be worse (better) all things considered, without being worse (better) for anyone. This could be so, even though we do not accept the inclusive view of benefiting. Therefore, *if* recessive egalitarianism is accepted—I am not saying that it should be—it had better be restricted to outcomes with the same number of individuals, as I have stipulated.

9

Prioritarianism and Its Problems

9.1 Prioritarianism and Impersonal Value

In (1995) Parfit puts forward an objection that applies to the kind of egalitarianism that I have outlined, *the levelling down objection*, and proposes an alternative view, *the priority view* or *prioritarianism*, which allegedly avoids this objection. I shall concede that my version of egalitarianism is indeed exposed to the levelling down objection, but argue in 9.2 that prioritarianism is vulnerable to worse versions of this kind of objection. In 9.4 I shall move on to consider another objection to prioritarianism which I find less compelling. On the strength of the first objection in particular, I conclude that my egalitarianism is more attractive than prioritarianism. In 9.3 I shall discuss how the inclusive view of benefiting bears on egalitarianism and prioritarianism.

Parfit distinguishes between two forms of egalitarianism: *teleological*, or *telic*, egalitarianism and *deontological*, or *deontic*, egalitarianism. Telic egalitarianism is about (un)just (in)equalities in respect of the benefits of outcomes, irrespective of whether they are produced by human actions, or by natural forces beyond human control. The egalitarianism that I have been outlining is telic. According to deontic egalitarianism, inequality is bad in itself only if it is unjust and 'injustice is a special kind of badness, one that necessarily involves wrong-doing' (1995: 9). Thus, on this view so-called *natural* inequalities—say, that some of us are born with a potential to be healthier, more intelligent, and so on than others—are not unjust and bad because they are not the result of any moral agent acting wrongly.

To my mind, its coverage of natural inequality makes telic egalitarianism the more appealing alternative. On the deontic view, no moral reason is given against *wishing* or *hoping* that, through the operation of natural or non-moral forces, some minority be afflicted with all the natural disadvantages, for instance all diseases, that would otherwise be more evenly spread over everybody. For were this wish or hope fulfilled, the outcome would not be unjust, since it would involve no wrong-*doing*, and as the more unequal distribution need not consist in a larger amount of harm, or in anyone being much more worse off, it may not be worse in any respect. In contradistinction, there would be moral reason not to *intend to bring about* this outcome since, were the intention to issue in this outcome, the outcome would be unjust and to that extent bad in itself. But, surely, there is something bad about this outcome itself, however it is brought about, that provides a moral reason not to hope or wish that it occurs as well as not to intend this. The natural view is, I think, that this badness stems from the fact that the outcome is more unjust.

In Chapter 7 I defended an extreme egalitarian claim, (E), to the effect that justice requires everyone to be equally well off, unless some autonomously choose (or would choose) to be worse off. I then defended an anti-inegalitarian interpretation of the value of just equality in Chapter 8 to the effect that it is impersonally bad in itself if some are unjustly worse off than others—that is, are worse off without having autonomously chosen to be so—and this badness detracts from the value that an outcome has in virtue of its amount of benefits, while just equality would add nothing to its value. Such an egalitarian principle needs to be combined with some principle of beneficence; otherwise, we cannot maintain that just equality at a higher level of welfare is better than just equality at a lower level. The principle of beneficence that I have defended in Part I is the inclusive person-affecting view that it is morally better if possible as well as independently existing individuals being benefited more. I assume that this principle accompanies telic egalitarian views like anti-inegalitarianism.

Consider now the levelling down objection, LDO. There are two populations, A and B, isolated from and unaware of each other: in A all individuals are equally well off, and in B all are also equally well off, though they are unjustly less well off than the members of A. Suppose that the latter suffer a misfortune that reduces the value of their lives to the level of B, so that both populations are now equally well off. On telic egalitarianism, this change is *in one respect* for the better, since it removes the intrinsically bad feature of some unjustly being worse off than others.

Certainly, in another way it is for the worse, since A are now worse off, and no one is better off. (We may even imagine that a levelling down makes *everyone* worse off, that it leaves everyone equally badly off at a level lower than the former level of the worse-off.) Given the principle of beneficence that telic egalitarians should endorse alongside their principle of equality, their view need not imply that the levelling down is for the better *all things considered*, when the two respects of beneficence and equality are balanced against each other. (It *never* has this implication if their egalitarianism is recessive.) Nonetheless, it apparently implies that this change is better *in one way*—as regards equality—although it is not better *for* anyone, but worse for some (or all). 'This implication', Parfit writes, 'seems to many to be quite absurd' (1995: 17).

The seeming absurdity might be due to the fact that they take for granted what Parfit calls *the person-affecting claim*: 'if an outcome is worse for no one, it cannot be in any way worse' (1995: 32). Thus, if the inequality between A and B has come about by the welfare of A rising after having been on a level with B's, and so the change is not worse for anybody (but good for some), it can be in no way worse, on the basis of the person-affecting claim (though telic egalitarianism implies, by contrast, that this change is in one respect for the worse). Similarly, if the change is reversed by levelling down, this can be in no way better, since the outcome is not (in any way) better for anyone. In other words, the person-affecting claim lays down:

PAC: An outcome cannot be better (worse) in any way or respect than another if it is not better (worse) *for* anybody.

Telic egalitarians have to concede that their view violates PAC and is hit by LDO. Their reply will have to be that this is not damaging. PAC presupposes that there are no impersonal values, with the exception of ones that have the same valence as personal values (like the impersonal value of sums or sets of benefits). If we acknowledge the existence of impersonal values that do not in this way mirror personal values, the violation of PAC follows as a matter of course. A theory of justice could hardly avoid acknowledging such impersonal values though, as I explained in Chapter 8, according to anti-inegalitarianism, the impersonal value of just equality in respect of benefits cannot exist without the personal value of benefits, and it cannot make the value of an outcome greater than the value of its sum of benefits. Some other theories of justice, whether they take justice to consist in equality or in getting what you deserve, assign to the impersonal value of justice a less dependent and more positive role.

Although telic egalitarianism necessarily conflicts with PAC, it will later be seen that if anti-inegalitarianism is taken to be recessive as long as it is confined to outcomes in which new individuals do not enter existence, it will comply with a weaker person-affecting principle with respect to such outcomes. But let us now direct our attention to the questions of what the purport of prioritarianism is and whether it can comply with PAC and escape LDO. As already foreshadowed, my answer to the latter question will be 'no' for (telic) prioritarianism.

Prioritarianism can be viewed as a way of rectifying the distributive shortcomings of utilitarianism. Suppose that we have a population of which one half is considerably better off than the other half, say, the former is at the level of 100 and the latter at 70. Suppose further that we could either increase the level of welfare of the better-off with 35 units, or the worse-off's welfare with 30 units. Then, according to utilitarianism, we should increase the welfare of the better-off with 35 units. This is so, irrespective of whether we take utilitarianism to be to the effect that we ought to maximize *the sum* of the benefits that individuals get, or *the average* of what they get. (But throughout I take utilitarianism to be the doctrine that we ought to maximize the sum of benefits because it is the more common and plausible form of utilitarianism.)

To many people, this is an unacceptable verdict. The morally correct judgment is instead that we should give the 30 units to the worse-off. After all, this will eliminate the gap between the better- and worse-off instead of increasing it to 65 units, at the price of reducing the total sum of benefits distributed by a mere 5 units.

In this connection, it is important to keep in mind the distinction between *benefits* and *resources* which generate benefits. Benefits have intrinsic value for us, whereas resources have only instrumental or extrinsic value for us, in virtue of producing what has intrinsic value. Resources have no value for us in circumstances in which they cannot produce intrinsic value, for example food which we cannot eat, or lodgings in which we cannot live.

As already remarked, it is normally resources that we distribute for we cannot distribute benefits directly. This might mask the distributive problem that I have presented due to diminishing marginal utility, the fact that resources tend to benefit the better-off less than the worse-off. Thus, imagine that we were instead facing the problem of giving either the better-off 35 resource units or the worse-off 30 resource units (say, money). Then utilitarianism might well imply that we should give the worse-off the 30 units because in their hands they may generate more benefits than 35 units would generate in the hands of the better-off, due to diminishing marginal utility. This goes to show that in many actual cases, utilitarianism will give the morally correct answer. But this is because of contingent facts, such as diminishing marginal utility. In cases in which diminishing marginal utility is not operational to a sufficient degree, say, in which 35 resource units benefit the better-off minimally more than 30 units benefit the worse-off, utilitarianism implies that we ought to give the better-off the 35 units. To many of us, this is morally unacceptable.

Prioritarianism offers a way to avoid this counterintuitive implication by means of a minimal revision of utilitarianism. The idea is that just as resources have a diminishing marginal *utility*, so benefits have a diminishing marginal *moral importance, weight or value*: they matter less morally the better off the individuals who receive them are (Parfit, 1995: 24). In one of Parfit's formulations, prioritarianism declares: 'Benefiting people matters more the worse off these people are' (1995: 19).

However, this formulation is at least equally well suited to a deontic version of prioritarianism: since it employs the event sense of 'benefiting', it can be read as being about the moral importance of *acts* of benefiting rather than about the moral importance of the benefits being contained in outcomes, as telic prioritarianism should be. We are interested in the telic form, since we want a prioritarian counterpart to telic egalitarianism. Telic prioritarianism should rather make the claim that benefits contribute more to the moral value of outcomes the more badly off those who have these benefits are. As Parfit puts it in a later paper, according to

The Telic Priority View, we have stronger reason to act in one of two ways, and this act would in one way make the outcome better, if this act would give people a greater sum of weighted benefits. (2012: 402)

Telic prioritarianism, then, is a view to the effect that the moral value of an outcome is a function not only of the size of the benefits and harms contained in it, but also of the moral weight or value that they get from their 'location' in it, from how well off the recipients of them are. However, this does not specify how telic prioritarianism differs from telic egalitarianism. The difference is that, while what matters on egalitarianism is how well off the recipients are in relation to others, what matters on prioritarianism is how badly off they are, *absolutely speaking*: 'It is irrelevant that these people are worse off *than others*. Benefits to them would matter just as much even if there *were* no others who were better off' (Parfit, 1995: 23). This disagreement about whether it is the absolute or relative position of recipients by reference to which benefits should be weighted is, as Parfit writes, 'the chief difference', or the essential difference between telic egalitarianism and prioritarianism.

We might ask: should we so understand it that, according to prioritarianism, there is a tacit assumption to the effect that the worse-off are *unjustly* worse off, that is, that their position is not just or autonomously chosen? Surely, like egalitarianism, prioritarianism must imply that the latter conditions are not met because it is implausible to claim that benefits to the worse-off have greater moral weight even if they autonomously choose to be worse off, or this is just because deserved. Prioritarianism is reasonably interpreted as differing from egalitarianism in that, like utilitarianism, it rejects justice along with deserts and rights. Conditions like deserts and rights can make it just that, independently of what other individuals have, one individual has a certain amount of benefits. But if these conditions are rejected, it is hard to see how justice could consist in anything other than an interpersonal relation, like individuals being equally well off. If there were only a single individual in the universe, and this individual was badly off, benefits to him or her would have greater moral weight on prioritarianism, but it is hard to see how this could be a matter of *justice*. For no amount of benefits bestowed could then be perfectly just—as is a distribution that creates a match with the recipient's desert level, according to a desert theory—or more or less just. So, presumably, prioritarians have to take it that justice is abolished as well, alongside deserts and rights.

However, prioritarianism is akin to egalitarianism in recognizing an impersonal value which does not simply mirror the sum of what has personal value, or benefits (cf. Persson, 2001: 28). A benefit in the lap of someone worse off has greater value than the same benefit in the lap of someone better off. But this greater value must be impersonal; it cannot be personal since, by hypothesis, the benefit is the same, irrespective of whether the recipient is better or worse off. If it were better *for you* to receive a benefit if you were worse off than if you were better off, it cannot be the same benefit. It may instead be a resource which, as remarked, normally generates bigger benefits in the hands of the worse-off. As Parfit notes, prioritarianism presupposes that we can speak of 'a roughly equal benefit, however well off the person is who receives it'. Otherwise, we could not ask 'whether some benefit would matter more if it came to someone who was worse off' (1995: 3).

Here is another way to bring out the difference between the personal value of a benefit and its impersonal, prioritarian value. A benefit is something which has intrinsic value for someone. This value, being intrinsic, must depend on intrinsic properties of the benefit. The prioritarian value, on the other hand, depends on the *relation* between this value and the welfare level of the recipient of the benefit; it is higher the lower this level is.

Like this relative value, the badness of unjust inequality in respect of the distribution of benefits cannot be a badness *for* the recipients.[1] If the value of the relation were of the

---

[1] Contrast Broome's notion of an 'individual good' which 'depends on the relation between one person's position and other people's' (1991: 181).

same kind as the value of the relata, relating them would affect the sum of this value. Thus, once we relate the smaller benefits of Lesslie to the greater benefits of Richie and conclude that Lesslie is thus and so much unjustly worse off than Richie, the badness of this unjust inequality would increase the difference in respect of personal value between Lesslie and Richie. And if the badness of this new and greater inequality in respect of personal value between them is also personal, it should also be factored in and pump up the inequality. Consequently, we would be caught up in a regress of an ever-increasing difference between Lesslie and Richie in respect of personal value, until we acknowledge a badness of the relation of unjust inequality in respect of personal values that is impersonal.

Therefore, in contradistinction to utilitarians, both prioritarians and egalitarians are committed to an impersonal value which can make the value of an outcome differ from the value of its sum of personal values or benefits. They differ in that prioritarians assert that this value is fixed by the relation between a benefit and the absolute position of the recipient of it, whereas egalitarians assert that it is fixed by the position of the recipient relative to others. However, prioritarians and anti-inegalitarians are alike in holding that their impersonal value is dependent on personal values, that it cannot be instantiated unless something is good or bad for individuals. Hence, they hold that an outcome cannot be good or bad in any respect, unless it is good or bad for someone.

Parfit holds that the prioritarian principle 'can be regarded as the only principle we need' (1995: 22), but that does not set prioritarianism apart from egalitarianism. In contrast to what I did earlier on, we need not construe egalitarianism as consisting of two principles, a principle of justice as equality combined with a principle of beneficence. Anti-inegalitarianism could be stated as a single principle such as:

> AI: It is always morally better if some are benefited, though benefits have a moral weight that is inversely proportional to their effect on the size of unjust inequality: the smaller they make it, the greater their weight, and in case of just equality, the value of benefits equals their personal value.

This is equivalent to a two-principle formulation which has it that an outcome is morally better if it contains (i) a larger sum of benefits, or (ii) less unjust inequality in the distribution of it, which detracts from the value of this sum. The essential difference between prioritarianism and egalitarianism is simply that, whereas prioritarianism weights benefits in relation to the absolute levels of the recipients, egalitarianism weights them in relation to how recipients unjustly fare in relation to others.

9.2 Prioritarianism, Levelling Down, and the Desirability of Welfare Diffusion

Let us now return to Parfit's most important and most discussed objection against telic egalitarianism, LDO. He claims that this objection has 'great force', but that it is not 'decisive' (1995: 33). I do not deny that egalitarianism is exposed to this objection, but shall argue that prioritarianism is also hit by it, in a more damaging way.

It will be remembered that LDO is to the effect that telic egalitarianism implies, implausibly, that a change, which consists in the welfare level of the better-off sinking towards the level of the worse-off, is in one respect better, though it is better for nobody (and worse for some). It is better in that there is less inequality—which is assumed to be unjust—and, as has been seen, on telic egalitarianism unjust inequality is bad in itself. The outcome might never be better all things considered, since the loss of benefits might outweigh the gain in respect of equality (as recessive egalitarianism implies that it always does when no new recipients are added).[2]

It cannot be denied that telic egalitarianism implies that levelling down is in one respect for the better, though it is not better for anyone. This is simply a corollary of the telic egalitarian thesis that unjust welfare inequality is something that is impersonally bad in itself. However, it can be argued that this implication is not counterintuitive, as Temkin has convincingly done (1993: ch. 9). Moreover, it can be shown that prioritarianism also implies that levelling down is in one respect for the better. This should not be surprising, since we have seen that prioritarians also are committed to acknowledging an impersonal value. Prioritarians would then be in an uncomfortable position to press LDO against egalitarianism. It is this line of argument that I shall now pursue (largely following my presentation in 2012).

When the better-off lose benefits so that their welfare level becomes closer to the level of the worse-off, this implies, on prioritarianism, that the average moral value of the remaining benefits of the better-off—and, consequently, the remaining benefits of the whole outcome—will increase because benefits at higher levels, with lower moral value, have been removed. According to prioritarianism, this increase in average moral value means that the outcome is in one respect better, though it is not better for anyone. Hence, prioritarianism is exposed to LDO.

Parfit, however, thinks that prioritarianism avoids LDO because prioritarians 'are more concerned for people the worse off these people are... it makes no difference... whether there are other people who are better off' (1995: 23). It is true that 'it makes no difference' to the prioritarian concern for the *worse-off* whether, or to what extent, there are other people who are better off, but it does not follow that prioritarianism is not exposed to LDO. This is because there is *another* respect in which levelling down is better, according to prioritarianism—a respect which 'makes no difference', according to either egalitarianism or utilitarianism. This is the higher average weight of benefits which, according to prioritarianism, determines the value of an outcome together with the sum of benefits. And this weight goes up because of what happens to *the better-off*: their loss of benefits that have lower weight.

---

[2] It should be noted, however, that the denial of the transitivity of 'better than' in Chapter 4 tends to strengthen the reason of beneficence not to level down, since some things that are qualitatively higher may be lost.

To see that prioritarianism implies that levelling down makes the outcome better in respect of the higher average weight of benefits, it is helpful to start by looking at outcomes in which the sum of benefits is constant, say, 100 units, and it is never the case that any recipient gets a different number of units than anyone else. It is just the number of recipients that varies in the *Series*: in the first outcome, 1:100, one individual enjoys all of the 100 units, in the second outcome, 2:50, two individuals each have 50 units, in the third outcome, 4:25, four individuals each have 25 units... and in the final one, 100:1, 100 individuals each have one unit. According to both egalitarianism and utilitarianism, all outcomes in the Series are equally good, all things considered.[3] But according to prioritarianism, the first outcome, 1:100, is worse than the rest, the final one, 100:1, is the best, and the outcomes in between are increasingly better than the first, all things considered.

The final outcome is the best, on prioritarianism, because each unit of welfare is received by someone who without it would be at the neutral level, so each unit has the maximal moral weight or value that it could have in the Series. By contrast, in the first outcome some units go to someone who would be at a very high level without them, say, at the level of having 99 or 98 units, so these units would have a comparatively low moral value. In other words, the average moral or prioritarian weight of welfare units is highest in the outcome 100:1, and lowest in the outcome 1:100. Since the sum of benefits is the same in all outcomes, it follows that the former is, all things considered, the best outcome and the latter the worst outcome, according to prioritarianism.

We might put this by saying that prioritarianism implies *the desirability of welfare diffusion*, DWD: it is better all things considered if a quantity of welfare is diffused as widely as possible, that is, distributed over as many recipients as possible, so that each recipient gets a minimal benefit. By contrast, utilitarianism and egalitarianism are indifferent with respect to whether a welfare quantity is diffused over many, or concentrated to a few recipients (according to egalitarianism this only holds as long as there is just equality of distribution). DWD implies that it is better if two individuals have one unit of welfare each than that one individual has two units, better if three have one unit each than that one has three, and so on. In other words, it is better if more individuals each benefit less than that fewer individuals each benefit more. This is the opposite of what the denial of the transitivity of betterness in respect of welfare in 4.2 would lead us to expect.[4]

It might be objected that prioritarians need not apply their doctrine to outcomes involving different numbers of individuals, as the outcomes in the Series evidently do. Parfit himself says that it cannot be applied to such cases and that we need different moral principles for such cases (2012: 440). This might be because it is thought that

---

[3] For the sake of simplicity, I am now bracketing complications that arise from the denial of the transitivity of the relation 'better (worse) than in respect of welfare' in Chapter 4.

[4] It should be noted that if it is burdens rather than benefits that are the subject of diffusion, it is not implausible to maintain that diffusion is desirable. This is what the disperse additional burdens view declares.

such an application presupposes that prioritarians are committed to the inclusive view that individuals can be benefited by beginning to exist—for example, the 99 extra individuals who exist in 100:1 being benefited by the fact that this outcome exists in place of the outcome 1:100—and that prioritarians are not in fact committed to this inclusive view of benefiting.

Now it is true that prioritarians are not necessarily committed to the inclusive view, but false that applying prioritarianism to the Series presupposes it. Note that the outcome 100:1 could have come about in other ways than by individuals being brought into existence: for instance, by transferring benefits from one individual at the level of 100 to 99 *pre-existent* individuals at the neutral (or zero) level, the 1:100 + 99:0 outcome. Even if they do not accept the inclusive view, prioritarians must admit that, if it arises in this way, their view applies to the outcome 100:1, that is, it applies to the comparison between this outcome and the outcome 1:100 + 99:0. But the *intrinsic* value of 100:1 is *the same*, irrespective of how it arises, and it is clearly better than 1:100 all told, since the average weight of benefits is higher, and the sum of benefits is the same—thus, the sum of weighted benefits is greater, to put it in Parfit's own terms.

To see that prioritarians are committed to the view that 100:1 is better all things considered than 1:100, note that the sum of weighted benefits of 1:100 + 99:0 is the same as that of 1:100, since the 99:0 add nothing to the former sum. So, according to prioritarianism, these outcomes are of equal value (whereas, according to egalitarianism, 1:100 + 99:0 is worse, since it involves an inequality which could be assumed to be unfair). Therefore, whether or not the 99 individuals exist, and we have a same number or a different number comparison with 100:1, is irrelevant to a prioritarian assessment of the outcome value. This is because it is not the relative position of the one at 100 to other existing individuals that matters for this assessment; as remarked, it is the weight of benefits in proportion to the absolute level of the recipients of benefits that matters. When there are no benefits, this weight must be nil. Consequently, we could make a same number comparison between the outcomes 100:1 and 1:100 + 99:0, concluding that, on prioritarianism, 100:1 is better all things considered; then compare 1:100 + 99:0 to 1:100, concluding that, on prioritarianism, they are of equal value, since the existence of individuals who have no benefits makes no difference on this view. Hence, 100:1 is better all things considered than 1:100, according to prioritarianism. A different number comparison would still be involved—namely, the comparison between 1:100 + 99:0 and 1:100—but it could not plausibly be claimed that this comparison relies on the inclusive view. Irrespective of the truth of this view, bringing into existence individuals who will be at the neutral level, at which existence is neither intrinsically good nor bad, will not benefit or harm them and, thereby, yield a reason for saying that this makes the outcome better or worse.

The fact that 1:100 and 1:100 + 99:0 have the same value on prioritarianism, but not on egalitarianism, brings out an important difference between these doctrines, namely that whereas egalitarianism is ultimately concerned about *subjects or individuals* who are unjustly worse off, (telic) prioritarianism is concerned about *the weight of benefits*.

The egalitarian concern is primarily about individuals being unjustly worse off than others, and their concern about the weight of benefits is derivative. Hence, egalitarianism can take individuals who have no benefits (or burdens) into account, while prioritarianism cannot. This is the reason why 1:100 and 1:100 + 99:0 have the same value on prioritarianism, but not on egalitarianism.

It seems undeniable that (telic) prioritarians are committed to holding the outcomes 1:100 + 99:0 and 1:100 to be of equal value because their sums of weighted benefits are the same. Yet, it seems strange, for in the outcome 1:100 + 99:0 there are 99 individuals who are badly off, slightly worse off than if they had been at the level of one. These individuals are missing in 1:100; so, it might seem that there must be a moral reason to change 1:100 + 99:0 to 100:1, which is lacking in the case of similarly changing 1:100. To be sure, if prioritarians endorse the narrow view of benefiting, they can maintain that there is a moral reason to change the outcome 1:100 + 99:0 to 100:1—that is, to benefit in the event sense the 99:0—which is lacking in the case of a change from 1:100 to 100:1, since nobody is here benefited in this sense. But if we set aside this view as having been refuted in Part I, the question is whether this view can be motivated in any other way.

I do not think that it can be as long as prioritarians stick to the idea that benefits have a moral weight that is *directly* relative to the *welfare level* of the recipients. Parfit introduces a view that he calls *claim* prioritarianism (2012: 437), and if such a view is to the effect that benefits to individuals have greater weight the worse off they are because this *gives* them greater *claims* to be benefited, it could motivate why there is a moral reason to benefit the 99 at 0. For in contrast to non-existent individuals, the 99 individuals could intelligibly be said to have such claims that benefiting them meets. But then the moral weight of benefits is not directly determined by the welfare level of the recipients; it is directly determined by the strength of their claims. However, such claims seem to be rights, which were rejected in Chapter 7. Besides, this type of view is better understood as a form of deontic rather than telic prioritarianism, since talk of claims is more natural in the context of moral agents who have corresponding duties.[5]

Irrespective of whether there is a moral reason to change 1:100 + 99:0 to 100:1 which is lacking in the case of similarly changing 1:100, however, it is indisputable that their sums of weighted benefits are the same and that they are less than that of 100:1. Since, on prioritarianism, 100:1 is then better than 1:100 all things considered, there must be some respect in which it is better. To repeat, this is that the average moral value of units of welfare is higher, since the recipients of these units in 100:1 are comparatively badly off. Contrast the reason why 100:1 is better than 1:100 with the reason why, for instance, 2:100 is better than 1:100. In the latter case the reason is that the sum of benefits is greater. According to prioritarianism, both 100:1 and 2:100 are better than 1:100 because their sums of weighted benefits are greater than they are in 1:100. But, as we have seen, there are two factors determining this sum, and 100:1 is better because of

---

[5] In Chapter 8 I used 'claims' in a less literal sense. Such uses could obscure the purport of claim prioritarianism.

one—the higher average weight of benefits—and 2:100 is better because of the other, the greater sum of benefits. Reference to these factors describes more precisely why these outcomes are better than 1:100.

100:1 will continue to be better than 1:100 in the same respect even if the number of recipients of a single unit of welfare in 100:1 is reduced from 100 individuals to 99, or 98 individuals. The total sum of welfare would be slightly smaller in these outcomes, the 99:1 and the 98:1 outcomes, than in the Series, but prioritarians would surely still judge the 99:1 and 98:1 outcomes to be better all things considered than the first outcome, 1:100. This is because the decrease in respect of total sum of welfare is reasonably outweighed by the much higher average moral or prioritarian weight of units of welfare in the 99:1 and 98:1 outcomes. If this increase in average prioritarian weight were not enough to outweigh the loss of one unit or two units, the prioritarian weighting of benefits would have to be so small that a worse-off individual must be very much worse off than a better-off individual in order to justify giving him or her two benefits rather than the better-off one.

However, if we gradually decrease the sum of welfare and the number of recipients in the outcome 100:1, we shall eventually reach a point at which, on prioritarianism, the outcome is no longer better all things considered. But it is nevertheless better in the same one respect, the respect of average moral value of units of welfare. Moreover, it will continue to be better in this respect even when we arrive at the outcome 1:1, in which there remains only one recipient with one unit. We might imagine that this individual is identical to the one who in 1:100 had 100 units. This brings out that prioritarianism implies that simply reducing someone's level of welfare makes the outcome better in one respect. Likewise, if there is a change from everyone's being equally well off at a higher level to them being equally well off at a lower level, prioritarianism implies that this change is in one respect for the better, since the average moral weight of benefits goes up. These consequences—which are obviously not consequences of egalitarianism—are quite unsavoury. They seem much more unsavoury than the consequence that the levelled down outcome is in one respect better which, I have argued, is a consequence that prioritarianism has in common with egalitarianism.

We have seen that Parfit claims that prioritarianism cannot be applied to outcomes in which individuals come into existence (2012: 440). But, as already explained, in order to vindicate this restriction it is not enough to reject the inclusive view of benefiting. For it could still be true that there is an *impersonal* reason of beneficence to add individuals who enjoy benefits because this increases the value of an outcome in respect of the sum of benefits. To exclude this application, you would have to adopt the narrow person-affecting view that we can only benefit individuals whose existence is independent of the benefiting action in conjunction with the view that all reasons of beneficence are person-affecting.

However, it is quite hard to deny that an outcome becomes better in respect of welfare if individuals with a high level of welfare are added to it. But if benefits added in this way, by adding individuals, add to the value of the outcome by increasing its sum of benefits, it is difficult to see how telic prioritarians could justify exempting the added benefits from the weighting that attaches to benefits received by independently existing individuals. Deontic prioritarians might try to justify such exemption by maintaining that only independently existing individuals can need, claim or have rights to benefits, but such versions of prioritarianism are irrelevant to the present discussion.

Prioritarianism, then, does not differ from egalitarianism in a way that saves it from exposure to LDO. Again, the essential difference between prioritarianism and egalitarianism is simply that, while prioritarianism weights benefits in proportion to the absolute welfare level of the recipients, egalitarianism weights them in proportion to the welfare level of the recipients relative to others. Levelling down makes the worse-off less worse off relative to others. That is the respect in which it is better, according to egalitarianism. But it also lowers the absolute welfare level of the better-off and, thereby, increases the average prioritarian weight of their welfare units. If the average prioritarian weight of the welfare units of the worse-off is constant (or increases because the welfare level of the worse-off also sinks, though less than that of the better-off), it follows that the average prioritarian weight of the units of the whole outcome increases. This is the respect in which levelling down makes the outcome better, according to prioritarianism.

It is easy to overlook that prioritarianism is exposed to LDO because it is natural to assume, as Parfit seemingly does, that if levelling down is better in some respect, this must be a respect which has to do with the position of the worse-off because it cannot plausibly have to do with the fact that the position of the better-off gets worse: 'If the better off suffer some misfortune, so that they become as badly off as anyone else, we do not think this is in any way a change for the better' (1995: 23–4). But this is exactly what prioritarianism implies; more precisely, it implies that the fact that the better-off lose benefits is in one way better *in itself*, and not because the worse-off become better off relatively speaking, as egalitarianism implies.

As mentioned in 9.1, anti-inegalitarianism can be formulated as *one* principle—AI—like telic prioritarianism. Prioritarianism says that an outcome is better than another if and only if the sum of *priority*-weighted (p-weighted) benefits is greater. The sum of p-weighted benefits is determined by two factors: (a) the sum of benefits, and (b) the average moral weight of benefits which is a function of the size of benefits and the absolute level of their recipients. Similarly, anti-inegalitarianism is to the effect that an outcome is better than another if and only if the sum of *equality*-weighted (e-weighted) benefits is greater. The sum of e-weighted benefits is determined by two factors: (a) the sum of benefits, and (b*) the degree of (unjust) inequality. According to anti-inegalitarianism, the strength of the (b*) factor subtracts from the value of the sum of benefits. When it is zero, nothing is subtracted. The value of just equality is not an independent value that could exist in the absence of benefits, and add a value over and above the value of the sum of benefits. It is instead a weight which operates upon the value of benefits, like the p-weight.

Imagine that, on the basis of this, I were to claim that anti-inegalitarianism is not exposed to LDO. Then it could be legitimately objected that this is a mere sleight-of-hand because the sum of e-weighted benefits is determined by the (b*) factor as well. Since the strength of this negative factor is reduced by levelling down, the outcome is in one respect better. But if this attempt to rescue anti-inegalitarianism from LDO fails, prioritarianism is also exposed to LDO, and to the related, more damaging objections outlined, because there is improvement in respect of the counterpart factor (b).

In reply to my objection that prioritarianism is vulnerable to LDO, Nils Holtug draws a parallel between the average prioritarian weight and the total or aggregate utilitarian's attitude to increases in average welfare (2010: 216). However, this parallel fails because total utilitarians are not committed to there being anything better—improvement in respect of any value—as regards outcomes in which the average level goes up, at the same time as the total welfare sum is constant or decreases, while telic prioritarians *are* committed to there being something better about outcomes in which the average prioritarian weight goes up, at the same time as the total welfare sum is constant or decreases. For instance, they are committed to holding that an outcome like 100:1 is better all things considered than the outcome 1:100 (because it is better than 1:100 + 99:0 which is of the same value as 1:100). Since this is so, there must be some respect in which 100:1 is better, though its sum of benefits is the same as 1:100, namely the higher average weight of benefits.

It is true that the sum of benefits of an outcome is determined by two variables, namely the number of individuals benefited and the average level of their benefits. So, aggregate utilitarians have a reason to be concerned about the average level—which is shown by the fact that when the individuals benefited are kept intact, this is all that they have to worry about. Consequently, it might be insisted that we could distinguish between two 'aspects' of the value of outcomes, according to aggregate utilitarianism. However, in the case of aggregate utilitarianism there is only *one kind of value*, the personal value of benefits, for the aspects to be aspects of, whereas in the case of prioritarianism the aspects pertain to *two kinds of value*, an impersonal value alongside the personal value, and an outcome could be better in respect of one kind of value, but not in respect of another kind, for example better in respect of an impersonal kind of value, but the same in respect of the personal kind of value, as happens in the *Series*.

9.3 Egalitarianism, Prioritarianism, and the Inclusive View

Since prioritarianism, like egalitarianism, is exposed to LDO, it violates Parfit's *person-affecting claim* (1995: 32) already mentioned:

PAC: An outcome cannot be better (worse) *in any respect* than another if it is not better (worse) *for* anybody.

However, once it has been noted, as I did in 9.1, that prioritarians, like egalitarians, are committed to there being an impersonal value of outcomes other than the value of the sum of benefits that they contain, PAC should not be thought to have anything going for it in the present context.

There is however a weaker person-affecting principle (weaker in the sense that a view can satisfy it even if it does not satisfy PAC):

> PAC*: An outcome cannot be better (worse) *all things considered* than another if it is not better (worse) for anybody.

If coupled with the inclusive view of benefiting and person-affecting reasons of beneficence, prioritarianism complies with PAC*. In case prioritarianism is instead combined with a denial of the inclusive view of benefiting and an endorsement of impersonal reasons of beneficence, its claim that welfare diffusion, like a transition from 1:100 to 100:1, is for the better all things considered, violates PAC*. I have however suggested that such impersonal views should be dismissed because they imply that what we should be morally concerned with is the boosting of sums of (weighted) benefits rather than with benefiting individuals (in proportion to how badly off they are).

However, even if prioritarianism is conjugated with the inclusive person-affecting view, there is a sense in which its concern about individuals falls short, since individuals on the neutral level will not morally matter according to it. For, as noted, it implies that the outcomes 1:100 and 1:100 + 99:0 are of equal value. Since what morally matters according to prioritarianism are benefits and their weight, individuals without benefits fall outside morality. The same is true of utilitarianism, but prioritarianism was introduced to repair the distributive shortcomings of utilitarianism.

The brand of egalitarianism that I favour, anti-inegalitarianism, could satisfy PAC* in outcomes with the same number of individuals, but hardly in different number outcomes. This is so if it assumes the recessive form. But it has surfaced how, according to anti-inegalitarianism, an outcome can be worse all things considered without being worse for anyone. For example, 1:100 + 99:0 is worse all things considered than 1:100, since it is significantly worse in respect of equality, but not worse for anyone and, of course, 1:100 is better all things considered than 1:100 + 99:0 without being better for anyone. Thus, in accordance with my stipulation in Chapter 8, recessive egalitarianism should not be adopted with respect to different number cases.

Consider an instance of what Parfit calls 'Mere Addition' (1987: § 142): to a population in which everyone is at a high level of welfare, such as 100, you add a few individuals at the level of one. That is, by the smallest increase of benefits you create a big (unjust) inequality. In such cases it is hard to deny that the badness of an increased inequality can outweigh the goodness of an increased sum of benefits, making the outcome worse all things considered, though it is not worse for anybody. Thus, such situations would refute recessive egalitarianism were it conceived to be applicable to them. This view could have plausibility only in same number outcomes in which big changes in respect of inequality must be created by great gains or losses of benefits. Here it has some plausibility to say that the latter always outweigh the former, though I do not want to commit myself to this view.

Such cases also show that anti-inegalitarianism is incompatible with a principle related to PAC* which states a sufficient instead of a necessary condition for an outcome being better (worse) all things considered, namely what Parfit calls *the principle of personal good* (2012: 404):

> PPG: An outcome is better (worse) all things considered if it is better (worse) for somebody and worse (better) for nobody.

Since PPG is false in some cases in which individuals enter existence, according to anti-inegalitarianism, it follows that in order to find out what outcomes we have moral reasons to bring about, we cannot simply look at how they benefit and harm individuals. There are impersonal moral reasons to prefer some outcomes to others, namely reasons of just equality.

However, it then seems that anti-inegalitarianism is committed to the view that, if there are a few living lives barely worth living, but many having enormously better lives, it would be better all told if the few at the very low level were to die a painless death, although this is slightly worse for them. The reason for this would be that the death of the worse-off would eliminate a huge inequality. But would it? Notice that the worse-off are now at an even lower level, the neutral level of non-existence instead of barely above it. Thus, the death of the worse-off has in fact increased the inequality as well as reduced the sum of benefits; hence, it is for the worse all things considered.

In this respect, anti-inegalitarianism and prioritarianism are in agreement. But in virtue of the fact that it implies DWD, prioritarianism countenances the difficulty of attaching too great a moral importance to the addition of individuals at low levels. This comes out as *better* than improving to the same degree the lot of already existing individuals at higher levels, not just as equally good as is true on utilitarianism. Suppose that a population, A, is located at a very high level, say 95. We then cause an equally big population, B, to exist and lead lives worth living, but at a low level, say 5. Prioritarianism implies not merely that the addition of B at the level of 5 would make the outcome better, but that it would make it *much* better than boosting the level of A to a similar degree, from 95 to 100, since benefits at a higher level contribute less to the moral value of an outcome. In fact, it implies that the smaller the sum of benefits to be distributed between A and B, the stronger the reason to add B as a recipient of it. But surely it is rather the other way around: the smaller the sum of benefits, the more dubious it is to add B rather than to give the benefits to A.

In view of the similarity of their implications for the elimination of those with lives barely worth living, it might appear that, if conjugated with the inclusive view of benefiting, anti-egalitarianism is also committed to the view that adding individuals at this low level would make the outcome better all things considered. Contrary to how it might appear at first blush, it might be contended that having B enter existence would not *create* a great gap between A and B in respect of welfare. Instead it would in fact slightly *reduce* the inequality between A and B by lifting B just above the neutral level of non-existence. If this is correct, anti-inegalitarianism would imply that the addition of B would be better than improving the welfare of A to the same extent, since this would increase inequality. Anti-inegalitarianism would then agree with prioritarianism and stand in opposition to utilitarianism which implies that these alternatives are equally good—surely a less implausible claim.

I think, however, that there are grounds for holding, as we are intuitively inclined to do, that the addition of B will increase inequality rather than reduce it and, thus, that it is not parallel to the elimination of B which does increase inequality. If it is unjust that B is worse off than A, we aggravate this injustice when, by eliminating B, we increase the inequality of welfare by reducing B to the neutral level of non-existence. (If this inequality is not unjust—if B autonomously chooses to be worse off and even to pass out of existence—there need not be anything wrong with the disposal of B.) But if the inequality between possible individuals at the neutral level of non-existence and actual beings at positive levels is not unjust, the outcome would not be made less unjust by lifting some of the possible individuals to a positive level of existence, even if this were to reduce the amount of inequality.

There are then two points at issue here: whether the creation of individuals at lower levels decreases inequality, and whether, supposing it does decrease inequality, the inequality decreased is unjust. My view is that doubt is called for on both counts. To begin with, it is doubtful whether inequality would be reduced by raising some possible individuals to a positive level. Suppose that we understand 'possible individuals' as the individuals whom the individuals existing at a given time, say, the present, could bring into existence.[6] Then the possible individuals who could be brought into existence by the individuals existing at t_1, the possible individuals at t_1, will be different in number from the possible individuals who could be brought into existence at later time, t_2, the possible individuals at t_2, when some of the possible individuals at t_1 have been brought into existence. The possible individuals at t_2 are likely to be more numerous, since more existing people can have more offspring. If this is what is meant by 'possible individuals', bringing individuals into existence might not have any impact on equality by changing the proportion between those who have worthwhile lives and those who are merely possible at the neutral level of non-existence. The proportion

---

[6] I take the number of possible people who existing people could bring into existence to be considerably smaller than Kagan does. He asks 'how many sperm-egg combinations are there with roughly 7 billion people in the world?' (2012: 219) and obtains an astronomical number, 3×10^{33}. But, as I see it, the number of people who could in fact come into existence is also limited by, for instance, the number of available wombs in which fertilized eggs could grow. The number then obtained is vastly smaller than Kagan's number. This point should also be kept in mind when the moral consequences of an inclusive principle of beneficence are considered (as well as the point that, in the actual world, only a smaller percentage of the smaller number of possible people could be given good lives without unacceptably lowering the quality of life of existing people).

might rather be roughly constant because as the class of existent individuals expands, so does the class of possible individuals.

Suppose instead that we try to fix the class of possible individuals by understanding it as 'the possible individuals at t_1, *and* at t_2, *and* at t_3, etc.', for every time at which it is possible for individuals to have offspring. Then the class of possible individuals will not expand as individuals reproduce and the population increases. The problem will instead be that this class of possible individuals appears to be indefinite or indeterminate because there is no definite time at which individuals will cease to be able to have offspring. Therefore, if this is the meaning of 'possible individuals', then again bringing individuals into existence will not in any determinate way change the proportion between those who have worthwhile lives and those who are merely possible.

Consequently, it is doubtful whether the inequality between possible individuals and actual individuals at some positive level could be reduced by the addition of new individuals with worthwhile lives. But then, if there is no reduction of inequality when new individuals with worthwhile lives are created, of course, the question whether this inequality is unjust does not arise. However—and this is the second point—it is also doubtful whether those who remain merely possible, but who would have had good lives had they existed, are subject to an inequality that is unjust or unfair. Can we plausibly claim that they unjustly or unfairly had smaller chances of coming into existence than those who did come into existence? Is coming into existence not more like a fair than an unfair lottery? Every individual who could possibly exist cannot have this possibility actualized and lead a good life, but at least as long as we do not introduce extensive genetic scanning of fertilized eggs and sort out some on unfair grounds, which of the possible individuals who actually begin to exist is largely a matter of chance.

The upshot is, then, that according to anti-inegalitarianism, there is no reason of justice to bring possible individuals into existence. There is however a reason of justice *against* doing so if these newcomers would unjustly end up on a lower welfare level than those who already exist. If this level is much lower than the level of the existent, this reason of justice would plausibly outweigh the reason of beneficence to cause them to exist, so that causing them to exist would be wrong, all things considered. It does not follow, however, that it would be right to dispose of these newcomers once they have commenced their existence, since this would increase the injustice inflicted on them. Rather, they should be made better off. By contrast, there is, according to prioritarianism, a stronger reason to bring such newcomers into existence than to improve the welfare of the existent to the same degree. In this respect, prioritarianism is even less plausible than utilitarianism, according to which these alternatives are equally good.

The fact that, according to my view, egalitarianism applies to the outcome of mere addition means, as emerged in 3.2, that it sits ill with views that there would be less moral reason to benefit individuals who exist thanks to the benefiting action, like McMahan's view that these benefits are non-comparative and as such have less 'reason-giving' weight than equivalent (comparative) benefits to independent individuals. For suppose that 100 independent individuals will exist in the future. We could give each of them an extra 20 benefits; otherwise, their level will be 80 instead of 100. We have to create another 100 individuals who will be at the level of 80 at least. The created individuals will have to be at that level if we spend the 20 extra units per head on the independent individuals. We could instead create another group of 100 individuals at the level of 90, leaving only 10 units per head for the independent individuals. According to my view, the latter outcome would be the one that we morally ought to produce because in this situation justice requires an equal distribution of benefits. But not so if non-comparative benefits have less reason-giving weight; then there would be a case for letting more than half of the total amount of benefits go to the independent individuals. Thus, there is a tension between my egalitarianism and McMahan's conception of non-comparative benefits.

Returning to the comparison between anti-inegalitarianism and prioritarianism, a corollary of what has been said is that, while prioritarianism facilitates the slide towards the repugnant conclusion via mere addition, anti-inegalitarianism to some extent counteracts it. It by no means blocks this conclusion, since if the welfare levels of the added populations are sufficiently close to that of the pre-existing population, the resulting outcome will be better all things considered. It will then also be plausible to hold that a transfer of welfare from the better- to the worse-off, which produces equality at a slightly lower level than the initial level of the better-off, will also be better all things considered. And then we are on our way towards a repugnant conclusion which should be stopped by the means that I recommended in Chapter 4.

However, prioritarianism aggravates this problem with the spectre of the repugnant conclusion—that is, it makes it worse than it is on utilitarianism—since it implies that one outcome in which many lead lives barely worth living could be better than another outcome in which many fewer lead very good lives, *even though the sum of welfare is smaller in the former* (cf. Holtug's 'super-repugnant conclusion', 2010: 254). Nonetheless, Chapter 4 presented a means of obstructing the repugnant conclusion—by denying the transitivity of 'better (worse) than in one respect/all things considered'—and as prioritarians can avail themselves of it, no less egalitarians and utilitarians, I shall not press this objection about the value of outcomes all things considered. But there is still the objection to prioritarianism that it implies that it is better *in one respect* to add new individuals at a lower level than it is to benefit existing individuals at a higher level to a corresponding extent, and in general better in one respect to diffuse welfare as widely and thinly as possible.

9.4 Is Prioritarianism Intrapersonally Applicable?

I shall now consider a problem which largely revolves around whether prioritarianism applies intrapersonally, that is, within the life of a single individual. But let me start by pointing out that because prioritarianism highlights the absolute level of the recipient, it cannot be appropriately sensitive to the difference that it makes to our moral intuitions whether there are other individuals at the same or different levels of welfare as the recipients of the benefits at stake. For example, if we consider what moral reason we have to bestow 30 units of welfare on Tom who is at the level of 70, it makes no difference to the value of the outcome, according to prioritarianism, whether there are other individuals who are (unjustly) better off, say, at the level 100. By contrast, according to egalitarianism, the presence of such individuals, say, Tim at 100, would strengthen the reason to give Tom the 30 units. I suspect that this is in line with the moral intuitions of many people, as it is with my intuitions. This is a point that I shall put to use in an objection to prioritarianism which also includes a choice between different allocations of benefits within a single life.

Imagine facing a choice between doing X which would give Tom 30 units of welfare if he turns out to be on the level of 70, or doing Y which would give him 35 units if he turns out to be on level 100. The probability that he will be on the level of 70 is the same as the probability that he will be on the level of 100, namely 50 per cent. Suppose that this is not a one-person case, but that there is also Tim, whose well-being we cannot affect, at the level of 100. Suppose further that we do not know whether Tom autonomously prefers that we do X or Y to him; so, we cannot appeal to respect for Tom's autonomy. In these circumstances, egalitarianism implies that we ought to do X, since this is guaranteed to put Tim and Tom on an equal footing as regards benefits (which we assume is what justice requires). Certainly, this means that Tom is robbed of the chance of getting the biggest benefit, 35 units, but robbing Tom of this chance is reasonably justified by the fact that the outcome of him being at 135 and Tim at 100 would be (unjustly) unequal.

In contrast, utilitarianism implies that we ought to do Y precisely because the expected benefit of this action is the greatest. On the other hand, prioritarianism seems to yield the same verdict as egalitarianism because the fact that 35 units are somewhat greater than 30 units is reasonably outweighed by the fact that the latter would be received by someone at a much lower level, 70 instead of 100.

Now consider what happens if, by removing Tim, we transform the case into a one-person case featuring only Tom—the first purely intrapersonal case. Egalitarianism now favours doing Y to Tom, just like utilitarianism does, because this produces the greatest expected benefit for him, and there is no longer any consideration of justice to outweigh this consideration of maximizing expected benefits. Unlike egalitarianism, but like utilitarianism, the prioritarian verdict remains the same despite the fact that the case has been transformed into a single-person case: apparently, prioritarianism still supports our doing of X, and continues to disagree with utilitarianism. According to prioritarianism, the presence of Tim is irrelevant, since what is distributively relevant is the absolute level of the recipient, Tom, and this remains the same, irrespective of whether or not Tim is present. Michael Otsuka and Alex Voorhoeve claim that this judgment is unacceptable because doing Y produces the greatest expectable benefit for Tom; it is what is prudentially best for him (2009: sec. 1).

They claim that prioritarianism treats this case of intrapersonal distribution in the same way as a case of interpersonal distribution in which the choice is between doing X which would give Tom, who is at 70, 30 units, and doing Y which would give Tim, who is at 100, 35 units. In both cases, they maintain, prioritarianism implies that we ought to do X (or, more guardedly, it implies that if this is the right thing to do in the interpersonal case, it is the right thing in the intrapersonal case, too). In other words, on prioritarianism 'intrapersonal and interpersonal tradeoffs have the same moral weightings applied to them' (2009: 177). Therefore, they conclude, this view cannot take on board 'a shift [which] occurs in the moral importance of benefits and burdens when we move from a case involving intrapersonal tradeoffs to a case involving interpersonal tradeoffs' (2009: 181). Intuitively, however, we take there to be a significant difference between an intrapersonal case and an interpersonal case, such that, whereas it is plausible to claim that we ought to do X in the interpersonal case, it is more plausible to claim that we ought to do Y in the intrapersonal case because this maximizes Tom's expectable benefits.

Their diagnosis of this difference is that

a single person has a unity that renders it permissible to balance (expected) benefits and burdens against each other that might accrue to her. A group of different people, by contrast, does not possess such unity. As a consequence, some forms of balancing of benefits and burdens that are permitted when these accrue to a single person are impermissible in cases where these benefits and burdens accrue to different people. (2009: 179)

In order to do justice to the shift in our moral intuitions which occurs when we move between intrapersonal and interpersonal cases, they assert that 'we need to invoke interpersonal considerations that are essentially relational, such as the intrinsic badness of inequality' (2009: 185).

But this conclusion cannot be right, since egalitarianism is exposed to a similar objection, though it comprises 'considerations that are essentially relational'. Changing the one-person case to a second purely intrapersonal case brings out the point: imagine that Tom will *first* be at 70 between the times t_1 and t_2 and *then* at 100 from t_3 to t_4—these periods being of equal duration—if we do neither X nor Y. But if we do X, he will certainly get 30 units at t_1 and be at 100 instead of 70 between t_1 and t_2, while if we do Y he will certainly get 35 at t_3 and be at 135 instead of 100 from t_3 to t_4. Between t_2 and t_3, he will be at 100 independently of our actions, either by rising to this level from 70, or by being kept at the level of 100. It might then be argued that egalitarianism is committed to the judgment that we ought to do X because Tom will then be guaranteed to be at the same level of 100 all through the period from t_1 to t_4. If we do Y, the distribution of benefits over this period will be unequal: 70 between t_1 and t_2, 100 between t_2 and t_3, and then 135 between t_3 and t_4. This inequality might be held to outweigh the greater of the total sum of benefits. It might be objected, however, that this judgment is counterintuitive, precisely because the sum of benefits is greatest in the latter distribution (which for that reason is favoured by utilitarianism).

This demonstrates that the fact that egalitarianism weights benefits in proportion to the relative position of recipients rather than their absolute position, as does prioritarianism, does not protect it from the sort of objection raised by Otsuka and Voorhoeve.

The fact that egalitarianism appeals to a feature that is 'essentially relational' does not mean that it is essentially *interpersonal*. This finding is not surprising since, as they remark in the long quotation above, the source of the objection is located in an inability to do justice to 'the unity' of a person's existence. The fact that the badness of unjust inequality is 'essentially relational' falls short of showing that egalitarianism captures this unity because the relation of equality could conceivably hold not only between different individuals, but also between different times in a single individual's life, in spite of the unity of the individual. It has not been shown that this unity rules out the application of the relation of equality.

Certainly, as noted in 7.1, there are problems with applying the relation of equality intrapersonally, to individuals at different times of their lives. What would be the relevant units of time between which equality should ideally obtain? Might we not in the end be pressed to the absurdity of requiring equality of welfare between every moment of an individual's life? However, we also saw that different temporal stages of people's lives could be so psychologically disconnected that the normal propensity for identification breaks down and creates a rationale for a demand for just equality between the disconnected temporal stages of a person.

At this juncture, it should be noted that there is an infelicitous ambiguity in describing, as do Otsuka and Voorhoeve, the relevant shortcoming of prioritarianism as being that 'it ignores the moral significance of the separateness of persons' (2009: 185). Saying that it ignores this significance, or 'fails to take seriously the distinction between persons', means in the words of Otsuka that 'it is insensitive to whether the life that goes well and the life that goes badly are possible lives of the same person or rather the lives of different people' (2012: 368). But this insensitivity could manifest itself in a tendency to assimilate either (a) interpersonal cases to intrapersonal cases, or (b) intrapersonal cases to interpersonal cases. (a) is what utilitarianism has been accused of when it recommends the maximization of benefits in the interpersonal domain no less than in the intrapersonal domain. It thereby treats separate persons as though they constituted a single super-person. Egalitarianism and prioritarianism meet this charge by weighting benefits in proportion to the absolute and relative position of recipients, respectively. But this might seem to leave them open to the opposite charge, (b): to explain why this weighting which is intuitively plausible in the interpersonal situation does not invade the intrapersonal domain, despite the apparent unity of a person. It is this second challenge to vindicate the significance of personal unity with which we are now concerned.[7] It is not clear why the difference as regards the way egalitarianism and prioritarianism propose to solve problem (a) should give egalitarianism an easier time with problem (b) than prioritarianism gets.

However, on behalf of egalitarianism it could be argued that it is not committed to supporting the doing of X in the second intrapersonal case. It could be claimed that the

---

[7] As Thomas Porter remarks (2012: 358; cf. also Parfit, 2012: 413), but Porter denies that there is a problem for prioritarianism on this score (2012: 359–63).

unequal distribution of 70–100–135 between t_1 and t_4 is not unjust or unfair if there is enough psychological connectedness between how Tom is in the period t_1–t_2 and in the period t_3–t_4 for him reasonably to regard his being at the high level of 135 between t_3 and t_4 as *compensating* him for being at the low level of 70 between t_1 and t_2. It can be prudentially rational to be prepared to undergo substantial sacrifices in the near future to reap later greater benefits under such circumstances. When we decide to make such sacrifices, we should not see it as a reason against undertaking them that they create an unequal distribution of benefits in our lives. Since this inequality would be autonomously chosen, it cannot amount to an injustice to us, as argued in 7.1. Similarly, if we autonomously decide to transfer some of our benefits to someone else who will thereby become better off than us, the fact that this transfer will create an inequality between us and the recipient is no reason against it because the fact that we autonomously choose the inequality ensures that it cannot be unfair to us.

Now if we egalitarians, instead of Tom himself, face the question of whether to do Y to Tom which will impose on him a sacrifice which he himself could rationally view as being compensated for by a later, greater gain, we would make a mistake were we to appeal to a relation of unjust inequality within his life which would have no place in Tom's own deliberation. The question is just what is prudentially best for him. Consequently, as long as we suspect no radical psychological disconnectedness in Tom's life between t_1 and t_4, we have no moral reason to do X rather than what maximizes Tom's benefits, that is, Y.

Although prioritarians do not believe in justice, as I suggested in 9.1, they can avail themselves of an analogous argument in the first intrapersonal case. They could maintain that if Tom himself were to encounter the question of whether it would be best for him to do X or Y, he would be mistaken to assign an extra prioritarian weight to the 30 units at 70 which would prevent him from being compensated for the lack of these units by getting 35 units later. Similarly, he would be mistaken to hold such an extra weight to be a reason against transferring some of his benefits to a better-off friend. The fact that these distributions are autonomously chosen undercuts the justification for assigning an extra prioritarian or other distributive weight to the benefits involved. Against this background, prioritarians could claim that when *they* countenance the question of whether to do Y that will impose on Tom a sacrifice which he could rationally regard himself as being compensated for by a later, greater gain, it would be wrong of them to introduce a prioritarian weight that would have no place in Tom's own deliberation. Therefore, like egalitarians, prioritarians could happily recommend the doing of Y.

In the course of arguing that prioritarianism is more naturally applied intrapersonally than is egalitarianism, Dennis McKerlie floats the idea of a prioritarian revision or re-interpretation of prudence, according to which

> What is best for the agent is receiving a smaller rather than a larger benefit, if the smaller benefit comes when he is badly off and if this choice makes his life better... The value of a life does

not just depend on the total amount of well-being that it contains; the value also depends on how the well-being is distributed across the temporal stages of the life. (2013: 139–40)

In terms of our example, this idea means that it would be doing X rather than Y which is expectedly best for Tom. But this is to confuse the impersonal, moral value of the prioritarian weight with the personal value of a benefit. Having 30 units of benefits at the level of 70 does not make Tom more better off than it would have made him had he received it at the level of 100; it does not make his life better *for him* to a greater degree.

We have seen, however, that people can autonomously choose a course of life that harbours fewer benefits than some alternatives. If such choices are made, respect for autonomy could justify that we do what is less beneficial for people. Thus, imagine that Tom is a dedicated, but somewhat misguided prioritarian, who wants to broadcast his pet doctrine by living it out in his own life. Then, if we knew this, we could justifiably do X. This is however not the situation that we are imagining; we are imagining that we do not know what Tom would autonomously prefer.

Under these circumstances, prioritarians should reason as follows in the first intrapersonal case: if getting 35 units at 100 is so good for Tom that it could outweigh the badness of going without the 30 units at 70—this is implied by saying that the former can be adequate compensation for the latter in the second intrapersonal case—then Tom ought rationally to run a 50 per cent risk of being at 70 and not getting the 30 units in order to have a 50 per cent chance of getting 35 units should he be at 100. Since, in his prudential deliberation, he himself should not take into consideration any additional moral weight of benefits received at the lower level, in making this prudential choice on his behalf other people should not do so, either. But then the morally right thing to do to Tom is Y which maximizes his expected benefits.

Parfit claims that 'it would be wrong to take, on this person's behalf, some of the risks that this person could rationally choose to take, if he or she made this choice for purely self-interested reasons' (2012: 423). I think, however, that what this morally justified greater caution or risk aversion on someone else's behalf comes down to is that we should avoid courses of action which seem *at odds* with what is expectably best for this person, even to a relatively small degree. For instance, we should avoid feeding people with sugary, fatty food, though we should allow them to feed themselves thus should they so prefer. If, however, a choice appears rational from a self-interested perspective, or prudentially best, it would be misdirected paternalism to overrule it in the interests of the subject, by introducing a prioritarian—or egalitarian—weight. These weights, being moral weights, are not in place when the individuals of relevance for a distribution of benefits are only ones within whose lives there is that amount of unity or identification that makes compensation possible.

The proposal made here amounts to saying that prioritarians could consistently supplement their view with conditions that remove the greater moral weight of benefits to the worse-off. These would be conditions to the effect that the absence of the benefits could reasonably be held to be compensated for by other benefits, so that subjects could rationally run a risk of not getting the former benefits in order to have a chance of getting the latter benefits, or that the subjects have autonomously chosen to be worse off. These conditions mirror the conditions under which egalitarians should hold that inequality of welfare is not unjust to the worse-off.

To sum up the argument so far. The problem that Otsuka and Voorhoeve raise does not have to do with respecting the separateness of persons in the sense (a). In contrast to utilitarianism, both egalitarianism and prioritarianism respect this separateness by their appeals to equality and priority, respectively. The problem for these doctrines is rather to account for the unity of individual persons in the sense of explaining why the factors which account for the separateness of persons in (a) do not creep into the intrapersonal realm in spite of the unity of persons. This is a problem that both egalitarianism and prioritarianism are up against, and I believe that their means of dealing with it could be similar. Thus, I do not see why prioritarianism has to have a greater problem with accounting for the unity of persons than does egalitarianism.[8]

However, even if egalitarians have to concede that prioritarians might be able to deal with the unity of persons in the same manner as they themselves do, the cases that we have examined in this section nevertheless show a significant difference between egalitarianism and prioritarianism which to my mind tells in favour of egalitarianism. Remember that whereas, according to egalitarianism, it makes a moral difference to a distribution within the span of Tom's life whether Tim is also present at 100, this makes no moral difference, according to prioritarianism. While giving Tom a 50 per cent chance of ending up at 135 could be morally right if he is alone in the universe, ensuring that he be at the same level as Tim, 100, might be morally right if Tim is also present, as implied by egalitarianism. But if, as I have argued, prioritarianism agrees with the former claim, it will have to stick to this claim even if Tim is also present. According to prioritarianism, Tim's presence is morally relevant only if he is a possible recipient of benefits, whereas he is also relevant as a point of reference, according to egalitarianism. Thus, an outcome in which there is a 50 per cent chance of Tom being at 70 and a 50 per cent chance of him being at 135, when Tim is at 100, remains better on prioritarianism than an outcome in which both are at 100. This is what utilitarianism, too, implies, but it seems to me counterintuitive.

Contrast a variation of this case in which Tim is a possible recipient as well. Suppose that there is a 50 per cent probability that Tim will be at 70 and a 50 per cent probability that Tom will be at 70, and that the same goes for their being at 100. Again, doing X will give the one at 70, be it Tim or Tom, 30 units, and doing Y will give the other one at 100 35 units (cf. Parfit's case 2, 2012: 405). In this case both egalitarianism and prioritarianism support the doing of X, unless it is known that—perhaps because they are enemies—Tim and Tom have agreed to run the risk of not being benefited should they be worse off in order to have the chance of getting the bigger benefit if better off.

---

[8] Although I agree with McKerlie (2013: ch. 5) that it is considerably more straightforward to apply prioritarianism than egalitarianism in the intrapersonal realm.

Then we should respect their agreement and do Y, but in the absence of knowledge of such an agreement, both views recommend X.

My overall conclusion is, then, that if we conclude that prioritarianism can solve the problem of the unity of persons—I do not need to insist on this, since I do not accept prioritarianism—it comes up against the difficulty that this solution is 'other-invariant', that its judgments about intrapersonal distributions are not sensitive to, or do not vary with, the presence of other individuals beyond the range of distribution, for instance that giving Tom a 50 per cent chance of getting 35 at 100 with the same risk of ending up at 70 is what we ought to do even if Tim is present at 100. By contrast to the former problem, the latter problem has to do with the defining difference between egalitarianism and prioritarianism, namely that egalitarianism focuses on the position of recipients relative to other individuals—who need not be possible recipients—whereas prioritarianism focuses on the absolute position of the recipients. The problem regarding the unity of persons arises not only for prioritarianism, but also for egalitarianism, and it seems that it could be solved for both in analogous ways.

10

Some Alternative Bases of Equality

10.1 Deflationary versus Selective Groundings of Equality

The chief objective of Part II has been to defend and develop the extreme egalitarian thesis that justice requires that everyone be equally well off, unless some autonomously choose (or would choose) to be worse off than others. This thesis has been established by a demolition defence that undermines grounds designed to make it just that some are better or worse off than others, these grounds being deserts and rights. The egalitarian view that I have defended is an anti-inegalitarianism to the effect that the impersonal value of just equality can be exemplified only if there are things of personal value, and it cannot make the value of an outcome greater than the set of its personal values, since just equality is not anything good in itself. But the unjust inequality of an outcome detracts from the value that it has in virtue of the benefits that it contains, and a difference as regards unjust inequality can make one outcome worse than another all things considered, though it is not worse for anyone, but better for some. However, this can clearly be so only when new individuals are added to an outcome; in same number cases recessive egalitarianism may not be unreasonable.

In Chapter 6 it was concluded that membership of the species *Homo sapiens* cannot serve to give human beings higher moral status or standing than non-human animals, or to 'upgrade' them to beings whose personal values contribute more to the moral value of outcomes. For this membership is not of intrinsic value, or even an intrinsic property of humans. If it had fulfilled these conditions, it might have seemed to be in a promising position to form the basis of human equality, of *all* humans having the same high moral value, since it could reasonably be taken to be a property that all humans possess equally. Even so, in light of the argument of 7.3, it can be seen that species membership cannot make all humans deserve or have a right to the same since—apart from not being anything of value—it is not anything for which humans are ultimately responsible (as I first argued in 1993). Thus, species membership cannot ground a claim that justice requires all humans to be equally well off. But, if it had been of intrinsic value, it could still, despite this shortcoming, have resulted in human well-being having a higher moral value, or adding more to the value of outcomes, than non-human well-being because of what in Chapter 6 I alluded to as its 'framing' effect.

Properties of beings that with greater plausibility than species membership can be held to be valuable usually vary significantly between human individuals. I am thinking of such properties as moral capacity, rationality, self-consciousness, and so on. For this reason they are unsuitable to constitute the basis of all humans having equal moral status. To overcome this problem of individual variation, Rawls has famously put forward the idea of a *range property* (1971: 508). To have a range property is to have some scalar property within a certain range, for instance to be inside a circle in virtue of being at a particular point within it. In the case at hand, Rawls proposes that the relevant range property is to have a moral personality above a minimal level or threshold. You have a moral personality if you have a capacity to have, or a potentiality to develop, a conception of what is good for you and a sense of justice (1971: 505). Everyone who has a moral personality to at least the minimal degree is 'within the range' and, thus, has equal moral standing; it is irrelevant that some have moral personality to a greater degree.

A first problem with this account is, as Rawls himself notes (1971: 509), that he has not justified zooming in on moral personality among the manifold of psychological capacities and dispositions that humans and other animals have. We have seen that there are other candidates, some of which, like sentience or basic experiential capacities, could endow a considerably larger class of beings with equal moral status. That is, an alternative proposal could be that all beings who have, or have a potential to develop, sentience or experiential capacities at least to the minimal degree that they are capable of enjoyment and suffering have equal moral status.

Another hitch, which Rawls also mentions, is that humans who are 'more or less deprived of moral personality may present a difficulty' (1971: 510). Cases in point are humans who are severely mentally retarded. He does not try to solve this problem. This is obviously a serious defect if the project is to supply *all* humans with an equal moral status. His goal might however be the less ambitious one of putting a subset of humans on an equal footing.

Even so, there are still problems ahead. First, what should count as a minimal degree of moral personality would seem to be arbitrary. This difficulty should not be taken lightly, since whether an individual falls on one rather than on the other side of the line drawn would make a great difference to this individual's moral status. Secondly, and of more relevance in the present context, no reason has been given why we should ignore different degrees of moral personality above the minimum. If degree of a certain capacity determines moral status to the extent that you must reach a certain threshold to have some moral status, why is it not the case that different degrees of the capacity above this threshold make moral status vary? Bluntly put, Rawls has not really solved the problem of variation.

Although Ian Carter clearly sees these deficiencies of Rawls's conception of a range property (2011: 548–50, as did Singer in 1979: 16–17), he advances a proposal which seems to face similar difficulties. Carter suggests that the solution to the problem of variation 'can be found in a particular justification for *evaluative abstinence*—that is, a refusal to evaluate persons' varying capacities' (2011: 550). He invokes a notion of respect—'opacity respect'—which involves a refusal to look further inside individuals once we recognize that they satisfy the requirement of a minimal degree of a moral personality (2011: 550-4). But this raises the question why we should adopt this stance of opacity respect towards people. As Carter himself puts it, the suspicion is that

> the commitment to evaluative abstinence in the public sphere is really nothing more than the outcome of a desire to avoid concluding that people are unequal as agents and that they ought therefore to have unequal basic entitlements.   (2011: 558)

In other words, the suspicion is that the appeal to opacity respect to justify human equality is circular because in order to defend this appeal to opacity respect we have to refer to our desire that people come out as equals. But we want to know whether this desire can be justified. So far as I can see, Carter does not do anything to allay this suspicion. It may be that his ambition is the more limited one of showing merely that a *politically liberal conception of justice* is committed to the adoption of opacity respect (2011: 554-60). Such a context-dependent justification is however insufficient for the present purpose of finding a ground for equality which is valid independently of ideological commitments.[1]

So far as I can find, we have to abandon the idea that there is any intrinsic property of some set of beings, whether it be human beings or persons, that could bestow on them an equally elevated moral value or status. The most plausible candidates for value-grounding properties are sophisticated psychological capacities, but of course there is great individual variation with respect to them. Furthermore, in Chapter 6, I argued that the value of these features is extrinsic or instrumental, not intrinsic. It is the *exercise* of such capacities that generates intrinsic value for their owners, that makes some things intrinsically valuable for them. As soon as there is the possibility of such exercises, there is the possibility of something—namely personal intrinsic value—that morally matters in itself, something that can make outcomes intrinsically valuable. But, strictly speaking, this intrinsic value belongs to lives, not to the individuals leading the lives. Therefore, they cannot endow humans or persons with intrinsic value. However, it is not necessary that humans or persons have a value that is intrinsic rather than extrinsic in order for it to make them worthy of something in the sense of deserving it. But, as I argued in 7.3, attribution of desert requires that subjects be ultimately responsible for their possession of the property that is the basis of their desert, and this is a condition that temporally finite subjects cannot fulfil.

There are, then, two values that are liable to be involved in attempts to ground the equal moral status of some class of beings. One is to the effect that this class of beings

---

[1] Richard Arneson (2015: 45-8), Thomas Christiano (2015: 58) and Lippert-Rasmussen (2016: 43-8) are uneasy about Carter's approach for these and other reasons. These writers also detail other grounds for being skeptical about other putative bases of equality discussed in the text.

all have the same value in virtue of some common natural—that is, non-evaluative or non-normative—property. The other is to the effect that in virtue of this equal value, they are worth the same treatment or existence—which I have interpreted to mean that justice requires that they be equally benefited or well off.

Kasper Lippert-Rasmussen distinguishes between these two aspects, but tries to forge them together in an account of the equality of persons. He writes that it is natural to combine the view that 'individuals should be equal in terms of what they are non-instrumentally concerned about' 'with the view that the equality of moral standing of persons is grounded in their capacity to be non-instrumentally concerned with things in a distinctive way' (2016: 51). Now I do not see why it should be granted that the latter capacity is the same in all persons rather than stronger in some persons than in others. But even granted this equality of standing, I do not see how the equality of treatment follows. For instance, why should we not rather maximize than equalize the total sum of what persons are non-instrumentally concerned about in the pertinent way? If it requires fewer resources to give some what they are non-instrumentally concerned about than others, this goal would justify the former getting more of what they are non-instrumentally concerned about than the latter.

Lippert-Rasmussen might want to reply (2016: 54) that it would not be *fair* to give some more of what they are non-instrumentally concerned about. But why would this not be fair if it takes fewer resources? If the reply is that this is unfair because some are just plain lucky to have non-instrumental concerns typical of persons that are more easily satisfiable—and even lucky to have concerns typical of persons—we are well on the way to a proposal like mine.

This proposal is not of the above 'dual-value' sort. Instead of basing equality of treatment of some group on the selection of some (intrinsic or extrinsic) value that they share—the first kind of equal value claim—I have contended that no feature (of value) can make any being worthy of better treatment than any other, since this presupposes ultimate responsibility for the possession of this property. This might be characterized as a *deflationary* vindication of egalitarianism or the justice of equality because it consists in demolishing any grounds designed to make it just that some be better treated than others.

The upshot is, more precisely, that it is unjust or unfair if some of the individuals for whom things can be intrinsically valuable have more of what is intrinsically valuable than others, unless these others autonomously choose to have less. For there is nothing that could make this just because this presupposes a possession of ultimate responsibility that is out of the reach of temporally finite beings. By itself this is enough to undermine what is offered by anthropocentric speciesism, the notion of a range property, or the appeal to various psychological capacities as grounds for a claim that justice requires equality of welfare within some selected class of beings. But the features offered also fail because they do not satisfy the joint requirements of both being something valuable and being common to all members of the selected class. As opposed to such *selective* egalitarianisms, the egalitarianism here advanced is extreme by ranging over *all* beings with a potential to acquire consciousness and, thus, to be subjects for whom things can be intrinsically valuable.

It might be wondered why the property of having sentience or consciousness cannot serve as the ground for a selective egalitarianism which is wide enough to be more or less co-extensive with extreme egalitarianism. This might be thought to be a property which is both valuable and shared equally by a large class of beings. George Sher's recent attempt to find a basis for equality appeals to something 'which is at least closely related to Singer's criterion of sentience' (2014: 84; 2015: 24). It is worth spelling out why such an account is defective, but first it should be observed that Sher's exposition is not free of ambiguity. It declares that it is 'the fact that each of us is a conscious subject—that each has a subjectivity of a certain sort—that underlies and supports our claim to moral equality' (2014: 79; 2015: 20). As he admits, this statement leaves it open 'whether what is doing the explanatory work is simply the fact that each of us *has* a subjectivity or...that each has a subjectivity with just the relevant features' (2014: 89; 2015: 28). The relevant features are specified to be '*the kind of structure that gives rise to a sense of time, reasons-responsiveness, and the interests that rational aims generate*' (2014: 90; 2015: 28)—in short, the subjectivity of a *person*. Sher confesses that he is inclined to come down in favour of the latter view, though he believes that 'even subjectivities that lack these features confer some moral significance on their bearers' (2014: 91; 2015: 29).

According to this interpretation, Sher's approach seems inconsistent with some of his claims. He remarks that it is a 'crucial fact that *having a subjectivity is an all-or-nothing matter*' (2014: 86; 2015: 26). This fact is crucial 'because it implies that the moral standing to which the subjectivities of different individuals give rise is all-or-nothing as well' (2014: 86; 2015: 26). But it is very implausible to maintain that the property of having the subjectivity or consciousness of a person is an all-or-nothing matter. Consider the development that we have all undergone from being foetuses with rudimentary consciousness to being full-fledged persons. Surely, this development does not feature a stage in which there is an abrupt change from a non-personal to a personal consciousness. This change is more likely to be gradual, developing consciousnesses by degrees acquiring the characteristics that are definitive of personhood, such as a more articulate sense of time and reasons-responsiveness. Moreover, this development normally continues after the—presumably vague—stage during which it becomes reasonable to hold that personal consciousness commences. But this means that Sher's proposed ground for equality countenances all the problems of gradation already reviewed.

What if he were instead to opt for subjectivity or consciousness *of any sort* as the basis of equality? Although he curiously claims that consciousness or sentience 'arguably admit of degrees' (2014: 86; 2015: 26)—despite the fact that he denies that the same is true of subjectivity—there is a sense in which they do not. If 'more conscious' is not confused with 'conscious of more', the phrase does not seem to make sense. Subjects can doubtless be conscious of more in the sense of having a wider array of possible objects of their consciousness, or of being conscious of more intense sensations of pleasure and pain, and so on. But if we rule out these possibilities of variation by stipulating that we are dealing with consciousness of one and the same object in every respect, it apparently does not make sense to say that the consciousness of it admits of degrees, or can be stronger or weaker.

Thus, we have eventually arrived at something which is an all-or-nothing matter. Could it serve as a basis for equality? No, because even if having consciousness itself is an all-or-nothing matter, it brings along *other* properties that are gradual, and these could plausibly be held to matter morally, or be of value. As mentioned, objects of consciousness vary in respect of both quality and quantity, and this plausibly matters morally. Furthermore, what morally matters is not having simply consciousness, but desires, and these obviously vary in degree of strength.

In 7.3 I noted that Singer takes advantage of this fact by means of his principle of equal consideration of interests (of the same strength). I added that, to my mind, Singer's move does not result in an egalitarianism worth its salt, since it allows benefiting the better-off more than the worse-off if their interests are stronger. The salient point in the present context, however, is simply that we need some moral principle to tell us how to deal with the variation in respects of other features, even if we have located *some* property of moral relevance which is an all-or-nothing matter (cf. Uwe Steinhoff, 2015: 170).

My proposal is the radical one that no variation as regards any features of sentient beings could make any of them worthy—in the sense of it being required by justice—of being better off than any others. No doubt, this proposal is too speculative and too divergent from common sense for the taste of many, but I see no alternative way of establishing an egalitarianism worth its name. If grounds that are designed to make it just that some are better off than others, like deserts and rights, are not demolished, it seems to me that the space left for equality would have to be very restricted indeed.

10.2 The Status of Inviolability or Not to be Harmed as a Means

I have proceeded on the assumption that the relevant equality of treatment concerns seeing to it that the individuals in question receive an equal amount of welfare. This might aptly be designated by the term 'equal concern'. But some egalitarians demand 'equal concern *and* respect' (to use a phrase popularized by Ronald Dworkin), and respect might cover treatment that does not mix well with a concern that everybody's level of welfare be as equal as possible. A case in point is respect in sense of refraining from *harming someone as a means* to a greater good, which will be discussed in this section.

Such respect is required by the 'inviolability' that Kamm ascribes to us, that is, 'the good of being someone whose worth is such that it makes him highly inviolable and also makes him someone to whom one owes nonviolation' (2007: 254). Notice that she talks about somebody being 'highly inviolable' rather than absolutely inviolable. For it is reasonably permissible to harm individuals by killing them as means to a greater good if the good is great enough, for instance the saving of millions of other lives. Likewise, you would think that their inviolability would also be higher if—contrary to what I contended in 7.4—it had been impermissible also to kill individuals as means to saving a few when this happens as a side-effect—and, indeed, to kill them merely as a side-effect.

Appeals to inviolability prompt the question of what could be the property of individuals which is the ground for the degree of inviolability that they in fact have rather than a higher or lower one. If it is the case that beings like us—whatever kind of beings we are taken to be—all have the same degree of inviolability, we must possess this property to the same extent; otherwise, some would be more highly inviolable than others. The preceding section enlarged on the problems of identifying any valuable property that we all share and of explaining how it could make us worthy of some type of equal treatment, for example the type that a particular degree of inviolability consists in.

Kamm seems explicitly committed to our having such an intrinsic property, since inviolability, as she conceives it, is 'victim-focused' (2007: 28). That is, on her view our being worthy of protection from being harmed as means to some greater good is based on some features that we possess as the victims of acts, and not on any features of the agents who act on us, as would be the case on a contrasting 'agent-focused' view of inviolability. Our alleged inviolability presupposes our having rights not to be harmed in certain ways, for instance a right to life that is violated when we are killed without our consent, and so on. But, as she realizes (2007: 251–2), even if we were to have a right to life, it could conceivably be permissible to infringe this right by killing one of us in order to prevent five others from being killed for the reason that this would minimize the total number of violations of rights to life. Under these circumstances we would not have the inviolability that she attributes to us.

As I have elsewhere (2013: 37–8) argued, inviolability in this sense cannot be victim-focused, but has to be agent-focused. Imagine that, out of respect for her inviolability, I do not kill Vic as a means of saving five lives, though I realize that this will lead to her and Tim being killed by somebody else as means of saving the five. Then my restraint does not make things better (or worse) from her victim-perspective: she will still be killed as a means of saving five. The difference lies in my agent-perspective: whether I be the one who executes killing or let somebody else do it. Therefore, I think that inviolability in the sense of a protection against being harmed as a means has to be agent-focused or based on facts about agency.

In the same book (2013: ch. 6), I also argued that it is not harder morally to justify harming as a means than as a side-effect. However, there I focused on how this idea is underpinned by causally based responsibility. But I would now like to supplement my earlier discussion by investigating some additional difficulties that crop up when means are intended. In the present context, it is important to have as good a case as possible for rejecting the notion of our having the status of inviolability, since equal respect for such a status would conflict with equal concern for everyone's welfare: it excludes proportionate concern for the welfare of the larger number of individuals who are harmed if nobody is allowed to be harmed as means to their benefit.

To have a specific target in mind consider the following *means principle* proposed by Tadros who subscribes to Kamm's inviolability (2013: 124–5):

whilst it may be permissible to pursue the good where this will have, as one of its side effects, some lesser harm to others, it is not permissible to pursue the good where others will be used as a means to achieve that good. (2013: 114)

Let me begin my critique of this sort of principle by drawing attention to a distinction between what might be called *causal* and *epistemic* means.[2] There are other kinds of means, for instance means that have conventional connections to their ends, like when making a long jump is a means of breaking a record, and means that have constitutive or part–whole connections to their ends, for example when acquiring a book is a means of completing or contributing to the completion of a book collection. Alongside causal means, these means could be lumped together as *factual* as opposed to epistemic means, but I shall here concentrate on causal among factual means.

Being a (necessary) causal condition for the realization of an end is necessary for being a (necessary) causal means to it. But there is also an epistemic dimension to causal means if they are to be intended: then they must be something that you can *ascertain* prior to, and thus independently of, ascertaining that you have attained the end (cf. Persson, 2005: 118–19). By contrast to factual means, epistemic means must be intended: while you can kill someone by means of accidentally firing a gun, or break a record accidentally by means of a jump, you cannot use something accidentally as an epistemic means.

If means are sufficient for attaining an end, their application can enable you to infer that you have attained it. But suppose that you cannot directly verify whether sufficient means have been successfully applied, or whether the end has been attained, but have to infer whether it has been attained from some other facts that you can directly verify that you have brought about. Then these other facts could also be epistemic means for you by means of which you could *tell* that the end has been accomplished. These means could consist in reliable side-effects of the end; for instance, in the much discussed case of a runaway trolley hurtling towards five people being diverted onto another track where it will hit only one person, the hitting of this person could serve as evidence that the trolley has been successfully diverted away from the five if the occurrence of this diversion cannot itself be observed. This kind of means could also consist in facts that include the end as a part, if the only sufficient means available to you are *more* than sufficient for the attainment of the end (this will be illustrated below). A common feature of both causal and epistemic means to an end is, however, that in order for them to

[2] This is a distinction that I only alluded to in my earlier discussion (2013: 157–8).

be intended as means it has to be possible to establish their realization prior to establishing that the end has been accomplished.

Now one question is: can the fact that somebody is harmed as an *epistemic* means of telling that a good end has been attained make an action easier to justify than an action would be if somebody is harmed as much as an intended *causal* means of attaining the same end? Since epistemic means can utilize other facts than causal conditions of the end, another question is: does the fact that someone being harmed is used as an epistemic means to tell that a good end has been achieved, with this harm as a side-effect, make an action harder to justify than it would have been had the individual been harmed simply as a side-effect, without this fact featuring as an epistemic means? I believe that consideration of the following three cases suggests that the answers to these two questions are 'no'.

To begin with, compare two situations. In the first situation I have to kill five innocent people in a room as a causal means of killing a dangerous terrorist: imagine, for instance, that all six of them are lined up with the terrorist at the back of the line, thinking that the innocents will effectively shield him. However, I have a high-power crossbow which enables me to shoot an arrow right through all six. But I am somewhat doubtful whether this act can be justified.

While I am deliberating, the first situation is transformed into the second situation: the six are spreading out at the same time as the lights are dimming. I would now have been able to shoot only the terrorist had it not been for the fact that I can no longer discern which of the six is him. So, I put a chemical on the tip of my arrow, whose result would be that were the arrow to pierce somebody's—anybody's—torso, the impact would make the chemical mix with the victim's blood, and poisonous fumes would be released that would instantly kill everyone in the room. By shooting this deadly arrow into anyone of the six, I can therefore ensure that I shall kill the terrorist. I could then use the killing of all six as an epistemic means to tell that I have killed the terrorist. Killing all six is not a causal means to this end because killing the terrorist is not an *effect* of killing everyone in the room: it is a *part* of it. But it seems dubious that this change would make the killing of the innocents easier to justify, so that my doubts about its justifiability may now be resolved. If this is sound, applying the epistemic means of killing all six to the end of killing the terrorist is not appreciably easier to justify than applying the causal means of killing the five innocents to this end as would happen in the first case.

Now consider the second situation being replaced by a third situation: as I am aiming at the person who happens to be nearest to me, the lights are getting brighter to the extent that I am now able to discern who the terrorist is—and it turns out that he is the one I happen to be aiming at! I would then have been in a position to kill just him had it not been for the fact that I had put the chemical on the tip of my arrow. But as things stand, if I shoot the arrow into him, the five innocents will be killed merely as a foreseen side-effect. Killing them is no longer an intended means for me in any sense. Yet, it strikes me as questionable whether this change will make the killing of them along with the terrorist any easier to justify. After all, the five would die in the same way, as a side-effect of killing the terrorist due to the release of the fumes.

However, by altering the situation from the first to the third via the second, there has been a transition from a situation in which I would have killed the five innocents as an intended causal means to killing the terrorist to a situation in which they would be killed merely as a foreseen side-effect of this end without the justification for killing becoming noticeably easier. So, the insertion of epistemic means in between the first and third situation appears to obliterate or blur the intuitive moral difference between harming as intended means and as foreseen side-effect.

If it is insisted that there is a moral difference somewhere, where would it be: between causal and epistemic means (situation 1 and 2), between epistemic means and side-effects (situations 2 and 3), or in both places? Choosing the third option would mean that instead of the bipartition of harming as a causal means and harming as a side-effect, we would have a tripartition, with harming as an epistemic means being sliced in between them as being less hard to justify than the former but harder to justify than the latter.

To check whether there is a moral difference between the first and second situation, a point about the first situation that Jonathan Bennett notably has made (1995: 209–13) should be emphasized. This is that harming the five is not strictly speaking a causal condition of killing the terrorist and, thus, need not be intended in order for the end to be intended. For if the five innocents had miraculously survived unscathed being pierced by my arrow, this would not have foiled my end of killing the terrorist. All I need to intend as regards the five is that my arrow passes through their bodies; their being harmed and killed could be merely a foreseen side-effect, as it is in the third situation. The difference between the first and the third—as well as the second—situation is that my doing something to the five is a causal condition of killing the terrorist. But, despite the conception of responsibility as causally based, it may be wondered why this should make the killing harder to justify in the first situation.

By contrast, the killing of the five must be intended in the second situation because I have to establish that I have killed all six in order to be able to infer that I have accomplished my end of killing the terrorist. Why is this not at least as morally important as the fact that killing the five is a causal condition in the first situation? Want of an answer to this question may lead us to place the killing of the five in the first and second situation on a par. In support of this ranking, it could be maintained that in both situations I have to intend to do as a means something to the five that kills them (even if I do not have to intend that they be killed in both of them). In the third situation I need only foresee that I shall do something to them that will kill them (cause the fumes to spread).

This claim raises the question of what it is about intending to do as a means something to somebody which kills them that makes this seem harder to justify. I am inclined to conjecture that this is what we have seen to be involved in the notion of intending something as a means, namely that this requires it to be possible to ascertain that the means has been applied prior to ascertaining attainment of the end. Notice, however, that this does not entail that it should be possible to ascertain that the means *causes death* prior to ascertaining that the end has been attained. If this is not possible, application of the means seems easier to justify.

Imagine, for instance, that killing the terrorist had necessitated as a causal means to it the removal of the five from the room—to get him in clear sight—but in a fashion that would expose them to radiation or pollution that will kill them much later. Intuitively, this removal seems easier to justify than shooting an arrow through them. The reason is, I surmise, that the causal link between being shot through by an arrow and dying is so close that we cannot help being convinced that someone is dying as soon as we observe an arrow passing through them. This closeness is the reason why we are prone to overlook that the death of the five need not be intended in the first of the three situations above. By contrast the causal chain between the removal of the five and their death is so long that observing that they have been removed will not convince us, before we can ascertain the death of the terrorist, that they will die from the removal. So, here we are not tempted to assume that their deaths must be intended along with the removal. Additionally, as I have argued elsewhere (2013: 154–6), a conception of responsibility as causally based makes us feel less responsible for an effect the less directly it results from our bodily act.

Consequently, the notion of intending to do as a means something to someone which kills them is too unspecific to capture the factor that gives rise to the impression of impermissibility. It needs to be supplemented by a clause to the effect that the causal connection between the intended act and death be so intimate that observation of the act makes the agent spontaneously conclude that death is occurring prior to concluding that the end is attained, and sometimes even so quickly that it is mistakenly thought to be part of what is intended. Here we also have the explanation why harming as means can be made to appear more acceptable if, as I did in 7.4, we imagine it to happen as a side-effect of another action of ours: it then appears more acceptable because it is preceded by the attainment of the end of saving oneself from being hit by the act of deflecting a boulder, an act to which the harming is less directly connected, so responsibility for it is reduced.

As confirmation of this diagnosis, consider the different kind of case in which you have to kill a single individual as a means of being able to perform *the distinct act of saving five*: for instance, you have to let go of a rope in which one person is hanging as a means of being able to grab another rope in which five are hanging. Compare this to the following situation in which killing the one is (more) clearly a side-effect of letting go of one rope as a means of being able to grasp the rope in which the five are hanging: the rope that you let go of will hit the one, who is standing on a narrow ledge below, causing him to fall to his death. It seems to me that the latter act need not strike us as easier to justify than letting go of the rope in which the one is hanging. I put this down to the fact that the fall of the one due to being hit by the rope, though (more) clearly a side-effect, might still be something that you will have to face before the saving of the five.[3] But if what drives our intuitions about impermissibility is the fact that the harm is so tightly connected to the means that we cannot help concluding that it occurs prior to concluding that the end is attained, it appears obvious that these intuitions are unjustifiable.

It might be pointed out that in none of the three situations earlier presented do I *use or treat* the five innocents as causal means in a harmful way. In the first situation I would indeed have harmed the five innocents as causal means of killing the terrorist—loosely speaking—but I do not use them as causal means in a harmful way. This is true, but is it morally significant? In fact, both the first and the third situation could easily be so revised that they become cases of using the five as means in the process of harming them (in the second situation they are already used as epistemic means). Suppose, for instance, that in the third situation the light has become stronger because the five have moved to new locations in the room where there is a light sensor. Then in picking off the terrorist, I would be using the five as causal means because of the effect that they have on the light. But this use surely does not make my act harder to justify.

The first situation could also readily be turned into a case of harmfully using the five as causal means: imagine that there is a magnetic field in the room that would make my arrow swerve so that it would have missed the terrorist had it not been for the fact that it had passed through the five. Then by shooting the arrow through the five, I would be harmfully using them as causal means to prevent the arrow from swerving. But it seems to me hard to believe that this causal difference could make any difference morally speaking.

To see this more clearly, let me try to unravel what the distinction between harmfully using individuals as means and harming them as means involves. If the bodies of the five are simply an obstacle that my arrow has to penetrate in order to reach the terrorist, I have to harm them as causal means to harming the terrorist (loosely speaking), but I do not use the five harmfully as means to this end. Likewise, if, as in the Nozick case discussed in 7.4, you are innocently falling down on me, and I am using my ray gun to annihilate your body, I am harming you as a means of avoiding being crushed by you, but I am not harmfully using you as a means. The reason is that you *are* the threat that I am striving to eliminate, just as the five *are* an obstacle that I am striving to overcome. Just as in the latter case, as originally presented, I need not intend that the course of *the arrow* is causally affected by its penetration of the five obstructive bodies—its course could be the same as it would have been had they been absent—so in the case of causing your disintegration, I need not intend that this event causes *any other thing than you* to change.

---

[3] It might be noted that, although the moral reason against refraining from benefiting is less strong than against harming, it is seemingly harder to justify—but not to the point of impermissibility, I think—not saving one by getting hold of a rope as a means of being in time to slightly *later* getting hold of another rope on which five are hanging than getting hold of the latter rope when we face a choice between getting hold of one or the other rope *at the same time*.

The difference between harmfully using people as causal means and harming them as causal means is not that in the former, but not the latter case we make causal use of some of their properties. For just as I am making use of those properties of the five bodies that neutralize the magnetic field when I am harmfully using them as means, so I am making use of their penetrability to the arrow when I am harming them as a means. The difference is that in the former case I do not use any properties of the five to cause a change in anything *other than themselves*, like the course of the arrow. Similarly, when I am using your vulnerability to the rays of my gun, I am doing it simply to cause *your* disintegration, not to change any other thing. My objective is to eliminate the threat that you pose, just as it is to overcome the obstacle that the five pose.

However, it is hard to see how it could make any moral difference whether we are using some features of people causally to affect just them or some other thing as well if this does not make any difference to who is harmed or benefited, or the degree to which they are harmed or benefited. To provide another illustration of this point, let me modify also the case in which you are innocently falling down on me. Suppose that you are carrying a hard and heavy backpack which by itself would kill me were it to land on me. This backpack cannot be dissolved by the rays from my gun, but the dissolution of you would change its trajectory, so that it would miss me. In these circumstances, I could use you—your disintegration—as means to avoid being killed by the backpack. Of course, I would still be harming you as a means of eliminating the threat that you are posing, but as a further effect of this, I would be changing the trajectory of your backpack in a way that is beneficial for me. But, surely, this additional benefit would not render my disposal of you impermissible, though I can now be characterized as having harmfully used you as a means of removing the threat that *your backpack* is presenting.

In this example I am assuming that if I do not cause you to disintegrate, but you land on me with your backpack, you will not be harmed. Things would be significantly different if you would then be crushed and die, that is, if you would die whatever I do. Then advocates of a means principle could plausibly claim that I could permissibly kill you as a means of saving myself. But as I am imagining the situation, you will survive this incident unscathed if I do not use my ray gun on you. In this scenario, your disintegration serves a dual purpose: it eliminates the threat that your body poses, and it serves as a means to eliminate the threat that your backpack poses. Its serving the first purpose is not sufficient to justify it: surely, I could not permissibly kill you if I would still be killed by the impact of your backpack. Its serving as a means to remove this threat is necessary for justification—and sufficient, it seems, if I am permitted to eliminate the lethal threat that you would pose were you to fall without the backpack, since your death's service as a means does not affect you for the worse.[4]

---

[4] It seems that I would be permitted to eliminate you in these circumstances even if the threat that you pose would not be lethal were you to fall without the backpack.

So, it seems that I am allowed to use you harmfully as a means to the same end as I am allowed to harm you as a means—that is, this distinction seems morally insignificant. Therefore, I do not think that it matters to its tenability whether a means principle is couched in terms of harming someone as a means or harmfully using them as a means. It is untenable whichever 'means' locution is employed.

There is however a further 'means' locution that should be mentioned if only to be scrapped. It is important to distinguish between using beings as means and using them as *mere* means, or *merely* as means (which is the locution employed e.g. by Christiano, 2015: 63–4, 66, in the context of equality). I believe that the latter use involves disregarding that beings have ends or interests, or that things can be intrinsically good or bad for them. Although it is as a rule wrong to adopt such an attitude to beings who have interests, it seems that it is not always wrong. Imagine that my proposed action will not affect your interests in any way; then it is not clear that it would be wrong of me to be oblivious to how my action affects your interests. For instance, if I am tailing you because I believe that you will lead me to a certain destination, I might be using you as a mere means, as I might use street signs or a GPS, but this does not seem impermissible. Moreover, even if my action does affect your interests, and it would be wrong of me to disregard this fact, it might be that my *action* is nevertheless not wrong because it happens to affect your interests in a morally justifiable fashion. Then it is only the *attitude* behind my action that is wrong (cf. Parfit, 2011: ch. 9).

Hence, I think that the notion of using someone as a mere means or merely as a means is infelicitous when the topic is what *treatments* are wrong. This topic calls for the notions of harmfully using someone as a means and/or harming them as a means. I have suggested that there is no noticeable moral difference between these and that whichever is employed in a means principle, it is indefensible. My conclusion is, then, that in a discussion of what should be the object of equalization we can set aside equal respect of anything like inviolability. As already observed, this is important in the present context because equal respect with this objective would not be a friendly accompaniment to equal concern for welfare. It is incompatible with a concern that everybody be as equally well off as possible, just as it is with a concern about maximizing welfare.

PART III
Philosophical Thinking about How to Live

11

On the Usefulness of the Principles of Beneficence and Justice

The extreme or deflationist welfare egalitarianism put forward in Part II might seem intolerably counterintuitive. It would certainly affront most people to be told that it is unjust that they are better off than, say, the maggots that may eventually consume their corpses. But, as remarked earlier, this principle of equality will not do as the sole moral principle; it needs to be supplemented with at least a principle of beneficence. Such a principle shorn of anthropocentrism has analogous counterintuitive implications by itself. For it could imply that we ought to concentrate our resources on making life slightly better for countless simple invertebrate animals, since this might conceivably maximize the sum of welfare in the world. Prioritarianism underlines this recommendation, and so does extreme egalitarianism, since it could decrease an unjust inequality as regards welfare. On the other hand, the denial of the transitivity of the relation of being better/worse than all things considered defended in 4.2 opens up the possibility of there being benefits of higher quality that cannot be outweighed by *any* finite amount of lower quality benefits. This supplies a welcome counterweight to the moral weight added to lower level benefits by egalitarianism and prioritarianism.

However, even though an inclusive principle of beneficence without distinctions between higher and lower qualities of welfare could in theory second far-reaching efforts to mitigate interspecies welfare inequalities in the name of extreme egalitarianism, it is in practice more likely to counteract such efforts. This is because it will be very costly in terms of loss of benefits, if at all feasible, to make non-human animals capable of anything approximating to our welfare level by improving their mental faculties and the external circumstances requisite for putting these faculties to use. The accruing gains in respect of just equality will surely be outweighed by the costs as regards the overall sum of welfare, even if we were to set aside that some of this welfare will be of a higher quality that cannot be outweighed by any amount of sufficiently low-quality welfare.

Furthermore, it is questionable whether it is even in principle possible to transform, say, maggots, to the degree that *they* would be capable of enjoying as much welfare as human beings, whether numerically the same organisms could undergo such a drastic metamorphosis. In Chapter 6 I left this sort of question unanswered, though I expressed doubts about the idea that species membership is an essential property of organisms. But if it is not even in principle possible to lift some species of organisms to our welfare level, it is not unjust that this does not happen. In practice, however, it matters little what are these limits of what is in principle possible, since we reach the limits of what we can technically accomplish and of what is morally justifiable all things considered much sooner. Still, if we imagine that we could technically raise the average welfare of some non-human animals to our average level without incurring unjustifiable costs (or that almighty gods could do this when they create a world), we (they) morally ought to do it. It is no more defensible to claim that it is morally justifiable that these non-human animals are on a lower welfare level because this is where they are naturally fit to be than to claim this with respect to human beings with congenital handicaps.

Since, in fact, only considerably more moderate measures to alleviate the huge natural injustice of interspecies inequality in respect of welfare are manageable, this is all that we could be morally required to undertake, though the current inequality is an intrinsically bad feature of the world. But there is also a huge unjust inequality with respect to welfare between members of the human species, and here, too, there is a tension between beneficence and justice. For the elimination of this injustice would necessitate, among other things, the removal of institutions and practices of rewarding socially beneficial behaviour and punishing socially harmful behaviour, and this is likely to be contrary to the overall good of society.

The differences in respect of human behaviour are due not only to differences as regards social background, but also as regards genetic factors. Therefore, in the absence of the application of wide-ranging techniques of genetic engineering ironing out genetic differences between humans, the task of providing them with an equally good social start, though truly Herculean, would not be enough to ensure that they all perform equally well. As long as human beings are as genetically dissimilar as they are at present, it would be highly detrimental to the overall welfare of society to remove incentives that encourage those with genetically based traits beneficial to society to make use of them, and to remove disincentives that deter those with genetically based traits harmful to society from acting on them. Nevertheless, such practices of rewarding and punishing nourish an inequality of welfare that is unfair, since it is ultimately based on features beyond the responsibility of those rewarded and punished.

Thus, humankind being in its current shape, there is bound to be a conflict between what reasons of beneficence and justice dictate because social arrangements that create unjust inequality in respect of the distribution of benefits are indispensable to promote a social order which overall provides most benefits. Admittedly, an extremely egalitarian conception of justice, with its denial of deserts and rights, widens the gulf between the demands of justice and beneficence; it would not be nearly as wide if justice had consisted in individuals getting what they allegedly deserve and having rights to.

Now, as the opportunities of amassing wealth grow with technological progress and social organization, the differences in respect of welfare between the most affluent and the destitute countries have tended to increase, as well as the differences within the affluent countries between their citizens. The most egalitarian human societies to date are probably hunter-gatherer societies in which the opportunities of hoarding property are severely restricted, and by far the longest stretch of human history in which all societies were of this type was the time of the greatest human equality as regards welfare, albeit on an average level that was pretty low. Since the concepts of property rights and desert have a strong hold on the human mind, it seems inevitable that the insatiable human desire for more wealth will egg humans on to take advantage of expanding possibilities of accumulating wealth by enriching themselves. There is little hope that humans in general will be converted to a doctrine of extreme egalitarianism and attempt to make the distribution of welfare as equal as justice requires it to be. Instead, it appears likelier that this distribution will as a rule become ever more unequal in step with the development of technology that creates new avenues for generating welfare.

Furthermore, if science were to offer biomedical means of enhancing various capacities, humans would probably prefer to implement the capacities that accentuate inequalities in favour of themselves, or in groups to which they belong, rather than capacities that diminish inequalities. For instance, the better-off will prefer enhancements that will tend to sharpen their competitive edge and extend their lifespan rather than enhancements that will make them more morally concerned. Biomedical life-extension has the potential of boosting the inequality between humans in respect of welfare to an all-time high magnitude. So, the discovery of biomedical means of transforming human nature might well issue in human inequality of welfare increasing rather than decreasing, despite the fact that they could offer means of achieving the latter. In other words, even if means of diminishing the tension between what the principles of inclusive beneficence and extreme equality recommend were available, they would not be employed to this end. They are rather more likely to be employed to increase the existing inequality in respect of welfare because human beings in general will not take to heart the extent to which justice demands equality.

By contrast, political equality to the extent that it is realized in liberal democracies is evidently feasible. But democratic societies still have a hierarchical structure, with the elected representatives having much more power than ordinary citizens, not to mention the fact that they are generally much better off. In fact, current democracies do not seem to represent such a radical break with our evolutionary past and the organization of hunter-gatherer societies, in which there were leaders, 'big men', but their power was limited by the fact that other men could rather easily form coalitions to usurp their power if their leaders flagrantly misused it.

As already observed, there are also aspects of the other main moral principle here defended, the inclusive view of benefiting and person-affecting reasons of beneficence, which appear counterintuitive. One of them is its denial of anthropocentric speciesism, which has the—to common sense—counterintuitive implication that we have reason to do a lot more to boost animal welfare. Another counterintuitive aspect is its implication that we could benefit beings by bringing them into existence and, thus, that there is a person-affecting reason to do so. In Chapter 3 I argued that part of the explanation of why we find this implication counterintuitive is that we are in the grip of indefensible views such as the act-omission doctrine and an adjunct theory of rights. But another part of the explanation is that we overlook the asymmetry between abilities and disabilities and, more generally, the small extent to which our acts can be credited for benefits when they result in individuals commencing good lives.

It was seen that when we bring congenitally well-endowed individuals into existence, we only achieve what will make them benefit *on condition* that many other factors kick in. In a world in which there are comparatively few individuals with a capacity to be benefited in proportion to the resources that could generate benefits, procreation might well be something that we have good moral reason to do. But in the actual, overpopulated world with an extensive unjust inequality as regards welfare, reasons both of beneficence and justice strongly recommend improving the lot of already existent beings rather than adding to their stock. Thus, the dual principles here proposed have counterintuitive implications not only in the present, heavily overpopulated world with an overwhelming unjust welfare inequality both within the human species and between this species and other species, but also in a contrasting world with a small population relative to its benefit-producing resources, though the content of these implications will differ.

One difficulty with the principles of beneficence and justice advanced in this book is, then, that they appear counterintuitive in the face of common-sense morality. This will of course make people in general disinclined to try to abide by them. Another difficulty is that the empirical facts relevant to their application are complex, elusive and non-quantifiable, which makes it hard to find out what these principles recommend in practice. Suppose that we wonder, to start with, whether the world in its present state— with a couple of billion humans living in abject poverty, the extinction rate of biological species being something like a thousand times faster than it naturally is, a natural order in which organisms fight with each other to survive and reproduce, and so on—contains more benefits than burdens and, consequently, whether its existence is better than non-existence from the point of view of beneficence. Then we shall find ourselves compelled to admit that our knowledge of the mental lives of other beings than ourselves is far too scanty to permit us to determine with any reliability whether this is so.

In fact, even as regards our own lives, we are hard put to gauge the benefits and burdens that they have contained up to the present (see e.g. Kahneman, 2011: pt. V). We are decidedly forward-looking creatures, filled with desires and hopes for the future, and ill-equipped to remember accurately the benefits and burdens of the past and balance them against each other. Moreover, they have a daunting internal complexity because they involve imprecise and disparate elements: exercises of autonomy and qualitative differences of felt well-being, which are either content-based, or due to an imprecision which enables greater quantitative differences to turn qualitative. This makes the business of assembling benefits and burdens and balancing them against each other hopelessly unwieldy.

There is however a general reason for suspecting that what is bad might have the upper hand in our lives. This is that beings are capable of experiencing stronger negative sensations and emotions than positive ones—this is sometimes known as a 'negativity bias'. The signal that something's going wrong in your body—physical pain—can be more intense and bring more suffering than the signal that something's going well—pleasure—can bring enjoyment. This is not surprising because when something goes wrong in our bodies, it often has a greater impact on our chances of survival than when something goes well. Bodily damage can easily be irreversible and render us less fit for the rest of our lives—if it does not kill us. Similarly, our greater susceptibility to being harmed than benefited makes it comprehensible that the negative emotion of fear is more widespread and could be considerably more intense than its positive counterpart of hope and longing. Fear could be intensified to terror and horror, but there is no counterpart to this intensification in the case of hope or longing. Likewise, in a world in which most of the time we risk losing more than we could reasonably hope to gain, and in which we compete with each other over scarce resources, it has survival value that the negative reaction of anger be more widespread and stronger than its positive counterpart of gratitude, since it will be more important to scare off attackers than to return favours done by do-gooders. Hence, it is to be expected that anger could stoke up fury and rage, but there is nothing corresponding to this intensity in the case of gratitude. However, I shall not hazard any opinion on whether these considerations suffice to justify the conjecture that even in the case of better lives there is in general a preponderance in favour of the negative.

Imagine, then, that we agree that it is beyond our power to find out whether or not, for all sentient beings, or even for human beings in particular, it is better from the perspective of beneficence that the world continues to exist in its present state than that it is destroyed. Now if we bring in the perspective of justice as equality as well, the case gets appreciably stronger for holding that the world's persistence in its current state would involve less good than bad, but due to the fact that the degree of unjust inequality is also a complex and non-quantifiable matter, as we saw in Chapter 8, there would still be a considerable uncertainty. Notwithstanding this, it seems reasonable to hypothesize that the outcome of the struggle for survival and reproduction that is the *modus operandi* of evolution is so gravely wrong from the point of view of justice as equality that it might be likely to outweigh a possible surplus of benefits over burdens.

Perhaps the spoils of the victors have a better chance of exceeding the losses of the defeated in the case of a highly successful species like *Homo sapiens*. Nevertheless, to determine whether or not it is better even for humans that the world continues to exist in its current state all things considered, after balancing beneficence and justice against each other in what has to be a wholly intuitive fashion, appears unmanageable. This might be comforting, since had it been feasible, the conclusion might have been resoundingly negative in this case as well.

There is however a further aspect to keep in mind, namely that affluent states to a considerable extent are responsible and blameable for the unjustly unequal distribution of global wealth because they could have done considerably more to rectify it without making painful sacrifices. Consider the so-called *ultimatum games* that experimental psychologists have people play to test the strength of their sense of justice. In these games, so-called 'proposers' are given some valuable resource such as food or money. Their task is to divide it between themselves and 'responders'. They may divide it any way they like, but if the responders reject the portion that they are offered by the proposers, neither proposers nor responders will get anything. Now responders will usually accept divisions that diverge from a 50–50 division if they are not too much to their disadvantage, say, 60–40 per cent divisions, but they will reject more drastic divergences, for example, 80–20 per cent divisions. Evidently, they are then prepared to sacrifice benefits to themselves to punish proposers who are perceived as glaringly unfair in their own favour.

This seems a reasonable reaction, but if so, there is also a case for saying that, for instance, it would be reasonable for the poorest 80 per cent of the Earth's population, who account for less than 10 per cent of the global wealth, to reject the distribution that the better off 20 per cent are offering them even if the alternative is that nobody gets anything because all are extinguished. This is an unsettling thought: that we in affluent countries thrive in a world that the poor might justifiably bring to an end because of our omission to make the distribution of welfare in it more just. Were they to refrain from so doing, they would show us a generosity that we do not show them.

But although we could undoubtedly have done more to improve the state of the world, the indeterminacy and uncertainty that we have considered kick in again. Along with the difficulty of predicting the consequences of alternative courses of action, they imply that it is exceedingly hard to decide with any tolerable definiteness what ought morally to be done to effect this improvement. This raises the question of the practical usefulness of a morality consisting of the inclusive view of benefiting and extreme egalitarianism. In view of our limited knowledge of the wider consequences of our actions, especially as regards the mental states of others, as well as the complexity of the values of outcomes with respect to both the amount of their benefits and the justice of their distribution, and the delicateness of balancing these values of beneficence and justice against each other, such a morality cannot deliver anything but the sketchiest advice about what ought to be done in concrete situations.

Even though I have not made much of a case for it here, I believe that moral reasons are based on desires, broadly speaking, on an altruistic desire to benefit others for their own sakes, and a desire to do what is just. The aim of this book has been to deliver a philosophically sounder account of the content of these desires. The conclusion has been that the altruistic desire should encompass the welfare of possible sentient beings, regardless of their species, and that, since rights and deserts are groundless, justice is largely a matter of equality. If those of us who have the two desires mentioned adopt this explication of their content, we shall be guided in roughly the right direction. At the end of the day, this might be all that can be reasonably asked of the normative output of moral philosophy: that it imbues the right sort of frame of mind for grappling with the startling complexity of many moral problems for those who are appropriately motivated rather than that it supplies anything like straightforwardly applicable rules.

Yet, our need for moral guidance now appears greater than ever. This is because our powers of action, due to the advances of scientific technology, are more far-reaching than ever. Thanks to the exceptional progress of scientific technology, human beings have colonized the whole planet and now number more than seven billion. No other species has been anything like as successful, or has transformed conditions on Earth to a remotely similar degree. But this phenomenal progress threatens to call forth a backlash. The emission of greenhouse gases from the fossil fuels, which have powered the technology that underlies our affluence, risks causing a devastating climate change, and the explosion of the human population and its growing consumption of natural resources are leading to a destruction of habitats crucial for biodiversity, like coral reefs and tropical forests, and overfishing of the seas. Although sophisticated technology and social organization have enabled more than a billion people to lead extremely affluent lives, roughly as many people live in abject poverty and misery. Weapons of mass destruction are in the hands of an increasing number of states—some of them arch-enemies—and may end up in the laps of terrorist groups. In a nutshell, humanity faces threats to its survival of a kind and magnitude that it never did before humanity became a threat to itself (for further discussion, see Persson and Savulescu, 2012).

All in all, humanity is up against moral problems of the greatest urgency, but these are large-scale problems whose solution presupposes a mind-boggling body of factual knowledge. The two principles here espoused, which are difficult to apply even to simpler moral problems and have to be balanced against each other in an entirely intuitive fashion, cannot supply much practical advice here. But although we cannot determine with any practically useful definiteness what a morality consisting of these two principles demands of us as regards these global challenges, we can be certain that it will be quite demanding for those of us who are better off if we put these principles in the framework of a denial of deontological doctrines—like the act-omission doctrine and the doctrine of the double effect—and of the unimportance of personal identity. This morality will be far too demanding for our naturally limited altruism and sense of justice.

Our moral dispositions have most likely evolved to make us fit for life in small, close-knit communities with a primitive technology that can affect only the immediate environment—the conditions in which humans have lived during almost all of their history. Humans are morally myopic and tend to be concerned only about individuals with whom they are personally acquainted and about problems of immediate urgency for them. So, they tend to benefit and avoid harming individuals close by, even though this means failing to benefit or harming a greater number of unknown individuals more distant. It is plausible to hypothesize that morality originated to promote cooperation within small groups so as to make them fitter in the competition for resources with similar groups, and natural adversaries and adversities. Such a morality did not need to cover procreation, since this was regulated by the strength of the desire to copulate and a high infant mortality. But if we are to bring to a halt an overexploitation of the resources of the Earth and a population growth that may eventually be catastrophic for human civilization and the natural environment, we need to cooperate on a global scale in the interest of beings distant in space and time on issues including reproduction. This necessitates ridding ourselves of our tendency to tribalism and discounting of the future.

Its demandingness relative to our natural motivational propensities is, then, a further problem with the morality in which this book lands. Since I have elsewhere (Persson and Savulescu, 2012) discussed the prospects of strengthening our moral dispositions by biomedical means, alongside the traditional moral reflection and education, so that we become more capable of coping with the global challenges mentioned, I shall not do so now. Let me just point out that I take it to be a fact that, for example, protracted reflection on the arguments against anthropocentric speciesism and ultimate responsibility and in favour of imaginatively putting ourselves in the place of others *could* increase our motivation to act according to a more inclusive morality. The products of a revisionary moral philosophy should then not be assumed to be motivationally impotent, though they will hardly suffice their own.

However, the fact that morality has been subjected to a significant revision is liable to undermine its authority. If a moral norm for a long time is followed regularly without being questioned, this by itself increases its authority. Human beings are disposed to be respectful of what has an aura of being traditional and age-old. Moreover, they are conformists, so to the extent that a norm is obeyed by a majority, this augments its authority. For these reasons, any significant moral revision is likely to have a hard time gaining a foothold and being widely accepted, but there are reasons why it will be especially hard for a revision such as the one here proposed to win broad acceptance.

Commonsensical moral distinctions often hinge on perceptually salient differences, for instance between what exists and what does not exist, what is alive and dead, what is human and non-human, what is caused and what is allowed to happen, and what is done or used as a means and what is done as a side-effect, and oneself and others. Such differences are taken to be grounds for differences as regards value, or responsibility and related features like deserts and rights. A morality, such as the one here proffered, according to which perceptually salient distinctions like these are declared morally irrelevant, will appear to many as too abstract and general to be taken seriously. To be sure, it appeals to *some* commonsensical moral ideas—this is essential if a revisionary morality is to be recognized as a morality—namely, that there is reason to do what benefits, and to distribute benefits justly. But due to the rejection of the moral relevance of the perceptually salient distinctions mentioned, these moral ideas take on an altogether novel shape.

It is easier for us to feel benevolence and sympathy for individuals who are present to our senses, especially if this has happened regularly and we have grown accustomed to their appearance—the so-called exposure effect. However, the revisionary morality here proposed asks us to extend these responses not only to human beings distant in space and time, but also to non-human animals, and even to possible beings who do not (yet) exist. Moreover, although this is something that I have argued for at greater length only elsewhere (2013), it asks us to shoulder as much responsibility for failures to benefit as for harmful acts, and to be prepared to forgo immediate benefiting or to cause smaller harm as a means to being able to benefit more. It also asks us to be impartial between our own interest and the interests of others (as I argue in 2005: pt. IV). Finally, it asks us to disregard the strong reasons of justice that our powerful intuitions about what individuals deserve or have rights to apparently supply, and distribute benefits in a more thoroughgoing egalitarian fashion.

Such a radically revisionary morality will inevitably suffer a loss of manifest authority. This is awkward, since by itself this loss is likely to make people less inclined to exert themselves to comply with this morality, but the problem of compliance is aggravated by the fact that this morality is also so much more demanding, largely due to the great powers of action with which technology has equipped us. A combination of loss of authority and greater demandingness is certainly unfortunate. In addition, it seems vain to hope that moral philosophers will come up with any metaethical theory that could strengthen the authority of morality by demonstrating the existence of moral reasons that bind us or are valid for us independently of our attitudes. In Chapter 1 some considerations against the existence of such objective reasons were adduced, but I argue this point more fully elsewhere (2005: ch. 9 and 2013: ch. 12). Hence, we could scarcely hope that any Kantian-like respect or awe for a moral law that is binding or valid independently of our attitudes will replace the authority derived from the force of tradition and make us motivated to act in accordance with a revised, more demanding morality. In order for this to happen, the case for objective reasons must be persuasive to most people, since otherwise the power of the conformist drive will not be activated.

Ultimately, a morality is pointless if it cannot be implemented, but it has transpired that the implementation of the inclusive morality proposed in this book raises several problems:

(1) It is counterintuitive to the minds of people who have been brought up on common-sense morality because it rejects the significance of perceptually salient distinctions that this morality features.
(2) It gives rise to problems of deciding what is morally right because (a) this requires knowledge of a vast number of complex and largely inaccessible empirical facts, and (b) values of outcomes both in virtue of the amount of benefits that they contain and in virtue of the extent to which their distribution of benefits is in accordance with justice as equality are multi-faceted, imprecise, and non-quantifiable; additionally, to obtain an overall outcome value these two kinds of value must be weighed up in a loose, intuitive fashion.
(3) It is very demanding especially for those of us who are better off and can do most to improve matters morally.

(4) It does not possess the authority of common-sense morality because (a) it is not supported by tradition or habit, (b) it rejects the strongest reasons of common-sense morality (reasons of rights), and (c) there is little hope to compensate for this loss of authority by the discovery of objective moral reasons that bind us independently of our attitudes, at least not by means that will be persuasive to most of us.

The practical usefulness of the inclusive morality here proposed is then doubtful; however, this is not to say that there is anything wrong with the *moral philosophy* that arrives at it. It would be *desirable* to have a morality which is doctrinally more definite, foundationally unshakeable, readily applicable, and motivationally realistic, but reality may not grant us what is desirable. Common-sense morality is certainly more motivationally realistic, perhaps also doctrinally more definite and readily applicable, but it is less suited to cope with the mega-problems of the world today, being formed by our long history of living as hunter-gatherers in tribes. This suitability is another desideratum of a morality of at least as great importance as motivational realism and applicability, but it is difficult to see how a moral theory could meet both of these desiderata.

The upshot is that it is hard to see how a proposed morality could satisfy two conditions that seem necessary for it to have a point, or function. (a) It must be possible for people in general to follow it, that is, it must be successful in respects that we have just seen that the morality here proposed fails. (b) It must promote the welfare of the collective endorsing it, for example by means of promoting peaceful cooperation within it—this being the evolutionary function of morality. But now the hitch is that in the technological, globalized world of today the moral mega-problems cannot be solved unless there is international cooperation that takes into consideration of not only the welfare of the present generation, but also the welfare of future generations. However, it is not easy to understand how morality could aim both to promote the welfare of this vast collective and to meet condition (a), of it being in general possible to follow it. It faces something of a dilemma of either being too demanding for individuals or jeopardizing their collective good. So, it is difficult to see how morality could have a point today.

12

The Point of Moral Philosophy

By claiming, as I did in Chapter 11, that there need not be anything wrong with a moral philosophy whose upshot is a morality as difficult to implement as is the inclusive morality here proposed, I meant to imply that moral philosophy could have a point, although it leads up to a morality that does not have a point. Although this is true, I shall now argue that, in an important sense, moral philosophy does not have any point because it is incapable of establishing *any* morality, with or without a point.

I think that, in this sense, moral philosophy has a point just in case it produces something like a *rational consensus* about what is morally right and wrong, and what is the ground and meaning of this. Specifically, this is an *intrinsic* point of moral philosophy because it is what its method of argument is designed to accomplish. Of course, doing moral philosophy can be a means to ends *external* to it, such as earning a livelihood, getting recognition for one's acumen, or getting the kind of intellectual stimulation that you can also get from a game like chess. But when I talk about the point of (doing) moral philosophy, I mean a point that is intrinsic or internal to it, something that it is uniquely designed to realize by its method of argument. Soon I shall also draw a distinction between a *primary* and a *subsidiary* intrinsic point of moral philosophy, and restrict my claim that it does not have any point to the former sense.

It follows from this characterization that if one day in the future moral philosophy has established a rational consensus about what is morally right or wrong in every possible situation that we shall ever face, and what is the ground and meaning of this, it will no longer have any intrinsic point. Moral philosophers could then retire with a clean conscience, and go to the beach or play golf. If it is complained that the morality they have established is hard to implement, they could retort that this is not their fault, or business. It is due to the factual conditions of the world.

A less triumphant, but still hopeful, scenario is that in the course of time moral philosophers gradually get closer and closer to the truth about morality without ever fully grasping it. This might suffice to save moral philosophy from being intrinsically pointless. A more realistic scenario is, I believe, that it remains as *inconclusive* as ever about its most important issues, that controversies about them continue to rage on indefinitely. I describe this scenario as realistic because it seems to project that the future will be like the history of moral philosophy since about 1970. This was when analytic or anglophone moral philosophy—the only kind with which I am sufficiently acquainted to make it an object of speculation—picked up speed after having been largely dormant for the first half of the twentieth century. So far the domain of moral disagreement seems not to have shrunk by any important moral problem having been finally resolved and removed from the agenda. Personally, I cannot think of a single instance of moral philosophy having definitely resolved a pre-theoretical disagreement about what is morally right or wrong.

Certainly, there is more or less a rational consensus about the *falsity* of many claims both in normative ethics and metaethics (e.g. that husbands own their wives and children and have a right to kill them if it pleases them, and that 'x is good' and 'I like x' are synonymous). But this does not mean that the domain of disagreement has decreased, at least for two reasons. The first reason is that moral philosophy is developing by becoming more precise, by sharpening its conceptual tools. New distinctions are incessantly drawn, and as a consequence moral claims are split up in more precise versions. Since some of these claims will be only marginally different, it will be hard for us to reach a consensus about which alternative version is the most plausible one. To do so we must appeal to shared moral intuitions. We do have a batch of common intuitions about what is morally right and wrong in many situations, for example about it being morally wrong to kill, torture, rape, and steal in most circumstances, and it being right in general to help those who are much more needy than ourselves. And the agreement would be even bigger if religion and other ideological prejudices could be disposed of—which seems improbable. But we are not likely to have shared intuitions about the rare, or purely imaginary, cases to which we need resort to settle more fine-grained philosophical disputes. Consequently, growing philosophical precision is not like more precise measurements of something's weight or length which do bring us closer to its real weight or length. This is why increasing philosophical precision is no reason to believe in the hopeful scenario of getting closer to a consensus about the truth.

Nonetheless, this process of conceptual refinement sharpens our understanding of the complexities of the phenomenon of morality, or our ideas of it, and since at least moral philosophers take an interest in such a sharpening of our understanding, this may be said to provide moral philosophy with an intrinsic point for them. But this interest seems dependent on a belief that the process of conceptual refinement brings them closer to a consensus about the truth. Consider this analogy. Suppose that there is a game like chess, but for which there are no tournaments. So, we do not explore its possibilities of moves and counter-moves in order to defeat particular opponents and win tournaments. We explore these possibilities because we believe that we might find a 'perfect' strategy which *no* opponent can defeat. After many centuries, it dawns on us that there is no such perfect strategy. Would we then continue to explore the complexities of this game, taking this to be of interest in itself? I doubt that we would do so with much zeal; knowledge of this complexity is seen rather as a by-product of finding the perfect strategy. Likewise, I would be inclined to regard the knowledge of the complexity of our morality or moral ideas as an intrinsic point subsidiary to the primary point of establishing a rational consensus about what is morally right and wrong.

The second reason to doubt that the extent of moral disagreement decreases is that conditions of modern life with accelerating speed confront us with new moral problems, or make old problems markedly more potent. Some of these problems are smaller-scale, like *in vitro* fertilization and organ-donation, while others are the moral mega-problems of our time, like anthropogenic climate change, the huge global economic inequality, and the threat of weapons of mass destruction. For reasons that surfaced in Chapter 11, these problems are hard to solve.

So, what I am suggesting is that moral philosophy is virtually incapable of extending our substantial pre-reflective moral agreement, our more or less universal consensus about what is morally right and wrong, or of boosting the authority of morality by putting it on a more secure foundation. Our moral disagreement is rather likely to expand due to disputes in moral philosophy and novel technological and societal circumstances. In other words, moral philosophy is most probably destined to be deeply inconclusive. Thereby, it will fail in respect of its primary intrinsic point. If it is not too esoteric, it might even be harmful, since by raising some questions—for instance, about the foundations of morality—that it cannot answer, it might undermine the authority of morality in the eyes of the public.

One reason why moral philosophy is hard put to extend moral agreement lies in genetically based or hard-wired features of our moral psychology of a sort already exemplified. These features make it difficult for us to take to heart philosophical revisions of common-sense morality, even though they may be intellectually convincing. Whether we are capable of taking seriously criticisms of hard-wired features might depend on how we score as regards personality traits like open-mindedness, and some people are evidently more closed-minded and conformist than others.

As outlined in Chapter 11, these hard-wired features also make it difficult for us to comply with a significantly revised common-sense morality which rejects them as unfounded, such as the one here presented. This problem of compliance has become more pressing because of aspects of modern life already alluded to, namely the instruments put in our hands by advanced technology and our societies with millions, even billions, of citizens intimately intertwined by trade and travel with similar societies all over the globe. For our moral psychology has plausibly been shaped for life in small, close-knit societies with primitive technology which allows us to affect only our immediate environment. By contrast, our modern life conditions stretch our moral responsibility far into the future and all over the Earth, and that is something with which we are evolutionarily ill-equipped to cope.

Philosophical problems often take the form of a conflict between commonsensical intuitions or convictions and philosophical arguments undercutting them. To take a couple of well-known epistemological examples: we are utterly convinced that we perceive a physical world existing independently of our perceptions, that the human beings around us, and many non-human animals, have minds or consciousnesses more or less similar to our own, and that our inductive inferences are by and large reliable. Yet there are powerful sceptical challenges to the justifiability of these convictions, to which there are no replies that have won anything approximating to unanimous acceptance in spite of centuries of efforts (for further discussion of these problems, see Persson, 2013: ch. 11).

These particular conflicts between commonsensical intuitions and philosophical arguments are extremely wide-ranging: they affect virtually every aspect of our lives. In the case of morality, some of the conflicts between 'gut and brain' are also rather wide-ranging—though not quite as wide-ranging as the epistemological problems mentioned—but some are more local. As remarked, we have a firm intuition to the effect that there is a strong moral reason not to take human life, that human life is of great value, but modern medical technology presses us to be more precise about the purport of this intuition. The reason for this is that it enables us to sustain biological life for months and years when consciousness is irrevocably lost, or when terminal illnesses or injuries are so grave that life becomes unbearably painful or severely restricted. This poses the question whether the biological life of a human being in itself is valuable, or whether it is only instrumentally valuable as long as it underpins consciousness of enjoyable or valuable objects. As long as life-sustaining medical technology was less well developed, this question was not practically momentous.

In turn this bears on the question of the conditions in which human beings have the right to request euthanasia. If biological life by itself is not valuable, such a right is easier to vindicate—by reference to respect for autonomy—in cases in which people request euthanasia when they foresee entering into persistent vegetative states, or future lives dominated by hardships. Similarly, there will not be any moral objection to using organs from human beings in persistent vegetative states for transplantation if they have given their consent in advance.

However, these moral problems also actualize another conflict between intuition and intellect of much greater moral scope and significance. This is the dichotomy between consequentialism and deontology, that is, types of morality that differ over whether or not they comprise some version of the act-omission doctrine and/or the doctrine of the double effect. As should be clear by now, I am convinced that there is no tenable version of these doctrines, but many are of the opposite opinion. And even those who are sceptical, like myself, continue to feel the force of these doctrines in their everyday lives.

I believe that this is evidence that evolution has wired us up to react in accordance with something like these doctrines. As mentioned in an earlier chapter, my hypothesis is that a conception of responsibility as being based on causality underpins them. This is clearest in the case of the act-omission doctrine, the doctrine of greater practical importance. But as was seen in 10.2, the fact that other conditions than causal ones can be intended as means stretches the doctrine of the double effect to other conditions which can be ascertained prior to ends as causal conditions usually can be. It is comprehensible why evolution should have equipped us with a conception of responsibility as causally based because it is easier for beings to attribute responsibility simply on the basis of physical causation than by reference to mental states—which is surely more accurate—since the latter requires greater conceptual resources. It is also easier to avoid harming than omitting to prevent harm that could be prevented because the latter could be an overwhelming amount in our current conditions of being amply resourceful, whilst many others are in great need. If the act-omission doctrine is untenable, some acts that are commonly thought to be impermissible, like active euthanasia, may become permissible, and acts of charity may change from being supererogatory to being morally required.

According to my view, the act-omission doctrine is linked to another sentiment that has a good claim to be hard-wired: the sentiment that we have rights to ourselves and to what we are first to occupy or appropriate of unowned natural resources, and what we manufacture out of these resources by our own labour. Contemporary technology and trade have vastly increased the means of hoarding property to the point at which the richest 1 per cent of the Earth's population have as much as wealth as the remaining 99 per cent, and the 80 richest *individuals* have as much the poorest 50 per cent (see https://www.oxfam.org/en/pressroom/pressreleases/2015-01-19). Without understanding the strong grip property rights have on us, it appears incomprehensible how we can put up with a world with such an enormous economic inequality.

Like rights, desert is a consideration of justice, as was discussed in Chapter 7: it is just or fair that you receive what you deserve in virtue of your good or bad conduct, just as it is just or fair that you keep that to which you have a right, and it would be unjust or unfair to deprive you of it. It is plausible to hypothesize that being equipped with a sentiment like desert increases our reproductive fitness because it can be seen as driving strategies like tit-for-tat, which arguably have this feature (see Persson and Savulescu, 2012: 33–6). Still, this sentiment has a downside: for instance, it can tempt us to excessive retaliation, which is particularly dangerous at present when weapons of mass destruction are increasingly available.

As was contended in Chapter 7, if the notions of rights and desert are rejected, we can derive a far-reaching egalitarianism, since it can no longer be claimed that it is just or fair that some are better off than others because they deserve to be better off, or have a right to more. Although such a far-reaching egalitarianism is too strong stuff for common-sense morality, notable egalitarian elements have begun to be incorporated into it during the last century. At least what might be called the official or public morality of Western democracies—as expressed by laws and leading political ideologies—is nowadays broadly egalitarian: it ascribes an equal worth or moral status to all (postnatal) human beings, which is thought to be higher than that ascribed to non-human animals.

It was argued in Chapter 6 that the idea of an elevated status of humans cannot be vindicated. By contrast, most moral philosophers would agree with the official morality that some differences between human beings, like race, ethnicity, and gender, are not valid grounds for moral differentiation. But from the fact that *some* differences between humans are not valid grounds for moral differentiation, it does not follow that *no* differences are. For example, differences in intelligence, rationality, or morality could justify differences in moral worth between humans, as they are sometimes adduced as grounds for elevating humans above non-human animals. Thus, the idea of an equal human worth or moral status above that of non-human animals is philosophically quite dubious, though it may be politically incorrect to say so. For this reason, it is also questionable whether this idea of human equality can be cited as an example of moral *progress*.

The change of public morality in the direction of human equality in the twentieth century can therefore scarcely be put down to the influence of contemporary moral philosophy. Granted, some philosophers of the past have undoubtedly influenced the current public morality and politics, for example philosophers like Marx, Mill, and Rousseau. As remarked in Chapter 6, Christianity may be part of the ideological background of the doctrine of human equality, but its pronounced outbreak in the twentieth century is probably due to socio-economic factors. In a globalized world with world-wide travel and trade, discrimination against races and ethnic groups will tend to be a hindrance. And when technology has made the difference in physical strength between men and women less important, and contraception has reduced the importance of their different reproductive roles, it is to be expected that men and women should come out as more equal. However, it should not be assumed that such-like socio-economic changes have obliterated all proneness to racism and sexism. Not least the rapid deterioration of Germany into brutal racism during the Nazi period should remind us that the official morality can be little more than a façade or veneer. Conditions like scarcity of resources and epidemics can rekindle competition and animosity between different racial and ethnic groups.

The cause of this is that underneath the egalitarian surface there is the aforementioned stratification of our concern for others. We tend to be concerned about people in proportion to how well acquainted with them we are and how much we have cooperated with them in mutually beneficial ways. The people with whom we are most involved in these ways include close kin, such as children and siblings; thus, they belong to those for whom we care most. We are virtually indifferent towards strangers whom we recognize to be different by means of racial features or ethnic markers like dress and language. In between these extremes, there are various groups of individuals with whom we associate in some circumstances and for whose welfare we have a smaller degree of concern. There is certainly a plausible evolutionary explanation for such a stratification of our altruism. For it would be risky for us to extend invitations to cooperation beyond those with whom we are well acquainted and to strangers who, for all we know, might be inclined towards free-riding and deceit.

Some philosophers believe that this partiality is to some degree morally permissible. For instance, Samuel Scheffler has claimed (1982) that there are so-called *agent-relative prerogatives or permissions* to the effect that we are allowed to favour ourselves and those near and dear at the expense of others. But even these philosophers would admit that this partiality can be excessive, as is manifested by the pejorative charge of the terms 'nepotism' and 'cronyism'. Other philosophers, most famously utilitarians, take a sterner, impartial line, as does the present author. Again, this is a dispute that shows no signs of being conclusively resolved.

By contrast, there is a related feature of moral psychology that probably no philosopher would defend. This is that our spontaneous capacity to sympathize with sufferers is *not proportional to their number*: it does not grow as the number of sufferers grows; in fact, the suffering of a single concrete individual can arouse as much sympathy as masses of sufferers before our eyes, not to mention masses that are merely known by description as opposed to acquaintance (cf. Persson and Savulescu, 2012: 30). Needless to say, this limitation of our sympathy has assumed greater moral significance now that our technological resources enable the more affluent to assist masses of deprived individuals.

Another bias of our concern whose rationality few if anyone would endorse has to do with time: *the bias towards the near future* (see Persson, 2005: ch. 15). We are spontaneously more concerned about positive and negative events in the nearer than in the more remote future. As will be discussed in Chapter 13, this tendency to discount the more distant future is not strictly a moral bias because it is in operation in the domain of self-interest or prudence as well, that is, when we deal with the impact of events solely on our own interests, but it is also morally relevant, or relevant to our concern for others.

Even if we are intellectually persuaded that the fact that, say, something is postponed until tomorrow by itself is not anything that makes it matter less, we cannot easily shake off a feeling to the contrary. Plausibly, we possess this temporal bias because it has served our reproductive fitness in the long period of the past when we possessed no capacity to make reflective probability judgments. Then it would be useful to be spontaneously disposed to care most about threats in the imminent future because it is generally most urgent to deal with them.

Let me now revert again to the fact that modern social and technological conditions, which empower us to affect the whole planet for centuries to come, make these hard-wired limitations on our concern more harmful than they were in the long past when we could affect nobody except individuals in our vicinity in the immediate future. For instance, the fact that we are dragging our heels in coping with anthropogenic climate change is plausibly at least partially due to these hard-wired features. Since these climatic changes are slow in the making, they leave us largely unmoved because the largest numbers of individuals who will suffer most from them will be unknown to us as they exist in the remote future, and possibly in distant countries. These factors 'bleach'—if they do not entirely block—our awareness of harm for which we are responsible.

But as regards anthropogenic climate change the conception of responsibility as causally based also has a role to play. According to my analysis (2013: chs. 3 and 4), underlying the act-omission doctrine is a feeling that we are more responsible for what we cause than for what we let happen because then we omit interfering causally with an ongoing process. But the fact that the causal chain between our bodily actions and the resulting harm is spatio-temporally extended also tends to make us feel less responsible for the harm that we produce (cf. Persson, 2013: 6.5). As observed in 10.2, the fact that the causal chain between our acts and the resulting harm is spatio-temporally extended prevents an automatic association of harm and our acts which occurs when the harm results instantaneously, as when you punch people in the face or stab them. Besides, the fact that the causal chain is spatio-temporally extended is likely to make the victims anonymous. As is well known, the climate harm that we cause by acts of ours that emit greenhouse gases is spatio-temporally exceedingly remote; so, this is a further factor that bleaches our sense of responsibility for the harm that we cause by these acts.

This factor is at work even in the case of modern technology that is specially designed to cause harm, such as weapons. It enables many modern weapons to circumvent hard-wired inhibitions against physical harming that are activated when we cause physical harm by means of more old-fashioned weapons—inhibitions consisting in our repulsion at the sight of blood, guts, and bodies writhing in pain and screaming. It is psychologically much harder for us to cause physical harm if we have to do it by means of knives and axes than drones and missiles. The availability of the latter kind of weapons, then, increases the risk that we shall stomach doing much more harm than we would otherwise do when it is in our interest to do harm—especially as we are also numb to large numbers of anonymous sufferers.

In contrast to modern weapons, anthropogenic climate change involves a further harm-bleaching causal factor, namely *a dispersal of causes and effects over many agents and victims*. Parfit's example of 'harmless torturers' illustrates such a dispersal (1987: § 29). In the bad old days, each one of 1,000 torturers causes each one of 1,000 victims excruciating pain. Then, in order to relieve the pangs of conscience of the torturers, new pain-producing devices are installed: instead of causing a single victim excruciating pain by increasing a painful stimulus 1,000 times, each torturer now increases this stimulus by one unit for all of the 1,000 victims, thereby causing only an *imperceptible* difference for each of the 1,000 victims. This will surely make the torturers feel less responsible and guilty, since they can all say to themselves that *individually* they cause no pain to anyone.[1] Yet, *together* the 1,000 torturers cause the same quantity of pain to their 1,000 victims as they did in the bad old days. The reason that the new arrangement will make them feel less responsible is that, according to the conception of responsibility as causally based, they take themselves to be responsible only for what they *individually* cause and disregard what a collective of which they are members causes.

However, large-scale diffusion of both agency and effects is precisely what happens with respect to climate change: the innumerable greenhouse gas emitting acts of each of us have only an imperceptible effect on the climate, but because there is such a vast number of us acting the total effect can be harmful to the global climate. Nevertheless,

---

[1] Even if they had caused a minimal pain to each of the 1,000 victims, they would still have felt relieved because, as remarked, while we are capable of feeling adequate sympathy for a single victim, we are not capable of feeling adequate sympathy for several victims in proportion to their number. Thus, the number of sufferers cannot make up for the reduced sympathy that we would feel for each sufferer in isolation.

each of us could excuse ourselves by thinking that individually we cause no measurable damage to the climate (and even if the damage were measurable, it would still affect anonymous individuals in the remote future which is something that makes us discount it).

There is yet another factor that contributes to making it hard for us to internalize that we may be acting wrongly when we perform greenhouse gas-emitting acts. This is that it is a rather recent discovery that everyday acts like driving, flying, and heating have a deleterious effect on the climate, that their emissions cause global warming by accumulating in the atmosphere as a layer that lets through sunlight but blocks the radiation of heat from the Earth's surface. By the time of this discovery, we had already grown accustomed to performing these acts in the belief that they were harmless. It is hard to break the habit of performing them and start regarding them as harmful. Something similar may be true of meat-eating: in many places for most of the past, meat-eating was regarded as a matter of course because it was necessary for survival. Then living conditions slowly changed to make it unnecessary for survival, whilst the production of the main portion of the meat consumed changed to cause animals more suffering. But by then people had got so used to eating meat that it is difficult for them to shift to seeing it as wrong for the reason that it occasions unnecessary suffering.

With respect to both anthropogenic climate change and meat-eating, collective action is indispensable to prevent the harm, but they differ in that, while the collective actions of single nations suffice to prevent some of the harm that meat-eating causes, international, world-wide cooperation—or at least cooperation that involves the biggest emitters of greenhouse gases such as China, USA, India, and Russia—is necessary to prevent climate change effectively. There are several reasons why such global cooperation is hard to establish: long-standing political and cultural differences—and even military conflicts—between the countries involved, the huge economic gap between the more and the less developed countries, the difference in their historical record of greenhouse gas emissions, the difference in the extent to which they are expected to be affected by harmful climate changes, the difficulties of surveying compliance with international agreements, and punishing defection, and the fact that future generations of the nations entering agreements might not consider themselves bound by them for the reason that *they* have not consented to them.

These factors might all serve as excuses for politicians not to try their hardest to reach international agreements, and to eschew responsibility for the fact that there has been no such agreement by blaming other parties. They have a motive for not putting the mitigation of anthropogenic climate change at the top of their political agenda, since it is bound to impose unpopular constraints on the present lifestyle of citizens—less driving, flying, red meat-eating, and so on—to prevent harms beyond their horizon of concern. In democracies unpopularity among voters is of course likely to cause politicians not to be elected or re-elected.

I have now reviewed a large number of arguably hard-wired features of our psychology that are morally relevant. Some of them are such that few or no philosophers would hold them to be justified or rational. This may be true of number numbness, the bias towards the near future and some components of causally based responsibility. But even without justification, these factors will continue to bleach our consciousness of the harm for which we are responsible, that is, they will make it psychologically difficult for us to appreciate the full magnitude of the harm for which we are responsible. Other features are such that moral philosophers are divided over whether or not they are justified. This is true of agent-relative permissions, desert, property rights, and the two deontological doctrines mentioned. With respect to such features, the philosophical discussion is liable to be ineradicably inconclusive. My suggestion is that this threatens to prevent moral philosophy from having its primary, intrinsic point by making it impotent to extend our rational consensus about what is morally right and wrong.

But in cases in which moral philosophers reach the same verdict—if there are any such cases—the situation may still be troublesome. Suppose for instance that they agree that some of the just-mentioned features that bleach our consciousness of the harmfulness of our greenhouse gas emissions are irrational. Then, as remarked, these features will still continue to influence the public and, thus, put obstacles in the way of international treaties to reduce such emissions. This problem of the philosophical morality being more demanding than common-sense morality will of course be exacerbated if more elements of this morality—for example, agent-relative permissions, the deontological doctrines, and the notions of rights and desert—are rejected and, as a consequence, morality becomes more demanding.

It might be further exacerbated if we take into consideration the metaethical probing of the grounds of morality by philosophers. As remarked in Chapter 11, human beings tend to be conformists, that is, they tend to act and react as most people around them do. If they have been brought up to act and react in certain ways because these are ways in which the majority of their fellow-citizens have acted and reacted for centuries, they tend to be highly respectful of these ways of behaving. Historically, this respect has often assumed the form of attributing these forms of behaviour to their deceased ancestors who are deified, or to some other gods. These gods may be thought of as watching over the observance of these ways of behaviour. Obviously, this may strengthen the motivation to observe them.

Now if these gods and ways of behaviour are thrown into doubt by philosophers, this is likely to weaken the respect for these ways of behaving and the motivation to observe them. Most of us have heard, from Dostoyevsky and others, that 'if God does not exist, anything is (morally) permissible', and most of us have heard from our teachers already as undergraduates that this is false. I do not dispute what we have been taught: there can certainly be things that are morally right and wrong even if no gods exist. There is indeed a plausible evolutionary account of the origin of morality that does not appeal to any gods. Yet, if the belief in a divine source of morality is given up, this might well weaken the *motivation* to comply with it. This might be because it is now realized that you may not be punished if you contravene moral norms, or you may begin to doubt that these norms are wise and well-informed.

Philosophy could then undermine respect for the authority of the traditional or received morality, and the possible revisions of this morality proposed by philosophy will lack this type of authority. Could metaethicists deliver anything that could restore the authority of morality? Of course, there are accounts that present moral norms as resting on objective grounds, grounds that are external to our subjective attitudes, but these accounts are, and are likely to remain, contested by metaethicists who take morality to be something subjective, expressive of our attitudes. However, this debate seems destined to be inconclusive by generating ever more subtle distinctions that promote bewilderment rather than conclusiveness. Thus, moral philosophy could lead to an undermining of the authority of morality that will drain our motivation to follow even those moral norms about which there is a pre-theoretical consensus that they are valid. It goes without saying that this is even more infelicitous if morality is revised in a more demanding direction.

But this drainage of motivation will occur only if moral philosophy seeps out of seminar rooms—which is a big 'if'. I mentioned earlier that a doctrine of human equality has gained a strong foothold in democratic societies in the twentieth century, though it is philosophically dubious. Perhaps we should take this fact as an indication that contemporary—at least analytic or anglophone—moral philosophy is debarred from having much impact on the surrounding society, for the reason that it is by and large too esoteric. Perhaps the time is past when more ground-breaking or cutting-edge moral philosophy could be sufficiently accessible to laypeople to have any noticeable impact on their behaviour. Anyhow, the intrinsic point of pursuing it, in its present state of being hopelessly inconclusive and esoteric, can only be the subsidiary one of promoting the development of the discipline of moral philosophy. Apart from that, it could have an external point, such as being a means to the fun, fame, and fortune of its practitioners.

This is meant as a conclusion about doing moral philosophy in the sense of doing *research*. You may instead use your knowledge of moral philosophy to carry out *campaigns* for moral causes. The distinction between these activities is admittedly fuzzy—making some work in applied ethics hard to classify—but it is roughly the distinction between arguing to find out what is morally right, or what is the ground or meaning of it being right, and arguing to persuade people to embrace what you think is morally right. Campaigning is something that, for instance, Peter Singer is famous for. Campaigners pick out some normative ethical position—in his case a form of utilitarianism—and employ it as a platform for their campaign. A campaign will only have an intrinsic point if it has a reasonable chance of being successful. If your platform diverges radically from the morality current in society—as does utilitarianism—this obviously increases the risk of failure, and the pointlessness of your campaign. But I am not here trying to assess the point of moral compaigns, which would be a daunting task, as there is an endless array of them.

If we want to have an impact on the moral behaviour of our fellow-citizens, another thing we could do is to sort out those hard-wired biases or reaction patterns about which there is something approaching a consensus that they are unfounded and look for effective means of counteracting them, whether these means be persuasion by argument or biomedical. Again, this is an enterprise the point of which I am not attempting to appraise here (but see Persson and Savulescu, 2012). My tentative conclusion is about the primary, intrinsic point of doing moral philosophical research at the present state of the art. It is that it will most likely lack such a point because it is becoming clear that it is bound to be hopelessly inconclusive, but at least it will hardly be harmful, since it will be increasingly esoteric.

This conclusion cannot but be tentative since, in spite of discouraging signs, moral philosophy might conceivably turn out to have intrinsic point by radically extending our rational consensus about what is morally right and wrong. But this is a scenario that, on the basis of the development of moral philosophy up to this point, seems unlikely to materialize. However, in the least unlikely version of this optimistic scenario the extension of the rational consensus will take the shape of moral philosophy ending up firmly vindicating the contested hard-wired reaction patterns embodied in common-sense morality rather than by conclusively refuting them. The reason for this is that these reaction patterns are so deeply rooted in our nature that most of us could not reconcile ourselves to them being irrational or unjustified. Nevertheless, there will remain some conflict between gut and brain, since all of the hard-wired reaction patterns will surely not be philosophically defensible. Moreover, the more this morality retains of these reaction patterns, the less well suited it will be to tackle the moral mega-problems mentioned. So, on the present—unrealistic—assumption moral philosophy will achieve its primary, intrinsic point, but the morality in which it issues will not have a point, according to the reasoning of Chapter 11. A somewhat better upshot, but still not very satisfying.

13

Beyond Ethical Inclusiveness
The Philosophy of Life

Moral philosophy is likely, then, not to have a primary, intrinsic point because it cannot produce a rational consensus about moral matters, and morality cannot have a point as things stand at present. A rational *consensus* is necessary, since morality is a collective code which, if valid, is universally valid for everyone capable of understanding it, independently of their particular aims, as opposed to individual codes of behaviour which are valid for individuals given their particular aims. Now, although morality, in virtue of its universal validity or applicability, could comprise aims like acting in such a way that you together with others produce the best outcome, it will also comprise, perhaps derivatively, aims that you could realize single-handedly. In the case of the latter sort of aims, if you are convinced that it is morally right to pursue them, you need not worry about whether other people agree. By contrast, in the case of the former, collective sort of aims, you do need to worry about their agreement because their cooperation is necessary to realize these aims. To pursue them without the cooperation of others could be useless.

I shall now consider philosophical thinking about how to live whose point is independent of generating a consensus because it is designed to issue in individual codes of behaviour, applicable to individuals who set themselves goals that they can realize single-handedly. So, although individual codes can be quite demanding, this is not an insurmountable problem, since they can have a point even if merely single exceptional individuals are capable of living by them; compliance by a majority of a collective is unnecessary. Nonetheless, as a side-effect, compliance with such a code can contribute to the collective goals of an inclusive morality such as the one expounded in this essay. That is, it can lead you to take on the sacrifices required by such goals, but for another reason than that they are required by this morality. Therefore, the meaningfulness of your contribution—say, the meaningfulness of your cutting down on activities that emit greenhouse gases—is not contingent on so many of your fellow-beings contributing that there will be a beneficial impact on the climate.

Now, suppose that you endorse the inclusive morality launched in this book, though it cannot be shown to be universally binding by being based on anything beyond your desires to be benevolent and just. And suppose further that nothing can be done to increase the probability that a majority will follow anything like this morality. Then, as will transpire, an individual code of the sort considered below could be of moral relevance for you by supplying you with additional motivation to pursue the cooperative aims of this morality. It could also boost your motivation in cases in which single-handed moral action is sufficient, but very demanding, like when you could save somebody's life at great risk to yourself.

As remarked in the Introduction, morality, albeit inclusive, does not encompass our conduct in so far as it affects only ourselves. It regulates our conduct merely in so far as it also impinges on other beings for whom things can go well or badly, which is what happens in most situations. Common-sense morality allows us to favour to some extent ourselves in such situations. I have argued elsewhere (2013) that this is because it endows us with rights to life, limb and property. Generally speaking, we are allowed to favour ourselves if we do not infringe the equally stringent rights of others. This means, for instance, that we are allowed to hang on to things to which we have rights even if others would benefit more from access to these things. But, as was cursorily explored in 7.4, in some circumstances, such as when we are innocently attacked, we also appear to be permitted to enforce our rights even when this results in the infringement of (at least) equally stringent rights of others. When rights and causally based responsibility are rejected, such matters must be settled by a revised morality which leaves no room for such preferential treatment of ourselves, like the morality which features the dual principles of beneficence and justice as equality proposed in this book.

While common-sense morality *permits* us to hold on to that to which we have rights, even if others would benefit more from these things, we are of course not *required* to do so. Quite the contrary, we are permitted to surrender some of these things to others even if they would benefit significantly *less* from this than we would, for instance to sacrifice our lives in order to save the limbs of others. But if we engage in such behaviour to an excessive degree, we would be regarded as unduly imprudent or irrational—that is, as failing to meet the conditions of being autonomous—rather than as immoral. Then morality in the shape of paternalism is called in to restrain us.

Since I do not believe that the distinction between self and others is rationally important, I am committed to holding that the use of the term 'moral', which rules out that benefiting others unduly at one's own expense can be immoral, rests on a trivial distinction. But even if the realm of morality were expanded to cover such exchanges between ourselves and others, there would be *a purely intrapersonal sector* that I think we would be loath to have it cover. For we could ask what, in light of the available information, it is rational for us to do in so far as this affects only ourselves in the longer or shorter run—and our 'successors' in the sense discussed in 3.1—bracketing the consequences for others.

In ancient Greece, by contrast to modern times, ethics comprised this intrapersonal dimension. The chief question of ancient ethics was 'How should I live in order to lead a good life?' where 'good' covered what is good for oneself as well as what is morally good and good for others. The discipline of reflecting on purely intrapersonal aspects of how we should live could be labelled *the philosophy of life*. Its aim is to find how to make things go best for each of us given the basic conditions of human life to which we are all exposed, whatever our particular circumstances. These conditions include the fact that our lives are radically beyond our control, a matter of good or bad luck. They are beyond our control by being dependent both on natural forces and on the behaviour of other moral agents. Moreover, since it is easier for us to be harmed than benefited, it is more likely that the factors beyond our control will affect us for the worse. This is something that we should keep in mind when we confront the largely uncertain and uncontrollable future.

The basic conditions of life also include that we age and eventually die, normally well within a century, but that death or serious illness could strike us down at any moment. Yet, most of the time we assume that this will happen in the distant future, and attend little to it, as we are wont to attend little to what we place in the distant as opposed to the more imminent future. The question to be answered by a philosophy of life includes, then, how to live in light of our mortality and vulnerability. This question takes us into such matters as the significance of our identity over time and the importance of different temporal parts of our lives, like whether it is rational to care more about the present and near future than the more remote future and the past. We shall see that contemplation of these matters could have the effect of weakening the opposition that moral motivation faces from self-regarding desires. If our moral motivation cannot be pumped up to the requisite degree, this would constitute an alternative strategy of easing the problem of living up to the demandingness of morality.

I am now going to contrast two attitudes to the fact that our fortune is largely beyond our control, one familiar from ancient philosophy, the other more familiar from modern life. Martha Nussbaum points out that 'a central preoccupation of ancient Greek thought about the human good' was that the 'rational element in us can rule and guide the rest, thereby saving the whole person from living at the mercy of luck' (1986: 2–3). Put a bit more precisely, her claim is: (a) 'the good life for a human being must to some extent, and in some ways, be self-sufficient, immune to the incursions of luck', and (b) 'the aspiration to make the goodness of a good human life safe from luck through the controlling power of reason' (1986: 3).

It is no doubt true that our life cannot be much good for us if it is greatly dependent on luck, say, if we need to be lucky to survive the day rather than unlucky not to do so. Even if we do survive for this brief period, we shall have undergone too much anxiety for our life to be much good for us during it. On the other hand, we certainly do not need *complete* control of what will happen to us in the future in order to lead a good life; then a good life would obviously be out of our reach. But, generally speaking, it is better for us to have more rather than less control over what matters to us.

We can roughly distinguish two ways in which our 'power of reason' can extend our control. It can inform us of means of controlling what is external to us or our will and mind. Our reason in the shape of scientific knowledge has been remarkably successful in this instrumental endeavour to tame the surrounding world and utilize its resources for our benefit, thereby reducing our dependence on luck. I shall call the attitude of striving to make our environment conform to our desires *heterarchy* (which means roughly the rule of something 'other').

However, this is not the sort of 'the controlling power of reason' that was, in Nussbaum's words, 'a central preoccupation of ancient Greek thought'. The ancient Greeks lived in a pre-scientific era, as all generations of human beings up to the last centuries have done. It was an era in which many threats to life and welfare—like epidemics, famines, and the effects of extreme weather and other natural catastrophes, which have been increasingly curbed by science—were rampant. So were social disorder and war. The 'central preoccupation' of ancient Greek philosophers was whether by means of 'the controlling power of reason' human beings could secure a good life in a world that was to such a great extent beyond their instrumental control.

The control that they sought was a control over *their own minds or attitudes* to the world. When the attitude of heterarchy fails to achieve its goal, because the surrounding world remains recalcitrant to our efforts to make it conform to the objects of our desires, an alternative option is to change our desires to remove the conflict or, in other words, to change our conception of what matters to us. This is *autarchy* ('*autarkeia*'), the attitude that forms the contrast to heterarchy. Autarchy is the attitude of striving to change our own affective and conative attitudes so as to make them conform to the world around us. Adapting these attitudes may be a more effective or manageable way of diminishing our frustration and unhappiness than moulding the world to match them. This aim of seeking attitudinal harmony with the surrounding world is an individual goal which can sensibly be pursued whatever fellow-beings aim for.

Autarchy was prevalent not only in ancient Greek thought, but also in ancient Asian thought. Think, for instance, of the Daoist core notion of *wu wei*, the way of non-action or non-interference, of having a will that is concordant with the outside world and shirks interference with it, smoothly adapting to it like running water. Or consider the central Buddhist doctrine that life is essentially suffering, the cause of which is unsatisfied or unsatisfiable desires; consequently, this suffering can only be alleviated by ceasing to have desires. Much later an updated version of it found expression in European philosophy by Schopenhauer's claim that the insight that the world-in-itself, or the essence of the world, is an unsatisfiable will to life can induce a renunciation of this will and asceticism which side with the highest moral virtue of being ready to sacrifice oneself for others (1819: § 68). This provides an illustration of a link between a—pessimistic—philosophy of life and morality.

Although autarchy was once a dominant philosophical attitude, it is now rarely the subject of philosophical discussion outside the history of philosophy.[1] It is also largely

---

[1] See Irvine (2009) for an exception. Irvine also alludes to something like my distinction between autarchy and heterarchy and notes the preponderance of autarchy in ancient times (2009: 86). By the way, the attitude of autarchy fascinated the young Wittgenstein. Ray Monk quotes for instance the following remark from a notebook of Wittgenstein's made on 11 June 1916: 'I can only make myself independent of the world—and so in a certain sense master of it—by renouncing any influence on happenings' (1991: 141).

absent from public awareness. Perhaps this loss of popularity is due to the fact that the physical world is now to such a greater degree more in our control than it was when natural science was in its infancy. We are now so accustomed to being able to transform the physical world to fit the objects of our desires that we do not bother to consider altering the orientation of our desires. But there is now a reason to resurrect the attitude of autarchy which springs from the increasingly ominous downside to our extensive exploitation of nature. On grounds of sheer probability, we should have expected there to be overlooked detrimental side-effects of this over-exploitation since, as already mentioned, there are indefinitely many more ways of damaging well-functioning arrangements, like organisms and eco-systems, than of improving their functioning to the same extent. Thus, arbitrary interferences with well-functioning systems are much more likely to damage them than to improve them. Therefore, their order or organization tends to decrease in the course of time because most arbitrary changes will damage them. This is a part of what is known as entropy.

In fact, it is arguable that contemporary science has *increased* the risk of global catastrophes (see Persson and Savulescu, 2012: 125–7). Anthropogenic climate change, environmental degradation, and the expanding availability of weapons of mass destruction have made the risk of the downfall of human civilization greater than ever. Moreover, despite the extraordinary advance of scientific technology, which has significantly augmented the life-expectancy of citizens in many parts of the world, our lives remain beyond our control in innumerable respects familiar since ancient times: we are still mortal, fall victims to diseases, accidents and crimes, suffer from unrequited love and humiliating treatments, and so on. As a matter of fact, we are frighteningly fragile; at every moment of life, we risk losing more than we can hope to gain. Indeed, we constantly risk losing everything life could offer, since we can quite easily die at any point of time. It is so easy to kill or seriously harm us that it is practically impossible for us to protect ourselves against all such threats.

Therefore, the attitude of autarchy merits as much consideration now as it received in antiquity. However, exaggerated claims on its behalf were then made. For instance, the Stoic Epictetus seemingly adopted an exceedingly optimistic view of the extent to which we can control our attitudes. In his *Enchiridion* or manual he proposes a stark dichotomy apparently consisting in that *all* our attitudes are in our control, whereas our bodies and everything external to them are beyond our control:

> Of things some are in our power, and others are not. In our power are opinion, movement toward a thing, desire, aversion (turning from a thing); and, in a word, whatever are our own actions: not in our power are the body, property, reputation, offices (magisterial power), and, in one word, whatever are not our own actions. (2004: § I)

To begin with, it is patently false that our bodies are *entirely* beyond our power or control; most of us are perfectly capable of moving them at will in various ways. (In this quotation 'actions' cannot include any bodily actions, since our bodies are said to be beyond our control.) If the world external to our minds were not to a considerable extent within our control, we would obviously not survive for long. On the other hand, some of our attitudes are irrational and outside rational control: although they have propositional content and in theory are within the scope of reasons, they do not in fact respond to reasons. Examples would be various phobias, like agoraphobia and arachnophobia. Furthermore, as we saw in Chapter 1, some of our attitudes are *non-rational*: they do not have propositional content and, thus, are not the sort of attitudes that can be formed on the basis of reasons; this is true of, for instance, our dislike of pain and liking of pleasure. These are attitudes which are not based on reasons and, thus, cannot be altered merely by reflecting on reasons. We are rather powerless as regards the direct control of such attitudes.

So, needless to say, autarchy in the sense of total control over our states of mind and independence of everything external to them—strict self-sufficiency—is not possible. Still, even though our control over our own minds is far from complete, we are in a privileged position with respect to them: we normally control them better than anyone else does. In addition, it is far from clear how much we can modify our mind-set by sustained reflection on philosophical insights and other mental exercises, like the prolonged, deep meditation of Buddhist monks. Further, scientific discoveries are likely to help us expand our mental control. Science will probably supply us with ever more effective means—of a neuro-surgical or pharmaceutical kind—of altering irrational and non-rational attitudes. Thus, the limits of our autarchic control over our own attitudes are not set in stone, but are fluid and changeable, and we can strive to push them back. Autarchy in the sense of a process of extending the control of our own attitudes is possible, though autarchy in the sense of having attained total control over them is not.

But to what attitudes of ours would it be *desirable* or *rational* to apply the policy of autarchy, given that there is a chance of such an application being successful because we have some measure of control over these attitudes? Epictetus seemingly suggests that the mere fact that *the object* of an attitude is beyond our control is a reason for trying to rid ourselves of the attitude. He advises us not to mind things beyond our power or control: 'Take away then aversion from all things which are not in our power, and transfer it to the things contrary to nature which are in our power' (2004: § II). For instance, 'if you attempt to avoid disease or death or poverty, you will be unhappy' (2004: § II) because it is beyond your control whether or not they will afflict you; so, be indifferent rather than averse to them. Likewise, you should not take unreserved delight in things which are not fully in your control, like your wife and children, because they might die at any moment.[2]

Epictetus surely goes too far if his claim is that we should care about something only if it is completely in our power and control, since this would not leave us anything to care about. Death might rob us of everything of value at any moment. It is true that we

---

[2] Similarly, Spinoza writes that 'our sorrows and misfortunes mainly proceed from too much love toward an object which is subject to many changes, and which we can never possess' (1677: pt. V, prop. 20. 5). In my terminology, Spinoza's *Ethics* is more of a philosophy of life than ethics, its main topic being autarchic freedom from the bondage of passions.

can *decide* and *intend* to influence the happening of events only in so far as we think that we have the power to do so. Hence, these conative attitudes would have to be dropped if we were to discover their objectives to be mainly beyond our control. In contrast, it would be absurd to claim that the emotional or affective attitudes of *fear* and *hope* should not be felt for things outside our control because it is logically possible to hope for and fear *only* what is outside our control. To the extent that the occurrence of events is within our control, we can simply *ensure* that they occur or do not occur, and that excludes having hope or fear as regards their occurrence (cf. Persson, 2005: 66–7).

Now it is reasonable to weigh in the extent to which it is within our power to ensure the materialization of various possible goals when we make up our minds about which of them to strive for. Imagine that you regard, say, excelling in doing philosophy and getting recognition for your excellence as roughly equally desirable. Imagine further that you face a choice between (a) whole-heartedly engaging in perfecting your philosophical ability and (b) spending some of your time networking to boost your chances of getting recognition for your philosophy. You judge that you will be likelier to achieve more excellence if you opt for (a), but likelier to receive more recognition if you opt for (b). When you take into consideration that success with respect to receiving recognition is more dependent on factors beyond your control than achieving philosophical excellence is, you estimate that the probability that you will succeed in achieving an extra bit of excellence is around 75 per cent if you opt for (a), while the probability that you will succeed in receiving an extra bit of recognition is only 60 per cent if you choose (b). Then it is reasonable for you to prefer (a) because the expected value of this alternative is higher.

Thus, if some states of mind are roughly as valuable as some external states of affairs that many of us desire, like fame and fortune, but it is to a greater extent up to us to guarantee the existence of the former, then Epictetus could claim that it is rational for us to aim for the former rather than the latter. As regards fame, that is, recognition by a large number of people, and fortune in the sense of exceptional wealth, these are to such a large extent dependent on factors beyond our control that it may well be irrational to desire them—the risk of ending up frustrated through no fault of our own would be too great. However, appreciation by a small circle of family and friends, which almost all of us need in order to feel happy,[3] since we are intensely social creatures, would not seem to be so much more dependent on factors beyond our control than our states of mind that it could fail to be rational to desire them. The same goes for a modest amount of possessions which cater for the basic necessities of life. This would yield an existence which is a far cry from the self-sufficiency to which Epictetus seemingly aspired, but it is still tantamount to an abandonment of the more extravagant materialist or consumerist lifestyle of affluent countries which threatens to deplete the natural resources of the earth.

---

[3] 'It is only a slight exaggeration to say that happiness is the experience of spending time with people you love and who love you', Kahneman (2011: 395).

It should be emphasized, however, that this does not gainsay the point earlier made that an event's being beyond control is by itself no reason to surrender positive or negative attitudes towards it. As remarked, the degree to which you believe something to be beyond your control can determine what kind of attitude you can intelligibly take to it, just as its being certain or uncertain relative to your evidence can. As long as you believe something to be beyond your control and uncertain in some respects, you could intelligibly feel fear or hope concerning it. To the extent that you believe it to be within your control, it will be a suitable object of decision and intention to bring it about, or prevent it. If you are certain that it has happened or will happen, you will rather be glad or sad, relieved or disappointed, and so on that this is so.[4] But whether or not something is within your control, like whether or not something is certain, does not determine whether it is desirable or undesirable, or a proper object of positive or negative attitudes. Hence, if awareness of 'disease or death or poverty' makes us unhappy or fearful, we need some other reason than that it is beyond our power to protect ourselves fully against them to pacify them, or be cured of the unhappiness or fear that they induce in us. This awareness is rather likely to aggravate unhappiness or fear.

To be sure, we could remove or reduce this unhappiness or fear by suppressing thoughts about the risks of these misfortunes. Then we might be less worried or unhappy, but there is a flipside to keeping these risks in mind. By reflecting on how vulnerable we are, how fragile our lives are, we can bring out with greater clarity what is of value in our lives. This is because we easily slip into taking for granted things that we are accustomed to having, friends, family, professional occupation, material possessions, and so on—so-called *hedonic adaptation*. An antidote to this adaptation or insensitivity consists in voluntarily turning our attention to the (perhaps slight) possibility that we might lose these things in the near future, for instance because we or our acquaintances die. Such cultivation of what I have elsewhere called *the sense of the precariousness of life* (2005: 229–31) is likely to enable us to appreciate better the importance that these things have for us, since it is a well-known psychological fact that people often do not fully realize the value of what they have until they have lost it.

Zooming in on such possibilities as that we might not wake up tomorrow is likely, then, to raise the question whether we are spending our time today in a worthwhile fashion. I do not mean that we should be encouraged to aim 'to live every day as though it were the last'. We should certainly not overestimate the presumably small probability of soon falling victim to some calamity and for that reason abandon long-term life projects. The point is merely that we should not be entirely unaware of the small possibility that we might soon go down, as we standardly are prone to be. Making vivid the ineliminable uncertainty about what the future has in store helps us to appreciate the value of features of our present lives.

---

[4] For a more detailed discussion of such matters, see Persson (2005: chs. 5 and 6).

It should however be admitted that the question of how to live our lives presents us with something of an unresolvable dilemma between pursuing long-term projects which tend to make life more worthwhile if they are actualized, but which are less likely to be actualized, and pursuing shorter-term projects which are more likely to be actualized, but which would make life less rewarding if you do not expire prematurely. It might seem that the best insurance against the vagaries of existence is some mixture of long-term and short-term interests, but what is the right mixture is probably a matter about which general advice is pretty useless. But notice that if your overarching aim in life is the autarchic one to see how things work out for you—what interests you develop and to what extent you succeed in fulfilling them—then you cannot be disappointed whatever happens to you.

The main point in the present context, however, is that awareness of life's being beyond our control by and large should not be suppressed but be kept alive to inform the formation of our life-plans. For it can teach us to be more content with what we have, or have had, and more modest in desiring improvements by bringing out both the value of the status quo and the importance of desiring objects that are less luck-dependent. Unrestrained desires for improvements breed perpetual discontent with the status quo, even if you are exceptionally lucky in respect of succeeding in satisfying these desires, because no matter how great your wealth, how high your status, how good your health, or how long your life, you can always imagine them to be greater, higher, better, and longer.

So much for the importance of availing ourselves of the technique of making vivid to ourselves harmful courses that our *future* might take. There is however also a retrospective form of this technique, which consists in our imagining ways in which *the past* could have been less generous to us, so that we would never have enjoyed the benefits that we have in fact enjoyed.[5] This act of retrospective imagination or visualization could inflate our pleasure of having had these benefits to counterbalance the sorrow of having lost them. For instance, you could contemplate the extreme improbability of your coming into existence—this is dependent on such improbable events as your parents having had sex on a particular occasion, with the upshot that a certain one of hundreds of millions of spermatozoa fertilized an ovum. The realization of how easily you could have failed to exist and been deprived of everything that your life has brought you should have a sobering effect on your complaints about things that you have missed or will miss at various times in your life.

Moreover, if you imagine in a lively fashion how easily you could have been much more unlucky in the past, or might be very unlucky in the future, this facilitates your putting yourself in the shoes of individuals who are less lucky than you and sympathizing with their plight. This shows how life-philosophical reflection on the precariousness

---

[5] Irvine calls these techniques 'negative visualization' and attributes them to the Stoics (2009: ch. 4). He, too, distinguishes a prospective form of negative visualization from a retrospective form (2009: 155).

of life could amplify moral concern for the welfare of others, as I suggested at the outset of this chapter. It is not just prudentially rewarding.

The sense of the precariousness of life, however, is counteracted by *the mechanism of spontaneous induction* (Persson, 2005: 104). We have a tendency, when we intuitively estimate the probability of events, to be strongly influenced by how available representations of them are to our imagination, by how easy it is for us vividly to imagine them happening, though this factor does not mirror their probability. This has been called *the availability bias* (Kahneman, 2011: 131). Thus, we tend to be oblivious to the small probability that a kind of event will occur if we are accustomed to it not occurring. To take an example already employed, we are normally oblivious to the small probability that we may drop dead within the next couple of hours. We feel certain that we shall not die soon and turn a blind eye to the minuscule probability of this fatal event. So, we shall in normal circumstances feel no fear of dying soon, since our emotions are geared to how vividly we imagine events. However, if, say, an accident happens that makes this small likelihood readily available to our imagination, it might for a considerable period of time—by the mechanism of spontaneous induction—make a great difference to our emotional reaction to this type of event happening again, though there is no change of its probability.

To cultivate the sense of the precariousness of life, we must then resist the mechanism of spontaneous induction. This will make us more immune to hedonic adaptation and more sympathetic to those who are unfortunate, but these benefits have to be bought at the price of being more disposed to feel anxiety. If contemplation of the precariousness of life is to be vivid enough to elicit a sharpened perception of what is of value in our lives, it will surely also have to be vivid enough to evoke some measure of anxiety for possible losses. Thus, there is a cost to representing vividly the precariousness of life, and we might wonder whether it is a cost worth paying.

This might have been less of a problem for Epictetus, since he apparently believed in something like the immortality of the soul. However, those of us who do not share such reassuring beliefs have to face up to a risk of dying and losing virtually everything at any moment, and the certainty of eventually doing so.[6] But there are facts that could console us, or diminish the anxiety that such thoughts occasion. First, this could be effected by internalizing the fact that it is in itself unimportant whether there is someone in the future who is identical to you. As indicated in 3.1, what matters is rather whether there is someone who instantiates the valuable properties that you would like to see instantiated (for further discussion of these matters, see Persson, 2005: pt. IV).

---

[6] Kagan claims that 'fear of death is inappropriate precisely because death is certain' (2012: 297). But I believe that fear is the negative counterpart not only of hope—which does indeed presuppose some uncertainty—but also of longing which does not (cf. Persson, 2005: 81–2). Just as you can long for a death that you know will occur at a certain time—say, if you are in agony—you can fear such a temporally fixed death if it will instead rob you of a good life. But in any case there are doubtless times when you can reasonably fear that you might die *too soon* to have had time to complete your most important life-projects. Kagan observes (2012: 302–3), as I just did, that we also have reason to feel fortunate or glad for the goods of life that we have received, but that does not rule out fear of dying sooner rather than later.

But, then, if you survive, you should not be satisfied simply because your allegedly precious identity has been preserved. You should instead feel a pressure to live to be the sort of person that you would like to be, a pressure that should grow as the time at your disposal to become this sort of person gradually runs out and as your ability to improve on yourself decreases when your psychological and physical assets deteriorate with advancing age. Consciousness of such an ongoing struggle tends to blunt your fear of death. Additionally, when you have lived longer, you will have had more time to bring across to others what you consider of importance in life. The fact that you will cease to exist should matter less to you if what you regard as important will survive you and have a chance of influencing other individuals.

Secondly, to keep things in proper perspective, it should be borne in mind that there are countless beings, human and non-human, who are unjustly worse off than you, and that you could easily have been as badly off as they are. To repeat, there was an overwhelming likelihood of your not even having been conceived. However, a retrospective form of visualizing of how easily things could have taken a worse turn for you will probably prove to be an ineffective counterweight to the experience of things going badly for you at present or in the imminent future because we are *biased towards the future*, that is, spontaneously more concerned about our weal and woe in the future than in the past.[7] It is readily comprehensible why evolution should have equipped us with this type of bias: whereas we cannot do anything to change the past, we can often affect the future, and it is crucial for our reproductive fitness that we do so. So, it is good for us that our attention is instinctively focused more on the future than on the past, but this does not imply that the fact that something will happen to us in the future rather than has happened to us in the past means that it will contribute more to the value of our lives. It is hard to see how the mere timing of something by itself could make any difference to its intrinsic value for us. Therefore, the bias towards the future appears to be an irrational attitude that would not be entertained by somebody who has internalized a clear-headed view of the facts.

It is however not difficult to comprehend how the bias towards the future works to make things of value for us in the future attract us more than things of value for us in the past. In contrast to space in which we can move in any direction—for instance, from left to right as well as in the reverse direction—time essentially has a direction from the future to the past: the past is what happens *before* or *earlier* than the present, and the future is what happens *after* or *later* than the present. This is an order that we are hard put to reverse even in our imagination. Thus, we can without effort imagine how things can run on from the present into the future—as exemplified by the mechanism of spontaneous induction—whereas if we attempt to imagine (or remember) events leading up to the present, we have to adopt a point of view *earlier* than these events from which we can look *forward* to them. This is an imaginative feat that takes greater effort than imagining things running on from the present into the future,

---

[7] For further discussion of the bias towards the future, see Parfit (1987: pt. II) and Persson (2005: ch. 16).

though it is nevertheless much easier than imagining events occurring in a backward order from the present into the past.

As a result, possible future events are more readily available to our imagination than past events to stir up our attitudes. In other words, the availability bias underlies the bias towards the future. As already noted, the latter bias has great survival value for us since, as we can often affect the course of the future, it is crucial that we pay close attention to how to do so in order to get it properly done. On the other hand, the bias towards the future has drawbacks, too, such as making us more fearful and sad about what death will deprive us of than about what we have been deprived of by not having been born earlier, but its advantages—including increasing the likelihood of escaping premature death—seemingly outweigh them.

This brings us to another temporal bias which is directed solely at the future: as mentioned in Chapter 12, we have a *bias towards the near future* which manifests itself, for instance, when we are relieved as something unpleasant due to happen to us in the near future is postponed, and disappointed as something pleasant in store for us in the near future is postponed, whereas the same postponement of unpleasant and pleasant events in the more distant future is likely to leave us comparatively unaffected.[8] There is a discounting of future events which is rational because it is as a rule true that, when an event is in the more remote future, it is less probable than what is closer to the present and, as noted, the lower probability of an event's occurring makes it rational to be proportionally less concerned about it. But it would be a mistake to think that the bias towards the near future consists in being less concerned about an event in store for us in the more remote future because it is estimated to be less probable. For we could be greatly relieved when an unpleasant event, such as a painful piece of surgery, is postponed for just a day, even though we take this delay to make it only marginally less probable (and what could prevent it is likely to be worse, such as death!). The nearness in the future of an emotionally or motivationally salient event is rather a circumstance which tends to make it more available to our imagination and, thereby, more prone to arouse our feelings or desires; thus, the availability bias is at work as regards the bias towards the near, too. As in the case of the bias towards the future, it is readily comprehensible why evolution should have equipped us with a bias towards the near: events in the near future are usually more important for our life prospects because they are more probable.

But the motivational force of a salient event that is vividly present to our minds is shown most clearly by the fact that nothing could exercise a stronger motivational influence on us than an event of this sort when we currently perceive it—perception being more vivid than imagination as long as the latter falls short of being hallucinatory. For instance, it is virtually impossible for anything to surpass the pull on our attention and the motivational impact of an intense pain that is currently felt. This mechanism could be termed *the bias towards the perceived* (cf. Persson, 2005: 183–4).

---

[8] For further discussion of the bias towards the near, see Parfit (1987: pt. II) and Persson (2005: ch. 15).

It is stronger than the bias towards the near future, as is shown by the fact that we might be willing to swap an acute pain that we are currently feeling for a somewhat greater pain in the imminent future.

If we were to succeed in overcoming these biases towards the perceived and (near) future, the vista of an apparently endless past and future in an equally spatially endless universe would open up as a frame of reference for our concern. From such a view-point, '*sub specie aeternitatis*' everyday states of affairs, whether good or bad, shrink almost to insignificance.[9] By contrast, if we view such states of affairs from a mundane, personal perspective that often does not range over more than the imminent future and the near vicinity, they would occupy a relatively large part of the frame. For this perspective cannot harbour states of affairs that are hugely more extensive in time and space. However, with a switch to a cosmic perspective which extends over more of the universe than the small patch on which the life of each of us plays out, and over billions of years, such vastly more extensive states of affairs become imaginable. In comparison to them, what we could accomplish in our lives dwindles to something so minute that our interest in them is drastically reduced. If we take into consideration the billions of years when we shall be dead, a few decades of welfare before we die are diminished almost to the point of disappearance. Likewise, if we imagine the billions of beings all around us striving to satisfy their desires, we shall be loath to join their ranks with gusto.

Also, a wider temporal perspective reveals starkly that when one of our desires has been satisfied, the felt satisfaction will not last for long, even if it is the satisfaction of a desire which has occupied most of our attention. It is likely to be replaced immediately by a desire for something else, or else we are seized with boredom—a psychological fact that Schopenhauer never ceases to stress. Such a forceful realization of the transience of satisfaction tends to sap the strength of our desires and, so, lets us off the treadmill of futile fulfilment-hunting. In contrast, if our time frame does not stretch much beyond the near future, we are disposed to be prodded by one desire after another without being aware of how little their satisfaction has to offer us. Additionally, if we compare being satisfied with being unsatisfied during a limited period of time, while being oblivious to a much wider time frame, this small amount of satisfaction can come out as being quite significant for us. Consequently, we rather desperately desire more satisfaction, and a longer life that could contain this satisfaction. But when we shift from this mundane perspective to a point of view *sub specie aeternitatis*, which encompasses billions of other creatures as well, an instance of satisfaction of this duration is reduced almost to nothing, relatively speaking. This is an exercise of subjecting our desires to autarchic control, as opposed to heterarchically attempting to make our surroundings conform to the unbridled desires that we have when we spontaneously

---

[9] This is another piece of mental exercise practised by the Stoics; for instance, Marcus Aurelius refers to looking at things 'from above' in *The Meditations*, book 9.30.

view things from a mundane perspective (cf. Persson, 2005: 224–7, and Persson and Savulescu, 2013).

If vividly and persistently represented, these considerations—about the unimportance of the survival of the self, the cosmic transience of everything dear to us, and the arbitrariness of our occupying our present station in life rather than another one of countless alternative stations, or no station at all—could help us to reconcile ourselves with our inescapable vulnerability. Self-sufficiency is certainly impossible; there is nothing completely within our control to which we can retreat, as Epictetus might have thought. But by bringing home to us the futility of being selfishly grasping and acquisitive, these considerations could open sluices for moral motivation like altruism and a sense of justice. They could push us towards a conatively detached state that, as already noted, among European philosophers Schopenhauer in particular has eloquently described (1819: § 68). It is a state in which self-regarding desires are, if not defeated, at least markedly muted. The more frugal way of life that naturally results is particularly apposite in the present world, strained as it is by overpopulation and overconsumption.

This state of detachment is different from being morally activated by the weal and woe of others, but it is harmonious with it in virtue of reducing the strength of self-regarding desires that oppose moral motivation. The philosophy of life links up with morality because, by bringing out how ephemeral and uncertain our own long-term good is, it makes it easier for us to risk it in the line of doing what we morally ought. Furthermore, since the look at things from above puts us among other beings whose misfortunes could easily have been ours, it invites us to imagine ourselves in their shoes, which is liable to enhance the motivation to treat them beneficently and justly. Still, although abiding by such an autarchic philosophy of life naturally manifests itself in actions in line with an inclusive morality, its aims are different, and its contributions to moral aims have the character of side-effects. A simple illustration of this kind of relationship would be if people stop eating red meat purely for reasons of health, and this has positive side-effects both on animal welfare and the climate.

Despite the fact that I have talked about the effect of an autarchic way of life on our welfare, its aim need not be to maximize or increase the welfare of our lives; it could also be to have attitudes that are more closely attuned to fundamental truths about human existence, an aim which strikes me as more becoming of a philosopher.[10] But whichever of these aims that you have for acting in accordance with an autarchic philosophy of life, it is an individualist strategy that can have a point whatever others do, or are capable of doing. There is no denying that life-philosophical instructions to overcome temporal biases, the belief in the importance of our identity, and the mechanism

---

[10] Contrast Irvine who writes: 'if you seek something other than satisfaction, I would inquire (with astonishment) into what it is that you find more desirable than satisfaction' (2009: 78). In ancient Greece it was seemingly assumed that the aims of pursuing truth and satisfaction could by and large be brought to converge. As opposed to this, I argue in (2005) that there is a considerable tension between these 'rationalist' and 'satisfactionalist' life-strategies.

of spontaneous induction, are exceedingly hard to live up to, as hard as those of an inclusive morality. But the difference is that the former can have a point even though only singularly exceptional individuals are able to put them into practice.

The conclusion about the bearing of this exploration of an autarchic philosophy of life on the problems of implementing the morality of inclusive beneficence and extreme egalitarianism is, briefly and bluntly, that it can help on the motivational side. It helps with mastering its demandingness, and side-steps the problem with faltering authority, since a philosophy of life has never been supposed to possess any objective justification. By its motivational input, it encourages a lifestyle that saves up resources for the use of an inclusive morality. However, it offers no assistance with the more epistemic problems of implementation surveyed in Chapter 11, that consist in the two principles of this morality being difficult to apply to concrete situations because of their great generality, the inexhaustibility and elusiveness of relevant empirical facts, and the complexity and imprecision of values, which have to be balanced against each other in a wholly intuitive fashion. Nonetheless, this step from an extravagant to a more frugal lifestyle would stop our positively contributing to the severity of the moral mega-problems, which are due to the extraordinary power of our scientific technology and the consequent explosive growth of the human population, and which in conjunction threaten to bring about the downfall of human civilization.

References

Anscombe, G. E. M. (1957) *Intention*, Oxford: Blackwell.
Anscombe, G. E. M. (1967) 'Who is Wronged?', *The Oxford Review*, no. 5.
Arneson, Richard (2015) 'Basic Equality: Neither Acceptable Nor Rejectable', in U. Steinhoff (ed.), *Do All Persons Have Equal Moral Worth?*, Oxford: Oxford University Press.
Ayers, Michael (1991) *Locke*, vol. II, London: Routledge.
Bennett, Jonathan (1995) *The Act Itself*, Oxford: Oxford University Press.
Blackburn, Simon (1988) 'Supervenience Revisited', in G. Sayre-McCord (ed.), *Essays on Moral Realism*, Ithaca, CT: Cornell University Press.
BonJour, Laurence (1998) *In Defense of Pure Reason*, Cambridge: Cambridge University Press.
Boonin, David (2014) *The Non-Identity Problem and the Ethics of Future People*, Oxford: Oxford University Press.
Bradley, Ben (2009) *Well-Being and Death*, Oxford: Oxford University Press.
Broome, John (1991) *Weighing Goods*, Oxford: Blackwell.
Broome, John (1999) *Ethics out of Economics*, Cambridge: Cambridge University Press.
Carter, Ian (2011) 'Respect and the Basis of Equality', *Ethics*, 121: 538–71.
Christiano, Thomas (2015) 'Rationality, Equal Status, and Egalitarianism', in U. Steinhoff (ed.), *Do All Persons Have Equal Moral Worth?*, Oxford: Oxford University Press.
Cohen, G. A. (1989) 'On the Currency of Egalitarian Justice', *Ethics*, 99: 906–44.
Crisp, Roger (1997) *Mill on Utilitarianism*, London: Routledge.
Crisp, Roger (2003) 'Equality, Priority, and Compassion', *Ethics*, 113: 745–63.
Dawson, Karen (1990) 'Introduction: An Outline of Scientific Aspects of Human Embryo Research', in P. Singer, H. Kuhse, S. Buckle, K. Dawson and P. Kasimba (eds), *Embryo Experimentation*, Cambridge: Cambridge University Press.
DeGrazia, David (2005) *Human Identity and Bioethics*, Cambridge: Cambridge University Press.
DeGrazia, David (2012) *Creation Ethics*, New York: Oxford University Press.
DeGrazia, David (2015) 'Reply to Critics of Creation Ethics', *Journal of Medical Ethics*, 41: 423–4.
Epictetus, *Enchiridion*, trans. George Long, Mineola, NY: Dover Publications, 2004.
Feinberg, Joel (1970) 'Justice and Personal Desert', in his *Doing and Deserving*, Princeton, NJ: Princeton University Press.
Feldman, Fred (1992) *Confrontations with the Reaper*, New York: Oxford University Press.
Feldman, Fred (1995) 'Justice, Desert, and the Repugnant Conclusion', *Utilitas*, 7: 189–206.
Feldman, Fred (2004) *Pleasure and the Good Life*, Oxford: Clarendon Press.
Ford, Norman M. (1988) *When Did I Begin?*, Cambridge: Cambridge University Press.
Frankena, William (1963) *Ethics*, Englewood Cliffs, NJ: Prentice-Hall.
Hare, R. M. (1952) *The Language of Morals*, Oxford: Oxford University Press.
Harris, John (1985) *The Value of Life*, London: Routledge & Kegan Paul.
Harris, John (1992) *Wonderwoman and Superman*, Oxford: Oxford University Press.
Holtug, Nils (2010) *Persons, Interests, and Justice*, Oxford: Oxford University Press.

Hume, David (1739) *A Treatise of Human Nature*, 2nd edn, P. H. Nidditch (ed.), Oxford: Clarendon Press, 1978.
Hurley, Susan (2003) *Justice, Luck, and Knowledge*, Cambridge, MA: Harvard University Press.
Irvine, William (2009) *A Guide to the Good Life*, New York: Oxford University Press.
Kagan, Shelly (1992) 'The Limits of Well-Being', *Social Philosophy and Policy*, 9: 169–89.
Kagan, Shelly (1994) 'Me and My Life', *Proceedings of the Aristotelian Society*, 94: 309–24.
Kagan, Shelly (2012) *Death*, New Haven and London: Yale University Press.
Kahneman, Daniel (2011) *Thinking Fast and Slow*, London: Allen Lane.
Kahneman, Daniel and Tversky, Amos (eds) (2000) *Choices, Values, and Frames*, Cambridge: Cambridge University Press.
Kamm, F. M. (1992) *Creation and Abortion*, New York: Oxford University Press.
Kamm, Frances (2007) *Intricate Ethics*, New York: Oxford University Press.
Kim, Jaegwon (1993) *Supervenience and Mind*, Cambridge: Cambridge University Press.
Lippert-Rasmussen, Kasper (2016) *Luck Egalitarianism*, London: Bloomsbury.
Locke, John (1689) *An Essay Concerning Human Understanding*, P. H. Nidditch (ed.), Oxford: Clarendon Press, 1975.
Locke, John (1690) *Two Treatises of Government*, London: Everyman Library, 1924.
Marcus Aurelius, *The Meditations*, trans. Martin Hammond, London: Penguin Classics, 2006.
McKerlie, Dennis (2013) *Justice between the Young and the Old*, Oxford: Oxford University Press.
McMahan, Jeff (1981) 'Problems of Population Theory', *Ethics*, 92: 96–127.
McMahan, Jeff (1988) 'Death and the Value of Life', *Ethics*, 99: 32–61.
McMahan, Jeff (1995) 'The Metaphysics of Brain Death', *Bioethics*, 9: 91–126.
McMahan, Jeff (2002) *The Ethics of Killing*, New York: Oxford University Press.
McMahan, Jeff (2008) 'Challenges to Human Equality', *Journal of Ethics*, 12: 81–104.
McMahan, Jeff (2009) 'Asymmetries in the Morality of Causing People to Exist', in M. Roberts and D. Wasserman (eds), *Harming Future Persons*, New York: Springer.
McMahan, Jeff (2013) 'Causing People to Exist and Saving People's Lives', *Journal of Ethics*, 17: 5–35.
Mele, Alfred (1995) *Autonomous Agents*, New York: Oxford University Press.
Mill, J. S. (1859) *On Liberty*, E. Rapaport (ed.), Indianapolis, IN: Hackett, 1978.
Mill, J. S. (1861) *Utilitarianism*, G. Sher (ed.), Indianapolis, IN: Hackett, 1979.
Monk, Ray (1991) *Wittgenstein—The Duty of a Genius*, London: Penguin Books.
Moore, G. E. (1903) *Principia Ethica*, Cambridge: Cambridge University Press.
Moore, G. E. (1922) *Philosophical Studies*, London: Routledge & Kegan Paul.
Nagel, Thomas (1979) 'Moral Luck', reprinted in his *Mortal Questions*, Cambridge: Cambridge University Press.
Nielsen, Kai (1985) *Equality and Liberty. A Defense of Radical Egalitarianism*, Totowa, NJ: Rowman & Allenheld.
Norman, Richard (1983) *The Moral Philosophers*, Oxford: Clarendon Press.
Nozick, Robert (1974) *Anarchy, State, and Utopia*, New York: Basic Books.
Nussbaum, Martha (1986) *The Fragility of Goodness*, Cambridge: Cambridge University Press.
Olson, Eric (1997) *The Human Animal*, New York: Oxford University Press.
Otsuka, Michael (2012) 'Prioritarianism and the Separateness of Persons', *Utilitas*, 24: 365–80.
Otsuka, Michael and Voorhoeve, Alex (2009) 'Why it Matters that Some are Worse Off than Others', *Philosophy and Public Affairs*, 37: 171–99.

Parfit, Derek (1986) 'Overpopulation and the Quality of Life', in P. Singer (ed.), *Applied Ethics*, Oxford: Oxford University Press.
Parfit, Derek (1987) *Reasons and Persons*, Oxford: Clarendon Press.
Parfit, Derek (1995) *Equality or Priority?*, The Lindley Lecture 1991, The University of Kansas.
Parfit, Derek (2011) *On What Matters*, vol. 1, Oxford: Oxford University Press.
Parfit, Derek (2012) 'Another Defence of the Priority View', *Utilitas*, 24: 399–440.
Persson, Ingmar (1985a) *The Primacy of Perception: Towards a Neutral Monism*, Lund: Gleerup.
Persson, Ingmar (1985b) 'The Universal Basis of Egoism', *Theoria*, 51: 137–58.
Persson, Ingmar (1993) 'A Basis for Inter-Species Equality', in P. Cavalieri and P. Singer (eds), *The Great Ape Project*, London: Fourth Estate.
Persson, Ingmar (1995a) 'Genetic Therapy, Identity and the Person-Regarding Reasons', *Bioethics*, 9: 16–31.
Persson, Ingmar (1995b) 'Peter Singer on Why Persons are Irreplaceable', *Utilitas*, 7: 55–66.
Persson, Ingmar (1995c) 'What is Mysterious about Death?', *The Southern Journal of Philosophy*, 33: 499–508.
Persson, Ingmar (1997) 'Person-Affecting Principles and Beyond', in N. Fotion and J. C. Heller (eds), *Contingent Future Persons*, Dordrecht: Kluwer.
Persson, Ingmar (1999a) 'Harming the Non-Conscious', *Bioethics*, 13: 294–305.
Persson, Ingmar (1999b) 'Our Identity and the Separability of Persons and Organisms', *Dialogue*, 38: 519–33.
Persson, Ingmar (1999c) 'Does it Matter When We Begin to Exist?', in V. Launis, J. Pietarinen and J. Räikka (eds), *Genes and Morality*, Amsterdam: Rodopi.
Persson, Ingmar (2000) 'Mill's Derivation of the Intrinsic Desirability of Pleasure', *History of Philosophy Quarterly*, 17: 297–310.
Persson, Ingmar (2001) 'Equality, Priority and Person-affecting Values', *Ethical Theory and Moral Practice*, 4: 23–39.
Persson, Ingmar (2002) 'Human Death—A View from the Beginning of Life', *Bioethics*, 16: 20–32.
Persson, Ingmar (2003a) 'Two Claims about Potential Human Beings', *Bioethics*, 17: 503–16.
Persson, Ingmar (2003b) 'The Badness of Unjust Inequality', *Theoria*, 69: 109–24.
Persson, Ingmar (2004) 'The Root of the Repugnant Conclusion and its Rebuttal', in J. Ryberg and T. Tännsjö (eds), *The Repugnant Conclusion*, Dordrecht: Kluwer.
Persson, Ingmar (2005) *The Retreat of Reason: A Dilemma in the Philosophy of Life*, Oxford: Clarendon Press.
Persson, Ingmar (2006a) 'Mill's Principle of Liberty and the Distinction between Self and Others', John Stuart Mill Bicentennial Conference, University College, London 5–7 April.
Persson, Ingmar (2006b) 'Consciousness as Existence as a Form of Neutral Monism', in A. Freeman (ed.), *Radical Externalism*, Exeter: Imprint Academic.
Persson, Ingmar (2007) 'A Defence of Extreme Egalitarianism', in N. Holtug and K. Lippert-Rasmussen (eds), *Egalitarianism: New Essays on the Nature and Value of Equality*, Oxford: Oxford University Press.
Persson, Ingmar (2009a) 'Rights and the Asymmetry of Creating Good and Bad Lives', in M. Roberts and D. Wasserman (eds), *Harming Future Persons*, New York: Springer.
Persson, Ingmar (2009b) 'The Origination of a Human Being: A Reply to Oderberg', *Journal of Applied Philosophy*, 26: 371–8.
Persson, Ingmar (2012) 'Prioritarianism and Welfare Reductions', *Journal of Applied Philosophy*, 29: 289–301.

Persson, Ingmar (2013) *From Morality to the End of Reason: An Essay on Rights, Reasons and Responsibility*, Oxford: Oxford University Press.

Persson, Ingmar (2014) 'Internal and External Grounds for the Nontransitivity of "Better/Worse than"', *Law, Ethics and Philosophy*, 2: 125–45.

Persson, Ingmar (2015) 'What Makes Death Bad for Us?', *Journal of Medical Ethics*, 41: 420–1.

Persson, Ingmar (2016) 'Parfit on Personal Identity: Its Analysis and (Un)importance', *Theoria*, 82: 148–65.

Persson, Ingmar and Savulescu, Julian (2010) 'Moral Transhumanism', *Journal of Medicine and Philosophy*, 35: 656–69.

Persson, Ingmar and Savulescu, Julian (2012) *Unfit for the Future: The Need for Moral Enhancement*, Oxford: Oxford University Press.

Persson, Ingmar and Savulescu, Julian (2013) 'The Meaning of Life: Science, Equality and Eternity', in T. Uehiro (ed.), *Ethics for the Future of Life*, Oxford: Oxford Uehiro Centre for Practical Ethics.

Platts, Mark (1979) *Ways of Meaning*, London: Routledge & Kegan Paul.

Pojman, Louis (1997) 'On Equal Human Worth: A Critique of Contemporary Egalitarianism', in L. Pojman and R. Westmoreland (eds), *Equality, Selected Readings*, New York: Oxford University Press.

Porter, Thomas (2012) 'In Defence of the Priority View', *Utilitas*, 24: 349–64.

Rachels, James (1986) *The End of Life*, New York: Oxford University Press.

Rachels, Stuart (1998) 'Counterexamples to the Transitivity of *Better Than*', *Australasian Journal of Philosophy* 76: 71–83.

Rachels, Stuart (2001) 'A Set of Solutions to Parfit's Problems', *Noûs* 35: 214–35.

Rawls, John (1971) *A Theory of Justice*, Cambridge, MA: Harvard University Press.

Roberts, Melinda (2002) 'A New Way of Doing the Best We Can: Person-based Consequentialism and the Equality Problem', *Ethics*, 112: 315–50.

Roberts, Melinda (2004) 'Person-based Consequentialism and the Procreation Obligation', in J. Ryberg and T. Tännsjö (eds), *The Repugnant Conclusion*, Dordrecht: Kluwer.

Sacks, Oliver (1985) *The Man Who Mistook His Wife for a Hat*, New York: Summit Books.

Savulescu, Julian and Persson, Ingmar (2016) 'Conjoined Twins: Philosophical Problems and Ethical Challenges', *Journal of Medicine and Philosophy*, 41: 41–55.

Scheffler, Samuel (1982) *The Rejection of Consequentialism*, New York: Oxford University Press.

Schopenhauer, Arthur (1819) *The World as Will and Representation*, vol. 1, trans. E. F. J. Payne, New York: Dover, 1969.

Sher, George (2014) *Equality for Inegalitarians*, Cambridge: Cambridge University Press.

Sher, George (2015) 'Why We Are Moral Equals', in U. Steinhoff (ed.), *Do All Persons Have Equal Moral Worth?*, Oxford: Oxford University Press.

Sidgwick, Henry (1907) *Methods of Ethics*, 7th edn, Indianapolis, IN: Hackett, 1981.

Sikora, Richard (1978) 'Is it Wrong to Prevent the Existence of Future Generations?', in R. Sikora and B. Barry (eds), *Obligations to Future Generations*, Philadelphia: Temple University Press.

Singer, Peter (1979) *Practical Ethics*, Cambridge: Cambridge University Press.

Singer, Peter (1993) *Practical Ethics*, 2nd edn, Cambridge: Cambridge University Press.

Singer, Peter (2011) *Practical Ethics*, 3rd edn, Cambridge: Cambridge University Press.

Skorupski, John (1989) *John Stuart Mill*, London: Routledge.

Spinoza, Benedict (1677) *Ethics*, New York: Hafner, 1949.

Steinhoff, Uwe (2015) 'Against Equal Respect and Concern, Equal Rights, and Egalitarian Impartiality', in U. Steinhoff (ed.), *Do All Persons Have Equal Moral Worth?*, Oxford: Oxford University Press.

Strawson, Galen (1999) 'The Impossibility of Moral Responsibility', reprinted in L. Pojman and O. McLeod (eds), *What Do We Deserve?*, New York: Oxford University Press.

Strawson, P. F. (1959) *Individuals*, London: Methuen.

Tadros, Victor (2013) *The Ends of Harm*, Oxford: Oxford University Press.

Taurek, John (1977) 'Should the Numbers Count?', *Philosophy and Public Affairs*, 6: 293–316.

Temkin, Larry (1993) *Inequality*, New York: Oxford University Press.

Temkin, Larry (2003) 'Egalitarianism Defended', *Ethics*, 113: 764–82.

Temkin, Larry (2012) *Rethinking the Good*, New York: Oxford University Press.

Temkin, Larry (2014) 'Intransitivity and the Internal Aspects View', *Law, Ethics and Philosophy*, 2: 145–58.

Tooley, Michael (1983) *Abortion and Infanticide*, Oxford: Clarendon Press.

Veatch, Robert (1986) *The Foundations of Justice*, New York: Oxford University Press.

Veatch, Robert (1993) 'The Impending Collapse of the Whole-Brain Definition of Death', *Hastings Center Report* 23: 18–24.

Velleman, David (2008) 'Persons in Prospect', *Philosophy and Public Affairs*, 36: 221–88.

Waldron, Jeremy (2002) *God, Locke and Equality*, Oxford: Oxford University Press.

Wikler, Daniel (1988) 'Not Dead, Not Dying? Ethical Categories and Persistent Vegetative State', *Hastings Center Report*, 18: 41–7.

Woollard, Fiona (2014) *Doing and Allowing Harm*, Oxford: Oxford University Press.

Index

Abortion 76
Act-omission doctrine 3, 17–18, 21, 88–9, 94, 99, 170, 238–9, 241
Altruism (sympathy, benevolence) 13–14, 102, 153
Anquetil, J. 68
Anscombe, E. 15, 35n
Anthropogenic climate change 241–4
Anti-inegalitarianism 172–4, 188, 194–5, 196–200
Armstrong, L. 68
Arneson, R. 210n
Asymmetry between abilities and disabilities 18, 93, 94, 228
Asymmetry between beginning good and bad lives 17–18, 88–99
Availability bias 256, 258
Autarchy 23, 250–61
Autonomy
　ambiguity of 5, 41
　aspect of welfare 4–5, 27, 40–5
　conditions for 6
　limits of 5–6, 41–2
　maximization of 67–8
　of choice to be replaced 87
　of choice to be worse off 149–50, 152–6, 161, 204–6
　respect for 6, 67–70, 143
　vs. well-being 42–5, 67–70
Ayers, M. 140n

Beneficence, *see* Reasons of beneficence
Benefiting
　comparative and non-comparative 16, 57–9, 63, 96, 98, 199–200
　event and state sense of 2–3
　inclusive view of 12–16, 66
　reason-giving and reason-cancelling weight 96, 98
　two analyses of 7–10
Bennett, J. 217
Berkeley, G. 133
Bias towards the future 257–8
Bias towards the near future 241, 258
Bias towards the perceived 258–9
Blackburn, S. 108
BonJour, L. 133–4
Boonin, D. 8, 9, 101–2

Boredom 4, 32
Bradley, B. 72n
Brain-transplants 79–87
Broome, J. 57, 59, 187n
Buddhism 250

Carter, I. 209–10
China 243
Christianity 137, 240
Christiano, T. 210n, 221
Cohen, J. 161n
Consciousness
　conceptual/cognitive 129–30, 133–5
　perceptual/sensory 129–33
　object account of 130–1, 134
　dependence on the physical 131–2
Crisp, R. 28n, 149n

Daoism 250
Dawson, K. 53
Death
　and end of existence 120–1
　badness of 48–52, 67–76
　moral insignificance of 126–9
　of a human being 18, 119–29
　of the brain 122–5
　two concepts of 126–8
DeGrazia, D. 6n, 13, 45n, 60n, 70, 71, 73, 98n, 120n, 123n, 125–6
Demolition argument 158–65
Desert
　and justice 156–7
　and rights 144, 157–8
　and ultimate responsibility 163
Desirability of welfare diffusion, DWD (*see* Prioritarianism)
Desire (*see also* Pleasure)
　occurrent and dispositional 51
　self-regarding 33, 41
Dimishing marginal utility 175, 186
Direction of fit (of beliefs and desires) 35
Disperse additional burdens view 17, 117–18, 176
Double aspect account of welfare 67, 74–6 (*see also* Things going well for someone)
Double effect, doctrine of 3, 21, 170
Dworkin, R. 156, 213

INDEX

Egalitarianism, (*see also* Anti-inegalitarianism)
  and beneficence 152, 174–5, 184, 225–7
  deontological (deontic) 183–4
  extreme 19–20, 149–50, 164–5
    counterintuitiveness of 225–7
  luck-egalitarianism 164
  recessive (moderate) 181–2, 196–7
  restrictive 149
  selective 20, 211–12
  teleological (telic) 183–4
Enjoyment
  and propositional pleasure 29–30
  intensity of 106–7
  interest and sensual 32
Epictetus 251–2, 253, 256, 260
Equality (*see also* Egalitarianism and Inequality)
  and mere addition 115, 177–8, 196–200
  ground for 156–65
  intrapersonal 153, 202–4
  of conscious beings 212–13
  of human beings 208–10
  of persons 211–12
  of welfare 150–1
  utilitarian (equal consideration of interests) 165, 213
  value of 150, 173–4
Essentially comparative view 12, 114–17

Feinberg, J. 157
Feldman, F. 29, 30n, 31, 35n, 120n, 121–2, 172
Ford, N. 55n
Frankena, W. 28n

Gametic principle 64–5
Garbo, G. 83
Germany 240

Harming (*see also* Benefiting and Means)
  easier than benefiting 7
  qualified and unqualified 9–10, 58
Hare, R. M. 108n
Harris, J. 49–50n, 64–5, 143
Hart, H. L. A. 90
Haydn, J. 106
Hedonic adaptation 254
Hedonism 31–3
Heterarchy 249–50
Holtug, N. 195, 200
Human beings (organisms)
  equality of, *see* Equality
  moral status of, *see* Moral status
  origination of 52–5
  species membership of 137–41
Hume, D. 133
Hurley, S. 161, 163n

Ill-being 4, 32
Images 133–5
Inclusive ethics, *see* Morality
Inclusive view
  of benefiting, *see* Benefiting
  of person-affecting reasons of beneficence, *see* Reasons of beneficence
Independent individuals 13, 96–7, 199–200
India 243
Indurain, M. 68
Inequality
  degree of 174–82
  global 230, 239
  human 226–7
  interspecies 225–6
Innocent bystanders ('by-fallers') 167–9
Innocent threats 165–70
Interest in future existence 49–52
Inviolability 213–15
Irvine, W. 250n, 255n, 260n

Justice (fairness), *see also* Egalitarianism and Equality
  impersonal value of 2, 20, 172–4
  principle of 2, 19, 150
  rejection of 165, 187

Kagan, S. 5n, 75, 198n, 256n
Kahneman, D. 70, 228, 253n, 256
Kamm, F. 157, 166n, 171, 213–15
Kim, J. 108n

Leonardo da Vinci 120n
Levelling down objection (LDO) 183–5, 188–90, 194–5
Liberty, Mill's principle of 41–2, 43–5
Life
  biographical 119–20, 122, 127
  biological 18, 119
  end of, *see* Death
Lippert-Rasmussen, K. 149n, 151n, 153n, 164n, 210n, 211
Locke, J. 6n, 120n, 133, 157–8
Loss aversion 70

McKerlie, D. 153n, 204–5, 206n
McMahan, J. 6n, 16, 17, 52, 57, 59, 69n, 70–1, 73, 74, 75, 82, 84, 87, 88, 89, 90, 92, 93, 94, 95–6, 97–8, 99, 126–7, 129n, 138n, 141n, 142–3, 151, 167, 199–200
Marcus Aurelius 259n
Marx, K. 240
Means
  causal 215–20
  epistemic 215–17
  factual 215
  harming as 169–70, 213–21

principle 215, 221
  using harmfully as 169–70, 219–21
  using as mere means/merely as means 221
Mechanism of spontaneous induction 256
Mele, A. 163n
Merckx, E. 68–9, 71
Mere addition, *see* Equality
Mill, J. S. 5, 28, 31, 34, 35, 41–2, 43, 45, 240
Mona Lisa 120n
Monk, R. 250n
Moore, G. E. 28, 35, 36, 108n
Moral status (standing)
  and moral significance 1–2
  based on actual/potential consciousness 1–2, 128–9
  'fit' and 'frame' model of 144–5, 208
  of human beings 19, 137–42
  of persons 142–3
Morality
  and ethics 1
  authority of 21, 232, 233, 234, 244–5
  demandingness of 21, 231–3, 234
  hard-wired features of 238–44
  inclusive 1, 233–4
  origin of 1, 231
  other-directed 248
  point of 22, 233–4
  revision of 232–3
Moral philosophy
  inconclusiveness of 235–44
  point of 22, 235–46
Mozart, W. 104, 105, 106, 112n

Nagel, T. 163n
Naturalistic fallacy 28
Negativity bias 229
Nielsen, K. 149n
Non-identity problem 99–102
Non-transitivity
  of being better/worse than 17, 114–18
  of sameness of supervenient properties 107–14
Norman, R. 28n
Nozick, R. 42n, 152n, 165, 219
Nussbaum, M. 249–50

Olson, E. 52, 120, 124–5
Otsuka, M. 201–3, 206
Oxfam 239

Parfit, D. 13n, 16n, 17, 30, 35, 36, 37, 58n, 82, 83, 84–5, 86, 99, 103–6, 107, 115, 127, 172n, 177, 181, 183, 184, 186–7, 188–9, 190, 192, 203n, 205, 206, 221, 242, 257n, 258n
Person(s)
  concept of 6n, 67
  separateness and unity of 202–3, 206

Person-affecting claim (PAC) 184–5, 195–6
  weaker person-affecting claim (PAC*) 196
Personal good, principle of (PPG) 197
Personal identity 11, 51–2, 79–87
  error-theory of 80–1, 84
  insignificance of 3, 6, 84–7, 256–7
Persson, I. 3, 5, 7, 27n, 28, 29, 30n, 32, 33, 34, 36, 37, 38, 41n, 42, 44n, 45, 54, 55, 56, 60, 64, 79n, 80, 90n, 104n, 107n, 116, 121n, 122, 125, 130, 139, 156n, 158, 160, 187, 215, 231, 232, 238, 239, 241, 246, 251, 254, 256, 257n, 258n, 260n
Philosophy of life 23, 249, 260–1
Platts, M. 35n
Pleasure (*see also* Enjoyment)
  aspect of well-being 27–40
  intrinsic desirability/goodness of 30–40
  desire for 30–40
    originally intrinsic 33–4
    incorrigibility of 34–40
  liking of 30
  truth-adjusted 31
  propositional and sensory 28–9
Pojman, L. 137n
Porter, T. 203n
Possible beings
  benefiting and harming of 57–66
  reference to 59–61
  their non-existence and non-conscious existence 61–3
Potentiality for consciousness 51, 53–7
Precariousness of life 249–56
  sense of 254, 256
Prioritarianism (the priority view) 20, 149, 183–207
  and desirability of welfare diffusion (DWD) 190–3, 197, 200
  and LDO 189–95
  and the Series 190–3
  deontological/deontic 186, 192, 194
  impersonal value of 187
  intrapersonal 200–6
  teleological/telic 186–7

Rachels, J. 119
Rachels, S. 114n
Rawls, J. 152n, 157n, 209
Reasons (*see also* Reasons of beneficence)
  normative irreducibility of 35–40, 45–7
  to do rather than not to do 58–9
Reasons of beneficence
  impersonal 11n, 13–16, 78, 102
  person-affecting (person-regarding) 6, 10–16
    inclusive view of 10–16, 66, 75–6, 77–8, 88–9
    narrow view of 12–14, 16, 101–2
Repellant conclusion 181

Replaceability
  of (conscious/sentient) beings 17, 77–9
  of persons 79–87
Repugnant conclusion 17, 20, 103–7, 114–16
Responsibility
  as a ground for justice 158–65
  backward-looking justification of 163
  causally based 21, 89–90, 165–71, 218, 238–9, 241–2
  direct 160, 162, 163
  forward-looking justification of 163
  ultimate 160–4
Rights
  and desert 144, 156–8
  basis of 157–8
  general and special 90
  negative 5, 19, 41–2, 89–90, 92
  to life (worth living) 49–50, 90–2
Ring species 19, 139
Roberts, M. 52, 59n
Rousseau, J.-J. 240
Russia 243

Sacks, O. 131n
Savulescu, J. 7, 55, 139, 231, 232, 239, 241, 246, 251, 260
Scheffler, S. 240
Schopenhauer, S. 250, 259, 260
Self
  concept of 49, 80–1
  division of 84–5
Self-defence 165–71
Sequence 176–7
Series, *see* Prioritarianism
Shakespeare 104, 105
Sharon, A. 80
Sher, G. 212
Sidgwick, H. 163n
Sikora, R. 95
Singer, P. 56–7, 77, 78, 79, 137n, 138, 165, 209, 212, 213, 245
Skorupski, J. 28n
Socrates 42
Species membership, *see* Human beings
Speciesism 19, 137–42, 208
Spinoza, B. 252n

Steinhoff, U. 213
Strawson, G. 163n
Strawson, P. 132
Sub specie aeternitatis 259–60
Suffering 4, 32
Supervenience 17, 107–9

Tadros, V. 162n, 166, 168, 169, 171, 215
Taurek, J. 15
Temkin, L. 11n, 12–14, 17, 112–17, 149n, 153n, 174, 176, 177, 179, 181
Theseus, ship of 121n
Things going well for someone (welfare)
  two aspects of 4–5, 27–45
Time-relative interest account 70–5, 87, 97–8
Tooley, M. 49–50, 90–2
Tversky, A. 70
Twins
  conjoined 55
  monozygotic 53–5, 88–90, 94, 97

USA 243
Utilitarianism, forms of 78, 185–6
Ultimatum games 230

Value
  dependence on mind 135–6
  extrinsic 33, 48–9
  intrinsic 33–4
  moral 2, 137–8, 141, 142, 144–5, 208
  personal and impersonal 2, 15, 30–1, 33, 187–8
  of non-existence 11, 61–2
  supervenience of 17, 107–8
Veatch, R. 126, 137n
Velleman, D. 91n
Venice 83, 104
Voorhoeve, A. 117, 201–3, 206

Waldron, J. 137
Well-being 4–5, 27–40
Welfare 5, 67, 150
Wikler, D. 126
Williams, B. 83
Wittgenstein, L. 250n
Woollard, F. 166n